TROPICAL DEVELOPMENT, 1880–1913

TROPICAL DEVELOPMENT, 1880–1913

Studies in economic progress

Edited by

SIR WILLIAM ARTHUR

Routledge
Taylor & Francis Group

LONDON AND NEW YORK

First published in 1970

Published in 2006 by
Routledge
2 Park Square, Milton Park, Abingdon, Oxfordshire OX14 4RN
711 Third Avenue, New York, NY 10017

First issued in paperback 2014

Routledge is an imprint of the Taylor and Francis Group, an informa business

British Library Cataloguing in Publication Data
A CIP catalogue record for this book
is available from the British Library

Tropical Development, 1880-1913
ISBN 0-415-38192-4 (volume)
ISBN 0-415-37988-1 (subset)
ISBN 0-415-28619-0 (set)

ISBN 13: 978-1-138-86516-7 (pbk)
ISBN 13: 978-0-415-38192-5 (hbk)

Routledge Library Editions: Economic History

TROPICAL DEVELOPMENT
1880–1913

TROPICAL DEVELOPMENT 1880–1913

STUDIES IN ECONOMIC PROGRESS

Edited by W. Arthur Lewis

LONDON

GEORGE ALLEN & UNWIN LTD

RUSKIN HOUSE · MUSEUM STREET

FIRST PUBLISHED IN 1970

© *George Allen & Unwin Ltd. 1970*
ISBN 0 04 330170 3

Preface

These essays were prepared during the year 1967–8 by members of my graduate seminar in the Woodrow Wilson School. We had been studying various theories of development, and also analysing the progress of less developed countries during the 1950s and 1960s. It seemed a potentially useful adventure to go back to an earlier period of prosperous world trade to see how these same tropical countries had reacted then. For most of the tropics modern economic development began in the last quarter of the nineteenth century with its revolutionary reduction of transport costs and heavy international flow of capital. A great many books tell what happened at this time in the leading countries of Europe, and also in the temperate 'countries of overseas settlement' – Argentina, Chile, Canada, Australia and others. But there is very little written about the tropics. It seemed useful to find out what we could about the tropics at the end of the nineteenth century; and if what we found seemed interesting, to write a book of our own.

Such an adventure is hazardous. The chief reason why others have not already written such a book is that the materials are sparse and the data are uncertain. We have searched diligently, but have no doubt not found all that exists, and not correctly interpreted all that we have found. We have therefore no doubt made mistakes, which others will correct. That is how History is served. Our claim is that it is valuable to compare what was happening simultaneously in countries all round the globe, which were producing much the same commodities, and reacting to the same stimuli.

There is also hazard in reducing three decades of the history of any country to twenty to thirty pages. Here we are deliberately selective. The reader would be bored if we were to cover exactly the same ground in each of twelve countries. So each chapter emphasizes some aspect of the development process which is not so fully treated elsewhere. This may be immigration, or n-achievement groups, or railway finance, or colonial policy, or botanic gardens, or the great man theory, or whatever seems specially relevant to that country. Thus the book is not as repetitive as it might be; but it follows that the expert on any country who reads only the chapter on that country is bound to find that a number of elements have been omitted which he would have preferred to include, but which have been treated elsewhere in the book.

The countries were chosen randomly, in accordance with the interests of individual students. Chapter 2 gives trade statistics for seventy-eight tropical countries, of which only twelve are treated

7

here. (Some other essays dropped by the wayside.) Though chosen randomly, the twelve have turned out to be a good cross section. They include each of the three less developed continents: three countries from Latin America, five from Africa and four from Asia. They include countries that did well and countries that did poorly; plantation economies and peasant economies; countries with long participation in international trade, and new beginners; export enclaves and countries where the income earned from exports really percolated through the economy. The main interest of the exercise lies in asking why different countries fared so differently, and though one feels that it would have helped to have even more countries (such as Burma, Malaya, Cuba, Peru or Mexico) our twelve have differed enough to make possible fruitful comparisons.

My introductory essay was written after all the others were in, and is based on them. It identifies the two principal questions which run through the book: what aided or hindered a rapid growth of exports; and how effectively was the wealth created by exports used to create the conditions for self-sustaining growth? Perhaps it should be read last, rather than first, since its numerous references to the succeeding chapters may not otherwise be wholly intelligible.

Each essay has been revised several times, with editorial advice from me, and in some cases from experts on the individual countries. Special thanks are due to two of my colleagues, Professors Stanley Stein and Robert Tignor; also to Professor Morris D. Morris, Mrs Kusum Nair and Mr Tarlok Singh. None of these is responsible for the final product. Mrs Marion O'Connor helped me with the editing, and Mrs Dorothy Rieger did mountains of highly polished typing with her usual patience and good humour.

With such a large number of writers some variation of quality is inevitable. But anyone who reads through this volume is bound to agree that I have been privileged in having such an exciting set of students for a seminar.

W. A. L.

Research Programme in Economic Development,
Princeton University.

Contents

Statistical Tables

Chapter 1

THE EXPORT STIMULUS

by W. Arthur Lewis

The rapid development of the tropical world began in the last quarter of the nineteenth century, in response to cheap transportation and the industrialization of Europe and North America. The tropics had participated in international trade for some centuries; Asia was famous for its spices, its silks, and in the nineteenth century its coffee; while tropical America supplied minerals, sugar and coffee; and Africa supplied leathers and palm oil. But it would take cheap transportation to effect a revolution in the quantities and types of goods transported.

The decisive change in shipping came in the second half of the nineteenth century. In 1850 most ships were built of wood, and depended on sails; by 1900 nearly all new ships were built of iron or steel, burnt coal, and in the course of a year could carry, per ton of cubic capacity, three to four times as much cargo over the year (ton-miles) as the ships of 1850. Over this period shipping freights were on the average halved, with the most spectacular falls occurring in freights to the Far East after the opening of the Suez Canal in 1869.

What new ships did for sea transport the railways did for inland transport. The technique of making good metalled roads had been mastered in Europe in the second half of the eighteenth century, but very few tropical countries had decent roads even in 1880; Ceylon is one of the few exceptions. With bad roads, production for export would be confined to a few miles from the sea coast or the river, except for luxury articles and precious metals. Expanding trade quickened the interest in good roads, and much progress was made in places like Burma, the Gold Coast or Malaya at the end of the nineteenth century, within fifty miles of the sea, without waiting for the arrival of railways. But vast continental interiors could not be tapped on any considerable scale, away from major rivers (there was virtually no tropical canal-building), until the railway arrived. What made the railways possible in turn was the growing willingness of private investors in Europe to invest in foreign countries. Foreign investment was a small stream in 1850, but by 1913 it had become a great river. Most of the money went into temperate countries in

Europe itself, North America, Australia or other regions of settlement from Europe. But substantial sums also flowed to the tropics, especially for railways, from about 1870 onwards.

Cheap transportation made it possible for the first time to move large quantities of cheap bulk commodities. Before the transport revolution trade with the tropics was confined to the few commodities that could pay heavy transport costs because no local substitutes were available, and the number of persons who could afford to pay these costs was so small that the trade was small. But between 1883 and 1913 the volume of tropical trade multiplied by three.[1]

The rapid growth of trade was due not only to cheap transportation, but also and even more to the growth of demand resulting from the increase in the national incomes of the leading industrial states. The industrial revolution reached its peak in Britain between 1850 and 1875 in the sense that this was the period of the biggest expansion of the iron and coal industries in response to railway building, to the conversion of shipping from wood and sail to iron and steam, the conversion of textile machinery from wood to iron, and the spread of machinery from the textile trades into other sectors, especially clothing and agriculture. This is also the time when the industrial pulse quickened in France, Germany, Belgium and the United States of America. Thus the foundations were laid for the great spurt of industrial production in the last quarter of the nineteenth century averaging, for the four leading countries taken together, just about $3\frac{1}{2}$ per cent per annum.

The demand for tropical produce increased at the same pace as world trade as a whole. The market was especially buoyant for cotton, oilseeds, cocoa, coffee, tobacco, hard fibres, bananas, rubber and various minerals; it was not so good for tea, and positively unfavourable to sugar. There was also a strong demand for rice in the tropical countries themselves, to feed the workers producing commercial crops. The literature dwells at length on the expansion of the temperate countries (Australia, Argentina, *et al.*) in response to the growing demands for primary products at the centres of the industrial revolution. We are apt to forget that equally strong pulses went out to the tropics.

The tropical countries were in varying states of readiness to respond to the opportunity now presented by expanding world trade, so the results were not everywhere the same. Table 1.1 compares the principal countries, and the totals for some of the smaller countries grouped together.

[1] See Chapter 2, page 46.

The degree of variation is quite remarkable. At one end we have the sugar colonies of Britain and France, many of whom were exporting less in 1913 than in 1883. At the other extreme are the Far Eastern rice-growing peasant economies, Thailand, Burma and Indochina, whose exports multiplied by between four and five, plus the peasant economies of West Africa, and the newly opened mines of Central Africa. In between is a degree of variety which emphasizes that development cannot be explained by any simple theory relying on geography, race, religion, culture, or political organization. The countries studied in detail in this volume, though chosen randomly, include all levels of performance both above and below the average, all the tropical continents, and all forms of economic and political organization, and are in this sense typical of the wide range of tropical experience.

The main purpose of the authors in tackling these countries was to seek answers to two questions. First, what factors in each country accounted for the rate of growth of exports: why was it so high, or so low? And secondly, what was the impact on the rest of the economy of the growth of exports? In answering the first question we have to examine why Venezuela did so poorly in terms of exports (an index of 146) in contrast to her next door neighbours Brazil (373) and Colombia (334); why Ceylon (523) ran so far ahead of Indonesia

TABLE 1.1: *Index Numbers of Value of Exports*, 1913

(1883 = 100)

Asia		America	
Thailand	539	Ecuador	439
Ceylon	523	Brazil	373
Indochina	426	Mexico	352
Indonesia	311	Colombia	334
India	235	Central	298
Philippines	212	Peru	297
		Venezuela	146
		West Indies†	118
Africa		*Tropical*	
West	548	*Total*	271
Central	498		
East*	372		
Egypt	257		

Source: Table 2.1.
* Eritrea through Mozambique; Sudan; Madagascar; Seychelles.
† Includes British Honduras and the Guianas; excludes Cuba, whose 1883 exports are uncertain.

(311) and the Philippines (212); and above all to probe the great enigma of India (235) whose low performance even then (as now) was so untypical of other tropical countries. The second question is more complex, since it is harder to measure the extent to which a country benefited from having a high rate of growth of exports. Here we are interested in those social and economic changes by which a country is converted from a subsistence situation, through export-domination, into relatively independent self-sustaining growth. Thus Brazil (373) laid for itself a better foundation than Ceylon (523) in senses which we shall duly explore.

Such country comparisons are not made directly in the individual chapters, though they are implicit in the analysis. The purpose of this first chapter is to pull together what we have learnt from these and other studies about the questions posed. The first section of this chapter therefore analyses the factors which determined why the exports of some countries grew more rapidly than those of other countries between 1880 and 1913. The second section is concerned with the extent to which the growth of exports became a base for general economic development.

I. PRECONDITIONS FOR AGRICULTURAL EXPORTS

We confine ourselves, in this section, to agricultural exports, since there is little to say in this period about mining, except that it grew rapidly after 1900. There are brief notes on mineral exports in Chapter 2.

It is convenient to approach the problem by asking what circumstances facilitated the growing of export crops by small farmers. This analysis then leads naturally to the additional conditions for large-scale enterprise. We thus begin with five topics: internal peace, water, transportation, economies of scale, and land.

Internal Peace. Farmers are reluctant to plant if their fields may be ravaged by soldiers; trade is handicapped by roving bandits; and investors stay away from areas where arbitrary seizure is possible. The maintenance of law and order is therefore the first condition for economic growth. This condition already existed in southern Asia by 1880, but was not yet universal in Africa or Latin America.

Southern Asia had all passed into Spanish, Dutch, or British control in 1880 (with minor French or Portuguese enclaves) and had thus stable political conditions, in contrast with northern Asia (China) or western Asia (the Near East). The European scramble for sub-Saharan Africa was, however, only just beginning in 1880.

16

It would take another twenty years or more to establish administrative and police frameworks strong enough to ensure that traders could pass unhindered on their lawful business. For the same reasons the railway came late to Africa. Exports do not begin to be significant until after 1900.

In Latin America the independence gained so much earlier in the century had in several of our countries failed to result in stable government. Such countries as Argentina, Chile, Brazil and Mexico had achieved fair stability, but others, notably Colombia and Venezuela, still suffered from internal war. Actually, the successive *coups d'état* do not seem to have had much direct effect on agricultural production during our period, since they were not generally accompanied by rioting or looting, and were not specifically directed against the agricultural classes. More important was the fact that a *coup d'état* might bring into power an irresponsible *caudillo* who neither understood about development nor cared about it, and who therefore failed to pursue the active policies which it required. His government would also not be creditworthy, and could not therefore raise money abroad for railways and other public works. This irresponsibility seems for example to have played some part in the retardation of Venezuela during our period, in contrast with its neighbours, Colombia and Brazil.

Some political scientists have advanced the thesis that it is economic development that brings political stability, in the sense that politicians will fight and disturb society if they are allowed to, and stop only when powerful economic interests put their foot down and insist on good political behaviour. We shall confine ourselves to noting that the tropical world was both much more stable politically and more developed economically in 1913 than it had been in 1880; which was cause and which was effect we do not have to decide here.

Water. The richness or poverty of a tropical agriculture depends more than anything else on water. Some of the crops which were profitable in this period require some water all the year round: tea, cocoa, coffee, rubber, bananas, sugar, oil palm. These need either some rain for most of the year, or else an easy source of irrigation. Areas where the rain falls only for a few months, and which also cannot be irrigated, are confined to annual crops: to very coarse grains (sorghum, millet), manioc, cotton and groundnuts if the rainfall is only about 30 inches; or richer grains (maize, rice), yams and tobacco where rainfall is more abundant.

One consequence of the growth of world demand for the crops

17

requiring perennial water was to increase the value of naturally forested country relatively to that of natural grasslands. Hitherto the tropical peoples had tended to prefer grasslands, and to move into the forested areas only when driven by war or population pressure. On the one hand, grasslands were very suitable for grains and cattle; on the other hand, wet areas tended to be malarial and, in Africa, to be infested with tsetse fly. The growth of world demand thus worked a revolution; the areas previously unfavourable now became relatively rich. Population started moving from the drier to the wetter areas, and this movement still continues today, especially in West Africa with its enormous southward migration.

Another consequence was to give new value to irrigation works, where natural conditions made this feasible. Here the response of governments was very varied. Small irrigation works (e.g. wells, dams) can be executed by the farmers themselves or by local authorities. The record of both is poor in this period. Larger works (e.g. big rivers) depend on central government initiative, which varied considerably. The government of Egypt did very well, that of India did moderately, that of Ceylon rather poorly. (Since all these were British colonial governments, their different performances illustrate very well the absence of a uniform British colonial policy.)

Given the importance of water, it was to be expected that the wetter tropical countries would respond faster to the new export markets than the drier countries. The coastal belt of West Africa would do much better than the areas north of the forest. The interior of north-east Brazil could not hope to compete with the better watered lands of São Paulo. Most notably, almost any south-east Asian country should do better than India. The Indian sub-continent has some small areas, where rain is well distributed through the year, which can grow coffee, rubber, tea or other perennials. But the great bulk of the sub-continent gets its rain over a short period; and half the continent gets 30 inches or less. Hence it was simply impossible for the agriculture of India as a whole to benefit greatly from the expansion of world demand for tropical products – unless very much more could be done by way of irrigation. When one compares Indian and Japanese progress in agriculture at this time, it must always be remembered that the climate of Japan is much more favourable to agriculture than the climate of India.

Transportation. Some improvement in transport facilities, roads, railways and harbours, was universally required of governments. Areas close to the sea, or served by navigable rivers, could flourish without much government activity (e.g. Lower Burma, the Niger

18

Delta, the Gold Coast) but even they were enormously helped by good roads. Continental areas needed railways as well as roads.

Here again, governments varied enormously. Roads fared worse than railways. A few governments laid down excellent road systems (e.g. Ceylon, Malaya), but in the larger countries railways were the responsibility of the central government, which could borrow money in the world's capital markets, whereas roads were the responsibility of provincial and local authorities, who were both poorer and liable to be less progressive. Thus India was well equipped with railways, but her roads remained execrable even in 1913. The colonial powers were in a better position to provide railways than the independent governments, because their borrowing powers in European capital markets were greater, but they varied widely among themselves. At one end of the spectrum was Britain building railways throughout her empire, and even producing some good road systems. At the other end of the colonial spectrum, Portugal did no more for transport in her colonies than she did at home. The independent countries varied just as widely, from Brazil equipping the State of São Paulo with excellent infrastructure, to Afghanistan continuing to live in the traditions of earlier centuries.

Economies of scale. This factor had little significance. Of the crops then prominent in international trade, only two – sugar and tea – required large-scale processing immediately after harvesting. All other crops required only elementary processing on the farm (coffee, cocoa, palm oil, rubber, copra) or else could wait until they reached a central mill (cotton, jute, peanuts). Nowadays the small farmer also grows sugar or tea, and sells his produce to a central mill, but there was very little of this before 1913; planting and milling of these crops was then most usually under single control.

Nowadays the scientific revolution in agriculture gives an advantage to plantations because they are quicker than small farms in adopting new techniques, especially in countries which do not have a proper agricultural extension service. This was not an issue in 1880. The only tropical crop to experience a scientific revolution before the First World War was sugar, which was already a plantation crop. In everything else the small farmers used the same seeds and got more or less the same yields as the big farmers. Except in sugar and tea, there was no technical reason for plantations.

Neither was capital a significant issue. Capital was needed for infra-structure rather than for agriculture. Small farmers were used to clearing land to plant food, and, agriculture being a seasonal occupation, had plenty of off-season time in which to clear additional

19

land for export crops, if this was necessary. In many areas the custom in planting tree crops was to clear land in the usual way for food, plant it with foodcrops, and also insert the seeds of the tree crop. The land would be abandoned in the usual way after two further croppings with food, by which time the tree crops would be well established. The trees might not bear until they were five years old or more, but there was no financial outlay in establishing them, or in waiting for them to bear.

Even plantations did not necessarily have a large financial outlay. Where labour was available and willing, the planter could lease a dozen acres to a worker to clear and plant foodstuffs and insert the seeds of a tree crop. The worker would keep all the food, and be paid in addition, at the end of the lease, a few cents for each tree which had been established. This system worked easily where the small farmers were short of land, as in Trinidad. Where labour was scarce, the system was not so easy to apply; nevertheless, Brazil worked this system with Italian immigrants. It seems, however, not to have worked with Indians or Chinese brought in on indenture. Here the plantation would need a lot of capital, since wages might have to be paid for as much as seven years before the trees began to bear. The London stock exchange developed a lively interest in plantation shares, especially for companies in India, Ceylon, Malaya and Indonesia. But this represents only a part of the large-scale agricultural enterprise which expanded in the tropics between 1880 and 1913. Many plantations were started on a small scale, and thereafter expanded through reinvestment of profits.

Entrepreneurship. Was the small farmer held back by lack of entrepreneurship? He did not want for a market, since there was no lack of traders to sell his produce to. These were not always natives of the country. Trade at the ports tended to be handled by foreigners, even in India and Latin America whose native traders had long experience of the import and export business. Internal trade was largely in native hands in Latin America, in India and in West Africa; but in East Africa it was handled exclusively by Indians and Arabs, in Burma mainly by Indians, and in most of south-east Asia by Chinese. The fortitude of some of these men was remarkable: roads were bad or non-existent, malaria and other diseases endemic, and the natives not always trustworthy. Nevertheless they would go right up into the back-country carrying consumer goods to exchange for exportable commodities. (The exclusion of the Chinese from the Philippines may have had something to do with the failure of small farming there to respond to the export stimulus.)

20

The enterprise of the traders was matched by that of the small farmers, where suitable opportunities existed. Indeed, some of these small-farmer achievements are astounding, if one is used to reading about the lack of initiative in traditional cultures. Take the case of the Burmese. In Burma the flat, wet lands of the Irrawaddy delta were largely unoccupied as late as 1870, when the rising demand for rice began to make itself felt. The British Crown claimed ownership of all empty lands, but was willing to sell at nominal prices to small settlers. So Burmese moved down from Upper Burma, squatted and cultivated, and by 1913 were exporting 2½ million tons of rice from what in 1870 had been little more than swamp.[1] The Gold Coast story is equally remarkable. The land suitable for cocoa was covered by apparently useless forest. So the Akwapim farmers (with a few Krobo, Shai and Ga) moved down from their hills, bought it, cut the trees and planted cocoa. The government was asked neither for roads nor for titles, and was indeed hardly aware that the foundations of what by 1913 was already the world's largest cocoa industry were being laid under its nose.[2] These two examples, involving migration over long distances into totally unprepared country confound any idea that small farmers lack initiative, or the desire to make money.

Given suitable land and roads, small farmers seem to have responded to export opportunities all over the tropics, despite enormous differences of race, religion and culture (Colombia, coffee; Thailand and Burma, rice; Ceylon, coconuts and rubber; Uganda, cotton; Gold Coast, cocoa; *et al.*). Therefore when trying to understand why one region went ahead faster than another it is best to begin by laying aside cultural explanations, or suggestions that one people is lazier or has more initiative than another. Further exploration will usually reveal some more concrete explanation, in terms of markets, prices or the nature and cost of inputs. However, when the analysis is complete one may still be left with a residual, indicating greater entrepreneurial response in some groups than in others. For example, in the Gold Coast cocoa was pioneered not by all the forest tribes, but chiefly by the Akwapim and Krobos. As Professor McClelland has put it, *n*-achievement is higher in some societies than in others.[3] He has however pointed out that this is not a genetic

---

[1] The story is told by J. S. Furnivall in *An Introduction to the Political Economy of Burma*, Rangoon, 1931.

[2] We owe our knowledge of this episode entirely to the researches of Miss Polly Hill, *Migrant Cocoa Farmers of Southern Ghana*, Cambridge, 1963.

[3] D. C. McClelland, *The Achieving Society*, Princeton, 1961.

but a historical phenomenon, subject both to historical explanation and to rapid change. The most common reason for low n-achievement in any group at any time is simply that opportunity has hitherto been lacking. Once new opportunities are created, it is only a matter of time before the group learns how to exploit them.

Land. The crucial constraint on peasant production for export was lack of access to land. At this period, when he was entering the market economy for the first time, the small farmer was not willing to switch from growing food to growing crops for export; the new crops had to be additional. To have switched would have been very risky, and the small farmer could not afford this risk, since if he could not feed his family he would have to give up his lands and possessions to buy food. By 1960, small farmers are so accustomed to selling on the market that many countries export raw materials at the cost of having to buy food, but this was not so in 1880. Hence the small farmer would grow for export only if he could cultivate more land (or resort to double cropping).[1] This would depend both on whether empty land existed, and also on whether he could have access to it. Empty accessible lands existed in such places as Sub-Saharan Africa, Burma, Thailand and Indochina, where the farmers did indeed produce large amounts for export. At the other extreme land was scarce in India or Java, where population was already dense, and where the small farmer's response was relatively small. In between, we have countries where there was plenty of empty land, but it was not made available to the small farmers (most of Latin America, Philippines, Ceylon). Here the response could come only from large estates and plantations.

Where empty wet land was available, the planting of permanent trees (cocoa, coffee, rubber, coconuts, etc.) suited the small farmer very well. He would clear an area as usual and plant it with food, intercropping with seeds or seedlings of the permanent crop, as has already been described. Another group of farmers who could make an easy transition to commercial farming were those, like the Burmese and the Thais, who were growing their normal foodstuff (rice) for export; all they had to do (given the availability of land) was to plant larger acreages than before. Those who would find the transition most difficult would be such small farmers as the Indians,

---

[1] This is in line with Adam Smith's position that the gain from trade derives from using surplus labour and natural resources (not from switching, as the classical economists later argued). See the excellent discussion in Hla Myint, 'The Classical Theory of International Trade and the Underdeveloped Countries', *Economic Journal*, June 1958.

who had barely enough land for their food supplies, which came first in their priorities. At this stage, therefore, the response of small farmers to the opportunities for producing for export is almost exclusively a function of the availability to them of additional land on which to plant the export crop; this is why the response is enormous in Burma, or the Gold Coast, or Uganda; is muted in Ceylon or Jamaica or the Philippines; and is virtually non-existent in Venezuela or India. Of course, as the farmers got used to a money income, they became more willing to buy their food in the market and to give their lands and time exclusively to export crops. One finds some evidence of this in India; and, after 1900, cotton acreage grows very swiftly relatively to food acreage in Egypt. But this was a risky business, involving also a change in cultural patterns, so initially the farmer wanted to be able both to grow his own food and to grow crops for export. Except for the plantations depending on imported indentured labour, major dependence on imported food is a phenomenon of the twentieth rather than the nineteenth century.

India remains something of a mystery. It is one of the four countries which were already overpopulated in 1880, the other three being Egypt, Java, and Japan. Egypt met her problem by irrigation, which increased the cropped area by 60 per cent, and made it possible to multiply cotton exports by two and a half; unfortunately, from 1900 onwards the growth rate of acreage ceased to exceed that of population, and output per head suffered. Java adopted a rotation system, which put the village rice lands under sugar for eighteen months in every fifty-four. Japan intensified productivity per acre; but her main solution was to plant mulberry trees on land not suitable for rice. Silk thus became her leading export; a major source of income for her small farmers, and the country's biggest source of foreign exchange. Only India seems to have been completely defeated by population density. She did some irrigation, but little in relation to total cultivated area; most of her small farmers continued to farm wholly for subsistence; and her agricultural exports were among the slowest growing in the tropical world. Chapter 12 tries, not with complete success, to find the reason why.

Large-scale farming. Most tropical countries had empty lands at this time, which could have been made available to small farmers, but this did not always happen. Perhaps the land belonged to large landowners, who either cultivated it themselves, or left it idle. Or perhaps it belonged to the state, which did not put in the infrastructure needed to open it up, or else on opening it up allocated it to plantations rather than to small farmers.

23

Governments were not at this time particularly interested in fostering small-scale agriculture. There are some exceptions, e.g. Uganda, Gold Coast, and Punjab. They were not hostile to the small farmers, but they seldom had positive policies to help. If they opened up new lands they were more likely to steer them towards large landowners and plantations (e.g. Egypt, Ceylon, Kenya, Brazil). Where landowners were holding land empty, as in so much of Latin America, governments might have adopted land-reform policies in the interest of making land available to small farmers, but the only government which actually did this was that of Jamaica, after 1890. In this sense the failure of small farmers to produce for export in several countries must primarily be blamed on governments and the powerful landed interests with which they were associated; except in sugar and tea, large-scale production was political rather than economic in origin.

One should also note the small number of cases where the peasant was deprived of even such land as he had to make way for expatriate agriculture. In Java the villagers were 'invited' to lease their lands to sugar companies on a rotational basis – one-third of their lands every eighteen months – and though this was supposed to be voluntary and rents were paid, and income was earned working as labourers for the companies, one may guess that the system would not have operated over such a wide area but for political pressures exerted on the villagers to lease their lands whether they wanted to or not. Africa was the continent where the least regard was paid to indigenous land rights, especially in central, east and south Africa. There was still plenty of land in relation to population, so the effect of confining Africans to reserves, e.g. in Kenya or in Southern Rhodesia, would not show up in restricted output until after the war. Then it would become clear that European agriculture had been established at the expense of the Africans.

In many Latin American countries most of the cultivable land was already divided up into large estates, whose owners were not willing to lease or sell to small farmers for independent cultivation. (Colombia was one of the exceptions.) The landowners of southern Brazil brought in large numbers of immigrants and established coffee plantations. The landowners of Venezuela neither encouraged immigration nor rented to their land-hungry peasants; so cultivable lands, suitable for coffee, remained empty.

The decision of some large landowners to leave their lands uncultivated, when the peasants around them are hungry for land, is something of a puzzle. One can see why they would not open up more land and hire more labour, since this would raise wages. But why would they not merely rent out land instead of hiring labour? It is usually assumed that the labourer does more when working for himself than when working for wages; from which it follows that if he owns no land, and if the technology is the same and there are no economies of scale, he can be made to produce a larger surplus in the form of rent than can be extracted by hiring him to work for wages. These propositions explain both why output per acre is higher on small farms than on large farms through most of Asia and Europe; and also why, where land is scarce, landowners rent it out rather than work it with hired labour. Of course, where land is plentiful it would be necessary to restrict the amount rented out, so as to maximize rent, but given the total area permitted to be cultivated, and the total work force, renting would yield a higher surplus to the landowner than would wage labour.

One cannot rent out land for permanent tree crops (nobody will make such investments on a short lease); so if one does not wish to sell the land (for political or social reasons), one must cultivate the land oneself. This would be one reason for having large plantations of tree crops. Another reason, applicable to arable crops as well, would be if the usual assumption that the worker will work harder on his own does not hold. It is conceivable that, where land is plentiful, the farmers are used to doing rather little work to satisfy low consumption standards. If in these circumstances it is possible to deny them land (e.g. to meet population growth) they will have to work on plantations, and it may then be possible, by paying very low wages, to make them work harder than they would on their own. Physical violence, where it exists, reinforces the argument, but is not a necessary condition. If the workers can be made to work harder on plantations, it will pay the landowners to combine to leave lands idle, and to rent small parcels to labour on condition that labour service is performed on the estates. Presumably some groups of landowners in Latin America and in southern Africa have argued in this fashion.

Asian landowners did not hold their lands idle; they rented them out to small farmers. Here the puzzle is why more of these landowners did not farm the lands themselves in large compact estates. This was done in Ceylon; many native landowners put their land into tea, or rubber or coconuts, and some well-to-do urbanites bought land for this purpose. One looks for people of this kind in India, the Philippines or Sumatra, but they are not numerous. Of course the estate is not an economic proposition unless its yields exceed those of the small farmer; but since there were so many expatriate plantations in southern Asia, it is legitimate to wonder why there were not more native plantations. Except perhaps in sugar, the new technology (tea, rubber) was not difficult to learn. Presumably the answer is that the entrepreneurial attitude was to be found in the towns rather than in the countryside; and that townsmen tended to invest in trade and in the professions rather than in agriculture; but this answer in turn only provokes the question why.

The expatriate plantation could not come into existence without government support. Empty land had to be made available, and this usually meant state land, sold for next to nothing, or leased at a minuscule rent. (The exceptions are the cases where the indigenous peoples were moved off their lands, as in parts of Africa, or pressured into renting, as in Java.) Empty land meant absence of labour, so the plantation could not exist unless the government did something to ensure it a labour supply. Where was this labour to come from? Small farmers who have enough land of their own to feed themselves are not normally willing to work for wages on plantations, and in areas where the small farmers are short of land (e.g. Venezuela) they are normally tied to the landowning aristocrats. How then could labour be found for the new plantations? By 1880 slavery had been formally abolished everywhere except in Brazil, Cuba and some parts of the Near East. Powerful capitalists might persuade their governments that the free small farmers should be forced to work on the new plantations, whether at the point of bayonet, or by dispossessing their lands, or by imposing taxes payable only in money, so that the farmers would have to seek wage employment. Parts of Africa and Latin America would continue to engage in these practices, with their culmination in the horrors of the Congo under King Leopold of the Belgians, throughout our period and beyond. However, liberal opinion in the major imperialist powers, Britain, France, and the Netherlands, was strongly hostile to such practices, and fought to limit them. The persons and lands of small farmers were less well protected in the domains of the minor imperialists, and of the independent states.

To meet the shortage of labour, several countries imported Indians and Chinese on indenture. Under his 'contract' the worker was committed to work for his employer for a period which varied up to seven years, and which was enforceable against him by criminal proceedings. The treatment of these workers varied immensely, according to the liberality of the government concerned. In some countries the workers' rights were protected tolerably well, under a system of inspection, to the point that most of the workers decided to stay on and work voluntarily when their contracts elapsed. In other countries the system differed only marginally from slavery. Opposition to the system built up steadily in liberal circles, and also in India, which finally prohibited contract recruitment in 1917. By that date several million Indians and Chinese were living outside India and China. Many of these were traders, but the bulk had come in to work as labourers on plantations, in mines, or in building railways, or were descended from such immigrants.

Tropical South America received very few Indians or Chinese in our period (the earlier guano industry of Peru had been based on indentured Chinese labourers, treated worse than slaves). There was some small West Indian immigration, mostly to build the Panama Canal. But the main source of immigrant labour was Europe, especially, but not exclusively, Italy. Here, also, governments varied in the amount of initiative they would take. Venezuela took none, while the government of Brazil had active subsidized recruitment to bring in Italians for the swiftly expanding coffee industry of São Paulo.

Government. Our analysis of the factors favouring development leads back to the government at several points. The government was needed for internal peace, for irrigation, transport facilities, opening up empty land and immigration. Under highly favourable circumstances, needing only law and order, development was possible even under an inactive government (Burmese rice, Gold Coast cocoa) but these were fringe situations, since development of the country's interior would require railways, and money could not be raised for railways without government support.

Looking at these governments in our period, it seems almost an accident whether the government would be helpful or adverse to development. This is true even of the colonial governments. These did not act alike; changed their policies from time to time (e.g. Indonesia, Belgian Congo) and did different things in different places. The British, for example, promoted white settlement in Kenya, but decided vigorously against white settlement in Uganda and West Africa. Much depended on the personality of the colonial governor, since a strong governor could decide whether to back settlers or African farmers, whether to build a railway or to keep out of public debt, whether to foster immigration of Indian labour or to ban it, and so on. Moreover, governors were not chosen for their opinions; they were chosen for the usual reasons – patronage, knowing the right people, seniority and so on. In the same way the behaviour of the independent governments in Latin America and elsewhere depended very much on the personality of the man who had acquired the central power. All tropical governments were unpredictable at this time, in the sense that one could not predict, when the governor's name was announced (in a colony) or when the president was elected or the general seized power (in independent Latin America), whether one was in for a period of *laissez-faire* or of vigorous government activity.

Conclusion. In the light of the foregoing analysis, we begin to understand why some tropical countries responded swiftly to the growth of world demand after 1880, while others did not. Response was swiftest where new land was available for cultivation, whether by large or small farmers, and where the government removed obstacles to access (ownership, transportation, irrigation).

Immigration was not needed to start the ball rolling, since small farmers had free time beyond that required for growing food, which they could devote to export crops. But the limits of this time could be reached or small farmers might be unwilling to work for wages, in which case expansion of plantations would require immigration.

The fastest growth would be found (just as in the temperate zones) in areas with new land plus immigrant labour (e.g. Malaya, Brazil, Ceylon) or areas with access to new land and surplus labour time (Thailand, Burma, Colombia, Gold Coast). The slowest growth would be in countries where little new land was cultivated, whether because the population was already dense (India, Java) or because the government did nothing to break the land monopoly (Venezuela, Philippines).

Empty wet land was thus the primary requirement for rapid growth through agricultural exports. Good government was a secondary requirement. If there were no obstacles to cultivating the empty land, as in West Africa, the government's role was minimal (law and order and transport facilities). But if the land was tied up legally, as in much of tropical Latin America, economic growth would also require vigorous government action to make land or labour available to potential cultivators. Also government promotion of irrigation or of immigration might become crucial.

Taking the governments of this period as a whole, the performance ranged from terrible to mediocre; none was really good, in the sense of giving high priority to development. Perhaps the most active was the American government after 1900 (Philippines, Puerto Rico). The British did well in Malaya and Ceylon, but held back the industrial development of India, and laid the foundations of tragedy in Kenya. The Latin American governments were committed to the interests of their backward landowning aristocracy, so the average man living under their rule was not significantly better protected than the average colonial. If the tropics at this time were behind-hand in scientific and industrial technology, they were equally behind in political philosophy and public administration. This was partly but not wholly a matter of subordination to vested interests. It is true that the common man had not yet begun to exercise political influence, as was already the case in Western Europe, so that his interests (as a worker or a small farmer) tended to be suppressed whenever they conflicted with the interests of richer groups. But beyond this it is also true that even the interests of the richer groups in development were not adequately served by their governments. The fact that governments have an important positive role to play in development was only just beginning to dawn.

II. RESULTS OF EXPORT GROWTH

The immediate result of the growth of exports was an increase in national income per head, shared in differing proportions by the various social classes. However, growth linked solely to bringing new land into cultivation is unlikely to be permanent; development consists not primarily of exploiting new natural resources, but rather of learning to use existing resources more productively. The test of permanent gain from agricultural exports is therefore not so much the immediate rise in national income as the extent to which this was used as an opportunity for a permanent increase in productive capacity.

To attain economic maturity a country must be transformed in various ways which could be extended into a long list. Four stand out. First it must modernize its agricultural system, so that it becomes capable of yielding an annual increase in productivity. Secondly, it must acquire a reasonable infrastructure (transportation, public health, schools, water supplies, public health, police, courts, etc.). Thirdly, it must grow its own domestic entrepreneurial and administrative class, so that it no longer depends on expatriate enterprise and administration. Fourthly, it must generate its own domestic finance (taxes and savings) so that it can maintain adequate public services and a high level of capital formation without external dependence. If it achieves these last three, the economy will also become diversified; in particular will develop new commodity exports, and will also industrialize, first to process some of its raw material output, secondly in substitution for imports, and ultimately also for export with or without its own raw material base.

If it is wrong to judge the tropical countries exclusively by the rate of growth of their exports during this period, it is equally wrong to judge them (as is often done) solely by the extent to which they industrialized. Much more important is the extent to which they laid development foundations, in modernizing their agriculture and in acquiring infrastructure, modern 'élites', and financial capacity. These were the foundations which Western Europe and North America had been laying for themselves for a century or more before their industrial revolutions; absence of these foundations rather than poverty, is what marked out the tropical countries in 1880, in comparison with the temperate countries, and the task before them was to use the income generated by growing world demand as an opportunity to raise their productive capacity in these senses.

In what follows we shall begin by seeing what can be said about the growth and distribution of income, and then continue with productive capacity and diversification.

The growth of income. Reliable national income figures do not exist for this period, but there is no doubt that income per head was raised by exports. For the tropics as a whole food supply kept pace with population growth, while exports increased at an average rate of 3·6 per cent per annum, with purchasing power (relative prices) in terms of manufactures exactly the same in 1908–12 as in 1879–83. In addition there was a considerable expansion of services, improvements in housing, schooling, etc.

To appreciate this performance one must put it into perspective. In this period the rate of growth of manufacturing was about 2 per cent per annum in the UK, about 4 per cent in Germany, and about 4½ per cent in the USA. Real gross domestic product per head grew by less than 1 per cent per annum in the UK, and by not more than 2 per cent per annum in Germany or the USA.

Some of the tropical countries must undoubtedly have matched the *per capita* growth of GDP in Western Europe (1·0 to 1·5 per cent per annum). Celso Furtado gives this opinion for Brazil, and he may be right, especially if one excludes the north-east region.[1] The evidence for Burma, Thailand, Malaya, Ceylon or the southern Gold Coast (to list only those which have been examined) yields the same results. The period 1880–1913 has to be regarded as one in which many tropical countries grew as rapidly as many of the industrial

[1] See Chapter 4, page 123.

countries. Many, many more grew just as rapidly in their *modern* sectors, and did not grow so rapidly overall only because their modern sectors were still small relatively to their traditional sectors.

We have seen that all tropical countries did not fare equally well. Even where growth rates of gross output were equal, there would be differences in the growth of mass standards of living, associated with population growth, and with whether the exports were coming from small farms or from plantations.

At this time natural rates of population increase were generally low, since the public health measures which would bring down the death rates were still in their infancy. The modal growth rate of population at this time, excluding immigrants, was probably between 1·0 and 1·5 per cent per annum. Growth was perhaps a little higher in one or two Latin American countries; lower in malarial parts of Africa; lowest of all in India, where massive famines might make the rate over a decade as low as 0·5 per cent per annum. But population growth in this period had adverse consequences only in the countries which were short of arable land – Egypt, Java and India, and in only two of these, Egypt (after 1900) and Java, did the cropped area fail to grow as rapidly as population.

The group of small farmers who benefited most were those working on their own lands, not subject to the depredations of landlords. They clearly benefited, despite the harsh exactions of traders and moneylenders, since they grew export crops voluntarily, and only because they were profitable. Most of them grew as much food as before, so the export proceeds were a net addition to their incomes.

The product of all this development was certainly not distributed equally; it never is. Some people were worse off, especially those whose lands were taken away to make room for expatriates, and those who were submitted to various forms of forced labour (including taxes which could be paid only by working for wages). However, those who were deprived of land or labour were relatively few in our period. Perhaps a majority of the population, still locked in subsistence production, was as yet quite untouched by the development process. Those who benefited were those who had joined the monetary sector of the economy, which by 1913 might account for from a quarter to a half of an Asian or African economy. This sector of farmers, traders, civil servants, *et al.* was probably not richer per head than it had been in 1830, since neither productivity nor the terms of trade had altered significantly, but it was much larger, both absolutely and proportionately; the increased product

31

per head of the population occurring mainly as a result of transfers of people from the subsistence to the modern sector, as modern development theory suggests.

Population grew fastest in the countries whose development resulted from immigration, and this must be borne in mind in assessing the growth of income per head. The immigrants clearly benefited, whether free or indentured. Though some indentured labourers were treated badly, most were better off than they would have been in India or China, and they so indicated by refusing to return home when their contracts ended, even though they were entitled to free passages back home.

The fact that much of the product of the plantations accrued to persons other than the plantation workers does not distinguish the tropical economies from other capitalist economies of the time. In such economies (as also in the state-ownership form of socialism) the workers get only a part of their product, the 'surplus' being used to finance the consumption of other classes, and public expenditure, and capital formation. From the point of view of economic growth, critical attention focuses on what is done with the surplus rather than on the fact that it exists.

A substantial part of the 'surplus' was remitted abroad (as also of the incomes of immigrant labourers), whether to families, to shareholders, or to meet charges on railway and public debts. But a substantial part was also reinvested in the country, whether in new private assets, or through payment of taxes to government, or through financing the expansion of railways and other infrastructure.

The word 'empire' is in its origins associated with payment of tribute, and many people take it for granted that the colonies of our time were paying annual levies to Europe. This had never been the case in the British colonies. It had been so with the Dutch, but by 1880 this system had ended. The only territory paying significant tribute in our period was the Congo, under the rule of King Leopold.

India was distinguished among British possessions by the large army which was quartered there, and maintained by Indian taxes. This probably took, along with pensions of retired officers, some 2 to 3 per cent of the Indian national income, but to what extent this fell on the traditional sector of the economy (through land taxes) or on the modern sector would be difficult to say. It is possible that some Latin American armies cost as much or more.

When all is said, it remains indisputable that the expansion of exports raised net national income per head between 1880 and 1913. One could see this among those small farmers who were growing for export, or by comparing the situation of the indentured labourers with what they had left at home. It can also be seen in the expansion of the towns, in the growth of a middle class, and in the improvement of infrastructure. As Chapter 12 shows, this is true even of India in our period.

Why is this so hard to believe? Or rather why was it so hard until about the middle 1960s, when the statistics began to put it beyond doubt that tropical countries had been growing as rapidly as temperate countries since the end of the Second World War? The reason is that the prosperity of the tropical countries in 1880–1913 was followed by a long period of depression stretching from 1913 to 1950. This resulted from the decline in the rate of growth of world trade, first because of the world war, then because of the dislocation of Britain and Europe in the 1920s, then because of the great depression of the 1930s, which was in turn followed by the Second World War. Tropical trade had grown in volume at an average annual rate of 3·6 per cent between 1883 and 1913. Between 1913 and 1929 the rate dropped to 3·1 per cent, and between 1929 and 1955 it dropped still further to 1·5 per cent.[1] Moreover the terms of trade had already turned adverse by 1929; averaged only 91 over 1926–9 as against 100 in 1910–13. Thus the whole period 1913 to 1950 is one of great depression for the tropics.[2] The rate of growth of their income declined, and with this also the rate of growth of their productive capacity. The myth spread that economic development was more difficult to achieve in the tropics than in the temperate zones, and writers invented many kinds of structural and ideological explanations, which were left high and dry after 1950, when world trade revived. The truth is the reverse: but for the great depression of 1913 to 1950 several tropical countries would already have reached self-sustaining growth by 1950.

Productive capacity. As we have said, what matters in the long run is not how large today's national income is, but the extent to which the proceeds are used to make possible self-sustaining growth at a reasonable level. This involves what is done to create a productive agriculture, infrastructure, a modern élite, and financial capacity.

Agricultural output grew fairly rapidly in this period by bringing more land under cultivation. This did not happen everywhere. In a few places population was already pressing on the land (Egypt,

[1] For these figures see my Wicksell Lectures, *Aspects of Tropical Trade 1883–1965*, Stockholm, 1969.

[2] Some Latin American countries began to emerge from this depression in the middle 1930s by promoting manufacturing for import substitution.

B

India, Java); in others land was ample, but it was not accessible to would-be farmers (e.g. Venezuela, Philippines). Governments failed to pass the legislation needed to make land accessible to farmers. In any case, agricultural reform means more than bringing more land under cultivation; more importantly it means learning how to get more output from given inputs year by year. This is a complex process. It involves agricultural research, extension, and for best results, a literate farm population. It requires a network of institutions to supply credit to the farmer, to market his crop, to store seasonal surpluses, to supply fertilizers and irrigation water, and so on. The farmer's incentives must also be safeguarded by protecting him against rapacious landlords and moneylenders. Here and there in the tropics one can trace the beginnings of an agricultural programme – quite a few agricultural experiment stations, some agricultural credit societies, and even some restrictions on moneylenders – but no tropical country came anywhere near to getting the measure of its agricultural problem. The farmers were richer in 1913 than in 1883 because they were cultivating more land in more profitable export crops, but they were not yet beginning to be modern farmers, aware of the scientific relationships between inputs and outputs, and carefully checking costs against benefits and risks. Consequently, when there was no more new land to cultivate (as in Egypt) or when world demand slacked off (as it did from 1913 to 1950) tropical agriculture would sink back into its stagnation.

We get a more favourable picture when we turn from agriculture to the foundations required for sustained progress in the urban economy. Infrastructure of course benefited both town and country, though the towns as usual got the lion's share. The improvement in infrastructure was substantial. Transportation improved most, but the whole range of public services was affected. Public administration was strengthened, especially in Africa, where internal peace was generalized. Towns expanded, with houses, water supplies, hospitals and schools. A whole new range of economic institutions made their appearance – markets, banks, insurance companies. The average tropical town of 1880 was already unrecognizable in 1913.

Where most governments fell down was in neglecting education. There was immense variation. Ceylon, with one-third of its children in school in 1913, must have been near the top for tropical countries, challenged only by one or two West Indian islands. These were not the days of mass primary education. From the development point of view, it is more important to have an adequate outflow from the secondary schools to man managerial and administrative positions.

34

Here the record was better: atrocious in Africa or Indonesia, not at all bad in Colombia, or India or Ceylon, if only in that the native supply was more or less adequate to meet contemporary demand. One can still see today the difference in development capacity between those countries which had already in 1913 a good supply of secondary schools, and those which had not.

This difference shows itself in many ways, of which the most obvious is that those not well supplied with secondary schools have to import intermediate personnel at high cost, and have the distorted wage and salary structures which this produces. However the aspect which now concerns us most is the effect on the size of the modern *élite*, our third topic. In order to develop, a country needs an entrepreneurial class and an administrative class. Both of these are recruited through the secondary schools or also through the universities, mainly, in the first instance, from the sons of landed gentry.

Tropical countries made more progress in creating administrative than entrepreneurial *élites*. This is partly a matter of tradition. The civil service had greater appeal than business for the graduates from secondary schools and universities. But it was also a matter of competition. In many countries foreign trade was in the hands of foreigners – Europeans, Chinese, Indians, or Arabs. There the natives had no trading tradition, and could not get trading experience because the foreigners tended to employ only their own kind. This was not much of a problem in Latin America, where the foreigners tended to become assimilated. But in Africa and south-east Asia the foreigners were to some extent a drain on the country (sending part of their profits out); more importantly were too interested in foreign trade, thus hampering the diversification of the economy; and more importantly yet, in the long run, were a source of racial tension which deflected the talents of young natives into political rather than economic activities and which, in the second half of the twentieth century, would provoke unspeakable acts of genocide. One has to beware of generalizations. Some of the countries in this volume already had a substantial entrepreneurial class by 1913, notably India, Brazil and Colombia. Others were near to the other extreme: Egypt, Uganda, Philippines, Indonesia. And some had made a small beginning: Venezuela, Ceylon.

The fourth aspect of productive capacity is financial capacity: savings and taxes. Here the performance was worst. It was not completely negligible, since enough finance was generated to pay for such infrastructure as there was. The railway companies, the ports, the irrigation facilities and other public works financed by foreign loans had to pay interest and amortization, and if they did not earn enough for these purposes out of their own revenues the government had to find the difference out of taxes. There was probably not much shortage of capital. Money could be raised for infrastructure in the world's capital markets, and the rate for credit-worthy governments was only about 5 per cent. Agriculture, as we have already seen, needed very little capital, and it was not hard to get cheap three months' finance for trade. More important was the fact that tax rates were low because governments' horizons were low. They spent so little on education, public health, agricultural extension and other public services that most of them could manage their current budgets with as little as 4 or 5 per cent of the national income in taxes. Their peoples did not learn (and their rich were not forced) to pay taxes, and so nowadays, when fulfilment of popular ambitions would require nearer 20 per cent to be taken in taxes, many governments have difficulty in educating their people as to the connection between taxes and public services. But one must not exaggerate the contrast between temperate and tropical countries. In 1913, modern industrial nations took only 8 to 10 per cent in taxes; the big jump came during and after the First World War.

In sum, the tropical countries greatly improved their infrastructure, but they did relatively poorly in creating a modern *élite*, or in learning to generate savings and taxes. The most tragic case was that of Egypt, whose rapid growth per head came virtually to a standstill after 1900, when the expansion of the irrigated area trailed off because Egyptians had not in the intervening period learnt how to do anything but grow cotton, and in particular had not taken the opportunity to develop an entrepreneurial class. Practically all the other countries remained rather dependent on foreign initiatives; and this would handicap them when foreign initiatives dried up during the long tropical depression from 1913 to 1950. Self-sustaining growth was nearer in 1913 than in 1880, but there was still a long way to go.

Much of the failure in education and in the creation of entre-preneurial capacity is attributable to governments and the interests supporting them. Some of it resulted simply from neglect, due to the prevailing *laissez-faire* economics of the day, which failed to appre-ciate the role of government in the development process. But some was also deliberate. Some of the colonial governments (but not all) discriminated against indigenous peoples in favour of metropolitan interests, or of local settlers; were hostile to providing higher education or employment in superior posts; and discouraged indigenous entrepreneurship. Many of the governments of independent countries, in Latin America or elsewhere, were no better since, in the interest of their landed aristocracy, they were hostile to social mobility and to the educational or business opportunities which would give rise to it. Whether the failure was due to ignorance or to vice, the net result was the same.

Diversification. In studying how exports serve as an engine of growth one would like to see how, by strengthening the economic base in the ways already described, they made possible the growth of a whole new set of industries. Alas, this is sometimes but not always the case. We must discuss separately service industries, other agricultural industries, and manufacturing.

Service industries are the least complicated case. These of course expand as export income increases. Trade, banking, professions, government service, transport, catering, entertainment, etc., respond to any income, whether derived from exports or not. Service industries tend to be neglected because they do not earn much foreign exchange, but they are important because they are the largest source of employment in the modern sector, and by far and away the largest employer of secondary and university graduates (up to 80 per cent in some economies). Their high education content is also why they have the highest *per capita* value added, despite a low ratio of capital to income. All tropical economies became more diversified, in this important service sense, as their export incomes grew.

Agriculture shows quite a different picture, for this is the era in which 'monoculture' became established.

The term is misleading, since it implies *cultivation* of only one crop, whereas what happens is a tendency to *export* only one crop. As we have seen, the small farmers did not at this time switch from food to export crops. They continued to be self-sufficient in food, and added the export crops.

Monoculture is natural to any region which is geographically homogeneous. Given the soil and the climate, one crop will be more profitable than all the others, and this will be so for every farmer in a geographically homogeneous region. To escape monoculture one must postulate either that the price of the commodity falls as more is produced, or that land is scarce (land scarcity alters the relative cost of producing crops with different factor combinations as relative outputs change), or else that the land is not homogeneous.

Large savannahs are homogeneous geographically (more or less) and come to be planted exclusively in cotton, cocoa, grain, etc.

37

Large countries are not homogeneous (Brazil, India) and even some quite small countries (Ceylon, Jamaica) have different soils and climates which support different crops.

Given plenty of land, geographical difference is necessary to escape monoculture, but it is not sufficient. For if one part of the country is specially suited to a particular crop, which happens to be very profitable, the country will tend to concentrate on developing that region. Labour and capital will flow there, leaving the other regions to be relatively depressed. If 1880–1913 sees the beginning of monoculture, it also sees the beginning of those great regional economic disparities which now plague so many tropical countries, with differences in rainfall so often the crucial factor.

In the meaningful sense, these disparities are due to insufficient internal migration, rather than to too much migration. Migration causes the total output of the poorer region to fall, but when we speak of disparities we are usually referring not to total output but to output per head, which would be equalized at the margin if internal migration were sufficient (some regions might be left with zero output and zero labour). Therefore, in studying regional disparities, one is really studying chiefly the obstacles to internal migration. It is, for example, clear why output rose faster in the state of São Paulo than in north-east Brazil. What is not clear is why more people did not migrate from north-east Brazil to enjoy the ever expanding employment opportunities of São Paulo.

The natural forces which tend to develop agriculture faster in one region than in others may also be reinforced politically. The people of the wealthier region tend to have disproportionate political power which they may use to bolster their region and its crop. Taxes may be set to their advantage, and government expenditures may be concentrated in their favour. The coffee planters of Brazil used federal funds to 'valorize' coffee, at the expense of other crops and regions. The sugar producers of Jamaica did not encourage expenditures that would open up lands suitable for peasant production of bananas, and the tea and coffee planters of highland Ceylon threw their political weight against measures that would develop the lowlands, where small scale agriculture was concentrated. Misuse of political power is one of the evils of monoculture. It can result in artificial discouragement of some potentially valuable regions, and some potentially valuable new crops.

This political evil probably exceeds the disadvantages of the risk of monoculture which are more often discussed. Insofar as the risk arises from cyclical fluctuation of prices, the fact is that the prices

38

of agricultural products tend to move together, so a country's foreign exchange receipts will not necessarily fluctuate less if it exports three crops than if it exports only one. More important is the possibility that the single crop may be wiped out by an epidemic disease (e.g. coffee in Ceylon), or by a catastrophic fall in prices due to the invention of some substitute (e.g. indigo, limes). It is worth while to pay something to avoid these extreme risks. But if one crop is very much more profitable than any other, as is frequently the case (since different crops require different soils and climates) it may be more economic to bear the risk than to insure against it.

We have been considering the forces making for monoculture, but the expansion of exports may also produce diversification. The first crop finances roads and other infrastructure which may open up varied country, with varied possibilities. Most governments then establish some kind of agricultural service, whose officers almost always bring in new crops and try them out (e.g. rubber, Malaya). Thus the development of one export crop may lead indirectly to others.

Exports also create demands for agricultural products, whether consumer demand or intermediate demand. Immigrant labourers and the new urban classes have to be fed, so there is a demand for food. Some exports are bagged, so there is a demand for jute; also farmers use timber, to the advantage of the forest industries.

The rise of the plantation industry created a large market for food, especially rice, which was met by the smallholders of Burma, Thailand and Indochina, who expanded their output for export. One of the puzzles is why the farmers in the countries where the plantations were sited (Ceylon, Indonesia, Malaya, Philippines) did not themselves grow more rice to sell to the plantation labourers. They were protected by transportation costs, and would surely have had the political support of the planters and their governments. Presumably, in Ceylon, wet zone farmers found coconuts and rubber more profitable, and dry zone farmers simply lacked water. The Philippine farmers were deprived of access to land. Why Sumatra has not developed a sizable export of rice to Java remains obscure; presumably as in Ceylon or Malaya the perennial crops have been more profitable.

Finally we turn to manufacturing industry. Here also agricultural exports help by paying for infrastructure, and by creating a professional and business middle class capable of starting new enterprises. Exports also create demand, both consumer demand and intermediate demand. Why then did so little manufacturing industry develop in those tropical countries which were enriching themselves through agricultural exports? Of the countries in this book only India, Brazil, Ceylon and Colombia made a significant start with industrialization.

We may list seven possible explanations:

1. The destructive impact of foreign trade.
2. The distribution of income.
3. The use of political power by foreign traders.
4. The need for infant industry protection.
5. The absence of coal and iron ores.
6. The superior profitability of agricultural exports.
7. The absence of a domestic entrepreneurial class.

Foreign trade may actually destroy existing industries rather than create new ones. The destruction of the Indian handicraft cotton-spinning industry by imports is the stock example; however this was over before our period begins. From 1880 onwards such local industries as existed tended to grow, not to decline.

The second possibility often suggested is that industrialization was hampered by the unequal distribution of income. In this model, the poor consume mass-produced factory articles, suitable for manufacture at home, while the rich consume types of commodities which cannot be made at home. The argument can be challenged in various ways (can even be reversed by alleging that it is the rich who consume manufactures while the poor consume mainly food at the margin). But we do not need to pursue such models since essentially what they set out to explain is a deficiency of demand for manufactures— whereas in our period there was no such deficiency of demand. The tropical countries were importing large quantities of textiles, shoes, bicycles, and other such commodities that could have been manufactured at home. Our problem is failure of supply, not failure of demand.

The third explanation postulates that foreign traders had a vested interest in imports, and so discouraged local manufacture. Those importers had a vested interest in imports who also owned ships, or owned factories abroad, or owned rights to popular brand names. Other importers could have hoped to invest in local factories, or to acquire distribution rights. The foreign traders in West Africa seem to have been hostile to domestic manufacture, but one may doubt the significance of traders' hostility in other parts of the tropical world.

This hostility, if it existed, was important not positively but negatively, in the sense that it was not what the traders did but what they prevented from happening that mattered. For the fourth proposition is that industrialization could not succeed without active governmental support, in the form of tariffs or subsidies, and this the traders prevented. The proposition leans heavily on the familiar infant industries argument. This in turn leans partly on economies of scale, and partly on the costs of learning. Despite the age and undoubted validity of this argument, one may doubt how important it was in 1880. For there were at that time no significant economies of scale in cotton manufacture, and no such long learning processes as would ensure the defeat of newcomers to the industry. Alfred Marshall made a big issue of external economies, but even as he was writing his treatise, and illustrating it from Lancashire, the Indian cotton industry was rising up to slay Lancashire. The Indian cotton industry had absolutely no tariff or quota protection. If India could manufacture as cheaply as Lancashire, why not also Ceylon, or Egypt, or Malaya, or Java or the Philippines?

The principal weakness of the tropical countries was lack of cheap iron ores and coal on which to base an iron and steel industry. This limited their range of manufactures of metallic products, at a time when wood was giving way to metals. It is true that pig iron could be imported for fabrication, but in the absence of tariff protection the comparative advantage would lie with the countries which produced pig iron. Absence of ores did not only foreclose an opportunity of employment. It also raised the cost of manufacturing non-metallic products, since the factories had to import their machinery from abroad, and therefore faced higher capital costs than their competitors in the industrial countries. This seems to have been one of the more important limitations on industrialization both in India and in Brazil, though India had ores, whose development was hindered by the imperial power.

Brazil is a particularly interesting case, since it is frequently contrasted with the USA. They are similar in that both developed through agricultural exports. In the period 1880–1913, Brazil probably did about as well as the USA was doing in the period 1850–90. In both cases there was vast immigration opening up new agricultural lands, and a rapid growth of agricultural exports. In both cases, too, the cotton manufacturing industry went ahead quite rapidly. And both had vast regional disparities which make it reasonable to compare only their leading regions. The big difference is that the USA had its own iron and coal industries throughout, providing an additional source of manufacturing employment, and

41

serving also as a base for a burgeoning engineering industry. Output per head in the state of São Paulo was probably not very different from output per head in Pennsylvania in 1890. Thereafter the steel industry galloped off in the USA, multiplying its output by seven in twenty years. This example Brazil could not follow for lack of cheap coking coal.

Given the fact that the mineral base was inadequate and that it was costly to import machinery, one has to face the question whether in those tropical countries where labour was scarce, the most profitable use of labour during the period of booming agricultural prices, 1895–1913, was not to produce agricultural exports and to import cheap manufactures from the industrial countries. This argument would certainly not apply to India, or Java, or Egypt, or any other labour-saturated country, but it is not implausible for the rest of the tropics. Europeans found it profitable to emigrate to produce agricultural commodities in Canada, Australia or Argentina; and Americans found it profitable at this time to move westward out of the urban industrial centres into agricultural production in the Middle West. It would therefore be absurd to assume that the tropical countries were misusing resources, or missing an opportunity, merely because they developed their agriculture rather than their manufacturing at this time.

The comparison with the temperate agricultural countries is not, however, all-persuasive. The price of tropical products, per manhour of labour time, was lower than the price of wheat or wool. Tropical farmers produced less food per head than temperate farmers, and therefore received less per head for the alternative commodities which they supplied in international trade. Temperate countries could therefore better afford to be in agriculture, since their agriculture had better factoral terms of trade. To upset this argument one must demonstrate an equal productivity difference between the industrial sectors of temperate and tropical countries. There was indeed some difference in industrial productivity associated both with lower skills and higher capital costs (due to poor maintenance, higher depreciation rates, the higher cost of imported machinery and the greater scarcity of capital). But skills can be learned, and the differential in capital costs is also reduced by the development process itself.

In any case, despite the superior factoral terms of trade of their agriculture the temperate agricultural countries (Australia, etc.) *did* develop significant manufacturing capacity to a greater extent than the tropical zone. This was probably associated with the fact that

42

they were better equipped for manufacturing – had better infra-structure, a wider range of economic institutions, a greater savings capacity, and above all a domestic entrepreneurial class. Where such a class had made its beginnings, as in India or Brazil, manufacturing industry did get off the ground, in contrast with countries where it had not, such as Egypt or Venezuela. Domestic entrepreneurship was necessary because the foreign entrepreneurs were mainly interested in foreign trade – not exclusively so (Indian initiatives in jute manufacture and in iron and steel were taken by British manu-facturers), but sufficiently so for it to be generally true that the nationals of the country were more interested in developing its manufacturing capacity than its foreign capitalists were. When one has been through all the other factors, one is left with lack of domestic entrepreneurship as the most powerful explanation of failure to make significant progress in manufacturing, since almost any Latin American or Asian country could have supported enough manufacturing to employ, say, 6 to 8 per cent of its population in factories in 1913, with moderate tariffs. One should not be surprised at the lack of domestic industrial entrepreneurship; it takes more than thirty years for such a class to evolve. Germany, for example, was still relatively untouched by the Industrial Revolu-tion in 1830, when both Britain and France had been modernizing rapidly for at least thirty to forty years.

This answer is not, however, completely unrelated to the defi-ciencies of governments in this period, since better governments would have done more to create the kind of atmosphere in which industrial entrepreneurship, whether domestic or foreign, could flourish. To expect this from the colonial governments would be asking too much; the British government made its hostility towards industrialization quite clear in India, and the other colonial powers were no less prejudiced. The independent governments had the opportunity to foster industrialization, and the government of Brazil did in fact give tariff support. But most of the independent govern-ments were more interested in the landowners than in potential industrialization, and neglected their opportunity. The full exploita-tion of import substitution would not begin until the 1930s in Latin America, and the 1950s in Africa and Asia.

III. CONCLUSION

The picture presented by this introductory essay, and by the suc-ceeding chapters on which it is based, differs significantly from the current view of the fate of tropical countries in the period 1880–1913. The literature of this topic is sparse, but such as it is, it is mostly sombre. The terms which occur most frequently are 'colonialism', 'monoculture', 'exploitation', 'low wages', 'sources of raw materials', 'drain', 'peripheral', 'unstable'. These terms are appropriate and true, but they represent only one aspect of what took place. Our picture differs not in omitting the sombre, but in adding the other features which are necessary for a balanced assessment of the period.

As we have seen, those countries which responded to the demand for exports did well. Their modern sectors grew as rapidly as the modern sectors of Western Europe, and if their overall growth rates *per capita* were lower, say, 1·0 to 1·5 instead of 1·5 to 2·0, this would be because their traditional subsistence sectors were still so large; they were starting from a lower base of development. If modern sectors had continued to grow at the same rate, without the interruptions of the First World War, the great depression of the 1930s, and the Second World War, the leading tropical countries would now be unrecognizable.

The period is probably more important for laying the foundations for future growth than for what it did for income per head at the time. The tropical countries were late starters; were essentially subsistence economies until the coming of the railway, in contrast with Europe or North America where the road and canal revolution of the eighteenth century had already created large market economies at least a century before, and where the agricultural revolution had already, before 1800, made possible a substantial industrial and urban class.

What the tropical countries did during 1880–1913 was to improve their productive capacity; to give themselves railways, roads, harbours, water supplies; to build towns, schools, hospitals; to sprout a professional and trading middle class; to improve their economic, legal and political institutions, and to establish new ones. The 'enclave' economy existed, with exports isolated from any development function; but this was not the typical pattern.

Not all seized their opportunities. Some were slow to respond to export demand, while others sold their exports but spent the money without significant improvement of their productive capacity. The interest of the story lies in these contrasts; in trying to discover why some moved faster than others, and to identify the obstacles in the way of benefiting from the expansion of agricultural exports. In this process one learns that the problems of economic development are not significantly different today from what they were at the end of the nineteenth century.

BIBLIOGRAPHY

Books

Furnivall, J. S., *An Introduction to the Political Economy of Burma*, Rangoon, 1931.

Hill, Polly, *The Migrant Cocoa-Farmers of Southern Ghana*, Cambridge, 1963.

Lewis, W. A., *Aspects of Tropical Trade 1883–1965*, Stockholm, 1969.

McClelland, D. C., *The Achieving Society*, Princeton, 1961.

Article

Myint, Hla, 'The Classical Theory of International Trade and the Under-developed Countries', *Economic Journal*, June 1958.

Chapter 2

TROPICAL EXPORTS

by Charles C. Stover

I. THE RATE OF GROWTH

Between 1883 and 1913 the exports of tropical countries grew as rapidly as the exports of temperate countries, i.e. at an average rate of 3·4 per cent per annum, in dollar value. The data for tropical countries are reproduced in Table 2.1 which is abstracted from Professor Lewis's Wicksell Lectures.[1] Data for world trade comes from Dr Folke Hilgerdt's revised series, which rises from $7·8 billion in 1883 to $20·9 billion in 1913 (import values).[2]

The dollar values of tropical trade can be translated into an index of quantities with the special price index number of tropical exports which is given in the same source.[3] Volume grows faster than value, since prices were lower in 1913 than in 1883. The growth rate of volume was 3·6 per cent per annum over thirty years.

TABLE 2.1: *Exports from Tropical Countries*

(US $ million)

	1883	1899	1913
AFRICA			
Angola	2·0	8·6	5·6
Belgian Congo	2·2	7·0	11·7
British Somalia	2·3	1·8	1·0

[1] W. A. Lewis, *Aspects of Tropical Trade, 1883–1965*, Stockholm, 1969. The years 1883, 1899 and 1913 are cyclical peaks. The tropics are here defined as countries lying between 30° N and 30° S. The most important 'underdeveloped' exclusions are Argentina, Chile, Uruguay, the North African countries (excluding Egypt), and the Near East. Table 2.1 is an expanded version of the table in the Wicksell Lectures.

[2] The original figures were published in quinquennial averages in the League of Nations's *Industrialisation and Foreign Trade*. The revised annual data can be deduced from W. A. Lewis, 'World Production, Prices and Trade 1870–1960', *The Manchester School*, May 1952.

[3] Lewis, *Aspects*, pp. 49–50.

(u s $ million)

	1883	1899	1913
AFRICA (*continued*)			
Cameroons	0·6*	1·2	2·9
Cape Verde	0·2	0·4	0·4*
Egypt	60·8	75·9	156·5
Eritrea	0·3*	0·4	2·3
Ethiopia	1·0*	0·2	4·2†
French Equatorial Africa	—	1·6	7·1
French Somalia	—	0·1	9·2
French West Africa	4·0	12·4	24·4
Gambia	1·0	1·2	3·2
Gold Coast	1·8	5·4	26·4
Italian Somalia	0·1*	0·1	0·4
Kenya–Uganda	0·3	0·6	7·2
Liberia	0·3	0·7	1·1
Madagascar	1·5	2·2	10·9
Mauritius	18·7	8·1	10·4
Mozambique	1·1‡	1·5	5·3
Nigeria	7·9	8·5	33·0
Northern Rhodesia	—	—	1·0
Nyasaland	—	0·2	1·1
Portuguese Guinea	0·3*	0·5	0·5
Reunion	4·5	3·7	3·2
São Tomé	3·0*	3·8	9·0
Seychelles	0·2*	0·6	0·8
Sierra Leone	2·2	1·6	6·7
Southern Rhodesia	0·1	1·3	2·0
Sudan	0·6	1·5	5·8
Tanganyika	0·3*	1·0	3·9
Togo	0·1*	0·5	0·6
Zanzibar	6·8	7·4	3·0
AMERICA, NORTH			
Bahamas	0·7	0·8	1·3
Barbados	5·6	4·1	2·6
British Honduras	1·1	1·3	1·4
Costa Rica	2·1	4·9	10·3
Cuba	70·0*	46·3	165·2
Dominican Republic	0·7	5·8	10·5
El Salvador	5·9	3·7	7·7
Guadeloupe	6·2	4·5	3·5
Guatemala	4·8	8·4	14·5

47

TABLE 2.1 (*continued*)

(US $ million)

	1883	1899	1913
AMERICA, NORTH (*continued*)			
Haiti	7·3	12·7	11·3
Honduras	0·8	2·7	3·3
Jamaica	6·9	9·2	11·0
Leeward Islands	2·8	1·8	2·5
Martinique	7·0	6·4	5·6
Mexico	36·9	71·4	130·0
Netherlands Antilles	1·3	0·9	0·9
Nicaragua	1·0	2·4	7·7
Trinidad	8·6	12·5	11·4
Virgin Islands	1·0*	1·0*	0·3
Windward Islands	2·7	2·0	2·9
AMERICA, SOUTH			
Bolivia	8·0*	11·6	36·6
Brazil	84·5	162·2§	315·6
British Guiana	15·4	9·4	8·3
Colombia‖	11·9	19·2	39·7
Ecuador	3·6	8·2	15·8
French Guiana	0·1	1·6	2·4
Paraguay	1·0*	2·3	5·6
Peru	15·0*	16·4	44·5
Surinam	0·2	2·2	3·8
Venezuela	19·7	15·0*	28·8
ASIA			
Brunei	0·1	0·1	0·1
Ceylon	13·9	32·8	72·7
French India	4·9	2·2	8·5
India	336·6	353·9	792·4
Indochina	15·7	26·6	66·9
Indonesia	80·2	100·9	249·4
Malaya¶	72·7	102·8	192·5
North Borneo	0·5	2·0	4·1
Philippines	24·1	14·9	51·2
Portuguese India	0·5*	0·8	1·0
Sarawak	0·7	2·5	3·3
Thailand	8·0	15·2	43·1

(US $ million)	1883	1899	1913
OCEANIA			
Fiji	1·7	2·3	6·9
French Polynesia	0·7	0·8	2·2
New Caledonia	0·6	2·1	3·1
Papua	0·1	0·3	0·3
Other	2·0*	3·0*	5·0*
TOTAL	1,020·0	1,274·1	2,768·5

* Interpolation or 'guesstimate'.　　　　† 1912.　　　　‡ 1884.
　§1900　　　　　　　　　　　　　|| Includes Panama in 1913.
　¶ Figures for 1883 and for 1900 are for Straits Settlements. These figures include a very large element of re-exports.
Source: Lewis, *Aspects*, pp. 47–8.

This growth rate was only slightly lower than that of world industrial production, which is estimated at 3·7 per cent per annum.[1] Thus it may be said that the 'engine of growth' of the tropical world (exports) was beating as powerfully as the 'engine of growth' of the temperate world (industrial production) before the First World War. The picture which emerges is of a world economy in which industrial production, trade in manufactures, the trade of tropical countries and the trade of temperate countries were all growing at about the same rate.

It was not a constant rate of growth. Besides the well-known Juglar cycle (peaking in 1883, 1890, 1899, 1907 and 1913), there was also the 'great depression', as a result of which the world economy grew faster after 1899 than between 1883 and 1899. The following are the average annual growth rates for world industrial production and for the volume of tropical trade.

	1883 1899	1899 1913
Industrial production	3·3	4·2
Tropical exports	3·0	4·2

The depression was already marked at the peak of 1890, which was weak, mainly because of depressed conditions in Britain and France;

[1] Lewis, *Aspects*, pp. 52–3. The difference is well within the margin of error.

49

world prices were significantly lower in 1890 than in 1883. They continued to fall in the first half of the 1890s, especially after 1893, when the USA experienced a major depression. After the turn of the century all the major industrial powers boomed simultaneously. At the same time the closing of the American agricultural frontier reduced the growth rate of American agricultural exports. Prices then zoomed upwards.

This secular 'Kondratieff' movement shows very clearly in the prices of tropical products. In Table 2.2 commodities are arranged in ascending order, according to the ratio of their prices[1] in 1913 to 1883 (the third column). The first column is the index of 1899 on 1883, and the second column the index of 1913 on 1899.

TABLE 2.2: *Price Index Numbers*

	$\dfrac{1899}{1883}$	$\dfrac{1913}{1899}$	$\dfrac{1913}{1883}$
Sugar	46	107	49
Tea	71	103	73
Palm Oil	62	164	87
Cocoa	91	96	88
Rubber	83	111	92
Rice	106	91	97
Coffee	96	102	98
Cotton	66	191	125
Hides	72	175	126
Tobacco Leaf	94	138	130
Jute	104	207	215

The downward trend of prices was uniform in the 1880s and down to 1895, except for coffee, which moved upwards in this period (mainly because civil wars in Latin America interfered with supplies). During the upturn after 1895, prices recovered ground in varying degrees, so fast in rice and jute that in these two cases the 1883 price was already surpassed by 1899.

We can also explain the cases at the top and bottom of the list. Sugar suffered from excess and subsidized supplies, especially in Europe; while tea suffered from the relative stagnation of demand in Britain, the largest user. At the other end of the table, both tobacco and cotton profited from the closing of the American agricultural

---

[1] *Source:* These are c.i.f. London prices, as published by the British Board of Trade. See the *Eighteenth Abstract of Labour Statistics*, London, 1926.

frontier by 1900, which reduced the growth rate of American exports of these commodities. Jute ate into the market for hemp (whose price rose by less than 50 per cent); this plus the growing demand for packaging materials, with growing internal and external trade, kept pressure on supplies. The prices of hides and skins also benefited from rising demands, especially since leading African and Asian suppliers were not as yet interested in animal husbandry.

The terms of trade varied relatively little over the period, except in the middle 1890s. An index of the price of manufactures[1] fell from 100 in 1883 to 92 in 1913. On this basis the commodity terms of trade were constant for rubber, deteriorated for the first four commodities in Table 2.2, and improved for the last six commodities. Individual countries fared according to their particular specializations and demands.

The great depression hit India worse than other tropical countries because the prices of some of its leading exports – cotton and wheat – declined much more sharply during this period than the average for other tropical exports. In terms of dollars India's exports rose only by 5 per cent between 1883 and 1899, whereas exports of other tropical countries were up by 34 per cent. Adverse prices reacted on output. Valued at constant prices[2] India's agricultural exports grew by $1 \cdot 1$ per cent per annum to 1899, as against $1 \cdot 9$ per cent per annum in the second half of our period. After 1899 India's exports grew as fast as those of other tropical countries, lagging agricultural exports beings compensated by rapidly increasing exports of metals and manufactures.

If we exclude India, the volume growth rate for other tropical countries is about the same as that of India in the second half, i.e. about $4 \cdot 2$ per cent but is raised sharply in the first half, to about $3 \cdot 9$ per cent per annum indicating that the great depression was not nearly so marked in other tropical countries as it was in India.

II. INDIVIDUAL COMMODITIES

Table 2.3 shows the relative importance of individual commodities in tropical trade, by listing them according to the value of each exported from tropical countries in 1913. These figures are not exact. They are based on figures published by Lamartine Yates,[3] who identifies the continents but does not always show enough data for us to make a precise exclusion of exports from non-tropical

[1] Lewis, *Aspects*, pp. 49–51.   [2] See Chapter 12, page 311.
[3] P. Lamartine Yates, *Forty Years of Foreign Trade*, London, 1959.

51

Asia, Africa or Latin America. The second column of the table indicates roughly what proportion tropical exports were of the total trade in each product; it will be observed that the tropical countries faced strong competition for about half the trade listed in the table.

TABLE 2.3: *Tropical Agricultural Exports, 1913*

	Value US $ million	Percentage of World Trade
Coffee	336	100
Cotton	300	33
Sugar	245	50
Rice	242	95
Vegetable Oils*	220	40
Rubber	210	100
Hides and Skins	170	33
Hard Fibres	150	60
Tea	133	100
Cocoa	84	100
Tobacco Leaf	40	30
Timber	36	7
Bananas	27	100

* Includes oilseeds.

In addition to the agricultural exports shown in Table 2.3 and other agricultural exports bringing the agricultural total to $2,130 million, the tropics exported about $370 million of minerals (including gold) and $270 million of manufactures in 1913. More than half the manufactures came from India, led by cotton and jute manufactures. The exports of minerals were already growing rapidly; they are 'guesstimated'[1] at 5 per cent of total exports in 1883, 13 per cent in 1913, 26 per cent in 1937, and 29 per cent in 1965. The relative share of manufactures, in contrast, was low in the inter-war period, and did not start to grow rapidly until after 1955.

It is not possible, without much labour, to show the growth of the exports of individual commodities from the tropics between 1883 and 1913. However, it is possible to calculate imports into the leading countries of the products in which the tropics were mainly interested. The result gives us not tropical exports, since exports from temperate countries are included, but the expansion of the market as a whole. This is done in Table 2.4. The first column

[1] *Aspects*, page 51.

shows the value of total imports of the commodity[1] into the UK, Germany, the USA, France and Belgium in 1913. The second column gives an index number of value for 1913, on base 1883, and the third column gives a quantity index number, using prices c.i.f. London. The commodities are arranged in order of the value index number, with those that expanded fastest at the bottom of the table.

TABLE 2.4: *Imports of Tropical Products into Five Countries**

	Value 1913	Value $\dfrac{1913}{1883}$	Quantity $\dfrac{1913}{1883}$
	$US million	1883	1883
Tea	74	1·19	1·62
Cotton	588	2·02	1·62
Coffee	229	2·21	2·25
Hemp, jute	134	2·48	1·55
Oilseeds, vegetable oils	482	2·55	2·93
Tobacco leaf	109	2·94	2·26
Rubber	186	5·39	5·85
Cocoa	54	5·68	6·45
Bananas	27	14·91	n.a.

* UK, Germany, France, Belgium and USA: Figures derived from annual trade reports of each country. Figures are as nearly as possible imports minus re-exports, but comparability is impaired by the different commodity definitions and the different concepts used by different countries. Quantities in the third column found by applying to values the price indexes in Table 2.2. Rice and sugar are excluded because in these two commodities imports into these five countries are clearly not representative of world trade as a whole.

Here follow some notes on individual commodities in the order of their importance to the tropics, as in Table 2.3.

Coffee. Coffee was exported exclusively from the tropics. In the middle of the nineteenth century it was grown fairly widely in Asia and tropical America, but the crop was very subject to epidemic diseases. Valuable plantations in Ceylon and India and Java were wiped out during the second half of the century, leaving coffee primarily a Latin American crop.

The biggest expansions occurred in Brazil, Colombia, Mexico and Central America. For reasons explained later in this volume, Venezuela notably failed to respond to expanding opportunities. Asian output actually declined. The main producing countries are shown in Table 2.5.

[1] 'Special' imports, i.e. imports less re-exports.

TABLE 2.5: *Coffee Production*

(thousand metric tons)

	Average 1881–85	Average 1896–00	1913
Brazil	296	530	727
Venezuela	35	60	64
Colombia	7*	33	61
Guatemala	17	39	42
Mexico	6*	23	37
Java	82	46	35
El Salvador	6*	15	29
Haiti	25*	31	26
Puerto Rico	20*	23	23
India	13*	10	13

* Interpolated.

Source: France, Institut National de la Statistique et des Etudes Economiques, *Annuaire Statistique, Rétrospectif*, 1951, pp. 417–18.

The *Annuaire*'s estimate of world production gives an annual average growth of 2·3 per cent in the first fifteen years, compared with 1·9 per cent in the second fifteen years. There is a similar break in prices, which held up until 1896, being in that year 42 per cent higher than in 1883, and then fell almost continuously until 1910. In other words the industry was prosperous and expanded rapidly until the middle nineties. Ever since then coffee has been in trouble most of the time. The first major commodity control scheme was the coffee valorization scheme adopted in Brazil in 1906. This story is told in Chapter 4.

Cotton. World production grew steadily during this period (by about 3·3 per cent per annum) but there were considerable shifts in the relative importance of main producers. The USA and Egypt expanded in the first half of the period, and were then constrained in both cases by reaching their extensive margins: by the closing of the agricultural frontier in the USA, and by slowing down of irrigation in Egypt. Main producers are shown in Table 2.6.

The price of cotton, in contrast, moved down sharply in the first half, and rose even more sharply in the second half of the period (see Table 2.2). This is explained partly by the much faster growth of manufacturing in the second half of the period, and partly by the deceleration of exports from the USA and Egypt. Production grew swiftly in India and in Brazil in the second half. In both these countries rapid growth of domestic cotton manufacturing was a actor, but rising prices also contributed to stimulating raw cotton production.

Sugar. The first half of this period proved extremely difficult for tropical producers. Beet production increased enormously; as can be seen in Table 2.7 it increased between 1882 and 1900 by 188 per

TABLE 2.6: *Production of Cotton*

(thousand metric tons)

	1881–85	1900	1913
USA	1,273	2,197	3,069
India	400*	536	919
Egypt	130	244	344
Russia	n.a.	n.a.	158
Brazil	30*	46	103
Mexico	20*	22	45

* Interpolated.
Source: *Annuaire Statistique, Rétrospectif*, 1951, p. 428.

TABLE 2.7: *World Production of Centrifugal Sugar*

(thousand metric tons)

	1882–3	1900–1	1913–14
Beet Sugar	2,114	6,090	9,035
Cane Sugar	1,917	3,563	7,683
Total	4,031	9,653	16,718
Cane producers			
Cuba	474	655	2,677
Indonesia	216	744	1,405
Hawaii	52	327	566
Puerto Rico	80	94	314
USA	145	283	279
Argentina	15	117	274
Mauritius	124	190	250
Australia	36	114	250
Peru	24	120	223
British West Indies	308	289	174

Source: International Sugar Council, *The World Sugar Economy, Structure and Policies*, London, 1963, Vol. 2, pp. 225–7.

cent, as against 86 per cent for cane sugar production. In addition, several of the leading beet producers were paying substantial bounties on sugar exports, which further depressed free market prices. These bounties continued until 1903, when they were eliminated by international agreement through the Brussels Convention – the first international commodity agreement about a tropical product.

The free market price of sugar fell almost continuously until 1902, when it reached 36 per cent of its 1880 level; thereafter it revived slowly.

Tropical production thus came to depend on the availability of very cheap labour, much of it imported from India or China on indenture, and also on high technology. Much effort was given to careful selection of high yielding and disease resisting varieties of cane, and also after 1900 to the breeding of new varieties of cane. In this period also the small sugar mills were steadily driven out by large central factories with lower labour costs and higher extraction rates. Producers who could not meet these requirements – cheap labour and high technology – were driven out of the business, notably in the British West Indian islands and in Brazil, which had once been the world market's two chief sources of sugar.

After 1900 the cane sugar industry fared better. The Brussels Convention checked the growth of beet sugar production, and world prices rose. But despite the quadrupling of production between 1882 and 1913, the output of cane sugar in the later year was worth less than twice as much as the output of 1882, when both are valued at current market prices.

Rice. Before 1870 Europe was the main importer of rice but, with the development of tropical plantation industries, Europe's share of world imports had by 1913 dropped to about 40 per cent. Italy and Egypt had ceased to be principal suppliers. Three south Asian countries, with well-watered and relatively underpopulated lands (Burma, Thailand and Indochina) had seized the opportunity to build up large export trades in rice. Between them these three accounted for about 75 per cent of world exports of rice.

On the demand side, the three largest importers were now the plantation economies of Malaya, Indonesia and Ceylon, whose demands were growing swiftly. But Asia as a whole was self-sufficient, and had a large export surplus to Europe, to North America, and to the plantation economies of Latin America. Table 2.8 gives a rough picture of world trade in rice at the end of our period.

Since the price of rice held up very well throughout this period, the three main Asian suppliers prospered exceedingly. In current dollar value, total exports from Thailand and Indochina were in

1913 respectively 539 and 426 per cent of exports in 1883. The index for exports from Burma to foreign countries was 300, but this understates the position, since it excludes Burma's exports to India.

TABLE 2.8: *World Trade in Rice, Average 1909–13*

(thousand metric tons)

Imports		Exports	
Malaya	920	Burma	2,438
Indonesia	450	Indochina	896
Ceylon	385	Thailand	792
Cuba	120	Others	1,324
Others	3,575		
	5,450		5,450

Based on P. Lamartine Yates, *op. cit.*, p. 73. Figures for milled rice or equivalent exports of Burma are shown net of exports to India.

Vegetable oils and oilseeds. If our index of imports by leading importers is a good guide (Table 2.4) world trade in vegetable oils and oilseeds grew at about the same rate as world trade (and tropical trade) as a whole. However, the tropical share was only about 40 per cent. The tropics had a monopoly or near monopoly of coconut, oil palm and groundnut products, shared the cottonseed market, and faced competition from linseed, rape, sesame, soya and olive oils.

It is not possible to distinguish the tropical trade in these products separately, but it seems to have grown very much faster than the temperate trade, and therefore than tropical trade as a whole. If palm oil is typical, the market was weak down to the second half of the 1880s. The price then started to climb slowly, and accelerated after 1905. The swiftest increase in production and imports came after the upturn in world industrial production in the second half of our period.

Tropical countries which benefited substantially included India (cottonseed, peanuts), Ceylon, Malaya, Indonesia and the Philippines (coconuts) and Nigeria (oil palm).

Rubber. The *Annuaire Statistique*[1] estimates that production of rubber grew between 1880 and 1913 from 11 to 125 thousand metric tons; Table 2.4 gives an index of imports into leading countries of 5·85 on base 1883, but the trade figures also include gutta-percha.

Rubber had been known for centuries, but did not become a

[1] *op. cit.*, p. 432.

57

commodity of major significance until the vulcanization process began to come into use in the second half of the nineteenth century. In the first half of our period, the demand was still primarily for use in making raincoats, shoes, bicycle tyres and household articles; the demand from automobiles, now the largest consumer, began at the end of the century, and rose swiftly.

In 1913 three-fifths of the world supply was still wild rubber, and the Amazon basin was still the largest source. The shift to Asia came at the very end of the century, when the plantation industry was launched in Malaya. Plantation growth was swift: from about 5,000 acres in 1900 to 1,250,000 in 1913. According to the *Annuaire* the chief producers in 1913 were:

	thousand metric tons		
Brazil	36	Indonesia	7
Malaya	27	Bolivia	5
Ceylon	12		

The wild rubber industry was destroyed as much by the slaughter tapping of forest trees as by the superior varieties and processing of plantation rubber. The slaughter tapped rubber industries were booming around 1900 (Brazil, Bolivia, Mexico, Peru, Nigeria, Belgian Congo, Ivory Coast), but were already on their way down in 1913.

Hides and skins. These were an important source of income to many tropical countries; in the aggregate about as important as the more glamorous oilseeds, and as tea and cocoa added together. Yet no statistics are available to shed light on the growth rate of this trade. According to Lamartine Yates, the share of the tropics in total trade must have been about one-third.[1] India and Brazil were the largest tropical suppliers, but some hides and skins came out of practically every tropical country, except for those parts of Africa from which animals were excluded by the tsetse fly.

Hard fibres. The main tropical suppliers, and their 1913 exports, as given by Lamartine Yates, were as follows:

India (jute)	US $105 million
Philippines (abaca)	25
Mexico (henequen, sisal)	13

---

[1] *op. cit.*, p. 116. He allocates 42 per cent to the three less developed continents, but this includes substantial supplies from Argentina, Uruguay, Morocco and the Union of South Africa.

Production of tropical hard fibres grew faster than that of their main temperate competitor, hemp. The *Annuaire Statistique* estimates that world output of hemp grew 70 per cent between 1876–80 and 1913. India's exports of jute just about doubled in volume between 1882–4 and 1911–13, and domestic consumption increased even faster. Mexican and Philippine production also grew nearly as rapidly. The price of hemp languished, but the price of jute doubled between 1883 and 1913, so hard fibres were an excellent market for the tropics in this period. The basic reason was of course that the trebling of world trade enormously increased the demand for packaging materials and ropes.

Tea. Tea did better than Table 2.4 suggests, because the table omits some large consumers, especially Russia, The Netherlands, and overseas countries of the British Empire. The *Annuaire Statistique* estimates that world production about doubled between 1890 and 1914; but for India, Ceylon and Indochina together it estimates an increase of 233 per cent. Production in Japan and Formosa less than doubled, while production in China actually declined.

Consumption per head grew rather slowly in Britain, which was taking in 1914 about 40 per cent of the traded supply. The swift increase of output therefore depressed prices. Nevertheless, tea production remained prosperous throughout this period.

Tea shared with sugar the distinction of being plantation industries, whose technical requirements rendered them unsuitable for small-scale farming. They were therefore associated with land alienation, immigrant capital, expatriate management and indentured labour.

Cocoa. This is still the smallest of the three tropical beverage industries; in 1913 it was worth only 15 per cent of the total of

TABLE 2.9: *World Production of Cocoa*

(thousand metric tons)

	1896–1900	1913
Gold Coast	1	51
Ecuador	18*	39
São Tomé	13	36
British West Indies	18	31
Brazil	16*	30
Venezuela	10*	18
Other	12	55
	—	—
	88	260

* Interpolated.

cocoa, tea and coffee together. It was a late bloomer, shooting ahead in the last quarter of the nineteenth century more for use in candy and pastry than as a beverage.

According to the *Annuaire Statistique* world output grew between 1891–5 and 1913 at an average rate of 6·8 per cent per annum. The main producers are shown in Table 2.9.

In 1900 cocoa was grown principally in Latin America and West Indies. Progress continued rapidly there, but the most spectacular event of the period is the phenomenal rise of the Gold Coast from nearly zero to first place within fifteen years; this story is told in Chapter 6.

With this flood of cocoa coming on to the market, the price moved downwards almost continually. Nevertheless, the value of imports into the leading countries multiplied more than five-fold between 1883 and 1913.

Tobacco leaf. Tobacco was grown widely in the tropics, but only Indonesia, India, the Philippines, Cuba, Mexico and Brazil exported significant mounts. Tropical trade was only about 30 per cent of world trade in 1913.

World trade in tobacco grew somewhat more slowly than world trade as a whole. As in cotton, the output of the largest producer, the USA, grew more slowly after 1900 than before; and the price then moved sharply upwards. Exports then rose rapidly for India, Indonesia, Cuba and the Philippines; but production was lagging in Brazil.

The *Annuaire Statistique* gives the following figures for production in 1913 (in thousand metric tons): Indonesia 75, Philippines 46, Cuba 33, Brazil 29, Mexico 12, Paraguay 8, Puerto Rico 7, Colombia 6, Central Africa 3. The volume of production in India was not known, but India exported 12 thousand tons in 1913.

Bananas. The banana is the only fruit traded internationally in large quantities which is wholly tropical. The trade began just before our period, and multiplied fifteen-fold in value between 1883 and 1913. This was one of the products benefiting from speedier shipping in the first instance (to the USA from the Caribbean) and later of refrigerated shipping (to Europe).

In 1913 exports came almost exclusively from the Caribbean and Latin America. According to Lamartine Yates the roll-call for the average exports of 1909–13 was (in thousand metric tons): British West Indies 310, Costa Rica 200, Honduras 200, Canary Islands 140, Colombia 107, Brazil 54, Total 1,275.

Declining trades. Exports of indigo were worth only about two million dollars in 1913, but had been worth thirteen times as much thirty years earlier. The trade is interesting in this study of economic growth because it is an example of a commodity whose market was destroyed by the invention of synthetic substitutes. Also badly hit was the trade in 'logwood' and other tropical dyewoods.

Another trade which declined sharply was that in opium, following an agreement between India and China in 1906 to eliminate India's exports to China altogether in ten years. India's exports of opium fell to $11 million in 1913, having been $54 million in 1883.

Mineral Ores. Exports of minerals increased faster from the tropics than agricultural exports. Several factors contributed to this. One was the fact that metal industries were growing faster than others. A second was the exhaustion of Europe's non-ferrous ores. Perhaps the most important reason was the development of internal transport systems in the tropics (especially railways) which were particularly valuable in transporting heavy mining machinery inwards, and heavy ores outwards. Also very important was the increased making of geological surveys as the revenues of tropical governments increased and they strengthened their administrations.

Nevertheless, in 1913 the number of tropical countries exporting significant quantities of minerals was still small. And the number of minerals involved was also small.

Mexico had been exporting minerals for more than three centuries, but her mining industries developed with great speed during this period especially copper, lead, zinc, silver and gold. Peru showed rapid gains in copper and silver; and copper also began to be important in Bolivia and in Northern Rhodesia.

Tin played a spectacular role in the prosperity of three countries, Malaya, Indonesia, and Bolivia.

Gold was mined in small quantities in many countries. Relatively large increases occurred in Mexico, the Gold Coast, Southern Rhodesia and India.

Oil did not become significant until after the war, except in Burma and Indonesia.

III. CONCLUSION

The growth of tropical trade did not reflect simply the growth of demand, since in about half their trade the tropical countries were competing with temperate countries. Tropical trade in some products grew faster than demand. This was important in minerals, and after the US agricultural frontier closed, also in cotton and tobacco. The

61

reverse was also true; tropical trade did not keep up with temperate competition in sugar or indigo.

Yet the net effect was that tropical trade grew just about as fast as industrial production in the leading industrial countries taken together, and supplied therefore potentially as powerful an engine of growth. Why some tropical countries reacted to their opportunities better than other tropical countries is the main question pursued in the chapters which now follow.

BIBLIOGRAPHY

Official Papers

Belgium. Ministère de l'Intérieure, *Annuaire Statistique de la Belgique*, 1884, 1901, 1914–19. Brussels.

France. Direction Générale des Douanes, *Tableau Général du Commerce . . .*, 1883, 1899, 1913. Paris.

——. Institut National de la Statistique et des Etudes Economiques, *Annuaire Statistique, Retrospectif*, 1951, 1966, Paris.

Germany. Statistisches Reichsamt, *Statistisches Jahrbuch fur das Deutsche Reich*, 1885, 1901, 1914. Berlin.

Great Britain. Board of Trade, *Eighteenth Abstract of Labour Statistics, 1910 to 1925* (Cmd. 2740). London, 1926.

——. House of Commons, *Sessional Papers*, 1887, 1902, 1914–16. 'Annual Statement of Trade of the United Kingdom', 1886 (Cd. 5148), 1901 (Cd. 1105), 1914 (Cd. 7968).

Books

Deerr, Noel, *The History of Sugar*, London, 1950.

Food and Agriculture Organization of the United Nations, *The World Rice Economy in Figures, 1909–1963*, Rome, 1965.

——, *The World Sugar Economy in Figures, 1880–1959*, Rome, 1961.

International Sugar Council, *The World Sugar Economy, Structure and Policies*, London, 1963.

Lamartine Yates, Paul, *Commodity Control*, London, 1943.

——, *Forty Years of Foreign Trade*, London, 1959.

League of Nations. Economic, Financial and Transit Department, *Industrialization and Foreign Trade*, 1945.

Lewis, W. A., *Aspects of Tropical Trade, 1883–1965*, Stockholm, 1969.

Todd, J. A., *The Cotton World, A Survey of the World's Cotton Supplies and Consumption*, London, 1927.

——, *The World's Cotton Crops*, London, 1915.

Wickizer, V. D., *Coffee in the World Economy*, Stanford, 1949.

——, *Coffee, Tea and Cocoa, An Economic and Political Analysis*, Stanford, 1951.

——, *Tea under International Regulation*, Stanford, 1944.

Wickizer, V. D., *The World Coffee Economy*, Stanford, 1943.
Wickizer, V. D., and Bennett, M. K., *The Rice Economy of Monsoon Asia*, Stanford, 1941.

Article

Lewis, W. A., 'World Production, Prices and Trade, 1870–1960', *The Manchester School*, May 1952.

Chapter 3

COLOMBIA

by Ralph W. Harbison

I. INTRODUCTION

The period from 1885 through 1914 was a critical one in the modernization of Colombia. Using *per capita* income as the indicator of economic progress, it was during these years that the Colombian economy made the transition from stagnation to persistent growth. Concomitantly, the political system of post-independence Colombia underwent a transformation from a state of chronic civil strife to one of unprecedented, if only temporary, stability. This essay aims at the elucidation of the dynamics of economic development and the modernization process in Colombia during this period of transition.

Colombia at the opening of World War I was in the final state of pushing herself onto a path of persistent economic growth. As near as is possible to extrapolate from the very shaky estimates available for later periods, *per capita* GNP was around US $110 and had been growing very slowly, perhaps at an average rate of $0 \cdot 5$ per cent per year, since sometime in the last half of the 1890s.[1] The population was approximately $5 \cdot 2$ million and was growing at least 2 per cent per year.[2] The basis for continuing far-reaching and fundamental economic change had definitely been established.

But how did the economic development of Colombia get started and what relation did it have to the more general process of modernization? There were several key actors in the drama, each of which, after a brief look at pre-1885 economic history, will be considered at some length. The major conclusion of that examination will be that the transition to growth in Colombia cannot be adequately described within the framework of a single model of economic development. Instead, the transition was the result of the simultaneous and fortuitous coming together of the 'right' – i.e. unique – mix of forces. Perhaps the role of each in the development process

[1] W. P. McGreevey, 'Economic Development of Colombia', unpublished Ph.D. thesis, Massachusetts Institute of Technology, 1964, p. 241.
[2] See Section IV below, especially Tables 3.1 and 3.2, p. 72

64

is most lucidly described by reference to a distinct pure theory or model, but each provides only a partial explanation of that process.

II. THE ECONOMIC BACKGROUND OF THE TRANSITION TO GROWTH

The economic history of Colombia before the period in question had been dreary indeed: stagnation beginning with the turbulent pre-independence decade (1810–20), worsening very likely to an outright decline beginning about 1845, which reached its trough about 1885.[1] At this point GNP *per capita* was probably substantially less than US $100.[2] The drama of the change in the rate of growth from negative to positive and the course of the upward creep of *per capita* GNP is, of course, the subject of this essay. For the moment, however, it is the major aspects of the stagnation after 1845 which interest us.

In general, the economy was of course very largely one of subsistence agriculture, unencumbered by anything we would term a modern sector and buffeted precariously by occasional waves of temporary export boomlets in tropical commodities.[3] Nevertheless, there was even at this time a highly significant artisan manufacturing class and a sizeable, though stagnant, gold-mining industry.[4]

In particular, after the abolition of the state tobacco monopoly in 1850, tobacco production and exports grew very quickly, beginning in the late 1850s.[5] Tobacco in its peak year of 1866–7 represented 51 per cent of the value of total exports; it declined slowly and irregularly from one-third to one-fifth of total exports between 1867–8 and 1874–5.[6] Expansion was so fast that the quality of the product was compromised and the very limited suitable soils were quickly depleted by overexploitation. The low quality, the opening

[1] McGreevey, *op. cit.*, pp. 25, 241.

[2] *ibid.*, Table V–C.

[3] R. C. Beyer, 'The Colombian Coffee Industry; Origins and Major Trends, 1740–1940', unpublished Ph.D. thesis, University of Minnesota, 1947, pp. 53 ff.

[4] *ibid.*, Table III, McGreevey, *op. cit.*, Table V–A, Table V–B.

[5] Production was stimulated not only by the normal incentives provided by free production but also by a fortuitous and simultaneous expansion in world demand, particularly in Germany, and a general rise in the world price. McGreevey, *op. cit.*, p. 117.

[6] Banco de la República, Bogotá, *XXXVIII and XXXIX Informes Anuales del Gerente a la Junta Directiva*, Segunda Parte, pp. 201, 216. See also Beyer, *op. cit.*, Table III.

C

of cheaper sources of supply in the late 1870s, and the revival of US production following the Civil War were the economic causes of the sudden collapse of the tobacco boom in the late 1870s and early 1880s.[1]

More important for our development drama than the severe decline of tobacco exports, however, was the extremely low growth generating potential of the tobacco export expansion in the first place. Tobacco in Colombia was grown on a small number of large estates located in the low and fertile tropical river beds and worked by landless peasants, many of whom ten years earlier had been legal slaves. The premium incomes from tobacco exports thus went entirely into the hands of a very restricted number of already wealthy landholders, and not to the workers.[2] Further, outside of transportation facilities from the lowland river valley to the coastal port, tobacco production for export required little or no capital either in the form of inputs, processing machinery, or social overhead investments, thereby setting in motion only the most minimal sorts of backwards and forwards linkages to other sectors of the economy.[3]

Like tobacco, quinine enjoyed a brief export boomlet in the 1870s and suffered a disastrous collapse in the early 1880s. During the middle 1870s, it regularly accounted for 15 to 20 per cent of the value of Colombian exports.[4] High costs of production in Colombia combined with the coming into production of Far Eastern sources of supply to cause the collapse.[5] In fact, the only sustained development in the agricultural sector was concentrated in exports of hides of cattle, which began an uninterrupted rise in the 1870s. This steady increase in exported hides was spurred on by the growing cattle industry, which itself was based since the early 1870s upon the expanding use of the barbed wire fence.[6] Unfortunately, however, the expansion of the cattle industry was quantitatively small and

[1] McGreevey, *op. cit.*, pp. 44, 118–19 and Table II–B. Beyer, *op. cit.*, pp. 53–5, and Table III.

[2] See McGreevey, *op. cit.*, pp. 130–2 for discussion of the effect of the tobacco boom on income distribution, and see also Chapter 6 *passim* for the contrast with coffe.

[3] J. P. Harrison, 'Colombian Tobacco Industry from Government Monopoly to Free-Trade 1778–1876', unpublished Ph.D. thesis, University of California at Berkeley, 1952, is the most complete study of the tobacco boom in Colombia. See especially pp. 356–7, for mention of the negligible linkages to other parts of the economy. In this connection, see also McGreevey, *op. cit.*, p. 167.

[4] Beyer, *op. cit.*, Table III. Banco de la República, *op. cit.*, pp. 201, 216.

[5] *ibid.*, pp. 53 ff.

[6] McGreevey, *op. cit.*, p. 132.

unimportant in comparison with the tobacco and quinine booms, and suffered from low growth generating potential in much the same way tobacco did.[1]

Although relevant statistics are extremely scanty, it is probably safe to hypothesize that incomes earned largely from the tobacco and quinine export trade were spent mostly on imports of finished, high quality manufactures and luxury items from abroad, with unfavourable effects upon the artisan 'cottage' industries.[2] The Census of 1870 claims that 300,000 persons, mostly women, representing 22 per cent of the economically active population, were engaged in artisan activities – predominantly the manufacturing of rough textiles, the weaving of fibre hats and bags, the making of sandals, and leatherwork. Demand for these items in domestic markets slackened in proportion to the increased imports of higher quality equivalents or substitutes and luxury goods from abroad. Both artisan income and the size of the artisan sector began to decline until, in 1925, only 200,000 persons representing 10 per cent of the economically active population, were engaged in such activities.

Finally, the period before 1800 was notable for what it lacked, i.e. any real progress in industrialization. The introduction of dependable steam navigation on the Magdalena River was tobacco's only contribution to social overhead capital. Local governments built a few mule roads and bridges, but the initial stages of significant investments in social overhead capital upon which to base a modern industrial sector came only later.

In summary, then, the period from 1845 to 1880 was characterized by few changes in the situation of the great majority of the population engaged in subsistence agriculture, except insofar as the declining artisan incomes affected this group. In addition, no net capital formation, technological progress or industrialization worthy of the name took place. Boom and bust in rapid and jolting succession in the two major tropical crops dominated the agricultural export sector. Given a growing population, the result was stagnation and probably declining *per capita* GNP. To judge from the commentary of the time, the country was thoroughly demoralized by the lack of forward movement.[3]

[1] Beyer, *op. cit.*, Table III.

[2] McGreevey, *op. cit.*, p. 47.

[3] See, for example: Miguel Samper, *La Miseria en Bogotá*, cited in Beyer, *op. cit.*, pp. 54–5; J. M. Henao and G. Arrubla, *History of Colombia*, English translation by J. F. Rippy, Chapel Hill, 1938, pp. 493–4.

III. THE POLITICAL CONTEXT: TRANSITION TO
SEMI-STABILITY[1]

The dominant theme of pre-1880 Colombian political history is chronic instability and devasting civil strife amounting to permanent revolution. Since nominal independence in 1811, the country had been ruled by over fifty different 'administrations'[2] under nine distinct basic organic laws or Constitutions,[3] and had been ravaged by at least seventy and perhaps as many as eighty revolutions, *golpes de estado*, and local rebellions. Since the initial emergence of coffee as an export crop in the 1850s, there had been three major civil wars, in the last of which (1876–7) 80,000 men died.[4] Yet the worst of the political system's legacy to the development drama was still to come in the Civil War of 1885 and the Thousand Days War of 1899–1903. In this final holocaust at least 100,000 men were killed and another 60,000 incapacitated, representing a minimum 4 per cent of the total population.[5]

Three main issues were at the root of most of the instability: the proper form of the governmental apparatus of the nation, the rights and privileges of the Catholic church within the nation, and the extent of governmental intervention in an economy in which real wages for the masses were falling.[6]

The political philosophy of the Liberals evolved in favour of a decentralized federal system which would foster the development of locally autonomous institutions and would severely limit the powers reserved to the national government; the disestablishment of the church and the quashing of its influence over national political and economic life; and a 'laissez-faire' detachment from economic activities on the part of federal authorities. The Conservatives came

[1] The most thorough political history of Colombia at this time is presented in the prize-winning work of J. M. Henao and G. Arrubla, cited above.

[2] Depending upon how one counts, at least this number are listed in Manuel Mansalve, *Colombia: Posesiones Presidenciales*, Bogotá, 1954.

[3] For details of the provisions of each of these basic laws and summaries of the historical context surrounding the promulgation of each, see W. M. Gibson, *Constitutions of Colombia*, Durham, N. C., 1948.

[4] J. F. Rippy, *The Capitalists and Colombia*, New York, 1931, p. 23. Hagen (*On the Theory of Social Change*, p. 379) implies this estimate may not be reliable; I can present no special reasons either to accept or reject the precise number. Even half the number of deaths would indicate a major civil conflagration.

[5] E. E. Hagen, *On the Theory of Social Change*, Homewood, Illinois, 1962, p. 379. Beyer, *op. cit.*, p. 135. *United States Army Area Handbook for Colombia*. Washington, D.C., 1964. Hereafter cited as: *US Army Handbook*, p. 386.

[6] McGreevey, *op. cit.*, pp. 129–30.

to favour a highly centralized republican system, which would permit only very limited local autonomy in the face of the more or less all-inclusive powers reserved to the national government; the close mutual support of the church and state, in particular the maintenance of clerical privileges; and active promotion of economic advance by the national government. Each of the major civil wars, and many of the local disturbances, were the result of one of these groups' rediscovering how intolerable life was under the other and resolving to attempt to take power for itself.

In general terms, the period from 1842 to 1884 was one of Liberal dominance, which reached its peak in the promulgation of the Constitution of 1865. So weak in structure and power was the national government after 1863 that it either would not or could not maintain law and order in the various states; something approaching anarchy prevailed in many areas. The reigning philosophy did not permit active and energetic involvement of the federal government in economic affairs. All the usual economic effects of political chaos made themselves felt; labour shortages, exorbitantly high interest rates and widespread reluctance to invest, delayed shipments of produce via interrupted lines of communication, and great physical damage inflicted by ravaging armies on the move.[1] The result we already have seen: this era of 'pure politics' under Liberal rule coincides almost exactly with the period of zero or negative growth of *per capita* GNP.

With the opening of the second administration of President Rafael Núñez in 1884, began a new period in Colombian political (and economic) history, standardly called the 'Regeneration'. Elected by a coalition of Conservatives and moderate Liberals, this liberal-turned-conservative took the first giant steps toward political stabilization and economic progress.[2] Prerequisite to all progress, however, was the putting down of a rebellion in 1885 initiated by Liberals who feared turncoat Núñez's increasingly Conservative policies. To consolidate his victory and enshrine in law his own political philosophy, Núñez in 1886 promulgated a new organic law, the Constitution of 1886, which, with some updating, codification and reorganizing, remains the fundamental law of the land

[1] Beyer, *op cit.*, pp. 134–5. Great Britain, House of Commons, *Sessional Papers*, Diplomatic and Consular Reports for 1878–9, 'Colombia', by Consul Mallet. From Miguel Samper *La Miseria en Bogotá*, quoted in Beyer, *op. cit.*, p. 141.

[2] See Section VIII below for summary of the effects this new era in politics had upon the influence of the public sector in these early economic advances.

today.[1] Symbolic of the general reorientation of national life which it fostered, the Constitution changed the name of the country from the United States of Colombia to the Republic of Colombia and reduced the individual sovereign states to mere departments. Relations with the Catholic church were normalized, both in the Constitution and in the Concordat of 1887, thus removing, although only temporarily, the divisive issue of church–state relations from the political arena. The church regained its independent but highly influential position in society and maintained its grip on the country's educational system.

To summarize:[2]

'Núñez's work ushered in a new phase of Colombian politics and attitudes towards the government's role in the development of the nation. Despite the fact that the positive and immediate results of his policies were limited, there began with Núñez and the Regeneration a new way of viewing the nation's problems. No longer was the nation's development in the hands of subsidized foreigners as under the early republican regimes. Nor was a spiritless laissez-faire depended on to raise the nation out of its backwardness [as under the Liberal regimes]. For the first time Colombians began to regard their problems as soluble by their own efforts, their development dependent on their own actions, their fate in their own hands. The change which took place in 1885 and 1886 was thus the important political "precondition" essential to the emergence of the transitional phase of Colombian development.'

But few of the advances of the Núñez years were fully consolidated until after the tortured upheaval of the century's end, the Thousand Days' War (1899–1903). This last revolutionary struggle was initiated by the Liberals who felt the squeeze of an increasingly severe depreciation of the currency and who sensed the vulnerability of a weakened government presided over by an old man, exhausted by illness. In the entire turbulent history of independent Colombia, no conflict had been so costly; all the painfully familiar effects of war descended once again upon the afflicted nation, only with greater vehemence and more disastrous results.

'This three-year struggle caused incalculable losses. On the battle-

---

[1] For text and summary of historical context of formulation and promulgation of Constitution of 1886, see Gibson, *op. cit.*

[2] McGreevey, *op. cit.*, p. 59.

fields, 100,000 men or more perished; thousands were maimed for life; commerce was ruined; communications were very difficult; production almost negligible; and paper money, issued in increasing quantities to meet the needs of government, depreciated so much that a paper peso was worth less than one cent gold.'[1]

Beginning in 1904, however, with the ascension to the Presidency of General Rafael Reyes, came a period of nearly thirty years of uninterrupted Conservative rule based upon an informal consensus between the two parties. The (Conservative) administration in power thus enjoyed the tacit consent of the opposition party to its right to rule, an unprecedented situation in the history of independent Colombia. This consensus and its predecessor, the 'Regeneration' under Rafael Núñez, cleared the arena for the establishment of the foundations of a new era of increasing income *per capita*.

IV. POPULATION, SOCIAL STRUCTURE AND HUMAN RESOURCE DEVELOPMENT

People of a nation – in particular, their changing numbers over time, their distribution throughout the national territory, the ways in which they are organized into social segments, and their efforts to upgrade their own productive potential – are perhaps the single most important ingredient in the development process. Tables 3.1 and 3.2 present the existing population statistics pertaining to Colombia and several of its key regions around the turn of the century.[2] A brief glance at these two tables makes clear the sharp regional disparities in the demographic history of Colombia during our period.

Statistics on the rural-urban distribution and racial breakdown of population are more scanty. In 1918, however, nearly 80 per cent of the population lived in rural areas,[3] and of the remaining 20 per cent only half (10 per cent total population) lived in the twelve major cities. In 1905, approximately 8 per cent of the total population lived in these same twelve major cities.[4]

On the basis of what little we know about the founding of towns

[1] Henao and Arrubla, *op. cit.*, p. 519. See also: House of Commons, *Sessional Papers*, Diplomatic and Consular Reports for 1901, 1902 and 1904, 'Colombia'.

[2] It should be noted that recorded immigration into Colombia was never significant during our period, with the total yearly gross inflow never exceeding 300 persons. (See McGreevey, *op. cit.*, Table I–C–1.)

[3] 'Rural' indicates towns of less than 1,500 inhabitants.

[4] *US Army Handbook, op. cit.*, p. 51. McGreevey, *op. cit.*, p. 95 or Tables I–D and I–E.

71

TABLE 3.1: *Population by Key Regions,* Census Years†‡*

(thousands)

Region	1851	1870	1905	1912	1918	1928
Colombia total	2,008	2,708	4,144	5,073	5,855	7,851
Gran Antioquia (Antioquia and Caldas)	225	366	945	1,165	1,343	1,721
% in Area	11·2	13·5	22·8	23·0	22·9	21·9
Boyaca and Cundinamarca	694	912	1,134	1,303	1,467	2,007
% in Area	34·6	33·7	27·4	25·7	25·0	25·6
Santander and Norte de Santander	374	433	550	607	678	924
% in Area	18·6	16·0	13·3	12·0	11·6	11·8
Gran Tolima (Tolima and Huila)	187	231	373	441	512	652
% in Area	9·3	8·5	9·0	8·7	8·7	8·3

* Population figures exclude those people living in Panama, who were, of course, part of the population of Colombia before 1903.

† As the growth rates presented in Table 3.2 show more clearly, the 1905 Census figures almost certainly exhibit severe under-counting; 2·6 per cent per year population growth seems extremely high for a country which at best could only have just barely begun to experience the typical sharp decline in death rates which in those days was predicated upon the initial rise in *per capita* income.

‡ This table is taken from McGreevey, *op. cit.*, Table I–A.

TABLE 3.2: *Average Annual Rates of Population Increase**

Region	1851–1870	1870–1905	1905–1912	1912–1918	1918–1928	1870–1912	1912–1928
Colombia total	1·6	1·2	2·6	2·3	2·9	1·6	2·7
Gran Antioquia (Antioquia and Caldas)	2·1	2·8	3·0	2·4	2·4	2·8	2·4
Boyaca and Cundinamarca	1·5	0·6	2·0	1·8	3·1	0·9	2·7
Santander and Norte de Santander	0·8	0·7	1·4	1·8	3·1	0·9	2·7
Gran Tolima (Tolima and Huila)	1·1	1·4	2·4	2·5	2·4	1·5	2·4

* Calculated from the population figures of Table 3.1, by the standard formula

$$P_0 e^{rt} = P_t$$

after 1880 and the composition of the labour force in the fledgling industries which sprang up around the turn of the century, it seems reasonable to claim that between 85 per cent and 90 per cent of the Colombian population was rural in 1880.

By this time, the racial composition of the population had likely stabilized after the severe processes of initial dislocation followed by prolonged fusion of colonial times, and it is safe to assert that the population was a new triethnic amalgam consisting of somewhat over 55 per cent *mestizos* (persons of mixed White and Indian, or White and Negro blood), somewhat under 30 per cent pure Whites, with the remaining 15 per cent divided nearly equally among Indians and Negroes.[1]

The social structure prevailing in Colombia at the turn of the century exhibited the typical stratification into two distinct classes. The major determinants of class status were racial derivation, family lineage or pedigree, and wealth. In fact, social stratification in Colombia during our period is perhaps best described as a caste system, not as a class system; entrance to the upper class or confinement to the lower class was determined by birthright, not achievement. Between these two basic strata, upward mobility was approximately zero, and downward movements rare. Colombians were born into a status group, became highly conscious of the basic distinctions early in life, and generally accepted as quite right and natural their given position in the vertical organization of society.[2] Because stratification was complete, social mobility nil, and all political and economic power concentrated in the hands of a small, wealthy, ultra-conservative, land-holding élite, the social structure of the country *taken as a whole* was hardly conducive to economic growth.

[1] No two sources agree precisely on the ethnic make-up of the population. The figures presented here are within the extreme one finds in the literature, but no claim is made that they do more than to indicate order of magnitude. See: *US Army Handbook, op. cit.*, p. 60; Rippy, *Capitalists and Colombia, op. cit.*, p. 22; Juan Luis de Lannoy and Gustavo Pérez, *Estructuras Demográficas y Sociales de Colombia*, Bogotá, 1961.

[2] Lannoy and Pérez, *op. cit.*, pp. 107–14. P. M. Holt, *Colombia Today and Tomorrow*, New York, 1964, p. 7, Gerardo and Alicia Reichel-Dolmatoff, *The People of Aritama: The Cultural Personality of a Colombia Mestizo Village*, Chicago, 1961, p. 137. Somewhere below the lowest rung of the social ladder around 1900 (and still there today) were the relatively small numbers of pure Negroes, located predominantly in the hot lowland river valleys and along the coasts, and the Indians, found in the most isolated rural areas of the highlands. It is safe to assert that these unfortunate souls were left untouched by the social and economic changes taking place in Colombia during our period; for this reason we are not further concerned with them here.

But the picture as a whole is deceiving, for there was a region of Colombia whose social organization provided a much more favourable environment for the advent of permanent economic growth. We shall call this region the Antioqueño culture area, and it comprised during our period all of the present day departments of Antioquia, Caldas, Quindio and Risaralda, a significant portion of Tolima, and the most north-easterly segments of Valle del Cauca.

Quantitatively those who called themselves Antioqueños numbered 395,000 in 1870, 525,000 in 1883, 923,000 in 1905, and 1,377,000 in 1918.[1] Since the 1880s, Antioqueños have consistently represented between a fifth and a fourth of the nation's total population.[2] Although the racial make-up of Antioqueños was by the middle of the nineteenth century not significantly different from that of other Colombians, and although cultural cohesion, not physical characteristics, distinguish them, these 'Yankees of South America' like to refer to themselves as *La Raza Antioqueña* (the Antioqueño Race).[3] Until recently 'being Antioqueño meant more to them than being Colombian'.[4]

This powerful cultural separatism had its roots in the Spanish colonization pattern in Colombia. Although the Spaniards came in the sixteenth century in search of gold, only in Antioquia did they find it in appreciable quantities. While on the Sabana around Bogotá the Spaniards soon became landed gentry and in the upper Cauca River Valley owners of cattle ranches, in Antioquia, by far the poorest, most hopelessly isolated and severely underpopulated part of the colony, they became initially owners and managers of mines which they worked with Negro slaves and Indians.[5]

But even in early colonial times, the supply of Indians and Negro slave labour was never sufficient, and the labour shortage quickly forced the Spaniards and Criollos themselves to dirty their hands panning gold in their small and widely dispersed claims. Wealth in Antioquia became increasingly associated with hard work and individual initiative rather than with the number of one's *peones* or the extent of one's landed estate, as was the case on the Sabana and in the Valley.[6] Further, and more importantly, the Antioqueño

---

[1] J. J. Parsons, *Antioqueño Colonization in Western Colombia*, Berkeley, 1949, p. 103.   [2] See Tables 3.1 and 3.2, p. 72.

[3] *US Army Handbook, op. cit.*, pp. 55–6.   [4] Parsons, *op. cit.*, pp. 1, 4.

[5] Hagen, *op. cit.*, pp. 29–30; also Chapter 15.

[6] *ibid.*, pp. 29–30. Parsons, *op. cit.*, p. 101. See also: Alvaro López Toro, *Migración y Cambio Social en Antioquia Durante el Siglo Diez y Nueve* (Centro de Estudios Sobre Desarrollo Económico, Facultad de Economía, Universidad de Los Andes), Bogotá, 1967, *passim* and especially p. 32.

society was never thoroughly integrated into the Spanish colonial social structure, and the class structure never solidified so completely around the nexus of race and family lineage as it had in the other areas. These two rather special characteristics of Antioqueño colonization paved the way for the early emergence among Antioqueños of a 'tradition of democratic work for all'[1] and a system of social stratification in which 'social distinctions [came eventually] to rest more on economic achievement than social class at birth'.[2]

In the post-colonial internal migration southward from the department of Antioquia (to what today are the departments of Caldas, Quindio, Risaralda, Tolima and the north-eastern segment of Valle de Cauca),[3] the early established pattern of small land-holdings staked out by individual families was relatively unhindered by the presence of the large agricultural and cattle *haciendas* prevalent in the two other major areas of Spanish colonization. The extreme difficulty of communications within the region (even in comparison with the truly dismal transportation system in the rest of the country) further aided the emergence of 'an independent yeoman class' imbued with the 'spirit of self-determination'. In short, in the Antioqueño culture area there emerged a 'democratic society of small freeholders on a continent dominated by traditional Latin latifundism'.[4] Or to put the anomaly in McClelland's terms, the distinctive Antioqueño social structure gave rise early to people possessed of 'n-achievement'.[5]

Suffice it to add for the moment that in a society in which 'title to a few hectares of land has become the ambition of every *campesino*',[6] there is a natural symbiosis between the production of a crop like coffee (ideally suited to small scale family cultivation often on the same land area used for basic subsistence agriculture), and the entrenchment of the pattern of small mountainside holdings by independent self-reliant pioneers pushing out a homesteaders' frontier. The social structure of the Antioqueño culture area provided the essential framework for a permanent economic expansion.

But such expansion is always predicated on the development of human resources to 'staff' it, and it was during our period that investment in education on a large scale began in earnest in Colombia.

During the colonial period, access to such meagre educational facilities as there were had of course been the exclusive privilege of

---

[1] Hagen, *op. cit.*, p. 2.   [2] *US Army Handbook, op. cit.*, p. 79.
[3] Parsons, *op. cit.*, p. 6.   [4] *ibid.*, pp. 97, 101, 111.
[5] D. C. McClelland, *The Achieving Society*, Princeton, 1961.
[6] Parsons, *op. cit.*, p. 111.

the very small ruling class,[1] and all pre-independence educational institutions were run by religious orders. With the advent of independence, however, the church's absolute monopoly in the educational field was broken, and some long-established institutions passed into government hands while others were created from scratch by secular authorities. Among these were the first teacher training institutes, opened in 1822.[2]

Since the support of these secular educational establishments was the responsibility primarily of the state and municipal governments from the beginning of the post-independence period, sharp regional differences in educational achievement – i.e. in per cent of children in school and in literacy rates – manifested themselves very early. Antioquia was consistently the most advanced region of the country during our period.[3] In both 1905 and 1918[4] Antioquia and Caldas together accounted for about 35 per cent of the total primary school students in the country,[5] but only 23 per cent of the total population of Colombia.[6]

The powers of the national government, exercised through the Dirección General de Instrucción Pública,[7] were generally limited to inspection of the schools, the gathering of statistics, and the oversight of what few funds the national government in a country plagued by perpetual civil strife could devote to educational purposes. The President in 1872 reported that, on urging of the Dirección General, an integral plan for the fostering of primary education throughout the country had been submitted to the states and accepted by all but Antioquia.[8] By fiscal year 1878–9, 5 per cent of the planned expenditures of the national government were for education (the State of Antioquia in fiscal year 1876–7 had devoted over 8 per cent of

---

[1] The earliest 'education' establishments in the country – the so-called *doctrinas* – is an exception to this general rule; these were schools started by the religious orders beginning in the early sixteenth century designed chiefly to convert Indians to the Roman Catholic faith. (*US Army Handbook, op. cit.,* pp. 150–1.)

[2] *ibid.,* p. 150.   [3] McGreevey, *op. cit.,* p. 153.

[4] These are the only two years for which this author came upon the pertinent figures.

[5] Calculated from Colombia, Departmento Administrativo Nacional de Estadistica, *Anuario General de Estadística,* 1905, Bogotá, p. 98, and Dirección General de Estadística, *Censo de Población, 1918,* Bogotá, 1924, pp. 408–9.

[6] See Table 3.1 above.

[7] Founded in 1826 and fundamentally reorganized in 1870, the Dirección General de Instrucción Pública was the precursor of today's Ministry of Education.

[8] Colombia, *Mensaje del Presidente de la Unión al Congreso Nacional,* 1872.

its budget to education),[1] and the President had sent a special message to Congress on the development of educational programmes in agriculture.[2] Thus even before the end of the Liberal period, the general need for development of human resources was beginning to be recognized.

A glance at Table 3.3 gives the further impression that resources devoted to primary education increased slowly beginning in the late 1880s and accelerated noticeably after the turn of the century. By 1912 the President of the Republic could report that some departmental governments were devoting over one third of their revenues to primary education and imply strongly that those departments falling short of this ratio were delinquent in meeting their responsibilities.[3] The enrolment figures for 1913 correspond to about 25 to 30 per cent of the children of school age.

For the years before 1914, the statistical record on the development of secondary and higher education seems sufficiently confused as not to merit any discussion here. In 1914, however, there were in operation in Colombia: 28 teacher training institutions with a total enrolment of 1,728 students; 58 public[4] secondary schools serving 6,283 students; 246 private – i.e. predominantly church-run – secondary schools with 18,095 students; 9 public universities with 1,576 students; 5 industrial training schools with an enrolment of 598 pupils; and 2 schools of art with 500 students. Including in these figures the data for primary schools and students, Colombia in 1914 could boast of 5,225 educational establishments with 335,480 students – excluding the private universities run by religious orders and the military training institutes.[5] In those nine universities, there were two faculties of medicine and natural sciences (314 students), three of mathematics and engineering (201 students) and one of agriculture (16 students).[6] Somewhat over 6 per cent of the entire population was enrolled in some sort of formal educational institution compared with less than half that ratio in 1879[7] and about 34 per cent of the men in the country claimed they could read.[8]

[1] House of Commons, *Sessional Papers*, Diplomatic and Consular reports for 1878, 'Colombia'.

[2] Colombia, *Mensajes Dirigidos a Las Cámaras Legislativas de 1878 por la Administracion Ejecutiva*. Hereafter cited as *Mensaje*, 1878.

[3] *Mensaje del Presidente de Colombia al Congreso de 1912*.

[4] Public is used here in the North-American sense to mean state-supported. The Spanish is *oficial*.   [5] *Mensaje*, 1914,. p. 254

[6] *Mensaje*, p. 246.   [7] See Table 3.3.

[8] Colombia, Ministerio de Gobierno, *Censo General de la República de Colombia, levantado el 5 de marzo de 1912*, Bogotá, 1912. This figure is probably high, as it represents response to a census question of the sort, 'can you read?'.

TABLE 3.3: *Primary School Enrolment, Selected Years**

Year	Number enrolled	Number of schools	Approximate percentage of total population†
1876	70,818‡		2·4%
1879	73,142‡	1,461	2·3
1882	71,070§	1,262	2·2
1883	72,338		2·2
1898	136,132		3·2
1905	165,062	2,117	3·5
1907	227,283	2,875	4·6
1908	236,985		4·8
1914	306,709	4,913	5·8
1918	340,335		5·9

* *Source:* 1876 and 1879: *Mensaje del Presidente de Los Estados Unidos de Colombia al Congreso*, 1879. Hereafter cited as *Mensaje*, 1879. 1882: *Mensaje del Presidente de la Union al Congreso Federal de 1882*. 1883, 1898, and 1905: *Anuario General de Estadistica*, 1905, op. cit., pp. 93, 98. 1907 and 1908: *Mensaje del Excmo. Sr. Presidente de La República e Informes de los Ministros del Despacho Ejecutivo Dirigidos a La Asamblea Nacional Constituyente y Legislativa*, 1907 and 1908. 1914: *Mensaje del Presidente de Colombia al Congreso de 1914*. Hereafter cited as *Mensaje*, 1914. 1918: *Censo de Población 1918*, op. cit., pp. 408–9.

† These percentages were computed by projecting population from 1870 at 1·6 per cent per year to 1911, and 2·3 per cent per year from 1912 to 1918, and dividing the enrolment figures by the population estimates. Needless to say, these percentages are only very approximate; nevertheless, they do point up a significant trend.

‡ Includes students in federally 'recognized' educational establishments at *all* levels.

§ Excludes Santander and Panama; beginning 1907 all figures presumably exclude Panama and before this time should include Panama.

All this of course says nothing about the quality of education (or the attendance ratios), and judging by the repeated attempts to bring in foreign professors and by the various reform and re-organization schemes which pop up at frequent intervals in Messages to Congress by the nation's chief executives, educational standards left much to be desired. Nevertheless, it appears clear beyond dispute that Colombia had laid the foundation for a continuing 'investment in man' well before the close of our period.

V. COFFEE IN ANTIOQUIA: THE LEADING SECTOR

The rapid growth of coffee as an export crop fuelled the engine of economic expansion during our period. Total production rose from about 107,000 sacks of 60 kilograms each in 1880, to 475,000 sacks in 1896, to over 1·1 million sacks in 1915. From a meagre 12 per cent of total export earnings in 1880, coffee grew to represent 55 per cent in 1896 and, while once falling as low as 31 per cent in the intervening period, coffee again accounted for half of Colombia's total exports in the period 1912–15. Over the same period (from 1880 to 1915) the total value of all Colombian exports more than doubled, with the increase heavily concentrated after 1908, so that not only did coffee's percentage share in exports expand dramatically but so did total exports.[1] Table 3.4 illuminates more generally this rapidly changing composition of exports during our period.

Further, expansion of coffee production was heavily centred in the Antioqueño culture area. In 1874 the present day departments of Antioquia and Caldas produced only 2·2 per cent of Colombian coffee while in 1913 the corresponding figure was 35·4 per cent. Between 1874 and 1913 the share of Colombian coffee production of the departments of Santander and Norte de Santander dwindled from 87·6 per cent to 30·2 per cent; the share of the neighbouring departments of Boyaca and Cundinamarca grew from 7·5 per cent to 18·7 per cent and the share of Gran Tolima (the departments of Huila and Tolima, much of this last one being in the Antioqueño culture area) jumped from 0·9 per cent to 5·5 per cent. Put slightly differently, coffee production over this forty year period was multiplied 150 times in the heartland of the Antioqueño culture area, 60 times in the area (Gran Tolima) containing a high proportion of people who called themselves Antioqueños, almost 24 times in the region (Cundinamarca and Boyacá) containing the capital and rich highland agricultural centre of the country, and only 3·25 times in the 'traditional' coffee area of the Santanders.[2]

Outside of public-sector policies and the initial stages of a revolution in transportation technology which were so important as to merit separate detailed consideration, what were the peculiar qualities of coffee and the special nature of the two basic factors of production – land and labour – which caused such a large expansion in coffee output in Colombia?

Because there are no significant economies of scale involved in its production, coffee is a crop extremely well suited to small-scale family enterprise in a frontier region. It is readily grown in conjunction with the usual subsistence staples such as maize, beans,

---

[1] Beyer, *op. cit.*, Table II.
[2] *ibid.*, Table XI. McGreevey, *op. cit.*, Tables II–F–1 and II–F–2.

TABLE 3.4: *Total Value and Percentage Composition Major Exports*

Colombia: 1877–8, 1906, 1910, 1915, 1919

Year	Total exports (thousands of pesos)	Coffee	Tobacco	Gold	Cattle hides	Rubber	Straw hats	Quinine	Bananas	Others
						Percentages				
1877–78	11,111	13·45	5·08	20·99	7·29	1·58	—	22·23	—	29·38
1906	14,481	42·40	4·66	20·59	8·65	3·21	2·86	—	3·38	14·25
1910	17,787	31·03	2·16	18·96	10·41	4·71	5·54	—	9·41	17·78
1915	31,579	51·54	1·07	17·27	11·70	0·84	3·10	—	6·33	8·15
1919	79,011	68·74	3·49	0·53	10·93	0·25	1·35	—	2·82	11·90

Sources: Banco de la República, Bogotá, *op. cit.*, pp. 201, 202, 216. (I am indebted to R. Albert Berry for bringing this source to my attention.)
Beyer, *op. cit.*, Table III.

and yuca.[1] It is a perennial plant, which comes into production three or four years after transplantation, and will continue to produce even after several years of neglect. The harvested crop is easily stored more or less indefinitely after simple processing requiring little or no capital equipment. All these characteristics substantially increase the staying power of coffee over that of many other crops in the face of cyclical trade depressions or the dislocations of civil strife. As a prominent Colombian neatly pointed out in an 1880 pamphlet, coffee is ideally suited to small-scale peasant agriculture because[2]

'without noticeable increase in the labour required by his maize and yuca, each settler can convert a portion of his land into a *cafetal*. . . . All the effort required is the digging of holes and the setting out of the transplants at the time of seeding the maize and yuca. The weedings that these crops demand will suffice for the coffee. After three years . . . the land will have been converted into a producing *cafetal* . . . which will give an income which could never be hoped for from a similar acreage of maize or yuca. . . .'

In sharp contrast to the earlier situation with tobacco, the availability of land almost uniquely suitable to the growing of coffee was never an obstacle to coffee production.[3] Coffee's requirements for land, however, are very different. Light volcanic soils are preferred; rainfall per year need be only 40 inches; and the average seasonal temperature range must be between 18 C° to 25° C. Hillsides between 1,000 and 1,800 metres elevation which are unsuitable for other tropical export crops are thus ideal for coffee.[4] Much of the land within the Antioqueño culture area fits this description perfectly; comparatively little outside that area does. Large amounts of suitable land, in conjunction with the particular adaptability of coffee production to small-scale semi-subsistence agricultural undertakings, and with the relative absence in the Antioqueño culture area of

---

[1] So much so that coffee has never represented more than one-third of total Colombian agricultural output and may have been only 10–15 per cent around 1900. (Beyer, *op. cit.*, Table XIII and R. A. Berry, *Agriculture in Colombia*, (forthcoming), Chapter 2.)

[2] Mariano Ospina Rodríguez, quoted in Parsons, *op. cit.*, p. 139.

[3] Tobacco-growing in Colombia was limited to the rich heavy soils of the highly tropical river valleys (particularly the Magdalena Valley), and the scarcity of suitable land was a powerful brake on expansion during the tobacco boom. McGreevey, *op. cit.*, p. 142. Beyer, *op. cit.*, pp. 160 ff.

[4] Beyer, *op. cit.*, pp. 94 ff.

the feudal traditions of the large landed estates, formed a critically important element in the huge expansion of coffee production.[1]

The other major input – people – was not less important, and insofar as there was a bottleneck to even more rapid expansion of coffee production in the Antioqueño culture area, the scarcity of labour was the cause.[2] Much of this area of Colombia has been sparsely populated, at least since colonial times. But beginning in the 1850s, there began a substantial internal migration of families southward within the Antioqueño culture area from the department of Antioquia into the frontier areas now comprising the departments of Caldas, Tolima and even north-eastern Valle del Cauca. This movement of people accelerated well into the period under discussion, and, in addition, the natural rate of increase of the population appears to have been higher in the Antioqueño culture area than elsewhere even around the middle of the nineteenth century.[3] Finally, we should keep in mind the anomalous nature of the population that was opening up the new lands and multiplying so prodigiously: independent and self-reliant, high in the 'need for achievement', less encumbered than most other Latin Americans by the oppressive feudal traditions of the large landed estate, and more blessed than their compatriots with a 'McClellandesque' creative personality.

As the foremost scholar of the coffee industry in Colombia put it:[4]

'In this combination of elements – the existence side by side of good untouched free mountain land and a large number of ambitious mountain farmers with a frontier blood in their veins – coffee operated like a catalytic agent. It provided an acceleration and enthusiasm which lifted the movement into a fever pitch making the participants feel that they were being beckoned on to a promised land to fulfil Colombia's historic destiny. There was no longer the least shadow of doubt that the magic product so eagerly sought in the chaotic period from 1850 to 1880 had now been found.'

[1] Government legal and administrative policies had much to do with the availability of land. The discussion of this aspect of the critical marriage of man to land is deferred until Section VIII.

[2] Beyer, *op. cit.*, pp. 60 ff.

[3] Parsons, *op. cit.*, pp. 69–96, 102–8. The information on population size, distribution, and growth rates presented in Tables 3.1 and 3.2 summarize what little quantitative material we have pertaining to the southward migration and high rates of population growth in the Antioqueño culture area.

[4] Beyer, *op. cit.*, p. 183.

Indeed there wasn't! The 63,000 bags of coffee produced in Colombia in 1878 and representing 0·8 per cent of the world's coffee production had been multiplied eighteen times by 1914, when the 1,060,000 bags of Colombian coffee accounted for almost 6 per cent of world production. In the decade following 1914, Colombian coffee production would again double. By 1930 it would be four times, by 1963 six times, as great as it was in 1914.[1] In short, by 1914 coffee had 'taken-off' and was well on the way towards accomplishing what earlier export crops had not been able to do – pull the entire Colombian economy with it off the ground. But why the success of coffee in generating growth?

Coffee in the Antioqueño culture area was successful in sparking permanent growth where other crops had failed because the effects of the coffee expansion on several other areas of the economy were pervasive and profound, not isolated and superficial. Coffee production enjoyed those backward and forward linkages to the rest of the economy which neither tobacco, nor quinine, nor cattle could claim.

First, we may hypothesize[2] that, because the expanded output of coffee came in large measure from the placing in production of new 'free' lands in small plots cleared and cultivated by independent peasant families, a higher proportion of the increased incomes from coffee went to the equivalent of wages, and a lower proportion of the income increment went into rent. However, an increase in tobacco output was possible only from more extensive and perhaps ruinous use of a small number of estates staffed overwhelmingly by Negroes in virtual serfdom: here, the higher proportion of the increase went to rent and the lower, if any, to wages. The lion's share of increased prosperity generated by coffee production was enjoyed by the large poor rural *mestizo campesino* class, not the small group of rich, white urban landlords. These peasants, in turn, certainly did not buy for themselves and their children foreign travel and foreign education or other 'luxury' imports symbolized by fine French marble or silk stockings. Since such items could not be produced in Colombia, if only as one commentator so picturesquely puts it 'for lack of Paris labels',[3] the use of tobacco-generated incomes to purchase these luxury imports had resulted in a long-term depression

[1] McGreevey, *op. cit.*, p. 86.

[2] See McGreevey, *op. cit.*, Chapter 6. The argument here is taken from his work. It should be emphasized that this paragraph is to be interpreted more as a hypothesis than as an airtight assertion of fact. To show the hypothesis false would require a detailed breakdown by category over our period of Colombian imports. Unfortunately this author has not been able to find the data necessary to construct such a table.   [3] McGreevey, *op. cit.*, p. 155.

and decline in Colombian artisan manufacture of basic textiles without compensating growth in another domestic sector. But coffee-generated incomes in the hands of the Antioqueño farmers were spent precisely on those 'necessities', symbolized by cheap cotton and wool garments (and perhaps rudimentary education of children), which could be produced most economically in increasing quantities at home. Further, since in contrast to tobacco, this coffee-income-generated increase in the demand for imports was likely concentrated on 'necessary' commodities in which there had been huge productivity increases in the industrial supplying nations, not only did Colombians gain from the consumption effects of trade. Spurred by the emergence before their eyes of a very substantial market for consumers' necessities, they were also quick to discern and to begin to exploit the profitable opportunities for domestication of those foreign techniques. The rapid expansion of coffee production redistributed income towards that segment of the population most likely to spend that incremental income on items characterized by high potential for the generation of domestic incomes – i.e. on domestic goods whose large-scale production could utilize modern low-cost technology – and not on imports.[1]

Second, coffee requires only the simplest of capital equipment to process. The only necessities are supply of bags in which to store and ship the dried beans, access to a depulper and, in case one prefers not to rely entirely upon the sun, a drying machine. Each of these items – depulpers, dryers, and sacks – is easily manufactured. Increased demand for the first two provided some impetus for the expansion of a primitive metallurgical industry, and the third sparked development of the crude plant-fibre weaving industries, initially in the depressed artisan homes and later in larger establishments in the towns.[2]

Finally, due to the inaccessibility of the best coffee growing areas in the *cordilleras* of Antioquia and Caldas, the expansion of coffee production had to go hand in hand, symbiotically, with a revolution in transportation.

[1] The income distribution hypothesis sketched above is not meant to imply that a society which consumes more grows faster than one which saves more; there simply is no information upon which to base even an educated 'guesstimate' as to the difference (if any) between the savings ratio of the owners of tobacco-generated incomes and that of the owners of coffee-generated incomes. Rather the hypothesis is based on the valid argument that the lower the propensity to import out of additional incomes, the higher, *ceteris paribus*, will be the domestic growth-generating potential of that income increase.

[2] McGreevey, *op. cit.*, pp. 168, 211–12.

VI. THE RAILWAY REVOLUTION

Until the forty years surrounding the turn of the century, transportation technology in Colombia was on the whole limited to exploitation of the river system and of the primitive system of mule trails leading either from the mountains to the rivers or around rapids and sand bars on those rivers. The laissez-faire Liberal philosophy enshrined in the Constitution of 1863 strictly limited the potential role of the central government in transportation to promotion and improvement of inter-oceanic routes and rivers. This theory, however, was compromised in practice, and even during the height of the Liberal period the central government undertook the construction of a few wagon roads and bridges. Not until after the Civil War of 1876 was railway construction even indirectly encouraged by the federal government, and then mostly through subsidies to the state governments who were responsible for contracting for the planning and building of the railway.

The overriding objective of the pre-1920 expansion of the railway network – the construction of the 'coffee railways' – was to facilitate access to the sea, thereby stimulating coffee exports, initially by building rail links around obstacles in the rivers and then by connecting the river bridgeheads to the hinterlands by rail. The overall effect of the construction of the coffee railways was fragmentary, or 'obviously centrifugal' in nature, not integrative. Railway construction divided the country further and made 'each of its component parts look outward'. Since it was cheaper to bring merchandise to Medellín from London than from Bogotá,[1]

'each commercial region, i.e. Bogotá or Medellín was more or less independent [of the other] and what it did not produce it brought in from abroad.'

However retarding the early railway expansion may have been to the economic integration of Colombia's major commercial regions, progress with regard to the primary objective of facilitating transport to the sea for greatly expanding coffee exports was substantial indeed. As the following table shows, the net number of kilometres of track in use expanded very rapidly, multiplying sixfold in thirty years.

[1] Luis Ospina Vásquez, *Industria y Protección en Colombia 1810–1930*, Medellín, 1955, pp. 237–40, 281–3. McGreevey, *op. cit.*, p. 53, and especially footnote 29 on p. 53.

TABLE 3.5: *Net Kilometres of Track in Use, Selected Dates**

Year	1885	1890	1898	1904	1905	1909	1914	1915
Kilometres of track	202	255	498	565	666	900	1,166	1,212

* Except for 1909, source of this table is McGreevey, *op. cit.*, Table III–B or Beyer, *op. cit.*, Table XII.

For 1909, source is House of Commons, *Sessional Papers*, Diplomatic and Consular Reports for 1910, 'Report on Railways in Colombia' by Acting Consul General Huckin at Bogotá.

The effect on transportation rates was equally dramatic: in 1880, with the New York price of coffee at US \$341 per ton, the cost of transporting coffee from Medellín to the Magdalena River was US \$70 per ton, or 20 per cent of the price received. In 1914, after the completion of the Ferrocarril de Antioquia connecting Medellín and the river, the New York price per ton of coffee was US \$343, but the cost of transport from Medellín to the Magdalena River had fallen 73 per cent to US \$19, representing only 5·7 per cent of price.[1] Another comparison of internal costs per unit weight of coffee for the nineteenth century with 1943 equivalents also shows that the proportion of the price represented by internal transport costs fell from around 20 per cent to 2 per cent or 3 per cent.[2] At a minimum, the expansion of coffee exports, involving the shift in the locus of coffee production westward to the Antioqueño culture area, would have been greatly retarded without these sharp reductions in freight rates. More likely it could not have occurred at all.

On the other hand, the railways could not have been economically viable without the coffee export expansion, since in their initial years, well over half, and occasionally as much as three-quarters, of the total outbound freight on the railroads was coffee. In short, coffee-export expansion and railroad construction in Colombia are a perfect example of economic symbiosis: neither could have lived long without the other, but together they wrought a very fundamental change in the Colombian economy.

VII. THE EMERGENCE OF A MODERN INDUSTRIAL SECTOR[3]

No longer are gold or coffee Antioquia's first pride and leading source of wealth. Today Antioquia, and in particular its capital,

[1] McGreevey, *op. cit.*, Table 7.   [2] Beyer, *op. cit.*, Table VII.

[3] For a short history of the abortive industrial 'stirrings' in the early nineteenth century, see: McGreevey, *op. cit.*, pp. 27–9; Ospina Vásquez, *op. cit.* (Chapters II–IV presents a much more extended treatment of this early period, and his Chapters V–VIII are the source of most of the information in this section.)

Medellín, is one of Latin America's largest industrial centres. Before 1915, Medellín was the only city in Colombia which had developed any significant modern manufacturing sector at all.

Industrialization began in Antioquia shortly after the turn of the century. Generated by the new coffee incomes, the expansion of demand, both for finished consumers' goods and for agricultural implements, was the fundamental determinant of the timing, location, and nature of these initial efforts at industrialization.[1] But the expansion of demand, though a necessary one, was not a sufficient condition even for this early stage of industrialization. Government economic policies certainly favoured the process, as did the anomalous nature of Antioqueño society and personality, and the falling profit margins in alternative uses of investment funds, especially in the traditional areas of Antioqueño investment, commerce and mining.[2]

In Antioquia, as in so many other areas of the world, textile manufacturing was the leading sector of the industrial expansion. Much of the labour force was young girls, recent arrivals from the rural areas,[3] and the sharp acceleration in the growth rates of the cities coincides with the initial stages of industrialization. Although the first large-scale water-powered textile factory did not open until 1906, since the late 1880s there had been growth of improved though still small-scale and family-oriented 'cottage' operations devoted to the manufacture of coffee sacks. In addition, several primitive tanneries and shoe factories, a few firms making ceramics (porcelain tiles), and several small foundries making agricultural implements were in operation in Antioquia by the 1890s. In 1901, a modern brewery in Medellín and a modern sugar refinery in Palmira began operation; a large candy factory (an affiliate of Bogotá's big chocolate industry) opened its doors in 1903; and the first successful steam dredge, placed in operation on the Nechi River in 1909, made gold mining in Antioquia economical once again.[4] Thus, although by the turn of the century, industrial development in Antioquia was still in its embryonic stages,[5]

'already an industrial future could be foreseen, based on the capacities which had stimulated or promoted the mining industries and

[1] McGreevey, op. cit., p. 211; Parsons, op. cit., p. 173.
[2] Ospina Vásquez, op. cit., pp. 308–10; Hagen, op. cit., pp. 373–6; López Toro, op. cit., passim.
[3] McGreevey, op. cit., p. 232; Parsons, op. cit., p. 173. Ospina Vásquez, op. cit., pp. 331–2.
[4] Parsons, op. cit., p. 57.   [5] Ospina Vásquez, op. cit., pp. 308–9.

which also had played a part in the development of the spirit of risk-taking and innovation. . . . Men of vision and enterprise were not lacking then in Antioquia.'

Entrepreneurial activities were increasingly in evidence in Bogotá, too, although such activities were so heavily concentrated around Medellín that Bogotá declined in relative importance as a commercial and financial centre. Here the leading industry was brewing, with significant intersectoral linkages to the glass industry. Intermittent and only partially successful efforts were made to revive, restructure, and reorient the government-sponsored basic iron and sulphuric acid industries which had failed in the early 1880s. The country's first cement plant was established in 1908 near Bogotá. Finally, Bogotá's traditional economic role as market place for a huge and rich agricultural zone made it the natural place for the food processing industries to emerge, and the beginnings in this area were in evidence shortly after the turn of the century.[1]

However significant these meagre beginnings may have been for later widespread industrialization, their aggregate size, as measured by either share in GNP or numbers employed, must have remained exceedingly small. Even in 1925, the year for which the earliest semi-reliable estimates are available, manufacturing, mining, and construction combined were the sources of about 15 per cent of GNP, and of that 15 per cent, the modern industrial sector accounted for just about half. In 1870 the aggregate share in GNP of mining, manufacturing, and construction, was probably about the same, but the modern sector accounted for less than 3 per cent of GNP.[2] In 1925, only 3·4 per cent of the economically active population was employed in the modern manufacturing sector (in 1870 the corresponding figure was 1·1 per cent while slightly over four times that number were classified as working in mining, manufacturing and construction).[3]

So the modern manufacturing sector was small, and its growth was retarded by the financial crisis of 1904 and then by the effects of World War I. There can be no doubt, however, that the initial stages of industrialization in Colombia, which set the stage for a more than 5 per cent per annum increase in manufacturing output in the twenty years following 1905,[4] were a response to the early coffee-export expansion and an integral part of the transition under consideration.

[1] McGreevey, op. cit., pp. 220–2. [2] ibid., Table 23.
[3] ibid., Table 24. [4] ibid., pp. 61 and 200.

VIII. THE ROLE OF THE PUBLIC SECTOR IN THE
COLOMBIAN TRANSITION

Not surprisingly, the transition to growth which took place between 1885 and 1915 coincided with a shift from the Radical Liberals' philosophy of laissez-faire to the Modern Conservatives' effective interventionism. In several areas, government fiscal and monetary policies, sometimes by mere chance but increasingly often by design, made substantial contributions to the economic changes of the transition period.

First of all, public policy had a significant effect upon the availability of land. Colombian law early recognized the right of the peasant family who had cleared a plot of public land to cultivate it and to enjoy the fruit of their labour. Even on some types of private land, the law recognized 'possession and usufruct as tantamount to unwritten title'.[1] Aside from this spontaneous but tacitly encouraged invasion of unoccupied public and private lands, there emerged in Antioquia during the thirty years following independence a group of speculative land colonization companies which, having acquired large acreages by various means, proceeded to recruit groups of colonos, to divide the holdings into small parcels, and to sell the land to them. Many of these companies were owned by the emerging commercial class of the cities who also controlled the departmental government. Although by the 1880s this form of coordinated communal colonization had largely given way to migration of individual families, the coincidence of interests of the pioneer-settler and the politician-businessman helps to explain how new lands came into the hands of the small farmer in Antioquia.[2] In addition, the chronic strife of the pre-1885 period left governments at all levels continually and desperately in need of cash, hence the motivation for selling land at low prices in order to raise the necessary revenues quickly. Finally, at least in the Antioqueño culture area, some care was apparently exercised in the disposition of public lands to prevent the accumulation of more than a certain specified maximum number of hectares in the hands of a single man.[3] All of this contributed to the establishment of that society of independent

[1] Parsons, op. cit., p. 97. See also: A. O. Hirschman, Journeys Toward Progress (Anchor Books edition), 1965, pp. 134–40. López Toro, op. cit., p. 26.

[2] See López Toro, op. cit., pp. 28–37 for the best summary description of the several methods of bringing farmer and land together in Antioquia.

[3] Parsons, op. cit., pp. 97–9.

small freeholders so central to the running of the engine of growth, the expansion of coffee exports.

One more aspect of government land policies deserves mention. Given the critical financial situation of governments at all levels and the increased activities expected of them after 1885, it was never possible to pay the monetary subsidies which would have been necessary to promote major transportation improvements. Instead and in supplement of the few direct monetary subsidies it could manage, the state often encouraged railway, road, and bridge construction by making grants of public lands to the contractor. Going rates were in the neighbourhood of 300 hectares for each kilometre of track, and 240 hectares for each kilometre of road, i.e. improved wagon trail.[1]

Second, in addition to these large subsidies in the form of land, both the departmental and federal governments made grants of money to specified development projects. The Departmental Assembly of Antioquia seems to have been the leader in this form of government intervention in the economy. Hoping to stimulate the production of an export crop, the Departmental Assembly, beginning about 1869, exempted cocoa, indigo, and mulberries from local tax payments. In 1876, the Assembly destined over 40 per cent of the budget of the department to railway construction.[2] Then in 1877, perhaps in reaction to the lack of induced response from the earlier tax exemptions, the Antioqueño Assembly began providing monetary prizes or bounties for the production of sheep, cotton, wine, and most significantly, for the planting of coffee trees. At a time when about 1·1 Colombian pesos exchanged for a United States dollar, the Antioqueño who planted coffee could claim from the departmental treasury four pesos per one hundred trees planted, up to a maximum of one hundred pesos.[3] In 1881 this system of provincial bounties was re-enacted and the prize list broadened.[4]

'All but one of the payments made in the two years following the re-enactment were for new coffee plantations. . . . Eighteen years later the prizes offered under the law of 1881 were cited as having been an important factor in setting off the Antioqueño coffee boom.'[5]

---

[1] Parsons, *op. cit.*, p. 100.
[2] House of Commons, *Sessional Papers*, Diplomatic and Consular Reports for 1876, 'Colombia', by Vice-Consul White at Medellín.
[3] Parsons, *op. cit.*, p. 111.   [4] *ibid.*, p. 110.   [5] *ibid.*, p. 138.

The newly reorganized national government under the Modern Conservatives also began a monetary subsidy programme. Although the earliest plans may have been approved in the late 1880s, given the fiscal situation of the government before the Thousand Days War, national government monetary subsidies could not have been effective until after the beginning of the Reyes administration in 1904. At any rate, the effort emphasized the promotion of industrial manufacturing enterprises, not agricultural export crops as had the earlier prize system of the Antioquia Assembly, and the subsidies actually paid out were heavily concentrated in the textile industry. During the Reyes years, mostly abortive attempts were undertaken to induce by subsidization or concessions the establishment of food preserving enterprises, lard, sulphuric acid, glass and paper manufacturing firms, and an oil refining industry. A subsidized match factory actually did come into production during this period. Outside of the textile industry, however, the central government policy of privileges, concessions, and direct monetary subsidies was only marginally effective at best in stimulating economic development.[1]

Much more effective than the subsidy programme in promoting economic growth were the central government's tariff and monetary policies. Throughout the period of the transition, tariff revenues accounted for between half and two-thirds of total central government revenues.[2] But of these tariff revenues, a very large percentage, e.g. 50 per cent in 1884[3] and about 30 per cent in 1905,[4] was set aside by statute for service on the national debt originally contracted in the 1820s and in default much of the time since.[5] Customs duties before the 1880s were normally levied according to weight, and not value, of the article and quite naturally given the Liberal abhorrence of protectionism, the pre-1880 tariff was viewed exclusively as the necessary, but evil, source of revenue. There was no attempt to protect domestic production (e.g. artisan textiles) by rate differentials and thus the potential domestic income-generating effects of the

[1] Ospina Vásquez, *op. cit.*, pp. 335–7.

[2] *ibid.*, p. 323.

[3] *ibid.*, pp. 235, 277.

[4] F. L. Petre, *Republic of Colombia*, London, 1906, p. 325. See also, House of Commons, *Sessional Papers*, Diplomatic and Consular Reports for 1909, 'Report of the Finances of Colombia', by His Majesty's Minister at Bogotá, Mr Francis Stronge.

[5] For a very condensed summary of the pre-1906 history of the national debt to foreigners, see Petre, *op. cit.*, pp. 320 ff., or 'Report of the Finances of Colombia', *op. cit.*

pre-1880 export expansions were dissipated in a rising tide of imports.[1]

After 1880, however, with the coming to power of the Modern Conservatives under Núñez, a sharp reorientation of tariff policy followed quickly. The desire of the Conservatives to promote industrial development was of course one reason for the shift towards a meaningful protectionism for articles which were, or could be, produced domestically. But it was not the only motivation for the shift for, beginning in the late 1870s, the fiscal situation of the central government became critical: outlays regularly were over twice as large as revenues.[2] Given this situation a sharp increase in duties on the type of articles most heavily imported – e.g. finished consumer goods – and a decrease in tariffs on primary products made good sense on purely fiscal grounds. Even so the effect on industrialization of the Núñez tariff reforms was minimal.[3]

By 1905, with the coming to power of Reyes, inflation had substantially weakened whatever effects the Núñez tariff policies had produced, and a new and this time undeniably effective tariff reform was enacted. In general terms, Reyes 'put teeth into the protectionist policy of Núñez'.[4] Import duties were raised about 70 per cent, with higher raises on those items whose domestic manufacture was being promoted by subsidies and the like – e.g. sugar, alcoholic beverages, tobacco products – and much more moderate increases, or even reductions, on certain key inputs to the infant industries, e.g. cotton thread.[5]

'The protectionism of Reyes raised the level of efficiency of the protectionist system sketched by Núñez; and as in the case of Núñez, the fundamental objective of this policy was not exclusively or principally economic. Support of manufacturing enterprises was an element, a very important element, in the reorientation that Reyes, and the group that surrounded him, wanted to give to the political and social life of the country. . . . The attempt was to divert attention from the political conflict. . . .

'It was not a matter of indifference . . . that the firms which were supported had the attractiveness of size, novelty, and of modernity. It was just this which in large part gave them political worth, and political worth was the essential thing. It is well known the special attractiveness to the popular imagination . . . which

---

[1] McGreevey, *op. cit.*, p. 159.   [2] Ospina Vásquez, *op. cit.*, p. 277.
[3] *ibid.*, Chapters VI and VII. McGreevey, *op. cit.*, pp. 159–60.
[4] Ospina Vásquez, *op. cit.*, p. 339.   [5] *ibid.*, p. 334.

highly mechanized businesses have in comparison with the more simple types.'[1]

Almost by accident, then, tariff policy, at least after 1904, gave a definite boost to the transition process, through its effects upon both political dynamics and infant industrialization.

Monetary policy was also an important influence. In order to make up the chronic central government deficits caused primarily by the high costs of civil strife, the first Núñez government in 1881 established the *Banco Nacional*, the chief purpose of which was to print money and then to 'lend' it to the government. The *Banco Nacional*, whose capital was entirely owned by the government, was given the exclusive privilege of issuing paper money, and by law its bills had to be accepted throughout the country in payment of all outstanding obligations.[2] The *Banco* lost no time in availing itself of its rights to create paper money, and a severe inflation, destined to last until 1903, quite predictably set in.[3] After 1890, as Table 3.6 will show, the inflation as manifested in depreciation of the currency could only be described as 'galloping'; by 1898 it had 'run-away' entirely.

TABLE 3.6: *Rate of Exchange, Colombian Pesos per Hundred US Dollars, 1880–1910*

Year	Rate	Year	Rate
1880	111	1900	260
1885	130	1901	2,260
1890	193	1902	4,600
1895	265	1903	9,070
1898	291	1909	10,000
1899	410	1910	103*

* New Pesos, after revaluation of the currency.
Source: McGreevey, *op. cit.*, Table 4.

But this inflation may well have exerted considerable expansionary influence upon coffee production in Colombia. Although the quantitative evidence is not complete enough to be conclusive, it appears likely that the money wage did not increase very much and

[1] Ospina Vásquez, p. 326.
[2] See Petre, *op. cit.*, pp. 305 ff., for a neat summary of the Bank's history, compiled from the Reports of the British Vice-Consul in Bogotá for 1901 and 1903. In addition, 'Report of the Finances of Colombia', *op. cit.*, contains more detailed treatment.
[3] Ospina Vásquez, *op. cit.*, p. 278.

that consequently, the real wage level, and with it real production costs, fell with the inflation and depreciation after 1880. However this may be, there is no doubt that the large coffee grower paid his expenses in the ever cheapening Colombian currency, and received his payments for the crop in hard currencies from abroad.[1] The result, at least before the mid-1890s must have been artificially high profits in coffee, and greater inducement to put land into coffee production than would likely have been the case without inflation. Between the mid-1890s and about 1910, the world price for coffee was extremely depressed and the Colombian coffee industry suffered heavily not only from the low prices but also from the ravages of civil war. But, even during the especially hard years preceding 1904, the run-away inflation may have minimized the damage done to the coffee industry, if only by prolonging the smaller growers' staying power in the face of economic and political adversity.

In summary, whether by accident or by design, the policies of the Conservative governments after 1885 and especially after 1903[2]

'worked an extraordinary change in the atmosphere of the country, not only in putting the political conflict on a different level but also in encouraging interest in progressive businesses. In a certain way, the formula of the radicals [Liberals] had been inverted: now it was not that liberty would bring us progress but rather that progress would bring us liberty.'

That indispensable ingredient of an economic take-off, a government both capable of maintaining law and order and committed to progress came into existence in Colombia for the first time after 1885.

IX. THE EXTERNAL ECONOMY AND THE TRANSITION

Conspicuous by its absence in the analysis so far has been any mention of the effect of external economic influences on Colombia's transition from stagnation to persistent economic growth, and on the whole the role of foreign capital as such in the transition in Colombia was surprisingly small. But economic forces centred outside of Colombia did make some contribution to the transition.

First of all, although his figures cannot be considered anything

[1] Beyer, *op. cit.*, p. 118, and Diplomatic and Consular Reports for 1904, 'Colombia', *op. cit.*

[2] Ospina Vásquez, *op. cit.*, p. 327.

more than indicators of the general magnitudes and directions involved, McGreevey has shown that the terms of trade between 1881 and 1915 were generally very favourable to economic growth.[1] His calculations point to a general upward movement in the net barter (or commodity) terms of trade beginning in 1882 and continuing through 1893. From then until the low point was reached at the turn of the century, the trend was downward, and was caused by the world depression in coffee prices. After the low point, the terms of trade were more or less invariant, until 1906 when another general upturn began and continued until 1915. Certainly the transition to economic growth, based as it was on a coffee export expansion, would have been less likely had the terms of trade been consistently worsening.

Second, the credit policies of the large buyers of Colombian coffee in the US and Europe were instrumental in fostering the rapid growth of the leading sector, production of coffee for export.[2] Given the political instability, government bankruptcy, and under-developed nature of the banking system, interest rates were very high even for prime commercial or industrial borrowers in the big cities. What extremely little domestic credit was available to coffee growers was at prohibitively high interest rates.[3] In fact most of the money needed by farmers to defray the costs of increased plantings of coffee was advanced by buying agents of huge New York and London coffee-importing houses, with only the potential crop and often untitled land as guarantees. By the time of the depression in world coffee prices following 1896, commitments to foreign creditors were so massive that, especially after the economic disruption caused by the Thousand Days War, some of the larger holdings actually fell into foreign receivership as Colombians found themselves unable to pay their debts.[4] The availability of credit extended by foreigners to coffee growers must have been an extremely important fuel for the engine of growth in Colombia.

Finally, direct foreign investment in Colombia is notable chiefly for the very marginal effect it had upon the early stages of the transition. Outside of the German-financed Bavaria brewery, opened in 1891 and located in Bogotá, the only foreign capital in Colombia before 1914 worthy of mention was British or American. American capital had been heavily concentrated in Panama,

[1] McGreevey, *op. cit.*, Table II–G.

[2] See Beyer, *op. cit.*, for an extended discussion of credit policies of the large coffee importing houses in US and Europe.

[3] Beyer, *op. cit.*, p. 165.　　　　　　　　　　[4] *ibid.*, pp. 128 ff.

especially in the Panama Railway; and after its secession in 1903 total US direct private foreign investment in non-agricultural enterprises in Colombia was in the neighbourhood of US $8 million. By 1913, this sum had dwindled even further, to the range of US $4 million, of which about half represented the land holdings of the United Fruit Company in the Santa Marta area.[1]

British capital investments in Colombia were considerably larger during the transition and, as Table 3.7 shows, were heavily concentrated in mining and railways. Average nominal return to the British investors in 1913 was only 3.4 per cent, considerably lower than the average returns to all British capital in Latin America in that year.[2] In railway investments in Colombia, the overall average return on capital was only 2·8 per cent although two of the British-owned railways were both profitable and central to the development of the transportation system: the Dorada Railway Company which built and operated the railway around the rapids of the middle Magdalena River, and the Barranquilla Railway and Pier Company, which built the short railway connecting the river port of Barranquilla to its seaport on the Caribbean. Despite low returns generally, however, the British invested in at least eleven of Colombia's railroads.[3]

TABLE 3.7: *'Nominal' or 'Par' Value of British Investments in Colombia*

(£ million, sterling)

Year	1881	1800	1913
Railways	0·57	1·79	3·26
Mining	0·40	1·69	1·76
Government bonds	2·10	1·91	3·39
Total	3·07	5·40	8·41

Source: J. F. Rippy, *British Investments in Latin America*, Minneapolis, 1959; 1880: Table 3, Table 5; 1890: Table 7, Table 8, Table 10, Table 12; 1913: Table 19, Table 15. See Rippy's 'Preface', pp. vii–viii, for justification for using 'par' values, and for rate of return calculations.

All in all, however, Colombia seems not to have been especially attractive to foreign capital during the transition. Even by 1914, foreigners owned at most 4 per cent of the total Colombian capital stock, and of that amount, 40 per cent was concentrated in transport investments.[4]

[1] Rippy, *op. cit.*, pp. 37, 59, 61.
[2] *ibid.*, Table 18.   [3] *ibid.*, pp. 116–19   [4] McGreevey, *op. cit.*, p. 76.

X. SUMMARY

Early on in this essay the reader was forewarned its principal conclusion would be that a unique mix of forces, each providing a neat illustration of a distinct pure and univariate theory of development but none able alone to account for the whole story, produced the transition in Colombia. Now we may see that the role played by the expansion of coffee production is most easily understood in light of a model of aggregate income determination in which exports, somewhat analogous to investment, fluctuate more or less independently of income, and imports and import substitution, somewhat analogous to savings, are a much closer function of income.[1] Hagen's emphasis on personality types and social psychology certainly makes more comprehensible the special place of Antioqueños in the development process.[2] The rapid increase in population and the beginnings of industrialization in Antioquia have the distinct flavour of a Lewis-type situation of surplus labour (primarily women from rural areas) being tapped by an embryonic modern textile industry. At one and the same time, the distinctly lagged response of the fledgling manufacturing sector to increased demand generated by coffee incomes is a superb example of Hirschman's concept of development as a chain of disequilibria,[3] while the interdependence underlying the balanced growth doctrine is brilliantly illustrated by reference to the coffee-railway symbiosis in Colombia. The political transformation following 1885 is a fine example of Black's stage in the development process in which a modernizing leadership is consolidated.[4] Finally, the socialist position (meaning only the position of those of the ardent economic interventionists who cannot conceive of progress except under the aegis of the state) puts the role of the public sector into a more meaningful perspective.

Economic development is an eclectic process. The only way to begin to understand what happened to reverse the stagnation and even decline in *per capita* GNP in Colombia after 1885 is to throw

[1] See H. C. Wallich, *Monetary Problems of an Export Economy*, Cambridge, Mass., 1950, pp. 195 ff.

[2] See Hagen, *op. cit.*, especially Chapter 15.

[3] See A. O. Hirschman, *The Strategy of Economic Development*, New Haven, 1958.

[4] Black himself, however, dates this period in Colombian history differently. See C. E. Black, *The Dynamics of Modernization*, New York, 1966.

D

elements of many pure theories into a melting pot, and then proceed to savour bits of each.

BIBLIOGRAPHY

Official Papers

Colombia. Departamento Administrativo Nacional de Estadística, *Anuario General de Estadística*, 1905. Bogotá.
———. Dirección General de Estadística, *Censo de Población, 1918*. Bogotá, 1924.
———. Ministerio de Gobierno, *Censo General de la República de Colombia, levantado el 5 de marzo de 1912*. Bogotá, 1912.
———. Presidente, *Mensaje* . . ., 1872, 1878, 1879, 1882, 1907, 1908, 1912, 1914. Bogotá.
Great Britain. House of Commons, *Sessional Papers*, 1876, 1901, 1902, 1904, 1905. Diplomatic and Consular Reports for 1876, 1900, 1901, 1904 and 1905, 'Colombia' (C. 1555, Cd. 429, Cd. 786, Cd. 1766, Cd. 2236).
———, *Sessional Papers*, 1909. Diplomatic and Consular Reports for 1909, 'Report of the Finances of Colombia' by Francis Stronge (Cd. 4446).
———, *Sessional Papers*, 1910. Diplomatic and Consular Reports for 1910. 'Report on the Railways in Colombia' by Victor Huckin (Cd. 4963).
United States. Department of Defense, *United States Army Area Handbook for Colombia*. Washington, D.C., 1964.

Books

Banco de la República, Bogotá, *Informe Anual del Gerente a la Junta Directiva*, Segunda Parte, Numbers XXXVIII, XXXIX. Bogotá.
Berry, R. A., *Agriculture in Colombia* (forthcoming).
Beyer, R. C., 'The Colombian Coffee Industry: Origins and Major Trends, 1740–1940', unpublished Ph.D. thesis, University of Minnesota, 1947.
Black, C. E., *The Dynamics of Modernization*, New York, 1966.
Gibson, W. M., *The Constitutions of Colombia*, Durham, NC, 1948.
Hagen, E. E., *On the Theory of Social Change*, Homewood, Ill., 1962.
Harrison, J. P., 'Colombian Tobacco Industry from Government Monopoly to Free Trade, 1778–1876', unpublished Ph.D. thesis, University of California at Berkeley, 1952.
Henao, J. M., and Arrubla, G., *History of Colombia*, translated and edited by J. F. Rippy, Chapel Hill, NC, 1938.
Hirschman, A. O., *Journeys Toward Progress* (Anchor Books edition), 1965.
———, *The Strategy of Economic Development*, New Haven, 1958.
Holt, P. M., *Colombia Today and Tomorrow*, New York, 1964.
Lannoy, J. L. de, and Pérez, G., *Estructuras Demográficas y Sociales de Colombia*, Bogotá, 1961.

López Toro, Alvaro, *Migración y Cambio Social en Antioquia Durante el Siglo Diez y Nueve* (Centro de Estudios Sobre Desarollo Económico, Facultad de Economia, Universidad de Los Andes), Bogotá, 1967.

McClelland, D. C., *The Achieving Society*, Princeton, 1961.

McGreevey, W. P., 'Economic Development of Colombia', unpublished Ph.D. thesis, Massachusetts Institute of Technology, 1964.

Mansalve, Manuel, *Colombia: Posesiones Presidenciales*, Bogotá, 1954.

Ospina Vásquez, Luis, *Industria y Protección en Colombia, 1810–1930*, Medellin, 1955.

Petre, F. L., *The Republic of Colombia: An Account of the Country, Its People, Its Institutions and Its Resources*, London, 1906.

Reichel-Dolmatoff, Gerardo and Alicia, *The People of Aritama: The Cultural Personality of a Colombian Mestizo Village*, Chicago, 1961.

Rippy, J. F., *British Investments in Latin America, 1822–1949*, Minneapolis, 1959.

——, *The Capitalists and Colombia*, New York, 1931.

Wallich, H. C., *Monetary Problems of an Export Economy*, Cambridge, Mass., 1950.

Chapter 4

BRAZIL

by Donald Coes

The period from 1880 to 1913 marks the culmination of Brazil's long history as a supplier of tropical goods to the world economy. This tradition had begun almost four centuries before, when the Portuguese shipped the first loads of pau-brasil, or dyewood back to their homeland. Sugar soon became the dominant economic activity, absorbing most of the capital invested in Brazil in its first century as a colony, and providing for the non-slave population what was perhaps the highest *per capita* income in the New World.[1]

The discovery of gold in 1695 and diamonds in 1728 in the interior province of Minas Gerais, as well as increasing competition from Caribbean sugar producers, shifted the focus of Brazilian economic life southward. Thousands of migrants were attracted from the declining North-East as well as from abroad. In the nineteenth century, gold and diamonds were discovered in several other parts of the world in greater quantities, and in Brazil itself coffee became a more promising export. Grown in the first part of the century on the slave-worked plantations in Rio and Minas Gerais, coffee had shifted south to the more efficient wage-labour plantations of São Paulo by 1880.

During the first half of the nineteenth century, Brazil had rarely had a favourable trade balance; European beet-sugar production during the Napoleonic wars and subsequent Caribbean production ruined Brazil's once lucrative market. The opening of the ports following independence and the granting of a preferential tariff had established British dominance in the import market which was to last until World War I, as well as to discourage and sometimes eliminate the few domestic enterprises which had been established.[2] Periodic loans from British banks had not solved the problems, and the *milreis* had been successively devalued.

All this was changed by coffee, which had been grown in Brazil for home consumption for over a century, but which had to await

[1] Celso Furtado, *Formação Econômico do Brasil*, Rio de Janeiro, 1959, p. 59 note.
[2] *ibid.*, pp. 114 ff.

the rise in incomes of the coffee-drinking North Americans before it was to assume real commercial importance. In 1861 Brazil had a trade surplus, the first of a long series which were to continue with few interruptions for seventy-five years, despite the balance-of-payments problems which arose from government borrowing.[1]

Coffee was to continue as Brazil's principal economic activity well into the twentieth century, but the São Paulo coffee 'cycle' was the last phase of economic development in response to external demand for Brazilian exports. World War I would encourage domestic manufacturing through the enforced separation from Europe and the United States, and autonomous growth would begin after the 1929 depression, when government policies maintained domestic employment as Brazil's capacity to buy abroad fell drastically, resulting in a period of import substitution industrialization.[2]

With the rise of coffee the economic centre of Brazil shifted southwards. Development had previously depended on sugar and cotton, both located in the North-East, but the prices of these two commodities fell very sharply after 1880 and, despite the rise of cocoa around Bahía, the North-East region remained depressed. Climate was the fundamental explanation of the failure of the North-East to share the prosperity of other tropical areas. The lucrative crops of this period all required a fair amount of rain. The North-East receives 50 inches along the coast, concentrated in a few months, but the rainfall drops to 25 inches and less as one moves inland, and also becomes uncertain, failing almost completely about once in every decade. The state of São Paulo, in contrast, receives more than 50 inches, more certainly, and better distributed through the year. As noted in Chapter 1, there was throughout the tropics a general shift of prosperity from the moderately dry towards the wetter areas; the decline of the North-East and the rise of southern Brazil is a part of this general phenomenon.

I. COFFEE

The leading producing area was at first the Paraiba Valley in the state of Rio de Janeiro, and contiguous areas in the states of São Paulo and Minas Gerais. A half century of coffee culture and the gradual decline of the slave population had begun to have an effect

[1] Brazil. Conselho Nacional de Estatistica, *Anuario Estatistico do Brasil*, 1939–40, Quadros Retrospectivas.

[2] Furtado, *op. cit.*, Chapter 21, and Werner Baer, *Industrialization and Economic Development in Brazil*, Homewood, Ill., 1965, Chapter 2.

well before the fall of the Empire, and abolition in 1888 was its death knell.[1] The brief resurgence of cotton culture in some areas during the American Civil War had proved a false hope, and the 1870s saw a shift in the centre of the coffee area southwest of the state of São Paulo which finally surpassed Rio's production in the 1880s. The growth of Brazilian coffee exports from then onwards is shown in Table 4.1.

TABLE 4.1: *Coffee Exports from Brazil, Five Year Averages*
(thousand 60 kg. sacks)

1878/9–1882/3	4,390
1883/4–1887*	4,952
1888–1892	5,324
1893–1897	6,763
1898–1902	11,222
1903–1907	12,684
1908–1912	12,520
1913–1917	13,049

* First six months.

Source: *Anuario Estatistico do Brasil*, 1939–40, p. 1375.

The rise of the São Paulo region as the world's greatest coffee-producing area was due not only to increasing American consumption or the favourable climatic conditions enjoyed by the state, but in large part to immigrants, especially Italians. Few Italians came until 1876, when 7,000 arrived, many of them going to work as *colonos* on the coffee plantations of São Paulo. Throughout the rest of the nineteenth century and the first few decades of the twentieth, São Paulo was to be one of the principal destinations of Italian migration. *Paulista* planters realized that immigration provided a more secure and dependable source of labour than did the dwindling slave population, and abolition in 1888 was far less a threat to the coffee culture of São Paulo than it was to the older plantations of the Paraiba Valley.

By the 1880s, 30,000 immigrants came annually, and more went to São Paulo than to any other state. From 1880 to 1913 nearly three million immigrants came to Brazil, more than half of them to São Paulo.[2] Although Italy contributed by far the largest share,

[1] S. J. Stein, *Vassouras, A Brazilian Coffee County, 1860–1900*, Cambridge, Mass., 1957, describes the growth and decline of a Paraiba Valley town.

[2] Brazil, Directoria Geral de Estatistica, *Recenseamento Geral de 1920*, Rio de Janeiro, 1922–9, Vol. 3.

102

there were numbers of Portuguese, Spanish, and Germans as well. Many did not stay; emigration records for the period are incomplete, but it has been estimated that only half of the immigrants stayed, and in some years exits were almost as numerous as entrances.[1]

Coffee was well established as Brazil's principal export by 1880. Over half of the total export revenue came from coffee, and second-ranking sugar accounted for only a tenth of export income. The success of coffee culture as Brazil's principal crop was due to a number of causes. Favourable climatic and topographical conditions, as well as the famous *terra roxa* (red soil) of the São Paulo region made the state ideal for coffee growing. The composition of exports is shown in Table 4.2.

TABLE 4.2.: *Exports from Brazil**

	Quantities in thousand metric tons		Values £000,000		Index Nos. 1911–15 on 1878–82		
	1878–82	1911–15	1878–82	1911–15	Quantity	Value	Price
Coffee	263·4	779·2	11·2	37·4	296	334	113
Rubber	6·9	36·8	1·1	11·1	534	993	186
Hides and skins	20·7	41·1	0·7	3·0	199	429	210
Yerba-mate	12·9	65·3	0·2	2·0	507	933	186
Cocoa	6·2	37·2	0·3	1·9	598	564	95
Tobacco	21·0	25·5	0·6	1·4	121	212	174
Cotton	21·0	20·9	0·8	1·3	99	168	169
Sugar	190·0	27·5	2·5	0·3	14	13	91
Other	..	..	2·0	3·1	..	155	..
Total†	..	..	19·5	61·5	255	315	124

* Annual averages. Values in pounds sterling.

† Price and quantity indexes given for total assume that prices of 'other' changed to the same extent as the weighted average of the eight commodities shown.

Source: Anuario Estatistico do Brasil, 1939–40, pp. 1375–80.

International coffee prices during the 1880–1913 period rose in the first part of the period, reaching a peak in 1893, when they began a precipitous decline, reaching a low between 1899 and 1903. Their recovery was equally rapid: by the end of the period they were at levels comparable to those of the late 1880s and early 1890s.

[1] Brazil, Directoria Geral de Estatistica, *Recenseamento Geral de 1920*, Rio de Janeiro, 1922–9, Vol. 3.

These price movements were not necessarily those felt by the planters. Steady depreciation of the *milreis* on the London exchange from 22 pence in 1880 to 7d in 1899 cushioned the effect of falling prices and permitted planters to shift part of the burden to others in the economy, particularly the import-consuming townspeople in the cities of Rio and São Paulo.

After 1900 it was no longer as easy to devalue as it had been a decade earlier; planters faced more political opposition from urban groups,[1] and in 1906 they turned to a coffee price support system known as 'valorization'.[2] Throughout the period, however, coffee remained a profitable venture, aided first by devaluation and later by valorization.

The chief factors in coffee production were labour and transport, accounting for about two-thirds of the total production costs.[3] For those who owned land, there was little difficulty in becoming a coffee grower. One hectare (about 2·5 acres) could support between 600 and 800 trees, which after a growth period of four or five years would produce an average of 11 sixty-kilo sacks annually for up to thirty years.[4] The land itself was usually about a fifth of the cost of establishing a plantation, depending on its quality and access to transport. Most of the necessary physical investment – workers' housing, drying platforms, storage areas – could be made with locally available materials. Nearly three-quarters of the cost of developing a plantation was the labour necessary for the preparation, planting, and cultivation of the young trees, as well as for the construction of the processing facilities. The few machines used for processing the coffee were often made in São Paulo, where a number of foundries, machine shops, and other firms serving the coffee sector had been established.

An aid to capital formation in the coffee sector was the possibility of a form of share-cropping with the European immigrants, as well as the subsidization of immigration by the state of São Paulo, which recruited *colonos* in Europe. Usually the immigrant was given housing and the right to all secondary food crops he grew while the land was being developed and planted, as well as a percentage of the first harvest or a payment by trees planted. In return, he was required to clear the land, plant and cultivate the young trees until

---

[1] Furtado, *op. cit.*, Chapters 29, 30.

[2] See below, page 121.

[3] Augusto Ramos, *O Café no Brazil e no Estrangeiro*, Rio de Janeiro, 1923, p. 197.

[4] *ibid.*, pp. 200 ff.

they matured, and to provide labour for other jobs on the *fazenda*. A considerable part of the São Paulo coffee culture was developed in this way, and landowners could thus become major coffee planters in four or five years.

Once the plantation was producing, the workers were contracted by the planters for the year. Wages were paid by the number of trees cultivated and the quantity of coffee harvested. As the fertility of the soil decreased, the yields of supplementary food crops planted between the rows of coffee declined and owners were sometimes obliged to pay higher wages to keep their workers.

About a fifth of the income of the coffee sector was spent on transportation to Santos,[1] though this of course depended on the accessibility of the plantation to a railroad. There was little immediate flow of the coffee income to other areas or abroad, since the workers had a relatively simple standard of living and produced much of their own food. The few demands for manufactured products, chiefly sacking for the coffee bags and cheap textiles for the workers, could be largely satisfied by local production, since the cotton textile industry was one of the few industries to develop during the coffee cycle.[2]

Due to the time lag of four or five years for tree maturity, short-term price movements had little effect on production, despite the enormous increase in production – especially in the last decade of the period – in response to high world prices. When coffee prices rose as they did in the early 1890s or again after 1908, large increases in income accrued to the coffee sector. It is difficult to tell what effect, if any, this had on wages, but most of the extra income was reinvested in further plantation development. Some of the extra income was undoubtedly spent immediately on imports: the only trade deficit in the whole period occurred in 1913 when coffee prices fell off from their 1912 peak and imports were still high, and in 1896 the trade surplus was nearly eliminated when coffee prices turned down from the high levels of the early 1890s.[3]

II. TRANSPORTATION

The rise of the coffee sector brought with it considerable growth and prosperity for São Paulo and contiguous regions. As we have

[1] Ramos, *op. cit.*, pp. 197 ff.

[2] See S. J. Stein, *The Brazilian Cotton Manufacture: Textile Enterprise in an Underdeveloped Area 1850–1950*, Cambridge, Mass., 1957.

[3] *Anuario Estatistico 1939–40*, Quadros Retrospectivas, Comércio Exterior.

seen, one of the chief costs of coffee production was transport to the port of Santos. Transport became increasingly important as the 'coffee frontier' moved westward across the state and further from the market-places. In the Rio de Janeiro area, coffee had originally been carried to the port by pack animal and ox-cart, but by the 1870s much of the coffee moved by rail. Compared with the slow, laborious ox-carts which trudged up and down the coastal escarpment separating the coffee growing highlands from the sea, the railroad was an incontestably better way to get the coffee to market. By the end of the Empire it was evident to most coffee-growers that railroad development was an integral part of the growth of coffee production. Railroads were expensive, even for prosperous coffee planters, and there is little chance that the state of São Paulo would have developed as it did without foreign investment in railways.

Particularly important in the development of Brazilian railways was government support, begun during the Empire and continued during the Republic. In 1852 the Empire had guaranteed 5 per cent per annum on the invested capital for railroads which it deemed important to the national interest. Other concessions were granted as well: free entry of all materials, monopoly carrying rights in certain zones, access to government lands, and the right to arbitration in disputes with the government. The result was a rapid expansion of the means of transport in the last half of the nineteenth century. Many of the railroads were actually built by state (or provincial, under the Empire) governments, and the guarantees by the government were an important stimulus in the construction of others.

The great expansion of railroads was not limited to São Paulo, despite their much greater profitability. Between 1870 and 1900, lines were opened in nearly every state, many of them simply narrow-gauge feeder lines which ran a relatively short distance inland from major ports. Many only stayed in business through the government guarantee, in contrast to the success of the railways in São Paulo. British capital was invested in many of the larger private lines, and some Belgian investments were made around the turn of the century.

One of the fundamental weaknesses of Brazilian railway development was the lack of any real national integration of the system, despite the profusion of companies and rapid development of individual lines. A number of different gauges were used, making it impossible to interchange rolling stock, and even today this problem persists. Since most of the railways were built to bring produce

106

down from the hinterlands to the ports, no railways ever linked the various regions of Brazil with one another. This may be one of the reasons for the relative lack of internal human movement from the less prosperous regions of the north to the rapidly growing regions of coffee culture. With the exception of the São Paulo railways, and a few lines serving Rio, the Brazilian railways never flourished as did those built at the same time and often financed by the same investors in Argentina and other nations. In part this was due to the terrain, but equally important was the lack of profitable bulk commodities outside the coffee regions. The fact that Brazilian exports were shipped from a number of different ports, from Belém at the mouth of the Amazon to Porte Alegre in the far south, meant that there was no central point like Buenos Aires or Chicago at which the various lines converged. Santos and Rio played this role in their respective areas, but their effect was limited to a few central states.

São Paulo was served by four major lines. The first was built by an English company in 1858, from Santos up the escarpment to São Paulo and north-west to Jundaí. All the traffic from São Paulo's interior to the port of Santos passed over this line, the most prosperous in Brazil. The government guarantee was soon unnecessary, and the railway was able to pay 10 per cent dividends while charging lower rates for coffee shipments than any other line. The Paulista railway was financed by a group of planters, and was similarly profitable. Two other major lines feeding the city of São Paulo, the Mogiana and the Sorocabana, were opened in 1875 and 1878. Both received a guarantee on part of their lines, but were built largely on private initiative.[1] A number of smaller lines were built, many of them simply feeder lines from large plantations connecting with the major trunk lines.

The government itself was responsible for the construction of some of the railways, and its policy had the strong support of the planters. To finance its undertakings, the government usually borrowed abroad, and about a third of the public debt by the end of the Empire had been incurred for the construction of railways and other improvements in the transportation system.[2] Despite the leading

[1] Instituto Brasiliero de Geografia e Estatistica, Conselho Nacional de Geografia, *I Centenario das Teriovias Brasilieras*, Rio de Janeiro, 1954, pp. 146, 150.

[2] Estimated from J. S. Duncan, *Public and Private Operation of Railways in Brazil*, New York, 1932, pp. 43–4, and Luis Pinto Ferreira, *Capitals Estrangeiros e Divida Externa do Brasil*, São Paulo, 1965, pp. 93 ff.

role of British capital in financing or directly operating many of the railroads, a number of the government loans were raised in France.

Although railroads were the principal means of transport which were stimulated by the prosperity of the coffee sector, the 1880–1913 period was also marked by the development of other parts of the infrastructure demanded by an export economy. The docks at Rio and Santos were expanded considerably, the latter becoming the world's largest coffee port. The mileage of telegraph lines was more than tripled between 1889 and 1913, even though over 6,000 miles had already been built during the Empire.[1]

Progress in water transportation was also evident. The great entrepreneur of the Empire, Baron Maúa, had founded several navigation companies in the 1850s and 1860s, including a line opening up the Amazon valley. Steamships augmented the capacity of these companies, and by 1889 steamships connected the whole coast. One of the provisions of the republican constitution of 1891 was the requirement that intercoastal shipments be made in Brazilian bottoms.[2] By 1913 most of the navigable rivers were provided with regular service – about 80,000 miles in all. Brazil probably enjoyed better coastal and fluvial service than it does today.[3]

Less was done to develop roads, other than those from plantations to a railhead where branch lines were too costly. In the central part of the country, in the states of Rio, São Paulo, and Minas Gerais, a number of roads existed, some of them built during the Empire, but no national network developed during this period – a situation which began to change only in the 1950s.

III. POPULATION

Brazilian population statistics are not always as accurate as they appear to be; nevertheless Table 4.3 gives a good idea both of total population growth and also of the relative development of various regions. São Paulo and the southern region grew fastest of all, as a by-product of coffee. The other swiftly growing region, Amazonia, was responding to a temporary boom in rubber, to which we shall come in a moment.

The slowest growing region was the North-East, hit by the decline of sugar. Given the surplus of labour in this region, it is surprising that the development of São Paulo and the south depended so much

1 *Anuario Estatistico*, p. 1345.
2 J. C. Oakenfull, *Brazil in 1911*, London, 1912, pp. 111–12.
3 *Ibid.*, p. 112.

on immigration from overseas. When one considers the large number of *nordestinos* who migrated south after World War I and in much greater numbers in our own time, it seems strange that the coffee boom did not produce such a movement. In part the answer lies

TABLE 4.3: *Population, by Regions*

(millions)

	1872	1920	Annual % Increase
Amazonia	0·33	1·44	3·1
North-East	3·33	7·91	1·8
Bahía	1·38	3·33	1·9
Central	3·28	9·06	2·1
São Paulo	0·84	4·59	3·6
Western	0·22	0·76	2·6
South	0·73	3·54	3·2
Total	10·11	30·64	2·3

Source: Anuario Estatistico, 1939–40.

in the poor state of internal transport – even today only two major roads link north and south. But probably even more important was the political structure of the North-East. Landowners were respected in part for the number of men their lands supported – many Brazilian writers characteristically refer to the social organization as 'feudal' and even after the legal reforms of the Empire which ended the semi-feudal status accorded to large tracts in the North-East, the rural population could often be tied to the land through debt, just as the *seringueiros* were in Amazonia. Any organized effort to recruit labour in the North-East met the opposition of landowners, who roundly denounced a plan of the Campos Salles government to move a number of people from Ceará to the south.[1] *Nordestinos* did migrate in fairly large numbers to Amazonia, in search of rubber, but those who went to the rubber regions were often recruited in towns, having already fled their subsistence plots in the interior and, unlike the Europeans in the south, often arrived in debt, sometimes spending the rest of their short lives attempting to break from the cycle.

The wave of immigration caused by the expansion of the coffee sector was one of the most profound changes to occur between the

[1] Caio Prado, Jr., *História Econômica do Brasil*, 8th revised edition, São Paulo, 1963, p. 217.

eighties and the First World War. São Paulo had agents in a number of European cities, and 'San Paolo' became a magnetic name to many Italians.[1] Immigration to the state increased to levels unknown during the Empire, and by 1900 nearly one-fourth of the population of the state was foreign-born.

But the impact of the immigrants on Brazil cannot be measured by their numbers alone. For many of them, work on the coffee *fazendas* was simply a temporary stage in their progress toward a more remunerative position. Many who had been tradesmen and artisans in their native countries went to São Paulo, not to harvest coffee, but to use their special skills and experience in a more prosperous land. The immigrants have sometimes been pointed to as examples of entrepreneurial or 'innovating' groups,[2] but if we look at them more closely, their role is not particularly surprising. The beginnings of industrialization in São Paulo cannot be credited to any one group: among those who founded some of the industries which were to be the nucleus for the import substitution industrialization of the thirties, one finds men of widely varying backgrounds, including a number of native Brazilians. Among the leading entrepreneurs were Italians like Francisco Matarazzo, founder of the largest corporate empire in São Paulo, Antonio Pereira Ignacio, a Portuguese immigrant who established large textile and cement plants. The Lebanese Jafet brothers became leading textile entrepreneurs, and expanded into other fields. But there were also native Brazilians among the entrepreneurs – a *paulista*, Antonio Rodovalho, established one of the principal paper companies. Another, Luis Queiroz, started a pioneering chemical firm. Several of the railroads had been organized by native *paulistas*, and the *paulista* Silva Prado family was active in textile enterprises and other firms.[3]

It seems difficult to select any particular group, either from among the immigrants, or from the *paulista* population as a whole, as the crucial entrepreneurial group. Those who responded to the growing opportunities offered by the growth of exports and the development of the São Paulo market came from widely disparate origins – planters and immigrants, Lebanese and native *paulistas*, Italians and Germans. When we remember that nearly a quarter of the population

[1] See Constantino Ianni, *Homens sem Paz*, São Paulo, 1963, for a study of Italian immigration to São Paulo.

[2] For example, by E. E. Hagen in *An Analytical Model of the Transition to Economic Growth*, quoted by Benjamin Higgins in *Social Aspects of Economic Development in Latin America*, Vol. I, UNESCO, Expert Working Group on Social Aspects of Economic Development in Latin America, Mexico City, 1960.

[3] H. F. Lima, *A Evolução Industrial de São Paulo*, São Paulo, 1954, Chapter 5.

of São Paulo in 1900 was foreign-born, and that many of the immigrants had a higher level of education, literacy, and familiarity with various technologies new to Brazil, it is not surprising that São Paulo industry bears the mark of the immigrant. Nor did immigrants restrict themselves to industrial enterprises in the city of São Paulo. Many of the *colonos* acquired a little land of their own, often in areas which had already been planted and were less fertile than the frontier areas.[1] Some succeeded in becoming large planters themselves: one Italian, Lunardelli, even came to be known as the 'king of coffee'. The development of urban centres, especially Rio and São Paulo, stimulated many immigrants to produce food crops, and much of the growth of agricultural production in the southern states was due to small farms established by Germans and Italians, a pattern of agriculture virtually unknown in the north.

IV. LAND

One of the striking aspects of the period from 1880 to 1913 is the fact that despite the rapid growth of certain exports, particularly coffee and rubber, as well as the lesser exports like cocoa, there was relatively little change in the basic distribution of agricultural property in Brazil, and hence in the relative distribution of income among groups, even though there were important regional redistributions of income, capital, and labour induced by the differential rates of growth of exports.

In terms of the pattern of land holding and occupation, Brazil was already an old country by the time of independence in 1822. Shortly after its discovery in 1500 the crown, using a Portuguese precedent, had instituted a system of *sesmarias*, or grants of large tracts of land to individuals considered capable of using them productively. Sugar production required substantial investments, and only a few people, often Portuguese nobility, were granted the largest tracts, some of which were the forerunners of whole states like Pernambuco. These grants, or *capitanias*, were subdivided, and all that was necessary for title to interior areas was the ability to populate them with sufficient cattle and a few slaves or followers to establish a kind of rudimentary occupation.

During the colonial period, much of Brazil's interior, even some of the vast regions now in the states of Mato Grosso, Goiás, Pará, and Amazonas, were claimed in this way. Usually it was done by groups of explorers, or *bandeirantes*, who went from São Paulo

[1] Caio Prado, Jr., *op. cit.*, pp. 254–61.

throughout Brazil in search of gold, diamonds and Indian slaves. Many of them asked for title to vast interior tracts, securing their claim with their men, who might be either slaves or poor free men allowed to use part of the land for their own purposes in return for maintaining the claim and caring for the cattle.

Paradoxical as it may seem in so vast and sparsely populated a country, much of the accessible land in Brazil had been claimed by the nineteenth century. The abundance of land in the early colonial period permitted a rather easygoing attitude towards property boundaries and even titles themselves. Land divisions were based on natural topographical features, rather than degrees of latitude or longitude, as in the United States, and by the mid-nineteenth century the confusion of ill-defined titles was beginning to be a difficult problem in the areas of denser settlement. Some of the confusion was ended in 1850, when the imperial government promulgated a law attempting to systematize land divisions on the basis of geometric measurement, although the law was never really implemented. More important was another section, requiring that all land be acquired through purchase, and threatening sanctions against illegal occupation of public land. The next major change came with the advent of republican decentralization following the fall of the Empire, when title to public lands passed from the federal government to the states.[1]

Only in the areas of European immigration in the three southern states did the smallholding, worked by its owner and his family, become important. Although some small-scale attempts to settle European immigrants in the states of Rio de Janeiro and Espírito Santo had been made in the early nineteenth century, it was in the hilly land north of Porto Alegre in Rio Grande do Sul where immigration had the greatest land settlement. First, Germans beginning in 1824 and then Italians in the 1870s populated much of the northern part of the state, as well as substantial areas of Santa Catarina and Paraná.

In the rest of Brazil the large estate continued to dominate the pattern of rural settlement, as it had for nearly four centuries. Much of this land, however, was unused, since the owners often had only enough men and resources to establish effective occupation, but never really to cultivate or settle it. Owing to the relative shortage of labour, a condition which continued in Brazil from the early days of Indian enslavement through the immigrant-worked coffee plantation system of São Paulo, landowners were usually glad to establish

[1] T. L. Smith, *Brazil, People and Institutions*, Baton Rouge, 1946, p. 259.

some relationship with itinerant settlers or *caboclos*. One common arrangement was a kind of sharecropping, or *parceiro* system, in which a part of the crop was turned over to the *patrão* in return for the land use. Much of the North-East's cotton crop was produced in this way. Another arrangement, common in the interior, was the assignment of responsibility for the landowner's cattle to a group of cowherds, or *vaqueiros*, who might in time even establish herds of their own, if they were able to buy or rent land from the owner, who was usually absent, preferring the life of the coastal towns.[1] The least prestigious status was simply that of the *aggregado*, or retainer, who might begin as a squatter and win acceptance by the landlord or an overseer in return for occasional work and perhaps some of the surplus which his subsistence agriculture might produce. Although there is little detailed information on the proportions of these various categories of farmer in Brazil's rural population, the 1920 census does show the extraordinary degree to which the land was dominated by large estates even at this date. Only about 20 per cent of Brazil's total area was enumerated in the census, but this is due to the extremely low percentages for the vast interior states of Amazonas (4 per cent), Pará (7), Maranhão (9), and Mato Grosso (13). Of the land counted, less than 4 per cent was in agricultural establishments of 40 hectares (about 100 acres) or less, and the average size of an agricultural establishment was over 600 acres.[2]

The rapid expansion of the coffee industry was no doubt facilitated by the easy availability of land for smallholdings in São Paulo and the south. Yet it cannot be maintained that the concentration of land was a serious obstacle to the production of other crops in other parts of the country, except to some extent in the already thickly populated North-East. The Brazilian landowner seems not to have conformed to the stereotype of the aristocrat holding land exclusively for prestige purposes and failing to exploit its commercial value. The failure of the North-East was an entrepreneurial failure to cope with a halving of the world prices of sugar and cotton by the end of the century,[3] rather than a simple case of land monopoly.

V. OTHER AGRICULTURE

As befits such a large country, with a wide climatic variation,

---

[1] Enclydes da Cunha, *Os Sertões*, 'O Homem', 15th revised edition, Rio de Janeiro, 1940, pp. 121–4.

[2] *Recenseamento de 1920*, Vol. 3, Pt. 1, pp. 32–3.   [3] See Chapter 2.

Brazil's agriculture was by no means monocultural. Coffee dominated the regions where it was suitable, but Brazil was also interested in most other tropical crops.

Food. As usual, food production was the major agricultural industry. Food farmers benefited from the expansion of the export industries, and seem to have kept up quite well with expanding demands and population. There are no records of domestic food production before 1920, but Furtado has suggested that supplies in this sector were highly responsive to the developing internal markets of São Paulo and Rio de Janeiro.[1] In most of these areas a wide range of subsistence farms had existed for nearly a century, but with the development of markets for surpluses and growing demand in the coffee regions, these areas were integrated into the economy of the central states of São Paulo, Rio and Minas Gerais. Italian and German immigrants established small farms in the southern states during this period, and by the turn of the century Rio Grande was regularly exporting a number of food products to Rio and São Paulo. One of the best known products of the region was wine, made in the hilly region north of Porto Alegre, the capital, from which it was shipped north. More important in economic terms were the exports of meat and wheat, in whose production the central and southern plains of the state gave Rio Grande do Sul a natural advantage. Foreign exports from the state increased as well, particularly cattle hides, whose export volume doubled between 1880 and 1913.

Sugar. In contrast with the prosperity of the central coffee-producing states, the period from 1880 to 1913 was one of stagnation, if not decline, for the populous states of the North-East.[2] In the sixteenth and seventeenth centuries Brazil had been one of the world's greatest sugar suppliers, enjoying a virtual monopoly until the Dutch and British began production in the Caribbean and in Asia. So tempting was the sugar trade that the Dutch seized Pernambuco in 1630 and were only expelled by the Portuguese in 1654. World prices had declined in the eighteenth century, and continued downward,[3] despite the temporary resurgence of prosperity caused by the collapse of Haitian production after 1789 when that colony revolted against the French. Although the area continued to

[1] Furtado, *op. cit.*, pp. 202–3.
[2] Maranhão, Piauí, Ceará, Rio Grade do Norte, Paríba, Pernambuco, Alagôas, and Sergipe.
[3] Roberto C. Simonsen, *História Econômica do Brasil 1500–1820*, São Paulo, 1937, p. 114.

export modest amounts of sugar, three centuries of sugar had exhausted the soil, eliminated the forests, and crowded out other crops. The equipment used for processing the cane was technically inferior to that used in the newer producing countries, and in many areas the *engenhos*, or mills, were no different from those built by the Portuguese during the height of the Brazilian sugar boom.[1] Deforestation resulted in widespread erosion, and much of the fertile land was washed away. Planters were reluctant to use land for anything other than sugar; even subsistence agriculture was eliminated, and unlike coffee, supplementary food crops could not be grown in the same areas with the cane. The absence of food crops, however, originated in the social and political situation, and not from natural or technical reasons. During the seventeenth and eighteenth centuries a number of fugitive slave settlements, or *quilombos*, grew up in the backlands where, free from the domination of sugar, the slaves planted a number of crops, including corn, beans, sweet potatoes, manioc, and bananas. In the sugar areas themselves manioc became the chief staple, since it could be grown easily and with little labour on land not used for sugar, but its nutritional qualities were low.[2]

Brazilian sugar production had grown during the Empire, although it lagged far behind the Caribbean, and the rise in volume was accompanied by a fall in prices. Some limited attempts were made to modernize the industry, and British investments financed a few central mills which bought cane from surrounding producers. Most of these mills had difficulty obtaining a regular and dependable supply of cane, and in the nineties began to grow cane themselves.[3] This concentration and integration of production continued throughout the period, but Brazilian production could not compete internationally, and the sugar sector attracted little foreign investment in comparison with the sums invested in Indonesia and elsewhere. Why Brazilian planters failed so signally in an industry where world production doubled is not clear; new technology simply passed them by.

Cotton. The other important cash crop in the North-East was cotton, which had been cultivated since colonial times for export to the growing markets of Europe. The sudden shortage of cotton in Europe during the American Civil war provided a strong stimulus to Brazilian cotton growing. The Manchester Cotton Supply Asso-

[1] Josue de Castro, *Death in the Northeast*, New York, 1966, Chapters 4 and 5 and Caio Prado, Jr., *op. cit.*, pp. 249 ff.
[2] Caio Prado, Jr., *op. cit.*, pp. 42–3.   [3] *ibid.*, pp. 252–3.

115

ciation even sent seed to provincial authorities in São Paulo, and by 1870 Brazilian exports, both from the North-East and from São Paulo, were about 45,000 tons a year.[1] Within a few years, however, world cotton prices began to fall, as American cotton returned to the European markets. Brazil was at a comparative disadvantage in the world market, partly due to poor transport, as well as to the generally poor quality of the cotton.[2] By 1880 production had fallen off considerably, and in some areas disappeared. But cotton prices revived very sharply after 1900, and the average annual output rose from 45,000 tons over the three years 1900–02 to 91,000 tons over 1911–13.

An important consequence of temporarily large supplies of cotton as world prices fell during the 1870s was the development of a domestic cotton textile industry, about the only manufacture of real importance in Brazil prior to World War I. Most of the mills were built in Rio and São Paulo, although the earliest ones were founded in the North-East in the 1840s and by 1885 the states of Rio, São Paulo, and Minas Gerais had thirty-three of Brazil's forty-eight textile mills.[3] Both water power and imported coal were easier to obtain in the south, and the growing population provided a better labour supply and market than did the stagnant North-East.

Cocoa. Although often grouped with the North-East, the state of Bahía was an exception to the pattern of decline in the north. Accompanying the growth of demand for coffee was the demand for cocoa, which in colonial times had been produced in northern Brazil in the Amazon region. In the mid-nineteenth century it was discovered that it flourished in the fertile and more accessible coastal lands in the southern part of the state. Following the severe drought of 1877 in the North-East, a number of migrants entered the region, and Bahian cocoa production doubled between 1880 and 1890 as new lands were cleared and planted. By the turn of the century over 13,000 tons were exported, and by 1913, more than 30,000 tons. Almost 20 per cent of the state's public revenues came from an export tax on cocoa, and the city of Salvador was a prosperous exception to the general decline in the north.[4] Unlike coffee, however, Bahía's cocoa production was not able to maintain its share of the expanding world market, despite the rapid growth of production. By 1913 African production, particularly that of the Gold Coast (Ghana) supplied nearly half the world demand.

[1] S. J. Stein, *The Brazilian Cotton Manufacture*, Cambridge, Mass., 1957, p. 45.
[2] *ibid.*, pp. 47–8. [3] *ibid.*, p. 21. [4] Caio Prado, Jr., *op. cit.*, pp. 248–9.

Tobacco. The state of Bahía was also favoured by its position as a leading tobacco producer, since the demand for this crop rose significantly during this period. Between 1880 and 1913 the value of tobacco exports more than doubled.

Rubber. The most spectacular chapter of Brazilian economic history at the end of the nineteenth century was the rubber boom in the Amazon basin. Rubber trees were indigenous to the region, and explorers had noted its use by Indians, although it was for a long time no more than a curiosity. In 1842 the process of vulcanization was discovered, and it became possible to use rubber for industrial purposes without alterations in its state due to temperature changes. In 1890 the pneumatic tyre was perfected, and the demand for rubber skyrocketed as the new automobile industries developed.

At the time Brazil enjoyed a natural near monopoly in the production of wild rubber, which was gathered throughout the Amazon basin. The production process was relatively primitive, and labour was the only significant input. Claims to certain zones along rivers were staked out and gatherers were recruited to collect the latex from trees along their paths and to coagulate it for shipment down river to Manaus and Belém. The 1877 drought drove thousands of *nordestinos* to the Amazon basin, and the governments of the Amazon states subsidized the passage of many others.[1] Even more than coffee culture, the expansion of rubber production demanded a large supply of labour. During the seventies and eighties, about 20,000 migrants a year went to the Amazon region from Ceará, one of the most severely stricken of the North-East states,[2] and it was this flow of labour which permitted the expansion of the industry after 1880.

Collectors (*seringueiros*) were often lent their passage to the rubber zones, as well as the necessary tools and food; in return they were obliged to pay off this debt from rubber earnings. The system soon developed into a vicious form of debt slavery. The owner of the collection rights (*seringalista*) in a certain area could easily keep his collectors in continual debt, since he was the source of necessary foodstuffs and supplies. Proprietors refused to hire collectors who owed debts to other proprietors, and in some cases guards were stationed at the mouths of river tributaries to prevent the escape of the gatherers.[3] The *seringalistas* themselves were often in debt to large commercial houses in Manaus and Belém, through which all the rubber traffic passed.

[1] Furtado, *op. cit.*, Chapter 23. [2] *ibid.*
[3] Charles Wagley, *Amazon Town*, New York, 1964, p. 194.

Despite the hardships of the rubber gatherers, the prospects of becoming wealthy through the discovery of a particularly good concentration of trees were appealing to north-easterners, and the population of the state of Amazonas grew more rapidly between 1872 and 1900 than any other state in Brazil, averaging more than 5 per cent a year. Owing to the structure of the industry, little of the income from rubber exports ever reached the *seringueiro*, who survived on manioc, fish, and the few animals he might hunt as he made his rounds. Since all the rubber was transported by river, the boom left no infrastructure like São Paulo's railways, nor did it result in any local food production. Most of the wealth which resulted from the boom was concentrated in the towns of Belém and Manaus, where today ornate and forlorn opera houses which once heard Caruso stand as monuments to the hopes of that spectacular age.

Although few noticed it at the time, the doom of the Amazon rubber boom was sealed in the early 1870s when wild seedlings were transferred from Brazil to Kew Gardens in London, and from there to Malaya and Ceylon. There rubber was grown on organized plantations, where the productivity per man and per acre was far higher than in the gathering system of the Amazon. Rubber prices and consumption continued to rise throughout the first decade of this century, but Oriental production rapidly overtook Brazil. As late as 1905 Brazil produced most of the world's rubber, and demand continued to surpass supply. The peak came in 1910, when rubber prices reached more than £600 a ton, and rubber alone accounted for over a third of the value of Brazil's exports. With increasing Oriental production the price began to fall, and by 1913 prices were half what they had been three years earlier. Prosperity was vanishing from the Amazon as rapidly as it had come.

VI. ECONOMIC POLICY

The importance of the large land holding, or *fazenda*, in Brazilian economic life was reflected in the politics of both the Empire and the 'Old Republic', as the series of governments from 1889 to 1930 has come to be known. With large numbers of people dependent upon them for the use of the land, or as an important customer, or as an influential friend, the landowners were able to wield considerable power, virtually controlling Brazilian politics. Before Vargas came to power in the 'revolution' of 1930, the number of votes cast in a presidential election was never more than 3 per cent

118

of the population.[1] The landowners were aided by a widespread sentiment in government, among urban intellectuals and in the military that Brazil's natural destiny was as an agricultural nation. Industry was not actively opposed, and there was widespread support for manufacturing using local crops, such as cotton textiles, but the primary interest of the Brazilian ruling class, both before and after the fall of the Empire, was in agricultural export. Despite the growing importance of urban groups, the republican constitution of 1891 strengthened the planters, and policies like the Taubaté coffee valorization plan were the natural result of republican decentralization. Exchange devaluation, despite its increasing unpopularity with the small middle classes of Rio and São Paulo, was another way in which the landowners used their political power to advantage.

Industrialization. The political history of the time should not be seen, however, as simply an exercise of the power of the export producers. There had been great hopes for industrialization among most Brazilians after the Paraguayan War, when the necessity of some minimal domestic industrial base and a more effective transportation and communication system became evident. Many believed that Brazil was on the threshold of a period of economic growth like that of the United States. Between 1880 and the fall of the Empire in 1889, the number of 'industrial establishments' (some were little more than one-man firms) had grown from about 200 to 600, with well over half the investment in them in the textile industry.

The textile industry was easily the most successful. By 1913 Brazil was producing over three-quarters of its domestic consumption of cotton textiles.[2] Other manufacturing industries begun in this period included chemicals, food preparation, clothing and metalworking. In most cases tariff protection was incidental rather than deliberate. Import duties were one of the chief sources of federal revenue, and the tariffs were intended more to raise revenue than to protect domestic manufacturers.

Government economic policy during the 1880–1913 period basically favoured the landowning rural aristocracy, as it did throughout the Empire, but the period was marked by a series of crises and debates over the proper economic conduct of the government. Rui Barbosa, the first finance minister of the Republic, was one of the group of Brazilians who expected a great industrial future for their nation, and his policies of tax reform, corporate

---

[1] Guerreiro Ramos, *A Criso do Poder no Brasil*, quoted by de Castro, *op. cit.*, p. 130.

[2] Calculated from figures in Stanley J. Stein, *Brazilian Cotton*.

legislation, and expansion of credit to industry through a reformed banking system were made with the objective of promoting industrial development. Unfortunately the rapid expansion of credit and a wave of speculation accompanied the establishment of the new government and, between November of 1889 and October of the following year, corporations were organized with a greater total nominal capitalization than during the previous three-quarters of a century.[1] Most of this was purely speculative, and the boom or *encilhamento* cane to an end in 1891, with the failure of a number of these hastily organized ventures.

The biggest industrial deficiency was the failure to develop a significant iron industry. This was not for lack of popular support. Even in the colonial period there had been attempts to develop a domestic iron industry, and one blast furnace built in 1818 functioned sporadically and uneconomically until 1895, but it was only in the 1890s that any real progress was made. In 1888 the 'Esperanca' furnace, with a capacity of six tons a day, was built, and a number of foundries and forges were established, chiefly in the iron regions of the state of Minas Gerais. By 1900 Brazil was producing about 4,000 tons of iron a year, which was about 15 per cent of annual iron and steel consumption at that time.[2] The main obstacle was the absence of cheap domestic supplies of coking coal; iron ore was abundant, and was exported, but coal was imported. If cheap coal had been easily accessible, Brazil would have taken off as an iron and steel producer, and her growth rate of industrial output per head could then not have been inferior to that of the United States. What held Brazil back in this area was not some cultural peculiarity, but simply lack of coal.

Coffee power. The rise of the coffee sector in the Brazilian economy had several political effects. Even during the Empire it had commonly been said that 'Brazil is coffee'. The fall of the slave-worked plantations of the Paraíba valley, and the rise of the more capitalistic system of São Paulo was decisive. It was this shift of the dynamic centre of the economy, as much as disillusionment with the ageing monarchy or the Comtian positivist doctrines then in vogue, which led to the Republic. The role of the court in the centre of Brazilian political life decreased, and the rise of the *paulista* coffee culture was accompanied by increasing demands for more regional autonomy

[1] Pinto Ferreira, *op. cit.*, p. 121.
[2] Edmundo de Macedo Soares e Silva, 'O ferro e o carvão na História, na Economía, e na Civilização do Brasil', p. 493 (in *Aspectos da Formação e Evolução do Brasil*, published by the *Jornal de Commercie*), Rio de Janeiro, 1953.

and decentralization. The inability of the imperial government to meet the growing demands of São Paulo and other states for better public services, education, and a more modern banking system strengthened the hand of those who advocated a new form of government more sympathetic to the new forces in Brazilian economic life.[1] Although the actual change in régimes was little more than a coup by military officers and some civilian sympathizers,[2] few mourned the passing of the Empire. The federal government which followed it seemed made-to-order for the *paulista* planters. São Paulo had already begun to subsidize European immigration as a source of labour for the coffee plantations in 1881,[3] and under the new republican constitution even greater initiatives were allowed the states. Regional banks were given the authority to extend credit liberally,[4] and the states were given greater taxing power than they had enjoyed during the Empire. Another privilege was the right to contract directly with foreign lenders for public borrowing. Even municipalities borrowed and, between the fall of the Empire and 1910, Brazil's foreign debt more than tripled.[5]

The new political power of the coffee-growing states culminated in the Taubaté agreement of 1906, one of the world's first major price support plans. Reacting to the fall in world coffee prices since the 1890s, the producers saw an opportunity to exploit Brazil's domination of the world market (Brazil produced about three-quarters of the world's coffee between 1900 and 1905).[6] Under pressure from the planters, the major producing states signed an agreement at Taubaté, São Paulo, to purchase coffee surpluses. The constitution had conceded states the right to levy export taxes, and under the terms of the agreement, a tax on each bag exported was used to finance the servicing of the loans contracted by the states to purchase the surpluses. Although one of the provisons of the agreement was the responsibility of the states to limit future production, there was little incentive for the planters to do so, now that the future of coffee production appeared secure. The fundamental weakness of the system – its encouragement of a misallocation of resources to produce coffee at an artificially high price – was not apparent for a number of years. Brazil's virtual monopoly on world production permitted the scheme to function in the short run, and in purely static terms, the plan seemed to be a success. Not

---

[1] Furtado, *op. cit.*, pp. 202–3.   [2] Caio Prado, Jr., *op. cit.*, p. 214.
[3] N. W. Sodré, *História de Burgesia Brasiliera*, Rio de Janeiro, 1967, p. 162.
[4] Pinto Ferreira, *op. cit.*, pp. 116–17.
[5] *ibid.*, p. 164.   [6] Sodré, *op. cit.*, p. 172.

until the 1920s was the damage apparent, when surplus stocks grew to comprise a third of total production,[1] and other countries entered the market under the protection of the Brazilian price umbrella. Only in 1929 would the whole structure come tumbling down, as the price of coffee fell to a third of its former level and foreign financing to purchase the continuing surpluses was suddenly unavailable.

Public finance. Following in the traditions of the Empire, the period saw a marked increase in the public debt. The government had already borrowed heavily for a number of causes: the Paraguayan War of 1864–70, the financing of several railways and roads, famine relief in 1877, and treaty obligations. Brazil's credit was good: during the nineteenth century it was the only American nation to honour all its debts (even some US states repudiated their obligations).[2] The new government continued the tradition, and between 1889 and 1913 seventeen foreign loans were contracted, most of them on the London Market. One was the famous 'Funding' loan of 1898, to consolidate older obligations. Government budgets of the period sometimes show a quarter of the expenditure devoted to the Finance Ministry; most of this represents debt servicing. Between 1884 and 1914 the debt of the federal government, states, and municipalities rose from £12m. to £162m.[3] Debt servicing became a major item in the balance of payments which, despite Brazil's consistently favourable trade balance, was reduced by this obligation, a problem compounded by increasing remissions by immigrants to their native countries.

The government of Campos Salles (1898–1902) attempted to restore some order in public finances. His orthodox but able finance minister, Joaquim Murtinho, faced with falling coffee prices, large government obligations, and a fiscal system which delegated many taxing powers to the states, balanced the federal budget, and even went so far as to sell two of the navy's ships.[4] Excise taxes and tariffs were raised and 20 per cent of the money supply was retired. The depreciation of the *milreis*, which had dropped from 27d in 1889 to 7d in 1898 (as domestic prices rose rapidly during the *encilhamento* and coffee and cocoa prices fell), was checked, and when Salles left office in 1902 the rate had risen to 12d. The Salles-Murtinho policies were maintained by the government of Rodrigues Alves (1902–06), and Brazil's foreign trade position improved as

[1] Furtado, *op. cit.*, p. 212.   [2] Caio Prado, Jr., *op. cit.*, p. 217.
[3] Pinto Ferreira, *op. cit.*, p. 164.
[4] N. W. Sodré, *História Militar do Brasil*, Rio de Janeiro, 1965, p. 165.

coffee and cocoa prices rose along with the rapidly increasing demand for rubber.

VII. NATIONAL INCOME

For Brazil as a whole this was a prosperous time. The volume of exports rose by 2·9 per cent per annum, the terms of trade moved in their favour, food production kept pace with demand, and the foundations of industrialization were laid.

Furtado has argued that the growth of Brazilian exports in the last half of the nineteenth century resulted in an increase in average *per capita* income of about 1·5 per cent annually, as rapid as that of the United States in the same period.[1] This is based on his estimate that real income originating in the export sector was five times as high at the turn of the century as it had been in the 1840s, and that real income as a whole multiplied by about the same amount in the fifty-year period. Given the growth rate of the population of about 2 per cent per annum, the *per capita* growth rate was thus about 1·5 per cent.

This estimate appears to be slightly high for the 1880–1913 period, even considering the inferential and tenuous way in which such estimates are made. It is also necessary to consider the regional variations, which were wide.

The coffee producing states of São Paulo, Rio, Minas Gerais and Espírito Santo turned in the best performance. Between 1880 and 1913 the value of coffee exports grew at an average annual rate of 4 per cent, while population grew at about 2·5 per cent. Food production kept pace with population; infrastructure grew at least as fast as coffee exports, and industry grew even faster. Furtado's assumption that real income grew as fast as exports is not unreasonable in these states. This would yield an average growth of *per capita* income of about 1·5 per cent per annum, comparable with that of the United States as a whole (though there were United States regions which grew faster, thanks to the mechanization of agriculture, or to the swift rise of iron and steel).

In the North-East there is no doubt that *per capita* income was not increasing; it was in all probability, declining. Cotton and sugar, the two chief exports of the region, earned only half as much in 1913 as they had in 1880. It is doubtful that there was any significant increase in productivity in the subsistence sector, which had suffered from the severe drought of the 1870s. Despite considerable migration

[1] Furtado, *op. cit.*, p. 177.

of the population to more productive areas, population increased at a rate of about 1·8 per cent annually between the 1872 and 1920 censuses. Given the decline in real income from the principal north-eastern exports, and assuming no productivity increase in the subsistence sector, it appears that real *per capita* income in the North-East may have fallen by as much as 0·5 or 1·0 per cent annually, even if we allow for a slight decline in the price of imports, as does Furtado, and some limited investment in railroads, shipping, and a few manufacturing establishments.

In contrast to the other northern states, *per capita* income in Bahía was at least stable, and probably increasing slowly. Although the population grew at about the same rate as in the North-East, 1·9 per cent annually, the value of the two principal exports, cocoa and cotton, increased rapidly, at about 2·5 to 3·0 per cent annually. They were a relatively small part of total Brazilian exports, however, and their effect on the whole Bahian economy resulted in a rate of growth of real *per capita* income which was probably around 0·5 per cent annually.

The three southern states had the most rapid rate of population growth outside São Paulo between 1872 and 1920, approximately 3·2 per cent yearly. Even so, real income apparently kept ahead of population growth, due in part to the development of small agriculture supplying the growing demands of São Paulo and Rio and to the favourable foreign demand for the two principal exports of the region, hides and skins, and yerba-mate, even though they were not among Brazil's major exports. Real income from exports grew at about 5 per cent annually, and the production of foodstuffs increased as well. Furtado's estimate of a 1·0 annual rate of increase of *per capita* income in the south in the last half of the nineteenth century is reasonable, and it may even have been higher in the 1880–1913 period.

Export growth had a greater impact on the economy of the Amazon region than anywhere else, since rubber gathering was the only non-subsistence activity in most of the vast region. Furtado argues that investments in the rubber sector may actually have had a 'negative multiplier effect', since other activities were abandoned and goods formerly produced locally were imported. Although this proposition might be disputed, there seems little doubt that the rubber boom had less permanent effect on the region than the development of exports in other regions. Due to the prospects of sudden wealth, migration into the region resulted in a rate of growth of population of about 3·1 per cent between 1872 and 1920.

124

The increase in real income from rubber exports averaged about 7 per cent annually over the 1880–1913 period, yielding a rate of growth of *per capita* income of about 4 per cent. Due to the structure of the rubber exporting system, however, and the decline in world prices after 1910, real *per capita* income in the Amazon region was already beginning to fall, and would not begin to recover until recent times.

We can conclude that *per capita* income in Brazil as a whole increased as a result of export growth during the period from 1880 to 1913. Only in the North-East is there definite evidence of a decline, and in some regions like the Amazon it increased rapidly. Furtado's estimate of an average rate of growth of 1·5 per cent for an earlier, overlapping period from 1850 to 1900 appears to be too high for the 1880–1913 period. This is due in part to an acceleration of the decline in the North-East at the end of the century, as well as to a slightly more rapid rate of growth of population. If one takes for the country as a whole, growth rates for export values of 3·5 per cent per annum, for food production of about 2·5, and for industry of about 4·0, national income will have grown by between 3·0 and 3·3 per cent, allowing also for fast growth of infrastructure. This would make the increase in *per capita* real income something of the order of 1 per cent per annum, comparable with say Britain or France.

Real income is not all; the increase in productive capacity is also important. By 1913 there was a nucleus for future industrial expansion in Rio and São Paulo. The state of São Paulo possessed an excellent railway network, and Brazil's ports and communications had greatly improved. The southern states had become a major food producing area, and Brazil had become one of the principal destinations of immigrants to the New World. As for human resources the record on illiteracy and primary education was very bad; but Brazil was meeting its own demands for secondary and higher education and had also created a substantial commercial and industrial class.

Yet many problems remained for the future. The North-East remained in decline. The participation of the population in national political life was extremely limited; literacy rates were little changed between censuses – most of the improvement can be attributed to Rio and São Paulo – and despite the existence of several professional faculties in Rio, Recifé, and São Paulo, as well as the military school, no truly national university existed. Outside the state of São Paulo, transport was still poor or non-existent. Brazil would wait for several decades before even recognizing these problems, and they still loom large today.

BIBLIOGRAPHY

Official Papers

Brazil. Conselho Nacional de Estatistica, *Anuario Estatistico do Brasil*, 1939–40. Rio de Janeiro.

——. Conselho Nacional de Geografia, Instituto Brasileiro de Geografia e Estatistica, *I Centenario das Ferrovias Brasileiras*, Rio de Janeiro, 1954.

——. Directoria Geral de Estatistica, *Recenseamento Geral de 1920*, Volumes I–VII. Rio de Janeiro, 1922–49.

United States. Bureau of the Census, *Historical Statistics of the United States, Colonial Times to 1957*. Washington, D C, 1960.

——. Department of Commerce, *Report on Trade Conditions in Brazil* by Lincoln Hutchinson. Washington, D C, 1906.

Books

Baer, Werner, *Industrialization and Economic Development in Brazil*, Homewood, Ill., 1965.

Castro, Josue de, *Death in the Northeast*, New York, 1966.

Cunha, Euclydes da, *Os Sertões*, 'O Homem', 15th revised edition, Rio de Janeiro, 1940.

Duncan, J. S., *Public and Private Operation of Railways in Brazil*, New York, 1932.

Furtado, Celso, *Formação Econômica do Brasil*, Rio de Janeiro, 1959.

Ianni, Constantino, *Homens sem Paz*, São Paulo, 1963.

Lima, H. F., *Evolução Industrial de São Paulo*, São Paulo, 1954.

Normano, J. F., *Brazil, A Study of Economic Types*, Chapel Hill, N C, 1935.

Oakenfull, J. C., *Brazil in 1911*, 3rd annual edition, London, 1912.

Pinto Ferreira, Luis, *Capitals Estrangeiros e Dívida Externa do Brasil*, São Paulo, 1965.

Prado, Caio, Jr., *História Econômica do Brasil*, 8th revised edition, São Paulo, 1963.

Ramos, Augusto, *O Café no Brasil e no Estrangeiro*, Rio de Janeiro, 1923.

Simonsen, R. C., *História Econômica de Brasil, 1500–1820*, São Paulo, 1937.

Smith, T. L., *Brazil, People and Institutions*, Baton Rouge, 1946.

Sodré, N. W., *História da Burgesia Brasileira*, Rio de Janeiro, 1964.

——, *História Militar do Brasil*, Rio de Janeiro, 1965.

Stein, S. J., *The Brazilian Cotton Manufacture: Textile Enterprise in an Underdeveloped Area, 1850–1950*, Cambridge, Mass., 1957.

——, *Vassouras, a Brazilian Coffee County, 1860–1900*, Cambridge, Mass., 1957.

United Nations. Department of Social Affairs, *Age and Sex Patterns of Mortality*, New York, 1955.

——, *Methods of Using Census Statistics for the Calculation of Life*

126

Tables . . . , with Applications to Brazil by Giorgio Mortara, New York, 1949.

Wagley, Charles, *Amazon Town*, New York, 1964.

Articles

Higgins, Benjamin, 'Requirements for Rapid Economic Development in Latin America: the View of an Economist', *Social Aspects of Economic Development in Latin America*, Vol. 1, edited by Egbert de Vries and José Medina Echavarría (UNESCO), Paris, 1963.

Macedo Soares e Silva, Edmundo de, 'O Ferro e o Carvão na História, na Economía e na Civilização do Brasil', *Aspectos da Formação e Evolução do Brasil*, published by Jornal de Commercio, Rio de Janeiro, 1953.

Chapter 5

VENEZUELA

by Frederick Norbury

I. INTRODUCTION

Although long considered a dank political backwater of the Spanish Empire in the New World, isolated from the fashion and favour of the royal court, the provinces which were later to form the independent Republic of Venezuela had become by 1800 among the most productive of Spain's agricultural dominions. By 1797 the most significant of the colonial restrictions on trade had been removed, and exports began a period of fairly rapid growth. This growth was interrupted and even reversed by the physical destruction and market disruption associated with the protracted wars of independence and the subsequent separation of the Venezuelan provinces from the federation of Gran Colombia. It was 1830, for example, before the human population regained the magnitude of the generally accepted figure estimated by Humbolt in 1804. The cattle population appears to have suffered even more severely. The growth of trade was again reversed during the Federal Wars which lasted from 1857 to 1863 – and the cattle if not the human population fell once again. On the whole the value of exports doubled between 1840 and 1880 and, by the latter date, a fairly high level of export earnings had been established. They amounted to almost 70 million bolívares, or somewhere between 7 and 8 US dollars per person. On a *per capita* basis, this was a higher level than that achieved by Venezuela's geographical and cultural neighbour, Colombia. And Venezuela ranked as the second largest exporter of coffee in the world.

In spite of this early start as a large-scale exporter of primary products, Venezuela appears to have benefited somewhat less (in economic terms at least) from the rapid expansion of the markets for primary products that began in the last quarter of the nineteenth century than a simple examination of the country's resource might lead one to expect. Between 1880 and 1913 the value of exports did not quite double (see Table 5.1); indeed in this respect Venezuela is near the bottom of the Latin American league, contrasting most unfavourably with her next door neighbours Colombia and Brazil.

128

Exports grew in value only at about the same rate as population (1·4 per cent per year). This growth rate is only slightly higher than that achieved from 1840 to 1880. Part of this phenomenon can be attributed to the sluggish performance of coffee which grew – by volume – at a rate of 1·1 per cent per year and by value at 1·4 per cent per year. (And it should be noted that these calculations may overstate the real growth rates since they are based on official figures which included a significant amount of coffee actually produced in Colombia but shipped through Venezuelan ports. Colombian production at the time was increasing at a very rapid rate.) Exports of cocoa grew somewhat faster, but not sufficiently so to brighten the aggregate figures.

TABLE 5.1: *Exports from Venezuela, Five Year Averages*

Quantities (thousand metric tons)*

	1878–82	1883–7	1888–92	1893–7	1898–1902	1903–07	1908–12
Coffee	37,660	40,606	46,299	44,240	42,925	44,623	48,567
Cocoa	4,542	5,943	6,858	7,985	7,805	13,565	15,950
Hides (thousands)	292	223	234	297	332	315	323
Cattle (thousands)	—	9,158	11,364	13,028	37,125	92,357	11,818
Balatá (tons)	—	—	—	—	541	1,216	1,940
Rubber (tons)	—	—	—	—	68	112	287
Gold (kilograms)	3,520	5,151	2,164	1,698	899	783	1,115
Tonka Beans	—	—	56	80	40	69	162
Dividivi	2,512	3,110	3,529	1,487	2,730	4,515	7,842
Wood	—	—	9,493	6,762	6,336	9,959	9,575

Value (thousand bolívares)

	1878–82	1883–7	1888–92	1893–7	1898–1902	1903–07	1908–12
Coffee	39,127	44,892	74,669	73,342	35,997	35,757	57,137
Cocoa	7,217	9,972	9,623	8,830	10,713	15,851	18,177
Hides	2,193	2,804	2,706	3,854	4,393	5,043	5,631
Cattle	—	1,015	1,174	1,365	3,609	6,699	1,080
Balatá	—	—	—	—	1,785	4,054	10,033
Rubber	—	—	—	—	415	766	2,825
Gold	11,500	16,876	6,237	4,098	2,359	2,146	2,807
Tonka Beans	—	—	396	539	106	136	948
Dividivi	376	317	433	166	291	447	611
Wood	—	—	431	292	199	378	393
Total	69,461	82,660	102,375	97,267	73,258	78,653	109,782

* With the exception of hides, cattle, gold, balatá, and rubber.

– = not available.

Sources: Venezuela, Ministerio de Fomento, Dirección General de Estadística, *Anuario Estadístico de Venezuela*, 1912, Caracas, pp. 336–9.

Ramón Veloz, *Economía y Finanzas de Venezuela, desde 1830 hasta 1944*, Caracas, 1945, *passim.*

E

This slowness of growth is not confined to exports; it is found also in many other indexes. We may note specifically transportation, population, education, banking and manufacturing, all of which are related to exports in a cumulative chain of cause and effect.

Why the Venezuelan economy did so poorly in this period is not easy to disentangle. We shall examine the three most plausible explanations – unfavourable geography, the monopolization of land, and the instability of government. But first we must see what actually happened in the leading economic sectors.

II. LAGGING DEVELOPMENT

Coffee. The most important export crop was coffee, earning 55 per cent of export revenue in 1913. The crop had expanded fairly rapidly in the middle of the nineteenth century, and continued to do so at a slower rate until the end of the century, when it stagnated, in contrast with neighbouring countries. Coffee cultivation made great progress in its early stages principally because it made use of the mountain slopes, land areas which had previously been worthless. By the 1830s yearly exports were 80,000 sacks; in the 1850s, exports had risen to a little less than 300,000, and in the 1880s exports averaged 700,000 sacks. Between the 1830s and the 1850s, exports grew at 7 per cent per annum; between the 1850s and the 1880s growth slackened to 3 per cent per annum. In the thirty-two years between 1880/81 and 1912/13, for which exports were reported by commodity, shipments varied usually between 500,000 and 900,000 sacks. The recorded exports divide evenly at a median value of 710,000, with no evidence of a temporal trend.

Looking at coffee revenues, the picture brightens somewhat, at least in the 1880s and the 1890s when rising coffee prices were an exception to the falling price trend of almost all other commodities. In terms of five-year moving averages, revenues doubled between 1880/81 and 1891/92; although coffee exports were increasing at 3 per cent per annum, annual revenues grew at 6 per cent. Export earnings were fairly constant in the first half of the 1890s but they started to fall off noticeably after 1897. In 1899, disaster struck: the price of coffee was half what it had been the previous year; the rains came late and the price of local corn, used for breadmaking, doubled;[1] and the government fell. Coffee revenues did not pick up again until 1910.

[1] Nicolas Veloz Goiticoa, ed., *Venezuela*, International Bureau of the American Republics Handbook, Washington, DC, 1904, p. 292.

130

Coffee was produced in the Andine states to the west and in the valleys of the central region, the two areas where most of the population lived. In the west, it was found on the fairly small landholdings characteristic of the region. In this area, coffee production began fairly early, being quite well established by 1880, and the land seems to have been cultivated rather intensively. In the central region, on the other hand, coffee was produced on large estates which monopolized the cultivable land in the region and were characterized then, as now, by great expanses of empty land. A great deal of this idle land was appropriate to coffee production. According to one observer, in fact, much of the idle land was superior in quality and better suited to coffee production than the land that was actually under cultivation.[1]

The great puzzle of Venezuelan development is the slow growth of the coffee industry between 1880 and the mid-1890s. In this period coffee prices were good, and output expanded rapidly in Venezuela's neighbours, Brazil and Colombia. The explanation is tied up with the distribution of land, in the sense that small farmers were denied access to empty lands. The large landowners, for their part, complained of shortage of labour, but would neither make lands available to small farmers nor engage in a vigorous immigration policy, such as Brazil's. This is the central problem when one tries to understand the relative stagnation of Venezuela in this period; the later sections of this essay try to probe it.

Cocoa. The most rapid expansion in this period occurred in cocoa, which just about quadrupled its production. It was still, at that, a pretty small industry, compared with, say, that of the Gold Coast, which started to grow cocoa only after 1880. Cocoa was never more than a poor second in the export trade of Venezuela in the nineteenth century. The eighteenth century had witnessed its growth and dominance in the European markets, and perhaps its point of saturation in the agronomy of Venezuela. The areas which will support cocoa culture are restricted as to climate and terrain. Temperatures may vary minimally from 80 degrees Fahrenheit; the climate must be moist and humid; the land must be well irrigated. Originally the bulk of the crop was produced in the coastal valleys,[2]

[1] Nicolas Veloz Goiticoa, ed., *op. cit.*, p. 153.
[2] Eduardo Arcila Farias, 'Evolución de la Economía en Venezuela', *Venezuela Independiente, 1810–1960*, Fundacion Eugenio Mendoza, Caracas, 1962, p. 369; P. L. Bell, *Venezuela: A Commercial and Industrial Handbook*, US Department of Commerce Special Agents Series Number 212, Washington, DC, 1922, pp. 55–6; and Veloz Goiticoa, *op. cit.*, p. 155.

for the most part on old and large estates from Puerto Cabello to La Guiara. With the introduction of coffee, cocoa was displaced from the central areas to the east near Carúpano and to the areas west of Puerto Cabello. The shift took place in the coastal areas alone; the literature does not support any change in the relatively small cocoa production in the lower Andes valleys. Since the climatic conditions for cocoa culture are restrictive and since the shift in land use has historical support, the hypothesis that cocoa production grew as much as possible seems admissible, even in the absence of detailed land use data. However, it is impossible to say with any degree of certainty that the empty land that existed could have been profitably devoted to cocoa production.

Cattle. Live cattle and hides and skins together make up the third item in the export list. The growth of exports was substantial, but was not outstanding, having regard to what was possible. Some cattle production took place in the valleys and foothills of the Andine states, but the cattle region par excellence was the Llanos, a broad plain stretching from the foothills of the coastal mountains southward toward the Orinoco River, containing an area of approximately 120,000 square miles. The cattle were of *criollo* stock, descended and somewhat naturally selected from the beasts originally brought by the followers of the *conquistadores*. The only care they received was round-up for market. Estimates of their numbers at various points in time ranged from over 8 million to less than 2 million. There were some technical problems associated with production. The reported reproduction rate – 200 per thousand in 1873 – is fairly low and the cattle suffered from disease and insects, especially ticks. The pasture which the Llanos provided was not of the highest quality and deteriorated severely during the dry season. But, on the whole, the cattle population density recorded at the turn of the century, approximately 50 acres per cow, seems unaccountably low, and for most of the period it stayed well under the level that the Llanos are reported to have supported in earlier times.

Forest products. Here again an opportunity was missed, especially that presented by the rubber boom, which largely by-passed Venezuela.

Great numbers of wild rubber plants existed in the dense forests of the Amazon and Guyana region which lay along the upper reaches of the Orinoco River. The areas were populated almost exclusively by various Indian tribes which, unlike those in the central and highland regions of the country, had never been incorporated into the colonial economy or even entirely pacified. These Indians provided the bulk of the initial labour force. Later on some mestizos would migrate to the area, but they tended to come for the harvest season and rarely remained on a permanent basis. The constraints on production were several. First, the labour supply was extremely limited. The census of 1891 recorded a population of only 45,000 for the entire Amazon territory.[1] Of this number, some 2,400 worked as rubber gatherers. The Indians displayed a quite predictable reluctance to work for wages, and could be induced to do so only by the grant of considerable credit in advance (as much as a thousand bolívares) and by being allowed to work on an individual basis. Second, the method of harvesting most frequently employed involved the total destruction of the rubber tree rather than tapping, so that year by year the rubber-producing potential of the region steadily declined. Thirdly, the most easily accessible rubber was harvested first, with the result that year by year the areas of rubber harvest shifted, becoming increasingly more distant from the transportation routes along the rivers. Consequently, transportation costs were increased. Fourth, as rubber gathering neared the Brazilian border, much of the product ended up in the hands of Brazilian traders who shipped it down the Amazon for export through Brazilian ports, thus placing the effect of these activities within the Brazilian economy.

In these circumstances the expansion of rubber production would have required the conservation of rubber trees so that they might be harvested on a semi-permanent basis. This would have meant the establishment of plantations, which in turn would have required a labour force that was unavailable within the region. The importation of such a labour force and its maintenance until plantings matured (six years) would have required considerable capital investment. The government could have assisted in the importation of rubber workers but, as long as the government did nothing to directly block such importation, it seems likely that private enterprise, if it had been sufficiently interested, could have done the job just as well. The most significant contribution that the government could have made would have been the construction of a railroad around the Atures rapids in the Orinoco River that made the rubber regions along the upper reaches of the river inaccessible to large boats. In any event, plantation capital was not forthcoming, and in its absence the railroad would probably have represented a relatively poor investment choice.

Most of what has been said about rubber would also apply to balatá and tonka beans which were harvested in the same region of

---

[1] Bell, *op. cit.*, p. 17.

the country under very similar conditions. The expansion of dividivi production, on the other hand, faced an even more serious problem. This tree from which the commercially valuable pods were obtained grew wild in the semi-arid regions along the Caribbean coast and at the foot of the southern slopes of the coastal mountains. It was thus located fairly near the centres of population, and easily carried to the ports. Although, due to its need to be located in dry regions, it might not have fitted readily into a pattern of subsistence agriculture as an income supplement, it could have been cultivated, perhaps by plantations, save for one serious drawback. A dividivi tree, once planted, requires approximately twenty years to reach maturity. If an investment with a twenty-year lag before benefits accrue is to be profitable within the time horizons of the typical capitalist, capital must have a lower opportunity cost than that which prevailed in Venezuela at the time.

Minerals. The country was rich in minerals, but the only mineral exported in significant quantity at this time was gold, and that industry almost died out during our period.

The gold industry declined for natural reasons – as the easily accessible veins were worked out. Meanwhile it had earned a quite considerable income, without however having much impact on the rest of the economy. The deposits were located in the unpopulated, malarial forests of eastern Venezuela, 150 miles from the Orinoco, the closest Venezuelan transportation route and the closest centre of population. The machinery to operate the mines was imported from the United States and Europe, and the food was imported from Trinidad. The labour force was made up of American engineers and West Indian miners, and most of their wages left when they did. The profits, though they often exceeded 1,000 per cent on invested capital, were expatriated to the owners in France and England. The government levied a 25 per cent tax on gold exports but, owing to the location of the mines, smuggling was fairly easy to accomplish, and the tax was frequently evaded. In modern terminology, linkages were weak, and apart from the small import and export duties collected, the mines were hardly a part of the national economy at all.

The most clearly documented case of governmental action interfering with the development of mineral resources is found in the case of the asphalt industry. Valuable surface deposits of natural asphalt were scattered throughout the country, the most important ones located in the Maracaibo basin and near the mouth of the Orinoco River. Various companies representing both British and American capital, predominantly the latter, had been formed to exploit these deposits, and large scale production got underway around the turn of the century. The ensuing history is more than vaguely reminiscent of that of American capitalism during the age of the 'robber barons'. The companies' experiences include stock frauds, swindles, law suits, and bribery. The difference in the Venezuelan case is that the government itself was one of the principal protagonists. Among other things, it changed the terms under which concessions were granted, charged the companies with non-compliance with agreed-upon provisions, and eventually – from 1904 to 1909 – assumed direct control of the most important deposits. The companies may not have been entirely blameless; there is some evidence that they may have become unfortunately involved in domestic politics and lost their gamble. In any event, the long-run significance of government action in this case should not be over estimated. Production in the richest holding resumed its earlier levels after 1909. Even as these events transpired, the growing availability of asphalt as a by-product of the petroleum-refining industry in the United States was destroying the very market at which Venezuelan production was aimed. And, in point of fact, governmental actions in this case did not prevent the inflow of foreign capital in the years immediately following 1909 that got petroleum exports started by 1914.

Other mineral development lagged for various reasons unconnected with the government. The petroleum deposits, for example, gained value only with the expansion of world demand, and they were developed at roughly the same time as the deposits in Mexico, which more or less enjoyed an ultra-stable government hospitable to the foreign investor under Porfirio Díaz up to 1910. The only significant exploitation of the fairly extensive coal deposits was actually carried out by the government itself. Production, however, was limited by weak domestic demand – the country had only eighty-seven steam locomotives in 1904 – and by the fact that the coal was low in quality. Often it had to be processed and combined with asphalt in order to become marketable. Copper production was carried out fairly efficiently by English capital, which built a railroad from the deposits to the sea. Production was most importantly limited by the size of the high-grade veins. The only production decline that occurred during the period was apparently in response to a fall in world prices for the product. Iron ore of a quality comparable to that in the Messabi Range in the United States had been discovered, but the deposits, though very large, were extremely isolated from existing transportation routes and would have required an enormous investment in order to be brought to market. If the ore in the Messabi

135

Range was comparable in quality and much more accessible to existing mills, Venezuelan ore will not have been competitive.

Transportation. It is not possible to say whether deficiencies of transportation held up economic growth; or whether the slow growth of output inhibited the demand for transportation. Probably each reacted on the other. The problem lay in internal rather than external transport. Port facilities apparently kept up with demand; at least there is no record of a shortage of such facilities significantly interfering with trade. Roads were execrable at the beginning of the period; and at the end of the period, although slightly improved, were still execrable. Cattle walked to market and coffee was hauled, surprisingly cheaply, on mule or burro back. In the more densely populated areas, there were some roads passable by ox-carts, especially in the dry season. From 1880 to 1892, about 1,000 widely scattered kilometres of railway track were constructed, but from 1892 until 1912 not one single kilometre of new trackage was begun. These lines were built to serve the export trade and, with one exception, each led from a port through the coastal mountains to the population centres in the interior; they did not interconnect.

Financial institutions. One bank was founded in 1877 to serve the financial needs of the government, and subsequently experienced a tortuous history of bankruptcy, reorganization, dissolution, and re-establishment. For most of the period, this bank, which was later to become the central bank of the country, was prohibited from engaging in private transactions. Two private banks were established in the early 1880s and seem to have been reasonably successful, though total deposits in 1915 are estimated at only 19 million bolívares or roughly 14 per cent of the value of exports in that year. These banks facilitated commercial transactions, issued some banknotes, and made short-term loans. Agricultural credit continued to be provided by the large import-export houses – mostly German – at a rate which has been disputed but which seems to have been at least 12 per cent per year.[1] There were no financial institutions for mortgage or other long-term credit.

The foreign exchange value of the currency was extremely stable throughout the period (at 1 bolívar = 19·3 US cents). Gold was the scrupulously-observed standard, silver coinage was restricted to protect its value, and bank notes were limited in circulation and fully redeemable.

Manufacturing. Even though the protective tariff had been accepted in principle and established in fact by 1896, domestic manufacturing

[1] Bell, *op. cit.*, pp. 225–6; and Veloz Goiticoa, ed., *op. cit.*, pp. 435–6.

developed very little. The government produced salt and matches. An unrecorded number of small shops and two mechanized factories produced shoes, with some surplus of rustic sandals (*alpargatas*) for export. Two cigarette factories existed. A brewery was established in 1894, a cotton-goods factory in 1899, and a cement factory in 1907. In a country which often had more cows than people and which was a major exporter of cocoa, both butter and processed chocolate were imported. Even shoes were often made with imported leather since – according to one account – the domestic product smelled when wet.[1]

Labour force. Approximately 65 per cent of the population made their homes in the cities and on the slopes of the 'agricultural zone', i.e. the coastal plains between the mountains and the sea and the mountain valleys of the Coastal Range and the Andes. Another 30 per cent of the population was distributed on the plains – the Llanos – between the mountains and the southern highlands. A scant 5 per cent were to be found in the forests. The first general census, taken in 1873, recorded a population of 1·8 million; the second, taken in 1881, 2·1 million, suggesting a growth rate of a little less than 2 per cent per annum. One more general census was taken prior to World War I: in 1891, recording a population of 2·3 million, More recent official estimates tend to diminish the totals, but the net result in terms of population growth from the beginning to the end of our period is a rate which varies from 1 per cent to never more than 2 per cent per annum. The absence of immigration contrasts markedly with Brazil. Immigration codes were carefully drawn up and laws were proclaimed to govern a flow of immigrants, yet in retrospect this activity hardly seems to have been worth the trouble. It appears that there simply was little immigration worthy of note. In 1881, for example, the net figure was exactly 584, and the figure for any year rarely exceeded 2,000. Some agricultural colonies of Europeans – German, Italian and Spanish – were established, but with one exception they failed to become viable economic units or to attract additional settlers. Some West Indian labour was imported for work in the jungle of the Orinoco basin and along the Caribbean coast, but according to contemporary accounts, it proved impossible to hold such labour in the interior of the country.[2] The Immigration Law of 1894, enacted during the period when not only coffee exports ,but coffee revenues as well, were stagnant, gave serious attention to the problem. It offered free passage and between 5 and 15 acres to each immigrant over ten years of age on the sole condition that a third of the land

[1] Bell, *op. cit.*, pp. 177–8.　　　　　　　　　　[2] *ibid.*, p. 32.

be put under cultivation within four years. A board of governors were to form a committee 'to do what was required'. No prices were stipulated; the proferred lands were not identified by any description whatever; titles could not, by provision of the law, be clear until the four-year period had lapsed, no land offices or agents were appointed to implement the applications for lots. Contract agents were busy in Bordeaux, Hamburg, Barcelona, Genoa and Las Palmas,[1] but no such practical activity was recorded in Venezuela in this period.

A code passed in 1903 barred the admission of West Indians as permanent immigrants, and by 1918 this discriminatory principle had been broadened to include all non-Europeans.

Education and training. The élite provided, of course, for the education of its own. The first university was established in 1721. A second was founded in 1810, and a third existed from 1890 to 1903. But the emphasis at this level was on theology, letters, and law; technical or business education was sparse. In 1896, the Polytechnic School reported an enrolment of fifty students, and the Engineering School, established by decree in January of 1895, opened its doors to forty-seven students in September of the same year. The curriculum of the Engineering School was designed to produce graduates in civil and military engineering, agronomy and architecture. By contrast, the liberal arts enrolment for the same year was over 1,000.[2]

The law provided for universal primary education and dictated the establishment of at least one school in each parish of the country. As is often the case, the law was not enforced. Literacy figures are unavailable, but expenditures on education declined from 1880 to 1913, both on a *per capita* basis and as a percentage of the national budget.

III. GEOGRAPHY

Before we examine other explanations of this low rate of economic growth, we must first consider whether the country's natural resources were not the limiting factor.

Venezuela is a very large country, about four times the size of Great Britain, with a population in 1913 of less than 2·5 million people. Nevertheless size is misleading. The country is blessed neither by configuration nor by climate.

On the west and north lie high mountains, belonging to the Andean range. Along most of the Caribbean coast these mountains rise

[1] Venezuela, Presidente, *Mensaje*, 1894.   [2] Presidente, *Mensaje*, 1896.

almost from the sea. Behind them is the vast plain of the Orinoco basin, up to 250 miles wide from north to south, and running almost the whole length of the country from east to west. Beyond the Orinoco, south and east, the land rises again to the Guiana highlands.

At this time the great majority of the people were settled in the lower reaches of the Andean highlands, some in the west Andes, but most along the Caribbean. On the map the Orinoco basin, flat and pastoral, looks like a tremendous resource, but it is not. In the wet season the plains become waterlogged, and several hundred square miles are covered with water. In the dry season the land is baked hard, and the grass withers away. In practice only the higher fringes of the plain adjacent to the Andes can be used throughout the year. The main industry is cattle ranching.

Across the Orinoco one enters the Guiana forests, whose main attraction in our period was as a source of rubber. The area is also rich in minerals, though this was not so obvious in our period. Very few people lived in this part of the country, which was inaccessible and malarial.

Agriculture – especially coffee, cocoa, and food – was therefore concentrated in the lower reaches of the Andes. This made transportation difficult. It is expensive to build railways over the sharp gradients of mountain country; and it is also difficult to maintain roads, since these are easily eroded by heavy rains.

The unsolved question is whether the expansion of the coffee industry was held up by lack of roads, and if so, whether this lack was due to the natural features of the country or to negligence on the part of the government. There is adequate testimony that there was plenty of land suitable for coffee, and much of this was in the coastal valleys, not too distant from actual or potential ports.[1] Not so certain is how easy it would have been to open up this land with roads. Railways were almost certainly unsuitable for much of this development, but most of the coffee had been planted before a single line of rail was laid. The evidence is not explicit on the subject of roads, but it is so insistent that cultivable coffee lands were being neglected that one is forced to conclude that development lagged for human reasons, and not because of natural features.

IV. LAND TENURE

The land tenure system in Venezuela had its origins in the *encomien-*

[1] Veloz Goiticoa, ed., *op. cit.*, p. 153.

das granted to the original *conquistadores* by the Spanish crown. In theory these grants merely charged the grantee with the responsibility of supervising the Indians' conversion to Christianity and civilization. By the nineteenth century the grantees owned the land as private property and the Indians, by now carrying various admixtures of Spanish and Negro blood, were bound to the land through a variety of mechanisms ranging from coercion to debt peonage. This was the *hacienda* system that was prevalent throughout Spanish America. In its Venezuelan version, the *haciendas* of the central region and the Llanos were very large and continued to expand as the century progressed, occupying neighbouring smallholdings, empty land, and even communal lands owned by the municipalities. This tendency toward concentration in land ownership is believed to have been more severe in 1900 than it had been a century earlier.

The first reasonably comprehensive land-tenure survey was not published until 1936, but it probably reflects fairly well the situation that existed in the period we are examining. According to this survey, 4·4 per cent of the rural property owners had 2,705,888 hectares, while 95·6 per cent had only 713,795 hectares. At the same time, roughly two-thirds of the population lived in rural areas, but only 10 per cent of the *campesinos* owned land, the other 90 per cent working on land owned by others. The latter category is residual and includes sharecroppers, cash tenants, wage workers, and squatters, the latter being especially numerous. The same census reveals that only 30 per cent of the 'appropriated' land (apparently land to which some legal title existed) was cultivated.

This distribution of land explains why small farmers could not get land to bring about a rapid expansion of exportable output, as they did in Colombia, or Burma, or the Gold Coast or elsewhere. The landowners made no move to rent land to small farmers, and the succession of *caudillo* governments made no move towards land reform. The *caudillos* of our period had no hostility towards the landed aristrocracy. No land tax was ever enacted, despite the frequently precarious financial problem of the government. No taxes were levied on agricultural exports. The empty lands to which the government held title were not distributed to the peasants. Banks were harassed, but there is no recorded harassment of the German import-export houses, the *hacienda's* source of credit. Despite the almost constant arrival of new *caudillos* in power, casting about for ways in which to enrich themselves quickly, most of the large estates came through the period untouched. Land was taken from those who had backed the losing candidate in a violent change of power, but apparently it was possible for most large landowners to back both candidates or switch allegiance at the crucial moment. In fact, succeeding *caudillos*, despite their humble origin, were incorporated into the high society of the capital as they arrived, and the membership of this society, composed in part of absentee landlords, remained largely the same both before and after the governmental change.

This tells us why there was no land reform; the *caudillos* were not egalitarian reformers. But why did not the *hacendados* cultivate their own lands more intensively? The traditional answer is that the *hacendados* are uninterested in economic gain. They do not exploit their land because they have not bought it for investment purposes. Land is purchased because there are few other outlets for consumption and land is one of the most important measures of status in the community. This view has been challenged. Recently the argument has been developed that economic historians have erred by analysing the *hacienda* as a sociological phenomenon rather than as an economic unit responsive to the dictates of economic rationality. From this viewpoint, Venezuela possessed such an abundance of land that land was in effect a free good. Output was roughly proportional to the labour supply employed. But a labour supply for a large operation of any nature was difficult to obtain. The average peasant, even the modern American farmer, if given a choice between working his own land and working for another, will readily choose the former as long as it will supply what he regards as a minimally adequate in-come. For a Venezuelan peasant, a very small lot of land might provide this. The *hacendado* could assure a labour supply only by denying the peasant the opportunity to obtain land of his own. His motivation to secure and hold land was in this sense entirely rational.

Though unwilling to lease or sell their lands to small farmers, the *hacendados* seem to have preferred to plant them rather than to hold them idle. The difficulty, as they saw it, was shortage of labour. Thus, the British representative in Caracas, Mr R. T. C. Middleton, writing about coffee in December 1877, noted

'One great drawback in the way of a yet further extension in the cultivation of what has become the chief staple of Venezuelan produce being, however, the scarcity of hands, and in some cases where the planting of new lands has been undertaken upon a scale disproportionate with the amount of labour procurable in the vicinity of them for the nurture of plants and gathering in of crops; and no proper account having been taken of a rate of wages necessarily on

141

the increase, but scanty profits, or no profits at all, having been realized. . . .'[1]

What seems strange is that the *hacendados* did not therefore do more to make a success of immigration. The most likely source of spontaneous immigration, the West Indies, was shut out by racial prejudice. To get immigrants from Europe required more positive steps, in support of recruiting agents, subsidization of passages, validation of contracts, etc. In effect, the government did practically nothing, beyond passing immigration codes. It would not have been easy to increase immigration. In the popular European image Venezuela was a hot, cheerless place, ridden with snakes and malaria. In addition, the character of the government must have been known in Europe. Tracts written to encourage immigration – there were some – go to great length to stress the existence of domestic law and order and the democratic qualities of the government. Something could have been done, however.

The task of the government would have been easier if the European agricultural colonies that were established had had a modicum of success which could have been reported in Europe to make Venezuela seem more attractive. These colonies suffered from many problems, but one of the most significant was their inability to obtain clear title to sufficient land of good quality and suitable location. It may be in the area of land access, rather than immigration, that government committed its greatest failing.

We may thus conclude that agriculture did not develop as rapidly as it might have done because the land tenure situation withheld land from the small farmers who might have cultivated it, while both the landowners and the government failed to do what was necessary for attracting immigrant labour. Both these failures depend to some extent on the deficiencies of government, since different governments would either have built roads and redistributed some lands to the peasants, or else have carried the *hacendados* along in a major programme of immigration. The search for explanations therefore leads us to the quality of Venezuelan governments.

V. GOVERNMENT

The most popular explanation of Venezuela's lagging development

[1] Great Britain, Foreign Office, *Reports by Her Majesty's Secretaries of Embassy and Legation*, 'Commerce of Venezuela for 1877', by R. T. C. Middleton, London, 1878.

is misgovernment. This was indeed an unfortunate time in the political history of Venezuela. Our period opens with the *caudillo* Antonio Guzman Blanco in the middle of his period of domination (1870–88). This was actually a relatively peaceful and ordered period, in which much money was spent on transportation, and coffee cultivation spread. But his overthrow was followed by a succession of rulers whose activities were unfavourable to development, until some twenty years later, when the presidency was seized by Juan Vicente Gomez (1908–35). Some of the intervening *caudillos* had longish terms. Cipriano Castro held office from 1899 to 1908, but he was a great plunderer, and his relations with foreign countries also discouraged foreign investment in the country.

Thus the governments were not all equally bad, but the period 1888 to 1908 was particularly unfortunate and what came before and after looks good only by comparison with what came in between.

The series of charges made against Venezuelan governments is endless: we shall consider only the most important of those which bear on economic development:

1. That the political violence associated with the arrival of new governments in power and their attempts to maintain power through force led to widespread property destruction that hampered the development of all economic activities. There does not seem to be much substance in this charge, which has more bearing on urban than on rural development. Soldiers steal food and slaughter a few cattle, but they do not uproot coffee trees. Destruction by armies cannot explain why the *hacendados* did not plant more coffee or cocoa.

2. That the public funds were stolen and squandered or deposited in European banks. Roads were so bad partly because money voted for roads was sucked up by politicians. A large army was maintained, draining off public funds – though against this must be set the fact that the army also performed some administrative functions which would otherwise have needed a civilian administration.

3. That the government's treatment of foreign investors, including its failure to meet payments on the external debt, and its harassment and expropriation of the asphalt companies, discouraged the inflow of foreign capital necessary for the development of the country's mineral resources. (This was reversed by Gomez.) The attenuated development of the railway system is due to governmental financial mismanagement, which made it impossible for the government to continue to guarantee the companies and so attract further capital

143

for railway construction. The government itself prohibited further construction in 1892.

4. That the government delayed the growth of the banking system in several ways. First, it failed to maintain the minimal conditions of order and security necessary for such a system to function. Second, the government itself periodically looted the established banks through the practice of forced loans. Third, the government reserved all mortgage credit activity to the national bank which it controlled, but then failed to make provisions for such credit ever to be actually granted.

5. Finally we come to the failing which emerged from Section IV: that the government neither redistributed land to small farmers, nor promoted immigration for work on the *haciendas*. This was probably the most important defect of all. Experience from other countries demonstrates that farmers need very little from a government to help them take up a profitable export crop like coffee. So long as land is available, not too far from the sea or rivers, they will plant the crop. Land was available not far from the sea; but the measures needed for men and land to get together were not taken.

Venezuela's experience is just another chapter in the age-old story of relationships between political adventurers and a landed oligarchy. The land-owners did not control the *caudillos*, but the *caudillos* were not hostile to the landowners. The *caudillos* did not harm the land-owners directly (e.g. by land reform) but also did not help them directly (e.g. by building roads or sponsoring immigration). Their antics were harmful to the development of the economy in the ways we have just enumerated, but they did not offend the landowners enough to stir the latter into establishing political stability. It is the modern capitalist – merchant, manufacturer or miner – who makes the effort to ensure political stability, and this class was still too small in Venezuela in 1900 to be able to have this effect.

VI. EPILOGUE

In many respects, 1913 is not a good demarcation year for a study of Venezuelan economic development. In 1908 a new dictator, Juan Vicente Gomez, took power in Caracas and began to effect basic changes in Venezuelan political and economic life. In some respects he behaved as a traditional *caudillo*. He was interested in wealth and women, and he amassed unprecedented quantities of both. He was not above governmental harassment of activities in the style of his predecessors. At one point he determined to achieve a personal

144

monopoly on cattle marketing in the country, and he did so, even though it involved driving entirely out of business an English company that had recently begun the export of frozen meat to Europe. But his behaviour in power represented a sharp break from what had gone before.

By 1913 his major accomplishments had all been political. He suppressed the regional *caudillos*, and established the first truly national authority that Venezuela had ever had. He secured his own hold on power, and brought about a greater degree of domestic order than Venezuela had ever enjoyed. The peace was coerced, a by-product of the tyrannical methods of a master politician, but it was nonetheless real.

In the years that followed Gomez brought order to the national treasury and a healthy balance to the books. He resumed regular payment on the external debt, which had often been defaulted before, and raised Venezuela's international credit rating. He guaranteed the security of the foreign investor in most endeavours and encouraged the inflow of foreign capital which developed the country's oil fields. And he spent massive sums on the improvement of the nation's transportation and communication facilities. The banking system flourished and branches of foreign banks were established. New manufacturing concerns began to be established at a rapid pace. Technical improvements in cattle production were supported, and eventually subsidies to encourage coffee exports were paid. Venezuela began to assume many of the trappings of a modern nation.

It has been debated whether the long continuance of Gomez's régime demonstrates that the economic forces favouring stability had now matured sufficiently to be able to impose their will; or whether it was a mere 'accident of history' that this particular strong man happened to be interested in economic development as well as in political power. Doubtless some element of both was present. There were economic groups in 1903 interested in a stable framework, but they did not put Gomez in power, and it is doubtful whether they could have removed him if he had proved indifferent to their interests. At the same time there was a good chance (though far from a certainty) that any dictator coming into power in 1908 would be conscious that the country was missing its opportunities, in contrast with its neighbours, and would recognize that it is easier to amass personal wealth in a developing economy than in a stagnant one. In a somewhat cynical sense, the tragedy of Venezuela lay in the fact that its political adventurers took over a century to learn this lesson.

145

BIBLIOGRAPHY

Official Papers

Great Britain. Board of Trade, *Wholesale and Retail Prices*. London, 1903.
——. Foreign Office, *Reports by Her Majesty's Secretaries of Embassy and Legation*, 'Commerce of Venezuela for 1877', by R. T. C. Middleton. London, 1878.
Venezuela. Ministerio de Fomento, Dirección General de Estadística, *Anuario Estadístico de Venezuela*, 1887, 1889, 1908, 1912, 1940, Caracas.
——, *Comentarios al VII Censo de Población de Venezuela*, Caracas, 1947.
——. Ministerio de Hacienda, *Revista de Hacienda*, September 1937, October–December 1937. Caracas.
——. Presidente, *Mensaje*, 1885, 1894, 1895, 1896. Caracas.

Books

Bell, P. L., *Venezuela: A Commercial and Industrial Handbook*, us Department of Commerce Special Agents Series Number 212,Washington, DC, 1922.
Bernstein, Harry, *Venezuela and Columbia*, Englewood Cliffs, N.J., 1964.
Gilmore, R. L., *Caudillism and Militarism in Venezuela, 1810–1910*, Athens, Ohio, 1964.
Lieuwin, Edwin, *Venezuela*, 2nd edition, London, 1965.
Marsland, W. D. and A. L., *Venezuela through its History*, New York, 1954.
Veloz, Ramón, *Economía y Finanzas de Venezuela, desde 1830 hasta 1944*, Caracas, 1945.
Veloz Goiticoa, Nicolas, ed., *Venezuela*, International Bureau of the American Republics Handbook, Washington, DC, 1904.

Articles

Arcila Farias, Eduardo, 'Evolución de la Economía en Venezuela', *Venezuela Independiente, 1810–1960*, Fundacion Eugenio Mendoza, Caracas, 1962.
Rasmussen, W. D., 'Colonia Tovar, Venezuela', *Agricultural History*, July 1943.

Chapter 6

THE GOLD COAST AND NIGERIA

by A. Baron Holmes

Until the Berlin Conference of 1885 and the rapid acquisition of territory that ensued, formal European control in West Africa was generally limited to the coast. After 1874, in what is today Ghana, Britain controlled the hinterland to the Pra River, although Ashanti remained independent. In Nigeria, Lagos had become a colony in 1861, but its hinterland was engulfed in intermittent warfare that resulted from the decline of Oyo as a unifying force among the Yoruba. In the Niger Delta, British consuls wielded varying degrees of formal and informal power, but the independence of the trade-oriented city-states had not yet been broken. Up the Niger River, Sir George Goldie's United Africa Company had begun to extend an informal influence. Formal protection was instituted as large-scale territorial annexation took place directly after the Berlin Conference: Ashanti and the Northern Territories in 1902, Yoruba-land during the 1890s, Eastern Nigeria in 1885, and Northern Nigeria in 1903.

However, as far as economic development and exports are concerned, dates of formal territorial acquisition by the colonial power tell very little. Development in the Gold Coast and Nigeria has been determined by the interaction of many factors whose significance varies widely from commodity to commodity. And despite important contributions by the colonial power in terms of peace, transportation, administration, and technology, the indigenous peoples were responsible for the burst of economic development that took place in the two decades before World War I. Because of their efforts and because of the crucial informal or incidental economic aspects of European hegemony, the story of formal conquest is relatively unimportant.

Until the 1880s, economic change was a matter of subsistence agriculture expanded by certain European and New World food crops after the Portuguese arrival in the fifteenth century, of population growth and migration, of the rise and fall of city-states or larger political groupings, of long-distance trade to the interior based on gold and kola nuts, and of post-fifteenth century slave-

147

trading with Europe, eventually suppressed during the first half of the nineteenth century by the British Anti-Slave Squadron and by the growth of legitimate trade in palm oil.

In 1880, palm oil and kernels dominated West African exports.[1] Even in the Gold Coast, gold constituted less than a fifth of exports. The trade in palm oil had expanded rapidly after the Napoleonic Wars when industrialization in Europe and the suppression of transoceanic slave trade in West Africa provided an important stimulus. The predominance of palm produce was interrupted before 1880 only by the short-lived cotton boom, experienced by cotton producers the world over in the effort to fill the supply gap created by the United States' Civil War.

After 1880 the situation was transformed, partly by an increase in the export of palm produce, whose price reached its lowest point in 1887, and then began to climb again; partly by the steady growth in cocoa output; partly by a temporary boom in rubber; and (in the Gold Coast) partly by mechanization of gold mining. Exports from the Gold Coast increased from £390,000 per annum for 1882–4 to £5,427,000 in 1913, an average growth rate per annum of 9·2 per cent. It is not possible to give a figure for exports from all of Nigeria. Exports from Lagos increased from £576,000 in 1880 to £882,000 in 1898; and exports by sea from the Colony and

TABLE 6.1: *Exports from the Gold Coast and Southern Nigeria, 1913*

(£ thousand)

	Gold Coast	Southern Nigeria
Cocoa	2,489	157
Cotton	1	159
Gold	1,656	—
Palm produce	225	5.126
Rubber	88	90
Timber	366	105
Tin	—	568
Other	620	894
	5,427	7,099

Source: Great Britain, *Statistical Abstract for the Several British Colonies, Possessions and Protectorates*, 1899–1913. B.P.P., 1914–16.

[1] H. J. Bevin, 'The Gold Coast Economy about 1880', in *Transactions of the Gold Coast and Togoland Historical Society*, Vol. 2, Pt. 2, 1956, provides a description of the Gold Coast exports, trade, transportation, and currency immediately before the period of our consideration.

Protectorate of Southern Nigeria increased from £1,608,000 in 1899 to £7,099,000 in 1913, the latter growth rate being 12·2 per cent per annum. Some considerable part of these high growth rates was due to the swift rise of prices after the turn of the century, but the growth in the volume of exports was also spectacular. Table 6.1 shows the composition of exports from both countries in the year 1913.

We shall begin this chapter by following the progress of individual commodities in each country separately, and shall end by considering certain general factors which promoted growth.

I. THE GOLD COAST

Around the year 1880, the exports of the Gold Coast consisted primarily of palm oil and kernels and of gold. Taking 1884 as an example, palm oil and kernels were 79 per cent of exports which totalled £467,000; gold constituted 14 per cent. The techniques of both the oil-palm and the gold industries were primarily extractive and were in African hands. European mining companies, spurred by the reports of M. Bonnat, started modern mining on the Gold Coast in 1878; however, in 1891 only one-third of gold exports came from European mines.[1]

During the 1880s, the price of palm oil fell and, despite the availability of kernels as a supplementary return to tree climbing, many villages did not find it profitable to carry palm produce to the coast.[2] Consequently, it is not surprising that many Gold Coast natives began looking for other profitable outlets for their energies, especially since the preoccupation with war and raiding had ended in the Gold Coast, below Ashanti, with the establishment of the Colony in 1874. Rubber, coffee, and cocoa, all in demand abroad, received attention, but cocoa and coffee were foreign crops and required a decade or more of experiments for introduction. Rubber, like gold and palm produce, was an indigenous natural resource and could be exploited by unskilled labour. *Funtumia elastica* trees grew wild in many regions of the forest, and required nothing more for export than tapping, simple processing, and transportation.

[1] R. Szereszewski, *Structural Changes in the Economy of Ghana, 1898–1911*, London, 1965, p. 29.

[2] 'The Omanhene of Akwapim informed the Governor that his people had almost ceased carrying palm oil and kernels to the coast as, after defraying the charges for transport, there was a loss upon the business.' Polly Hill, *The Migrant Cocoa Farmers of Southern Ghana*, Cambridge, 1963, p. 167.

During the 1880s the rubber industry developed slowly, the largest export being 1·5 million lb. worth £69,911. In 1890 exports jumped to 3·4 million lb.[1] with a value of £231,282; the peak was reached during 1898 and 1899 when 5·99 and 5·57 million lbs. were exported at a yearly value of £552,000 and £556,000.

Three factors seemed to determine rubber exports. One was price; between 1886 and 1899 the average value of a pound of rubber exported doubled.[2] Between 1900 and 1902 the price fell almost to half of the previous peak but revived by 1910, surpassing the previous peak by 12 per cent. From 1911 to 1913 the price again declined. Price was the primary determinant of output before 1900, but the very process of tapping the trees in a lethal fashion made it impossible to get large yields in following years. Slaughter tapping, the second determinant of output, was the rule of the day because tappers had no training in techniques designed to preserve the life of the trees. Thirdly, after 1900 the increasing opportunities offered by cocoa made rubber tapping less inviting. By 1910, the year in which prices approximated the 1899 peak, exports were only 3·22 million pounds as opposed to 5·57 in 1899. Labour in the Gold Coast appears to have pursued profit-making in a very rational way. The obvious declines in rubber and palm oil must be attributed directly to the more favourable opportunities available in the cocoa industry.

Cocoa is not indigenous to West Africa and it must be cultivated as a perennial tree crop; the difficulties in establishing its growth have no parallel in the exploitative, extractive industries: e.g. palm produce, alluvial gold, and rubber. On the other hand, cocoa flourished in the Gold Coast without rigorous or exacting methods of cultivation. It appears to have withstood moderate attacks of disease and pests and, after taking into account costs of transport, losses through disease and pests, and foregone opportunities during the non-bearing period, the yields paid a handsome return to all factors involved. Cocoa, as a consciously cultivated crop, shared many of the characteristics that made rubber, palm produce, and alluvial gold successful exports for small-scale operations. It did not require extensive research for minimum adaptation to local conditions. It required unskilled labour, available in substantial amounts at the prices offered; but it did not require 'scientific methods of agriculture' to achieve substantial returns. During its

[1] Before 1895, re-export of Lagos rubber is included. See S. La Anyane, *Ghana Agriculture*, London, 1963, p. 46.

[2] The changes mentioned are not actually prices but refer to export valuation per ton and involve the imprecision of changes in quality.

early years it could be intercropped with food, an advantage that greatly reduced the cash cost of establishing cocoa farms.

The Department of Agriculture played an absolutely vital role in distributing cocoa seeds and plants, and in demonstrating basic techniques to the Akwapim and Krobo peoples, but it did not have sufficient resources (men or money) to introduce precise, exacting or complicated techniques to large numbers of people. It had to rely on the 'grapevine' of information passed from one farmer to another. The basic techniques of cocoa-growing were fortunately simple enough for this method of transmission; therefore the efforts of a few persons proved to have a high multiplier effect in terms of information communicated. Significantly, acceptance of more complicated or less obviously profitable methods concerning disease control and curing techniques was not widespread.

Introduced into the Gold Coast first during the 1860s and later during the 1870s and 1880s cocoa spread slowly at first in the Akwapim region, and did not expand rapidly until the low palm-oil prices of the middle eighties drove the farmers to seek another source of cash income. Even then considerable experimentation was necessary before cocoa finally established itself as a viable crop. Polly Hill[1] tells the dramatic story of how the Akwapim farmers first planted cocoa in their own hill country, and then, seeking more land, migrated across the Densu River to buy low-lying forest lands from the Akim peoples. The Akwapim were prepared for this adventure by their previous experience. It was they and the Krobos who had cultivated the only oil-palm plantations in the Gold Coast. They had travelled far for the rubber trade, for portage in the Ashanti wars, labour in the building of the Sekondi railroad, and skilled work throughout West Africa. The inadequacy of their own hill country, in terms of the ratio of men to cultivable acres, contributed to their restlessness.

During the 1890s the industry was expanding rapidly in terms of acreage, but most of the output went to the local demand for seed. Exports started in 1891 with 80 lb. In 1893 there were 3,460 lb. exported, and from then until the First World War the increase was rapid and continuous. By 1900 536 tons, valued at £27,300, were sold, and by 1904 more than 5,000 tons were exported. Exports in 1913 were 50,600 tons worth £2,489,000. The Gold Coast had become the world's foremost cocoa producer.

In marked contrast with cocoa, gold was produced for export through precise techniques that required the introduction of capital

[1] *op. cit.*

equipment, management, and transportation. The Ghanaian gold industry is a perfect example of an expatriate-owned and expatriate-run capital-intensive enclave that exploits local resources with minimal employment of labour. The value of gold to the economy has been the taxes and customs duties, royalties and rents, wages and transportation levies paid by the industry. The labour supply of the gold mining industry was determined in large part by opportunities for agricultural production, and by 1913 cocoa was driving up wages in the mines and bidding away labour at harvest time. Also the gold industry made possible the Tarkwa-Kumasi railroad. In these senses the enclave both contributed to and competed with the rest of the economy.

The crucial factor in the growth of gold exports was the railway, which reached the mining areas in 1903. Exports grew from less than £100,000 to £255,000 in that year, and then jumped to £1,656,000 in 1913. The reason for this was the heavy cost of transporting mining equipment to the mines via the Ankobra River and human portage. According to Ward[1] the extension of the railway from Sekondi to Tarkwa 'brought the cost down with a run from £25 per ton to £2 per ton'. The extension of the cocoa, oil palm or rubber industries, within fifty or so miles from the sea, did not depend on modern transport, but the gold industry, with its heavy equipment, could not expand without the railway. Of course, once the railway was built all other industries benefited from it.

On the assumption that actual export development cannot exhaust the information available for our understanding of the process of economic growth, a few words are in order concerning industries that did not grow. Cotton was the object of substantial development efforts in which the British Cotton Growing Association and the government both spent manpower and treasure in largely sterile attempts to establish a cotton industry. But since the more suitable climate and soils were in the north, the crop could not be profitable until modern transportation became available. Coffee, at one time expected to be the principal native export crop, initially was stifled by disease. As soon as cocoa profits became apparent, coffee never again competed seriously with cocoa. Plantation rubber, although cultivated by a handful of European and native enterprises, was not important. In an attempt to develop profitable rubber cultivation, as opposed to exploitation of wild trees, exacting research into tree types, tapping techniques, and disease control was carried out by the Agriculture Department;

[1] W. E. F. Ward, *A History of the Gold Coast*, London, 1948.

however, the research began after 1900 and was not sufficiently successful to induce large foreign investment in plantations or to convince Africans that rubber was more remunerative than cocoa. Foreign investment in rubber remained limited,[1] and native rubber planting remained restricted to areas either unsuited to cocoa or complementary to cocoa. Other feasible crops like sisal, citrus, and copra received minor attention but remained negligible either because their production was obviously more profitable abroad,[2] or because existing opportunities engaged local factors at a higher return.

It should be noted that export development in the Northern Territories was seriously constrained by transportation costs. However, the very limited nature of opportunities for local labour made development of some export desirable, and substantial efforts were made by BCGA and the Department of Agriculture to increase cotton yields and to develop growth of cotton as a cash crop for export. Experiments were also made with groundnuts and sisal. Not until the year 1912 was a government stock farm opened to develop the livestock of the Northern Territories. While the government officials were searching for ways to increase profitable exports in the Northern Territories, the profit-conscious members of the labour force solved the problem by migrating to Ashanti and the Colony for work as labourers either in the mines or on the cocoa farms. Despite major reductions in transport costs with the railroad from the coast to Kumasi and a road from Kumasi northward, given the low productivity of existing industries,[3] export from the Northern Territories was not feasible on a large scale, and labour migration was a reasonable utilization of resources.

In conclusion, a few generalizations are apparent from a review of export developments in the Gold Coast between 1880 and 1913. First, there was substantial growth in exports, the value of which increased from less than half a million pounds sterling during the

[1] 'In 1911 there were 12 European rubber plantations.' S. La Anyane, *Ghana Agriculture*, London, 1963, p. 12.

[2] 'Most tropical fruits do remarkably well here and but for the excessive cost of production and transport, an export trade might be developed.' Gold Coast *Agricultural Report*, 1908, W. S. D. Tudhope, Director of Agriculture.

[3] Cotton yields per acre at the Tamale Agriculture Station, 26–48 lb. seed cotton per acre in 1909, grew to a still unsatisfactory 77 lb. per acre in 1913 after efforts by the BCGA and Government Department of Agriculture. Gold Coast *Agricultural Reports*, 1910, p. 36, and 1913, p. 56. Even with the peak yield 77 lb. per acre 'there is little likelihood of this crop being profitable as a single cultivation'.

153

early 1880s to more than 5 million pounds sterling in 1913. Second, the factors determining output vary enormously both over time and by commodity. For gold, transportation was the binding constraint before 1900; for cotton, there were many inhibiting factors that can be summed up as low yields, marginal prices, high opportunity costs; for cocoa the constraints were at first introduction and development of the crop, then awareness of its prospects and availability of seeds and seedlings; finally labour and transport. Third, agricultural development for export by native farmers is subject to the same wide range of production costs and yields that is true for a plantation enclave or for a farmer in an advanced country. Just because the locus of research and innovation in methods of production lies heavily in the hands of external agents does not mean that production coefficients are fixed or that price, transportation costs and acreage are the only relevant variables. Fourth, export development, then as now, was determined by factor availabilities. This is true just as much in the past as at present. For example, cocoa once introduced, and adapted to local conditions, achieved yields that drew available labour away from preparation of palm produce. Finally, limitation of analysis to development that took place (ignoring unexploited potential) or to the modernizing influences of capital and railways (ignoring the potential of pre-capitalist development) unnecessarily constrains our understanding of the process by which a region pursues achievement of its economic potential.

III. NIGERIA

Like Ghana, Nigeria experienced rapid growth in the value of exports between 1880 and 1913, but the economy was not transformed to the same extent. In 1913 exports were only about 50 per cent greater than those of the Gold Coast, although the population was about ten times as large. The new commodities which were to bring large incomes to the western and northern peoples after the first world war had not yet taken hold. Palm produce was still 64 per cent of Nigeria's exports in 1913, whereas it was now only 4 per cent of exports from the Gold Coast. Cocoa and rubber developed slowly in the Western areas, and not until 1912 did the railway reach Kano, opening up the vast hinterland of Northern Nigeria, with its potential in cotton, groundnuts and livestock.

Palm oil and kernels were produced all along the coast of Nigeria and into the immediate interior. Nigeria is fortunate in having a substantial network of rivers, creeks and lagoons that formed a widespread natural transportation network, and allowed deep penetration into parts of the interior, along the rivers, long before the advent of the railway or the motor road. Because of its unique river system, its relatively concentrated stands of oil-palm trees, its absence of alternative exports, and its trade-oriented political structure, the Niger Delta dominated the palm-oil trade. Dike[1] offers a breakdown for the year 1828 by region:

'4,461 cwt. from the regions around Sierra Leone and the Gambia, 7,350 cwt. from the Gold Coast, and 114,335 cwt. from the Bights of Benin and Biafra; but the export from the Bight of Benin was almost nil so that the 114,335 can be assigned almost entirely to Delta ports.'

Even after 1893 when peace came to the Lagos hinterland, the Delta exported approximately four times as much oil as Lagos and an almost equal amount of kernels.[2]

In the Lagos region, the political organization of the hinterland failed to provide coherence to the palm produce trade.

'The Oba of Lagos were unable to supply the European merchants with the amount of oil that the Delta traders could expect from rulers there; unlike the Delta chiefs, the Oba of Lagos had no political control over any of the palm-oil producing country and could not act as primary middlemen for the palm-oil trade.'[3]

The frequent wars of the nineteenth century arising from the decline of the Oyo kingdom led to both trade stimulation as a means of gaining strategic war materials and trade discouragement for strategic and materialistic reasons. Patrick Manning's estimates support his conclusion that 'in general the patterns of (palm produce) export trade seem to have been little disturbed by the sweeping political changes of the era'. His estimates do not suggest any marked export increase after Sir Gilbert Carter's 1893 peace mission in Yorubaland.

An important role in the palm trade was played by the freed

[1] K. O. Dike, *Trade and Politics in the Niger Delta 1830–1885*, Oxford, 1956, pp. 50–1.

[2] This general estimate is by Patrick Manning, 'Some Export Statistics for Nigeria, 1880–1905', *Nigerian Journal of Economic and Social Studies*, July 1967.

[3] J. H. Kopytoff, *A Preface to Modern Nigeria*, Madison, Wisconsin, 1965.

slaves from Sierra Leone, Brazil, and the West Indies, who acted as middlemen for the European merchants in Lagos and Badagry; however, it is difficult to estimate how much trade they drummed up in addition to that which would have taken place in their absence. This question is much more clear for cotton exports where the initiating role of the Sierra Leonians is well documented.

The first competition to palm produce came from rubber, chiefly during the 1890s. Rubber shares the extractive character of the palm industry, with the important exception that unskilled labour could destroy the natural resource through careless exploitation.[1] Rubber exports from Nigeria grew during the 1880s and became important when price rose sharply from 1894 until 1899. Slaughter tapping is indicated by the fact that exports from Lagos Colony declined after a peak of 6·5 million lb. in 1896 to 4·4 million lb. in 1897 and 3·8 million lb. in 1898, while the value paid per pound rose 40 per cent. The price continued to rise through 1900, but the quantity exported fell to 0·6 million lb. A similar path was followed in the Protectorate of Southern Nigeria (today's Eastern Region and part of the Mid-Western Region). In 1900 there were 2·3 million lb. rubber exported from the Protectorate, but by 1902 exports had declined to 0·9 million lb.; by 1904 exports had risen again to 2·4 million lb., falling again in 1905 (despite a rise in price) to 0·8 million lb. The wholesale destruction of the wild *Funtumia elastica* trees was unfortunate since at least 8 million lbs. of rubber would have been available yearly if better rubber-tapping techniques had been known and accepted. The natural supply of wild rubber slowly became supplemented by cultivated rubber, partly on expatriate owned and managed plantations and partly on native plots. During the first decade of the twentieth century, the Agriculture and Forestry Departments of both Nigeria and the Gold Coast experimented with various rubber plant types and with various methods of tapping the trees in order to raise yields; in addition, the Departments distributed plants and seeds of *Para* and *Funtumia* rubber trees to encourage the establishment of communal and individual plantations. By 1907, there had been established in the Central Province 1,629 communal plantations, containing 992,878 trees.[2] In 1911, the Director of Agriculture[3] surveyed the

[1] W. N. M. Geary, *Nigeria under British Rule*, London, 1927, pp. 56–8, cites an estimate that 'in 1899, 75 per cent of the rubber trees had died'.

[2] Southern Nigeria, *Annual Report* on the Forest Administration for 1907, p. 8.

[3] Southern Nigeria, Supplement to the *Annual Report* of the Agriculture Department for the year 1911, pp. 4–8.

agricultural development of Nigeria and found that seven rubber plantations had been established, three belonging to natives. These plantations contained from 10,000 to more than 100,000 trees and seedlings each. A beginning had been made toward development of a rubber industry based on scientific techniques, but it received little encouragement from a price structure, which remained unfavourable to Nigerian rubber from the end of World War I to the beginning of World War II.

Quality proved to be as much of a problem as quantity; like cocoa and palm oil the rubber offered for sale by peasants was of poor quality and could command only the lower prices. Practically every report by the Forest and Agriculture Departments of the Gold Coast and Nigeria mentioned the necessity of demonstrating efficient techniques of processing to peasant producers, and a major portion of the extremely scarce manpower of the departments was continuously devoted to processing demonstration. In Nigeria, rubber-tapping and rubber-processing techniques were the essence of the message of the government in the Central Province of Southern Nigeria. It is significant that for rubber, cocoa, and palm oil European buyers were willing to accept low quality produce, for sale either as low grade or for further processing to attain high quality. Because of the ability of the peasants to sell low quality produce at reasonable prices, they were able to by-pass one technical obstacle that favoured the establishment of plantations. As early as the first decade of this century, it was already apparent that communication of techniques would be the major task of any agricultural or forestry department. The initial establishment of cocoa, rubber, and palm-oil industries depended heavily on the fact that export production was feasible for peasants without the dissemination of and acceptance of exacting or precise techniques.

In Nigeria as in Ghana cocoa has proved enormously successful. Cocoa was introduced in Nigeria during the 1870s, both at Calabar and Bonny,[1] but the ecology of south-east Nigeria is not favourable to cocoa. It soon reached the Western Region; by 1880 J. P. L. Davies, an African, had a cocoa farm at Ijan, close to Agege, and located on the lagoon for purposes of accessibility. In addition to

---

[1] Buchanan and Pugh (*Land and People in Nigeria*, London, 1955) cite *Tropical Agriculture*, Vol. XXIII, p. 172, as giving 1874 as the date of introduction of cocoa to Eastern Nigeria, by a chief called 'Squiss Bamego'. R. E. Dennett claimed that cocoa was introduced into Calabar by an African named David Henshaw between 1870 and 1880; 'Agricultural Progress in Nigeria', *Journal of the African Society*, Vol. 18, p. 280.

the spread of cocoa that must have taken place from the Davies farm, the government botanical station at Ebute Metta, established in 1887, began in 1893 to distribute cocoa seeds.[1]

In 1886 only 25 cwt. were exported. In 1896 exports were up to 61 tons, exceeding exports from the Gold Coast, which in that year were only 39 tons. But planting was proceeding more rapidly in the Gold Coast. By 1900 the Gold Coast was exporting 536 tons, as against Nigeria's 202 tons (of which rather more than half came from the West). And in 1913 Nigeria had reached only 3,600 tons, compared with the Gold Coast's 50,600 tons. One can see how slow Nigeria was to develop cocoa when one recalls that Nigerian exports are now around 190,000 tons a year.

Cocoa was not well suited to the Eastern Region. The main reason why the Western Region was so slow in planting the crop seems to lie in the political history of this area. The vast hinterland of Lagos had been in the throes of many years of warfare and general disruption. When Sir Gilbert Carter brought peace in 1893, fighting had been going on intermittently for a century, and, as a consequence of the fighting, the population of the hinterland had been removed from many areas and was generally concentrated near the safety of cities like Ibadan and Abeokuta. Vast areas that today are under cocoa, food, and kola cultivation were then empty, and much was covered by forest. According to R. A. Akinola,[2] the villages surrounding Ibadan were established generally after the pacification of Yorubaland in 1893, as dispossessed farmers from war-devastated towns and domestic slaves of important war-chiefs moved outward from Ibadan to escape deteriorating soil conditions near the city. This migration, forced by the impossibility of proper fallowing near the cities, appears quite different from the profit-conscious movement of the Akwapim and Krobo in the Gold Coast. Because the attention of the people of the hinterland had been more on survival and war-making than trade and profit-taking, and because no centre for agricultural demonstration existed like that at Aburi, the post-war reaction of the Yoruba to export opportunities was slow. Those who sought profit from export must have

[1] J. B. Webster, 'The Bible and the Plough', in the *Journal of the Historical Society of Nigeria*, December 1963, claims that Davies first introduced cocoa to Nigeria. Regardless of which theory is accepted, the Davies farm proved the most important since Agege cocoa would spread through Yorubaland. The Agriculture Department also played a part in distributing cocoa to the Yoruba.

[2] 'The Ibadan Region', *Nigerian Geographical Journal*, December 1963. See also A. L. Mabogunje and M. B. Gleave, 'The Changing Agricultural Landscape in Southern Nigeria', *Nigerian Geographical Journal*, Vol. 7, June 1964.

concentrated mainly on known products like cotton and palm oil. All factors seemed to inhibit rapid expansion of Nigerian cocoa: concentrated population, limited awareness and expectance of European goods, unfamiliarity with cocoa cultivation but long familiarity with other export crops, and transportation difficulties (away from the important Ogun River). The combination of uninhibited land, empty through forced depopulation; concentration into large urban centres; and lack of acquaintance with cocoa made necessary a gradual introduction through migration of labourers to Agege for 'on-the-job-training' with cocoa and through propagandizing by missionaries, government officials, and traders.[1] The fact that the inhabitants of the interior, with the possible exception of the Abeokuta vicinity, were less exposed either to trade or to new crops and techniques of cultivation than were the Akwapim and Krobo of the Gold Coast probably slowed their reaction to the opportunities introduced.

To some extent (and J. B. Webster claims the extent to be significant), development of the cotton industry was due to an attempt by the Christian Missionary Society to introduce an export industry to Yorubaland, chiefly Abeokuta, during the 1850s and 1860s. Cotton had long been grown by the Yoruba for their own manufacture of cloth. The first Sierra Leonians reached Yoruba country in 1839; by 1842 there were 200 to 300 Sierra Leonians in Abeokuta and by 1850 approximately 3,000 in the Egba capital.[2]

Through a combination of the efforts of the Sierra Leonians, who were conscious of the possibilities of profitable export, and of the CMS and its missionaries who followed the doctrine of the Bible and the Plough, an export cotton industry was established in Abeokuta during the early 1850s. The first cotton gin reached Abeokuta before 1852. Between 1852 and 1859, exports doubled each year. By 1859, two to three hundred gins and five to six presses were at work. The American Civil War greatly stimulated production. Exports climbed to 1·5 million lb. in 1870. But thereafter prices fell sharply. Yields were so low because of unfavourable climate and soil conditions that the industry could not survive the low levels to which prices fell in the last quarter of the nineteenth century.

[1] Webster, *op. cit.*, pp. 427–33.

[2] Kopytoff, *op. cit.*, pp. 44, 150–1. Kopytoff provides a comprehensive history of the activities of the Sierra Leonians between 1830 and 1890. For the period after 1890, see J. B. Webster, *The African Churches among the Yoruba 1888–1922*, Oxford, 1964, and E. A. Ayandele, *The Missionary Impact on Modern Nigeria*, New York, 1966.

During the first decade of the twentieth century, the efforts of the British Cotton Growing Association revived the industry that the CMS had established in the 1850s. 'A power ginnery with annual capacity of more than 2 million lb. was set up at Abeokuta. The main areas of production had shifted slightly to the east, i.e. in the areas just being settled. Ilugun and Ishan were the main centres. The principal problem in this area was the lack of quick transport to Abeokuta.'[1] This cotton revival must be attributed primarily to two factors: the new railway that reached Ibadan in 1901 and the enterprise of the BCGA which had been formed in 1902. Prior to the building of the railway, cotton had been carried by canoe down the Ogun River and the railroad must have reduced the cost of transport, particularly for areas not served by the river. By 1906, ginneries had been established along the Lagos railway at Abeokuta, Eruwa Road, Ibadan, Iwo, and Oshogbo, and on the Niger at Lokoja and Shonga.[2] In addition to providing ginneries at central locations, the BCGA, having decided that cotton should be grown on peasant smallholds rather than plantations, carried out experiments and provided improved seed to the peasant producers. The Elder Dempster shipping company agreed for a time to take cotton free of freight, and the Alake and Council of Abeokuta offered prizes for the best fields while the *Egba Gazette* published instructions concerning cotton cultivation.[3] At the ginneries, the BCGA bought cotton at fixed prices of a minimum of 1d per pound. Interestingly enough, the very failure of cocoa cultivation to expand rapidly in Yorubaland made possible the development of the cotton industry, since similar efforts on the Gold Coast were blocked wherever cocoa could be grown or wherever labour had the desire to take advantage of earning wages on the cocoa farms.

In Northern Nigeria, cotton export was prohibited by transportation costs except for a few regions near the Niger and Benue Rivers and, even in these regions, all the inhibiting factors of low yields and low prices that limited the exports of Southern Nigeria were relevant. In 1912, Lamb, the Director of Agriculture in Northern Nigeria rejected emphatically the argument that the long experience of the Hausa with cotton production meant a great future for exports from the north. In 1913, he ventured the opinion that 'unless we

[1] Mabogunje and Gleave, *op. cit.*, p. 11.
[2] Frederick Shelford, 'Ten Years' Progress in West Africa', *Journal of the African Society*, Vol. 6, p. 347.
[3] William McGregor, 'Lagos, Abeokuta and the Alake', *Journal of the African Society*, Vol. 3, 1903, p. 479.

can introduce a variety of cotton with at least twice the gross return per acre that existing types give, I see little prospect of a great future for cotton in this country'.[1] Eventually, through years of research, the Department of Agriculture was able to introduce varieties like the American Allen type that improved the competitive position of cotton. Despite limitations, 56,796 cwt. were exported in 1913 at a value of £159,223. The chief explanation for the exports in the face of low yields is that Northern Nigeria had a substantial population with few other opportunities for export.

As with cotton, the export of groundnuts was prohibited by transportation costs until the advent of the railway to Northern Nigeria in 1911 and 1912. Climate and soil appear to have been better suited to groundnuts than to cotton over much of the area then served by the railway. Lamb suggested:

'The prevailing very light sandy loam soil is generally incapable of producing heavy cotton crops without manure; (on the other hand), the conditions for groundnuts are well-nigh ideal over large tracts of the Northern Provinces where a light sandy loam generally predominates, the high temperature also being most favourable.'[2]

As soon as the railroad reached Kano, groundnut exports from Northern Nigeria increased from 2,518 to 19,288 tons, the latter being worth £174,716 (some stockpiling had taken place in anticipation of the railroad). After the slack years of the First World War, groundnut exports increased rapidly, with more than 100,000 long tons exported during the late 1920s and over 600,000 long tons in the boom year 1963. The latter figures indicate the tremendous potential that existed and show how the farmers moved to take advantage of the export possibility, as soon as transport became available.

Northern Nigeria had also substantial unutilized potential in its livestock, potential that was being lost not only because of transportation costs but also because of the failure of the cattle Fulani to look on their herds as a capital investment to be exploited for profit. Exports of hides and skins in 1913 were £166,414 and £30,800 respectively, a substantial increase over the £151,161 and £17,671 figures for 1912 when the effect of the railroad[3] had only recently

[1] Northern Nigeria, *Report of the Director of Agriculture*, 1913.
[2] *op. cit.*, 1912, p. 11; 1913, p. 5.
[3] Not all of the hides and skins exported should be credited to the trade-creating powers of the railway. Lugard, in his *Annual Report for Northern*

F   161

been felt. Buchanan and Pugh estimated in 1948–9 that Nigeria had 7 or 8 million cattle, owned almost entirely by the cattle Fulani, a nomadic, pastoral people of the north; Scott cites a 1940 estimate by the Director of Veterinary Services that the total of livestock approximated 5 million cattle, 10 million goats, and 4 million sheep. It is difficult to specify precisely the size of the cattle stock before the First World War, and even more difficult to calculate the potential for exports of hides and skins; however, it is certain that the potential was many times larger than exports. Disease must have caused enormous losses, but unwillingness to treat cattle as an investment[1] and poor methods of curing the hides reduced the exploitation of potential substantially.

The remainder of the agricultural exports of the Northern Region were composed of minor products like shea butter and shea nuts, benniseed, Arabic and copal gum, and a little rubber from the southern provinces. Shea nuts, used for the production of butter substitutes, soap, and candles, grew in importance as new areas were tapped by the Baro–Kano railroad lines; in 1909–10, shea nut exports were worth £90,850 (as estimated at the government station at Idah).[2] Benniseed, with a peak of 1,209 long tons in 1913 and a value of £9,000 gained importance slowly over time and after World War II was valued at more than £1 million, an important export for the pagan tribes of the Middle Belt.

Nigeria's only mineral known during this period was tin 'discovered in 1884 by a trading agent, Sir William Wallace, but not assayed until 1902 when Wallace, then a political agent, sent a sample to London. Between 1902 and 1912, an area of 3,816 square miles was split up among 70 companies with an estimated capital of over £4,000,000'.[3] During the early years, the main deterrent to large-scale production was the cost of transportation. Before the advent of the railway, the ore was carried 200 miles to Loko on the Benue, where it was loaded on steam-launches to Forcados, an ocean port. The ultimate solution after a short period of rail transport on the Lagos–Ragachikun route, was the building of a light

---

Nigeria 1905–6 (p. 429) mentions 'that the Arabs export to Tripoli a million skins at a value of £87,000. There will be no difficulty in diverting this trade to the south'.

[1] Northern Nigeria, Veterinary Department, *Annual Report* 1914 by F. R. Brandt: 'It is seldom that a Fulani owner, especially in the eastern part of the country, sells cattle unless he is in immediate need of something', p. 8.

[2] Northern Nigeria, Agricultural Department, *Annual Report*, 1910–11, p. 718.

[3] McPhee, *op. cit.*, pp. 56–60.

railway from Zaria on the Kano–Lagos route to the Bauchi Plateau tin fields at Bukura in 1914. The tin exports grew slowly from 11 tons in 1906 to 1,529 long tons in 1911; 4,142 tons in 1913; 6,174 tons in 1914; and 15,129 tons in 1929. In 1913, tin exports were worth £568,000. Tin, however, did not play nearly as important a role in Nigeria as gold played in the Gold Coast, either in providing revenue or in making rail transportation feasible economically. In 1913 tin was 9 per cent of Nigerian exports while gold represented 30 per cent in the Gold Coast.

III. FACTORS AFFECTING EXPORT DEVELOPMENT

The development of these countries after 1880 cannot be explained to any major degree simply by favourable changes in international prices. In fact the price movement of these thirty years was not particularly favourable to West Africa. If we take the average of 1881–3 as 100, c.i.f. London prices in 1911–13 averaged for palm oil 96, cocoa 81, timber 69, rubber 123, and cotton 119. It is true that transport costs had fallen significantly, both at sea and inside West Africa. Still, it was not high prices but the spread of new knowledge, both of crops and of techniques and the improvement of the political and economic environment to which the African farmers were responding.

In what follows we examine some but not all of the factors relevant to the development of the export trade.

Geography and natural resources. In a region poorly endowed with man-made factors of production, the influence of natural factor endowment is inevitably very great.

Let us start with minerals. Only two were exploited in this period. Ghana's gold proved important during 1900–13 in facilitating construction of the Sekondi–Kumasi railway, and in assuming a sizeable share of the tax burden. Nigeria's tin played a much lesser role at this time.

Up to 1880 the main source of cash income lay in exploiting the natural vegetation; the wild growing oil-palm, rubber, shea nut and mahogany trees offered an easily realizable potential for export of a considerable magnitude. Except for the short-lived cotton boom of the 1860s, West Africans did not take to cultivating crops for export until after 1880.

Both the Gold Coast and Nigeria had ample cultivable land in relation to population; even today both countries are probably still underpopulated relatively to their agricultural resources. The southern regions are much better endowed with rainfall, and ever

163

since 1880 the perennials which they can grow – cocoa, coffee, oil-palm, rubber, bananas, coconuts – have been more profitable in export markets, in terms of labour requirements, than the crops of the north – cereals, cotton, tobacco, groundnuts. Hence the great disparity between northern and southern incomes which still persists throughout West Africa.

In addition the development of the northern province for export could not begin until the arrival of the railway, which in both the Gold Coast and Nigeria is after 1900. The north had for centuries traded across the Sahara, but only luxury items could survive this transportation cost, so the volume of this trade was very small. The coastal regions had both an advantage and a disadvantage. The disadvantage was that the tsetse fly ruled out animal transportation, and forced reliance on human portage. The advantage was water transport. In the Gold Coast the Volta bypasses the crucial forest region, but the Tanosu and Ankobra rivers did give access to the forest, and the nature of the terrain made human portage fairly easy between the cocoa region and the coast. Nigeria was even better endowed with rivers, creeks, and lagoons; of particular importance were the Niger Delta creeks, which tapped the vast oil-palm regions of the east, and the Ogun River, which opened up the Abeokuta hinterland. In attributing growth of exports to modern transportation, one must not forget that there was substantial production for export, using human portage, rivers and creeks, before the arrival either of the railway or of the motor road.

Transport costs have been estimated by Gould[1] for the beginning of the twentieth century in the Gold Coast. They run as follows in pence per ton mile:

	Pence
Cask rolling of palm oil	14·5
Cask rolling of cocoa	23·0
Hand cart	22·0
Head loading	30·0–60·0
Lorry (pre-1914)	20·0
Railway (1903)	11·3

For comparison export f.o.b. prices per ton were (in pounds):

	1900	1913
Cocoa	£44·6	£44·3
Palm oil	15·0	23·0
Groundnuts	6·7	9·1
Rubber	146·3	176·1

[1] Peter R. Gould, *Development of the Transportation Pattern in Ghana*, Evanston, Illinois, 1960, p. 25.

At these prices, cocoa, rubber, and, later on, palm oil could bear the cost of human portage for a fair distance – say, up to 50 miles.

Railway transportation would halve the transport cost, and so extend the distance from the coast, but exportation could start without it. The Gold Coast cocoa industry began in an area well suited to human portage, and a considerable network of roads was created for this purpose. Probably all the 26,000 tons of cocoa exported in 1910 were carried to the coast by human porters and barrel rollers. During the next year a branch of the railway reached the cocoa area, and in its first season carried 20,000 tons to Accra, of which some must be attributed to stockpiling.

Having noted the important magnitude of trade that developed without modern transportation, it is necessary to give proper credit to the railroads.[1] By 1913, the Gold Coast and Ashanti had 227 miles of rail transportation, Southern Nigeria 467 miles, and Northern Nigeria 445 miles. Additionally, the Gold Coast Colony had 332·5 miles of road in 1911 of which 190 were suitable for motor traffic; the largest portion of these roads were a cocoa network converging on Accra and Nsawam from Aburi, Dodowa, Kibi, and Asamankese and two feelers from the coast towards the palm and cocoa areas of the Central Province from Saltpond to Insuaim and Winneba to Nsaba.[2] Away from the rivers, railroads, and roads, vast areas of potential were being left idle because of insufficient transportation to market centres. Not until the road and lorry era of the 1920s were the empty regions exploited.

The Pax Brittanica. Although the term is horribly imprecise, the concept of a *pax* is a useful catch-all for a number of quasi-governmental factors affecting development. It is important to note that the formal imposition of British rule is not a useful indicator of the introduction of beneficial effects. The most important benefits are: end of warfare and raiding, hence security for settlement and cultivation away from urban centres; termination of unauthorized interference with trade; governmental expenditures for development purposes; and non-governmental accompaniments of colonial rule.

---

[1] Peter R. Gould, *op. cit.*, pp. 20–37.

[2] K. B. Dickson, 'The Development of Road Transport in Southern Ghana and Ashanti since 1850', *Transactions of the Historical Society of Ghana*, Vol. 5, Pt. I (1961), discusses the development of a road network, particularly after 1890 when Governor W. B. Griffith appointed an Inspector of Trade Roads, and after 1901 when Governor Nathan began to press for 'roads good enough for motor-cars and traction engines'.

British rule brought peace and security to the Gold Coast and Nigeria, both of which had been troubled in the past by wars, trade disputes and slave-raiding. In 1874, the British proclaimed a colony on the Gold Coast below the Pra and ended the incursions of the Ashanti. Peace made possible the establishment of the cocoa plantations, which, like the coffee plantations of the 1860s, might have been destroyed in war or might have been unfeasible for reasons of security. Ashanti was taken under British rule in 1900 after a short period of generally ineffective informal protection.

In Nigeria, the effects of the peace that the British brought to Yorubaland in 1893 were most important, since large areas had been emptied of people fleeing from war. The effect of British rule – formal and informal – in the Delta is more complicated. Palm oil exploitation does not require the same degree of security that is necesssry for cultivation of a tree crop like cocoa. In addition, the nature of the indigenous authority structure met the requirements of the trade, and, despite the frequent but generally short interruptions of trade that occurred, enough security was provided to maintain the trade at a high average level for almost a century. It is not at all clear whether the firms were able or willing to offer higher prices and a more extensive trade network than the native traders had done; the Royal Niger Company, for example, had to rely on arbitrary licensing and taxes to eliminate competition from coastal traders. In Northern Nigeria, the conquest of the Fulani emirs in 1903 certainly had the beneficial effect of providing security to many groups that had been the target for decades of slave raids and to people who had seen many wars (although it is probably true that the Fulani rule of the nineteenth century represented, relative to pre-*jihad* times, comparative peace and security).

Imposition of British rule also meant the end of unpredictable interference with trade. The importance of previous interference is hard to generalize since it must have ranged from absolute destruction of the trade, especially that involving strategic war materials, to careful profit-maximization by the interfering party. Unquestionably, interference raised costs by increasing risk and lowered profits through the frequent seizures and customs levies. The interference with trade by the tribes between Ibadan and Lagos is a history in itself, and it is difficult to say how much this interference reduced the palm-oil exports of the Lagos hinterland. Because the middleman in Nigeria and the Gold Coast was African, the alternatives open to the trader must have been limited before 1900; therefore, the traders, despite profit margins lowered by interference, would not abandon the trade until the net benefits had fallen below those of the limited alternative possibilities. The European trader generally had much better alternatives available for time and capital, and required higher standards of security; but, since the European middleman in the interior replaced African trading efforts or initiative rather than acting to extend the scope of trade,[1] the imposition of British rule does not qualify as an important stimulus to trade on the grounds that it enabled the European middleman to penetrate the interior.

Perhaps the most important effects of British rule were in the creation of infrastructure, especially railways. Not until the British gained control of and responsibility for a region were they willing to guarantee loans for economic development expenditures, particularly on railroads. The railroads created trade that eventually made possible repayment of the original loan, but only the willingness of the British to lend the capital for railway construction made this sort of economic self-sufficiency possible. Therefore, the imposition of a *pax* meant that a government was established with the ability to borrow for long-term capital projects and the willingness to tax for some development expenditures and important administrative services. With the British rule came certain incidental benefits like larger missionary expenditures on education and more extensive mercantile efforts toward trade creation, the net effect of which is certainly open to debate in the form that it took place.

The trade network. The effect of traders on exports depends on the extensiveness of the trade network, on the exchange terms offered by the traders, and on incidental services provided. The establishment of European trading posts along the coast, whether in the forts of the Gold Coast or the hulks anchored at the mouths of delta creeks, led to the development of a widespread network of African middlemen who carried trade into the interior. While disease, particularly before the discovery of the protective powers of quinine in 1854, barred European entry into the interior, African middlemen proved their ability to break bulk and to stimulate an enormous amount of extractive production for export. The penetration of the interior by European mercantile firms during the last

---

[1] This is certainly open to question, but the effect of trade redistribution does seem greater than that of trade creation. C. J. Gertzel in 'Relations between African and European Traders in the Niger Delta, 1880–1896', *Journal of African History*, Vol. 3, No. 2, 1962, notes that European firms attempted unsuccessfully to enter the hinterland of Opobo after the deportation of King Ja Ja in 1887, and sold their interior factories to the Opobo chiefs in 1893.

167

half of the nineteenth century involved both trade creation and some trade redistribution away from the African middlemen.[1] The use of power launches must have opened a larger trade up the Niger than had been possible by native canoe.

In the Lagos region, the trade activities of the Sierra Leonian middlemen was quite important. Not only did they deal in the usual oil-palm produce, but also they created the trade in cotton. Their dual connections, both with the European world of Lagos and with the African communities of Yorubaland, made it more possible for them than for European or inland Africans to carry on a continuous trade.[2] On the Gold Coast long experience with the slave trade created a substantial network of groups interested in trade,[3] and, during the palm-oil, rubber and cocoa trades, there was no evidence that distaste for trade was a factor of importance. In fact, for Nigeria and Ghana, interest in the profits from trade seems to have been foremost for both individual and community. Many – perhaps most – of the nineteenth century wars had trade disputes as a central cause.

Little information is available on the precise price offerings to the producers. Details of trading margins (given various producer elasticities of supply) and of price stabilization practices would help to explain the reaction of producers to changes in external demand. In addition, the effects of the trust system must have varied according to their terms of lending, the nature of the production concerned, and the borrowing habits of the producers. Whether credit was a matter of convenience or of necessity would have to be established by detailed study; however, the use of credit seems to have been quite widespread, and it seems to have been necessary for the operations of the African middlemen.

Finally, the effect of the traders depended on whether they offered incidental services like explanation of techniques of production or

[1] For the story of European penetration of the interior of the Niger Delta and of European-African rivalry for the palm-oil trade, see Flint's *Sir George Goldie and the Making of Nigeria*, London, 1960; Dike, *op. cit.*, and J. C. Anene's *Southern Nigeria in Transition, 1885–1906*, Cambridge, 1966.

[2] Kopytoff, p. 171, notes that the connections of the Sierra Leonians in the interior made it possible for them to get some produce through even during the unsettled times of the 1870s. Ayandele, *op. cit.*, and Webster's *The African Churches Among the Yoruba* both discuss the crucial trading activities of the Sierra Leonians.

[3] For a discussion both of general trade in the nineteenth century and of the particular role of the Kwahu, see Peter Garlick, 'The Development of Kwahu Business Enterprise in Ghana since 1874—An Essay in Recent Oral Tradition', *Journal of African History*, Vol. 8, No. 3, 1967.

encouragement of purchase of equipment designed to raise productivity. The role of the Sierra Leonians in stimulating cotton production and processing has already been discussed. At a later date, the BCGA provided a vital function by purchasing all cotton at a fixed price, issuing high-quality seed, and offering copious advice on proper methods of cultivation. On the Gold Coast, the Basel Mission during the 1850s and 1860s opened a trading company in Accra to handle its produce, built a road from Akropong to Accra, and hired a wheelwright and a bullock-trainer to cut down on transport costs.[1] Later, the Gold Coast government carried out trading activities from Aburi so that price differentials could be established to encourage better quality cocoa and so that technical assistance could be joined with marketing, a concept somewhat like that behind co-operative marketing societies. Traders, like missionaries and government officials, were often a source of innovation. J. P. L. Davies brought cocoa to Agege. Rubber-traders were responsible for introducing cocoa to the Ashanti region. Their success in these regards is supporting evidence for merger of extension work and marketing.

The influence of traders on exports is undeniably great. The structure of the trading sectors, its extensiveness, the pricing practices employed, and the incidental innovations introduced must be precisely determined for each commodity or region to explain the extent of exchange. The trade sector is one of the weakest areas in our understanding of development during this period.

Agricultural technology. Until the establishment of British rule around the turn of the century, experimentation of a systematic variety was rare and was the product of *ad hoc* testing by missionaries, traders, or government officers. The agricultural station of the Basel Mission, the Danish plantations and other experimental gardens during the nineteenth century made rudimentary tests of various vegetables and of certain cash crops like cotton, coffee, and cocoa.[2] Unfortunately, the early efforts were not backed by the resources of tax revenues and tended to be somewhat transitory. It is likely that distribution of seed was one consequence, even if techniques for cultivation had not been entirely perfected. Systematic methods of research began with the establishment of the Aburi agricultural station in 1890.[3] Other experimental stations during this period

[1] Webster, *op. cit.*, p. 424.

[2] See Anyane, *op. cit.*, pp. 12–15 for the work of the Danes, and pp. 15–30 for the work of the Gold Coast Department of Agriculture.

[3] See W. S. D. Tudhope, *The Agricultural Department of the Gold Coast Colony: A Short History of Its Institution and Development*, Accra, 1911.

were the Christianborg Coconut Plantation 1901, the Aburi Rubber and Kola Plantation 1902, the Tarkwa Agricultural Station 1903, the Lalolabo Cotton Farm 1904, the Kumasi Agricultural Station 1906, the Assuantsi Agricultural Station 1907, and the Tamale Agricultural Station 1909. Because of their late establishment, limited discoveries were made during the period. The Lalolabo farm claimed great progress with cotton.[1] The government stations at Aburi, Tarkwa, Kumasi, and Assuantsi discovered methods of rubber tapping less injurious to the trees and more productive over the long run. Cocoa-fermenting methods were vastly improved over the initial methods employed by the farmers. And perhaps most important of all, experience was gained in classifying both plant types and pest or fungus varieties. Some of the improved plant types were grown for distribution and methods were designed to deal with many of the pests and fungus growths.

In Nigeria, the development of the Agriculture Department took place at a somewhat later date. Although the first botanic station was started in Lagos in 1887 and another was established in Calabar in 1903, no agriculture department was founded until 1910. A forestry department of sorts had been formed in 1897, and, during the first decade of the twentieth century, agriculture was within the domain of the forestry service.[2] Northern Nigeria had no agriculture department until 1912, and no veterinary service until 1914. As a consequence of the late start, only the experiments of the forestry service with rubber and other tree crops were providing useful information before 1913. Some interesting results were achieved with cotton during the first years of testing, but the breakthrough with exotic Allen cotton took place during the war. One of the explanations of the slow growth of cocoa must be the lack of a seed and seedling distribution station in the interior of Yorubaland. Perhaps the most striking fact of all is that no research took place on oil-palm trees, diseases, methods of cultivation or of processing until 1907, and no seeds were distributed until 1928; this oversight was one of a number of factors in the decline of the Nigerian palm-oil export dominance.

Purposeful dissemination of know-how was determined largely by the extensiveness of the governmental agricultural and forestry services, particularly given the fact that peasant smallhold agriculture was to be the basic organizational unit of production. In

[1] W. H. Himbury, 'Empire Cotton', *Journal of the African Society*, Vol. 17, p. 271.
[2] R. E. Dennett, *op. cit.*, pp. 266–7.

the process of disseminating information, the departments were assisted by missionaries, traders, other governmental officials, and by various travellers who passed on new ideas about farming. It is important to note that, in a country relying on peasant smallhold production, certain messages are easy to communicate and others quite difficult. If the method proposed is simple, unlaborious, and obviously profitable, then the word tends to get around quickly. This was the case for initiating cocoa cultivation. Local farmers frequently broke into the Aburi garden to steal pods and would come from miles around to see demonstration methods of cultivation and processing. Because of the profitability involved, seeds were quite easy to distribute, but laborious methods of cultivation were not easy to sell. Complaints in the annual Agricultural Department reports were frequent concerning the unwillingness of natives to adopt the practice of uprooting and burning diseased trees. One could provide at length examples of relative success and failure of extension messages, but the general conclusion is that the less desirable the message, the larger the service required to disseminate the idea or induce its acceptance. Neither the Gold Coast nor Nigeria had a large agriculture or forestry service; the Gold Coast service, for example, grew from two to twenty-seven during the years 1890 to 1911, and its budget in 1914 was a mere £16,674. The most effective work done was that of plant and seed distribution. Between 1904 and 1910, the Gold Coast Department distributed more than a million cocoa seeds, 1·6 million Para rubber seeds, 15·8 million Funtumia rubber seeds, and a few hundred thousand plants of the same varieties.[1] In retrospect, the distribution of rubber seeds did not bring great results, but future profitability could not have been foreseen at the time. For cotton, the BCGA established central ginning facilities and performed an invaluable service in raising cotton yields, both through experimentation and instruction and through provision of quality seed. The history of attempts to improve methods of dealing with disease, of extracting rubber from wild trees, and of processing rubber and palm oil is a rather complicated and discouraging one; tedium of methods proposed and lack of profit rather than failure to communicate appear to explain failure of the extension work.

It evolved, partly through conscious policy of the colonial government and partly through the impersonal functioning of the market mechanism, that neither the Gold Coast nor Nigeria developed

[1] See W. S. D. Tudhope, *op. cit.*, pp. 15, 19–20, for listing of staff and table on plant distribution.

171

plantation sectors of any considerable importance.[1] On the Gold Coast, the primary explanation for the failure of plantations seems to have been the competition of the cocoa industry that bid up the price of labour and limited the pool of labour available to plantations. Despite this problem, by 1911 there were twelve European rubber plantations in active operation, most in the Western Region away from the main development of the cocoa industry. It must be said that the potential existed in 1913 for future development both of rubber and palm oil and of cocoa, the former two on plantations and the latter in peasant smallholdings. Some initial developments took place in Ghana toward establishment of European palm-oil plantations. In 1910 Lever Brothers established kernel-crushing plants at Opobo and Apapa in Nigeria and later in Sierra Leone. The Palm Oil Ordinance of 1913 empowered the Gold Coast governor to grant processing monopolies over areas with a ten-mile radius. In 1914 the governor was empowered to lease land for oil-palm cultivation for a period of ninety-nine years. The experiments in Nigeria and Sierra Leone lost £50,000 in 1913 and were closed during the war. Similar experiments were initiated with cocoa and with cocoa and rubber. The war brought an end to most of these developments.[2] In Nigeria a similar handful of plantations were initiated, some native and others expatriate. On a tour through Southern Nigeria during 1912, W. H. Johnson surveyed plantations established in the Central and Eastern Regions. Mr MacIver and Miller Brothers maintained rubber plantations while the African Association had rubber and cocoa.[3] Apparently, in 1907, Lever Brothers requested the right to erect mills and to acquire land for planting; their reception was discouraging and in the following year they modified their request: this time they did not ask for land but merely for an exclusive right to build mills and lay down monorails. The Nigerian government answered with a direct refusal.[4] The refusal of the Nigerian government to allow lease of oil-palm lands

[1] W. K. Hancock, *Survey of British Commonwealth Affairs*, Vol. 2, pp. 188–200 and 240–6, discusses the relative advantages of plantations versus peasant agriculture and surveys efforts to improve the technical operation of palm-oil processing by peasants.

[2] Anyane, *op. cit.*, pp. 32–3 and 42, and David Kimble, *A Political History of Ghana: The Rise of Gold Coast Nationalism, 1850–1928*, Oxford, 1963, pp. 46–7.

[3] *Report* by the Director of Agriculture on his tour through the Western, Central, and Eastern provinces, pp. 4–8.

[4] Hancock, *op. cit.*, p. 190. Unfortunately Hancock does not explain why other companies were allowed to establish plantations. Perhaps it was large oil-palm plantations that were found unacceptable.

for plantations led to the rapid decline in Nigeria's share of world exports of oil and kernels, since plantations elsewhere developed high-yielding trees and high-yielding techniques of oil extraction. Nigerian production techniques remained highly inefficient, with low productivity per man.

IV. CONCLUSION

Unquestionably both Nigeria and the Gold Coast made tremendous progress with development during the period 1880 to 1913. The value of exports had increased enormously. Peace had been established and law and order were widespread. A competent administrative service had developed. The network of traders, which had been solidly established before 1880, had further penetrated the interior, offering incentives to production, introducing new plants and techniques, and providing credit. Transportation was extended beyond the previous use of desert caravans, head portage in the tsetse zone, and canoe transport on rivers and creeks. A basic rail network had been laid out; a rudimentary start had been made with road transportation; and important expenditures had been made on harbour improvement. Substantial capital had been invested in gold and tin mines. As for agriculture, labour had been transformed into capital in the form of maturing acreages of cocoa and rubber. Understanding of basic techniques of production and dissemination of those ideas had made substantial progress, although it was apparent that peasant producers calculated the desirability of certain techniques differently from the valuations made by the officers of the extension service or the managers of expatriate-owned and expatriate-run plantations. Very few expatriate plantations were established, but in a number of cases it appears that their introduction had commenced before the advent of the war. Important initial efforts had been made in agricultural research, and the rudimentary methods for disseminating information had been adoped.

But there were two significant failures. One was the failure of the government to raise enough in taxation to provide better infrastructure. The government's sights were low; they did not extend much beyond the maintenance of law and order and the promotion of agricultural exports. Most of the income generated by rapid development was immediately consumed. Africans built some solid houses, but beyond this capital formation was relatively low. At this time the Americans or the Japanese were raising very substantially their

173

productive capital, both private and public. More progressive governments would have made a greater contribution to infrastructure.

The other great failure springs from the same source; this was
the failure to spend substantially on education. The governments
left education almost exclusively to the missionaries. These did well
in view of their limited resources, even to the extent of establishing
perhaps half a dozen secondary schools by 1913. But their resources
were meagre. In consequence the country's need for trained manpower was met mainly by importation, not just of university
graduates, but of secondary and technical personnel – of secretaries,
nurses, mechanics, clerks, and other intermediate grades. This was
perhaps the greatest failure of the West African governments, since
the cost of importing intermediate personnel and the shortage of
this kind of manpower continued to be a brake on economic
development right up to the end of the Second World War.

Closely related to the meagre expenditures on education was the
inability of Africans to achieve a dominant role in commerce. The
continuing power of European import-export houses and the
incipient appearance of the Lebanese in the pre-war decade relegated
Africans to the place of petty traders and factors for foreigners.
The emasculated stature of the African trading class inhibited local
accumulation of capital. Without a capitalized commercial élite or
a government that would tax to accumulate investible capital, Ghana
and Nigeria were unable to follow the path of India and Japan
where wealthy merchants moved into industry. Not until the 1920
trade collapse was the fate of the African merchant made clear, but
the pre-war combination of inexperience in large-scale commerce,
of strenuous European trading opposition,[1] of limited capital,[2] and
of sociological constraints on entrepreneurship foreshadowed the
outcome.

In a sense, the people did better than their governments, for their

[1] Gertzel, *op. cit.*, pp. 365–6, notes that Ja Ja and Nana were removed largely
because they attempted to trade directly with Europe: 'By removing Ja Ja and
Nana, the administration was removing the only Delta Africans who had the
resources even to attempt to establish an African export trade, as had a few of
the Sierra Leonian merchants in Lagos.' But she adds, 'it is difficult to say
whether Ja Ja could have maintained a profitable direct trade with Europe'.

[2] Gertzel in 'Commercial Organization on the Niger Coast, 1852–1891', in
Historians in Tropical Africa, Salisbury, 1962, pp. 289–304, places heavy emphasis
on shortage of capital as the reason for the failure of small companies in the
Delta. She mentions also their inability to buy trade goods cheaply. See also
P. T. Bauer, *West African Trade*, Cambridge, 1954, and Michael Crowder,
West Africa under Colonial Rule, Evanston, Ill., 1968, for analysis of the failure
of African traders.

story is one of responding to economic opportunities – in palm oil, cocoa, rubber, cotton – in unfavourable circumstances: the virtual absence of modern transportation facilities. It is a story to be pondered over by those who believe that economic development needs a particular set of Western institutions and ideas if it is to flourish.

BIBLIOGRAPHY

Official Papers

Gold Coast. Agriculture Department, *The Agriculture Department of the Gold Coast Colony: A Short History of its Institution and Development* by W. S. D. Tudhope. Accra, 1911.
——. Agriculture and Botanical Department, *Annual Report*, 1903 to 1913 inclusive.
Great Britain. Colonial Office, *Northern Nigeria Report, 1900/1–1911.* Annual Reports) London.
——. House of Commons, *Sessional Papers*, 1884, 1897, 1899, 1914–16. 'Statistical Abstract for the . . . Colonies . . .', 1886 to 1896 (C. 3874), 1882 to 1896 (C. 8605), 1884 to 1898 (C. 9459), 1899 to 1913 (Cd. 7786).
Northern Nigeria. Agriculture Department, *Annual Report*, 1912, 1913, 1921.
——. Veterinary Department, *Annual Report*, 1914.
Southern Nigeria. Agriculture Department, *Annual Report*, 1910 to 1920, excluding only 1916.
——. Forestry Department, *Annual Report*, 1907, 1910, 1911, 1912, 1913.
——. Forestry and Agriculture Department, *Annual Report*, 1909.

Books.

Anene, J. C., *Southern Nigeria in Transition, 1885–1906*, Cambridge, 1966.
Anyane, S. L., *Ghana Agriculture*, London, 1963.
Ayandele, E. A., *The Missionary Impact on Modern Nigeria, 1842–1914*, New York, 1967.
Bauer, P. T., *West African Trade*, Cambridge, 1954.
Boateng, E. A., *A Geography of Ghana*, Cambridge, 1959.
Buchanan, K. M., and Pugh, J. C., *Land and People in Nigeria*, London, 1955.
Crowder, Michael, *A Short History of Nigeria*, New York, 1962.
——, *West Africa under Colonial Rule*, London, 1968.
Dike, K. O., *Trade and Politics in the Niger Delta, 1830–1885*, Oxford, 1956.
Fage, J. D., *Ghana*, Madison, Wis., 1961.
Flint, J. E., *Sir George Goldie and the Making of Nigeria*, London, 1960.
Foster, P. J., *Education and Social Change in Ghana*, London, 1965.

Galletti, R., Baldwin, K. D. S., and Dina, I. O., *Nigerian Cocoa Farmers*, London, 1956.

Geary, W. N. M., *Nigeria under British Rule*, London, 1927.

Gould, P. R., *Development of the Transportation Pattern in Ghana*, Evanston, Ill., 1960.

Hancock, W. K., *Survey of British Commonwealth Affairs*, Vol. 2, Oxford, 1942.

Helleiner, G. K., *Peasant Agriculture, Government and Economic Growth in Nigeria*, Homewood, Ill., 1966.

Hill, Polly, *The Migrant Cocoa Farmers of Southern Ghana*, Cambridge, 1963.

Kimble, David, *A Political History of Ghana: The Rise of Gold Coast Nationalism, 1850–1928*, Oxford, 1963.

Kopytoff, J. H., *A Preface to Modern Nigeria, The Sierra Leonians in Yoruba, 1830–1890*, Madison, Wis., 1965.

Lucas, C. P., ed., *A Historical Geography of the British Dominions*, Vols. 2 and 3, Oxford, 1905 and 1913 respectively.

McPhee, Allan, *The Economic Revolution in British West Africa*, London, 1926.

Szereszewski, R., *Structural Changes in the Economy of Ghana, 1891–1911*, London, 1965.

Ward, W. E. F., *A History of the Gold Coast*, London, 1948.

Webster, J. B., *The African Churches among the Yoruba, 1888–1922*, Oxford, 1964.

Wills, J. B., *Agriculture and Land Use in Ghana*, London, 1962.

Articles.

Ajayi, J. F. A., 'Henry Venn and the Policy of Development', *Journal of the Historical Society of Nigeria*, December 1959.

Akinola, R. A., 'The Ibadan Region', *Nigerian Geographical Journal*, December 1963.

Bevin, H. J., 'The Gold Coast Economy about 1880', *Transactions of the Gold Coast and Togoland Historical Society*, Vol. 2, No. 2, 1956.

Dennett, R. E., 'Agricultural Progress in Nigeria', *Journal of the African Society*, Vol. 18, 1918–19.

Dickson, K. B., 'The Development of Road Transport in Southern Ghana and Ashanti since 1850', *Transactions of the Historical Society of Ghana*, Vol. 5, Pt. 1, 1961.

Garlick, Peter, 'The Development of Kwahu Business Enterprise in Ghana since 1874: An Essay in Recent Oral Tradition', *Journal of African History*, Vol. 8, No. 3, 1967.

Gertzel, C. J., 'Commerical Organization on the Niger Coast, 1852–1891', *Historians in Tropical Africa: Proceedings of the Leverhulme Intercollegiate History Conference*, Salisbury, 1962.

——, 'Relations between African and European Traders in the Niger Delta, 1880–1896', *Journal of African History*, Vol. 3, No. 2, 1962.

Greenstreet, D. K., 'The Transport Department: Its First Two Decades, 1901–1920', *Economic Bulletin of Ghana*, Vol. 10, No. 3, 1966.

Hanna, Marwan, 'The Lebanese in West Africa', *West Africa*, April and May 1958.

Himbury, W. H., 'Empire Cotton', *Journal of the African Society*, Vol. 17, 1917–18.

Howes, F. N., 'The Early Introduction of Cocoa', *African Affairs: Journal of the African Society*, January 1946.

Mabogunje, A. L., and Gleave, M. B., 'Changing Agricultural Landscape in Southern Nigeria: The Example of the Egba Division, 1850–1950', *Nigerian Geographical Journal*, June 1964.

McGregor, William, 'Lagos, Abeokuta and the Alake', *Journal of the African Society*, Vol. 3, 1903–4.

Manning, Patrick, 'Some Export Statistics for Nigeria, 1880–1905', *Nigerian Journal of Economic and Social Studies*, July 1967.

Oguntoyinbo, J. S., 'Rainfall, Evaporation and Cotton Production in Nigeria', *Nigerian Geographical Journal*, June 1967.

Shelford, Frederick, 'Ten Years Progress in West Africa', *Journal of the African Society*, Vol. 6, 1906–7.

Udo, R. K., 'Patterns of Population Distribution and Settlement in Eastern Nigeria', *Nigerian Geographical Journal*, December 1963.

——, 'Sixty Years of Plantation Agriculture in Southern Nigeria, 1902–1962', *Economic Geography*, October 1965.

Webster, J. B., 'The Bible and the Plough', *Journal of the Historical Society of Nigeria*, December 1963.

Chapter 7

KENYA AND UGANDA

by Bryan Devereux Hickman[1]

Although it is impossible to choose any one or more factors to explain economic development for a region, one can pick out a few key factors that serve as a touchstone for understanding the economic aspects of development in East Africa during the three decades before 1914. The first is that the geographical character of the region discouraged early contact between coastal traders and the interior. Much of the land between the coast and Lake Victoria, with the exception of highland areas, is arid. The inhospitable coastal hinterland and the lack of a river network like that of Nigeria limited trade to high-valued items like ivory and, to a limited extent, slaves. In addition, the region was not known to contain any minerals; hence no immediate economic justification for a railroad was available. The second key factor is that, despite the minimal development of the region, a railroad costing £5·5 million was built, largely for strategic reasons related to the Nile and the events of the Anglo–Egyptian Sudan.[2] Once the railroad had been completed, every thought turned to finding a means of making it economically viable. The means of development are explained by the final key factors: the inter- and intra-tribal wars engaged in by the Masai, which depopulated huge areas of the cool Rift Valley and the neighbouring highland regions, thus inviting thoughts of European settlement; and the rapid discovery of and development of cotton as a native crop in Uganda.

These four factors: the geography of the region, the building of the railroad long before effective demand, the depopulation of large areas of the Rift Valley during Masai raids and intra-tribal wars, and the rapid expansion of cotton in Uganda serve as a focus for understanding the full range of factors and events determining the development of East Africa between 1880 and 1913.

---

[1] The author would like to thank Peter Matlon for his help in preparing this chapter.

[2] See Ronald Robinson and John Gallagher, *Africa and the Victorians: The Climax of Imperialism*, London, 1961, pp. 350–1.

178

I. EAST AFRICA IN 1880

In 1880 the interior of East Africa had experienced little contact with Europeans. The area from the coast to the highlands of the interior, and the region to the north – about one-half of the total area of the country – was arid and sparsely settled. The land rose to the hills and plains inhabited by the Kamba, who were an agricultural people with some cattle. To the west lived the Kikuyu, raising both crops and livestock. In the Great Rift Valley, from Kilimanjaro to Mount Elgon, the pastoral Masai grazed their cattle on the rich highland plains. The Kavirondo area, around the north-eastern area of Lake Victoria was more densely populated by agriculturalists. The interior of the future East African Protectorate, now known as Kenya, excepting the arid lands immediately behind the coast and to the north, was suited for agriculture, because of its fertile soil and a warm, humid climate. For all the beauty and richness of the land, however, the inhabitants existed at a bare subsistence level, troubled by warfare and disease, living simply in little huts. Low productivity methods of cultivation provided meagre and uncertain returns. The variability of the rainfall led to recurring famines, causing great hardship for the peoples of this region of East Africa.

Economic activity above the subsistence level before 1880 was limited to the coastal cities of Mombasa, Malindi, and other smaller towns which had been settled by Arabs and Indian traders hundreds of years before. They carried on an extensive trade with Asia – exporting ivory, horn, cloves, and slaves, and importing consumer trade goods. Banking and finance in this early export-oriented economy were controlled by the Indian population, while the plantations were mostly run by Arabs.

The geography of Uganda was as varied as that of the East Africa Protectorate. From lowlands near the lake, the land rose slowly to a plateau of tree savannah to the north. It was the area near Lake Victoria that was most densely populated, for here the environment was particularly favourable. The soils were deep and rich; the rainfall was reliable[1] and well distributed throughout the year. Agriculture was particularly rewarding, lifting the population well above a

---

[1] C. C. Wrigley in *Crops and Wealth in Uganda*, Kampala, 1959, pp. 1–2, notes that 'more than half of Uganda enjoys a virtual certainty of a minimum of thirty inches and that only two areas in the south-west fail to enjoy virtual certainty of twenty inches. Points on the shore of Lake Victoria have as high as 74 per cent probability of obtaining water requirements twice a year.'

merely subsistence level. As C. C. Wrigley points out, 'The main source of food was not an annual, soil exhausting crop like maize or millet, but a banana grove which, once mature, yielded fruit all the year round and went on yielding it from year to year ... it was said with some, but not very much, exaggeration, that one old woman could feed ten old men'.[1] There were none of the worries of shifting cultivation, little need to clear and break new ground, none to store harvests, and there was practically no threat of famine. The high productivity of agriculture meant that the Baganda, living west and north-west of Lake Victoria, could spend more time and resources in raising their standards of living. They were well clad, had bigger, better, and cleaner houses than their neighbours, and had better weapons. With no markets, however, they could not produce for sale, so they developed a military machine for extracting livestock and women – the two most valued goods – from their neighbours. By the mid-1800s trade had opened up with the coastal populations by way of Arab caravans. Cloth, ornaments, soap, glass, and china were imported. Only slaves and ivory could be exported profitably, and the military machine was strengthened in order to ensure a supply from neighbouring tribes. Division of labour had reached the point at which not only were there warriors and food growers, but also potters, carpenters, and even smiths who could repair firearms. It was this relatively advanced civilization and economy which attracted British attention, when once contact had been made.

British involvement in East Africa before 1880 was centred on the Island of Zanzibar. In the years preceding the area's development, Britain's concern grew as a result of commercial interests in the Indian trade that dominated the Island, and became more intense in the 1870s with efforts to put an end to the East African slave trade. The necessity for British enforcement of a treaty negotiated with the sultan of Zanzibar in 1873, which closed all slave markets in the sultan's dominions, led to close political ties between the British and Zanzibar governments. British commercial enterprise was reluctant to venture into the limited opportunities of the mainland of East Africa. Only in transportation and communications did British private interests take an active lead – laying the groundwork of the infrastructure which was later to play an essential role in the growth of East Africa.

Transportation and communication systems were established in two stages. The first was the establishment of ties from Zanzibar and the coastal trading centres of Europe and other points in the

[1] L. A. Fallers, ed., *The King's Men*, London, 1964, p. 18.

British Empire. This occurred in the 1870s with regular steamship service between Aden and Zanzibar. The second stage, which was to draw heavily on public investment in the late 1890s and early 1900s, was the laying out of an internal transportation system through the interior of continental East Africa. It was early recognized that the primary growth potential for the area lay not at the coast but in the highlands and great lakes regions. Until the second stage of development took place, however, these areas were separated from the ports of the coastal settlements by a very crude and often broken chain of trails and caravan routes. The result was limited and extremely costly transport.

II. THE UGANDA RAILROAD

The lethargic pace of British expansion in East Africa ended abruptly in 1884. In that year a group of private commercial interests from Germany established treaties with tribes of the interior, annexing a large portion of land west of Dar es Salaam for 'exclusive and universal utilization for German colonization'.[1] In response, the British East Africa Company was established in 1886 on the basis of a fifty-year lease from the sultan of Zanzibar. Within two years the company had a charter as the Imperial British East Africa Company. Spurred on by the desire to control the headwaters of the Nile, as well as by competition with the German administration, the British sent expeditions into the north-western region over the next six years which led to the declaration of the Uganda Protectorate in 1894.

Beset with problems, the Imperial British East Africa Company was unable to meet the need for improved internal systems of transportation. With only a quarter of a million pounds sterling, it was far undercapitalized for the job it faced. Policy was ill defined, resources poorly used, and the company was under political pressure to over extend itself by trying to establish a base in Uganda rather than concentrating its limited resources on development of the coast. In 1892 the company faced near bankruptcy and had to retrench – at which time the missionary community in Uganda cried for help. Fighting in Uganda between rival Christian factions and Muslims drained the company's already low financial resources and revealed the weakness of its peacekeeping and administrative capabilities. Bankruptcy was declared in 1893, and in 1895 the British government withdrew the company's charter. That same

[1] Leonard Woolf, *Empire and Commerce in Africa*, London, 1920, pp. 235–7.

181

year, the Foreign Office took over the administration of the Protectorate which had been declared the year before. At last the resources of the British government were brought to bear in East Africa. And the form it most dramatically took was the Uganda Railway.

The decision which committed the British government to the constructon of the 600 mile railway line lacked a clear economic justification. A report presented to Parliament in 1895 estimated the total cost of the proposed line at £2,240,000.[1] Against this expense were set the economic benefits which were expected to flow from bridging the transportation bottleneck between Lake Victoria and the port of Mombasa.

An examination of the comparative price ratios between several key commodities in Uganda and in Mombasa during the pre-rail period underlines the potential for increased trade that the railroad planned to tap.[2] For example, ivory sold in Uganda at the rate of 3 shillings per pound as compared to 10 shillings per pound in Mombasa. Wheat in Mombasa which had to be imported from India sold for £10 per ton. In Uganda the price was £2 10s per ton. With rail shipment costs of 1d per ton mile, a reasonable profit could be made. Other products with favourable price ratios were maize, millet, rice, and simsim. Products not yet developed but in which it was believed Uganda had a comparative advantage were tea, coffee, rubber, and most importantly cotton. Each of these commodities enjoyed a large and growing demand on the coast, either for consumption or for export, but transportation costs of between £100 and £300 per ton placed a decisive obstacle in the way of large-scale production. Also recognized in the decision to build the railroad was the anticipated reverse flow of goods into the Lake Victoria region.

The decision to construct the railway was made in 1896, and work began in 1897. By 1899 the railway had been extended to Nairobi, and in 1901 it reached Kisumu on Lake Victoria. The cost estimates prepared six years earlier soon proved to be unrealistically low.[3] Working expenses in the first year alone were £367,927, with no revenue. During the second year, expenses grew to £600,488,

[1] Great Britain, House of Commons, *Sessional Papers*, 1895, 'Report of the Committee Appointed to Consider the Question of Railway Communication with Uganda,' August 1895 (7833).

[2] Great Britain, House of Commons, *Sessional Papers*, 1893–94, 'Report on Mombasa–Victoria Lake Railway Survey', (Cd. 7025).

[3] Great Britain, House of Commons, *Sessional Papers*, 1912–13, 'Statistical Tables Relating to the British Colonies . . .' (Cd. 6400).

partially offset, however, by the first trickle of income from passenger and goods traffic. The total capital cost of the railway was £5,925,909. Neither this nor the interest costs of nearly two million pounds sterling were ever repaid to the British treasury.[1] Not until 1905 did receipts exceed working expenses; thereafter the railroad turned handsome profits which were used for general administration purposes by the Protectorate government.

By the first years of the twentieth century, two major developments had taken place in the East Africa and Uganda Protectorates. One of these, as we have seen, was the construction of the railway, with the opening of the interior as a result. The other was the establishment of administrative control, first on the coast, then along the route of the railroad, and finally into the frontier districts. From July 1895 to March 1904, nearly £2,000,000 were spent by the East Africa Protectorate government apart from the railroad expenditures.[2] Of this, over 31 per cent had been spent on the military. The proportion of military expenditure in Uganda, with the continual civil strife, followed by a mutiny of Sudanese soldiers, was even greater. Of the remainder, most was absorbed by administration – a proposition which was to become particularly expensive in the East Africa Protectorate due both to the lack of African rulers of the sort who might be the bases for a system of indirect rule, and to the prospect of white colonization. Little money was left for investment in productive projects, or even for the basic social overhead capital.

At this point, the policies of the two protectorates took considerably different tacks, and hereafter we shall treat each protectorate separately. In the East Africa Protectorate a policy of white immigration to farm and otherwise develop the country was undertaken, whereas in Uganda African agriculture was encouraged and white immigration limited.

III. KENYA 1901–13

Sir Charles Eliot, Governor of the East Africa Protectorate, soon realized that the railroad was far more expensive than originally had been envisaged and that some positive policy was necessary to make it pay. The Protectorate administration was virtually forced to take a hand in development since the railway was financially its liability.

[1] M. F. Hill, *Permanent Way*, Nairobi, 1949, p. 243.
[2] House of Commons, *Sessional Papers*, 1905, 'Annual Statement of Trade' (Cd. 2626).

At the same time the whole character of the Protectorate had begun to change – it had an importance of its own and was no longer merely an area to be traversed to reach the rich interior. In point of fact, the railway did not pass through the richest portions of the East Africa Protectorate, but it did offer a series of points from which they were accessible. To the administrators of the Protectorate, great areas of fertile highlands appeared vacant along the railroad, and a colony of European farmers to develop them seemed the obvious solution. Export crops would balance the trade deficit as well as pay for the railway. Africans would provide the necessary labour.

Eliot did not believe that large-scale cash-crop production by the African population was possible, and never considered the idea seriously. It seemed possible in Uganda where there lived a prosperous and settled agricultural people, well organized and eager to adopt new methods. But the East Africa Protectorate was inhabited by pastoralists and by agriculturalists who appeared unable to produce a surplus because of the sub-optimal agricultural conditions which they accepted in order to achieve security from raiding enemies. There were no widely recognized chiefs through whom the Protectorate administration could work, and there was little organization or central authority among the tribes. Eliot had neither the experience nor the imagination to envision what new crops, improved methods and seeds, and an assured market might do to the old tribal agriculture. Development of African agriculture seemed an impossibility to him; at the same time the rich highlands were so inviting that he settled upon the idea of white colonization as a seemingly ideal policy for the East Africa Protectorate.

At the end of 1902 there were less than a dozen European settlers on the edge of the Kikuyu. But in that year the Crown Land Ordinance was enacted, making possible alienation of land on 99-year leases. By the middle of 1903 over one hundred settlers were established in the region, raising cereals, coffee, potatoes, fruit, and livestock in the highlands and cotton, fibres, tobacco and sugar at lower elevations. Besides settlers from the British Isles, recruiting efforts by the administration brought in a large flow of South Africans, anxious to resettle after the Boer War, as well as a few from North America, Australia, Germany and Romania.[1]

A host of problems faced the new settlers. Few of them had enough capital. It was estimated that at least £500 was necessary to set up a good farm, and that it could take as long as ten years to make it pay. Only a few, wealthy settlers had that much money or

[1] E. Huxley, *White Man's Country*, London, 1935, p. 93.

184

could wait that long. A great deal of experimentation would be necessary to select and develop the most profitable lines of production, and quite often settlers exhausted their resources before establishing successful farms. For all the recruiting efforts, the government land office was inefficient – slow to survey land, slow to issue deeds, and insistent upon many petty regulations, so that many arriving settlers had to wait months before even starting to get established.

The decision by Sir Charles Eliot to encourage European immigration was motivated by the objective of making the railroad pay, coupled with the relative emptiness of the depopulated Masai grazing and raiding zone. According to Wrigley,[1] native occupation was defined by the line of outermost settlement with exceptions being made to give all land adjacent to the railroad to Europeans, to move the Masai out of their homelands in the north of the Rift Valley, and to move approximately 5,000 Kikuyus from an area occupied north of Nairobi. To what extent the vacant lands were fallows rather than empty is a subject of dispute, but it was not until the inter-war years that land shortage began to be felt by the Africans.

Despite early efforts to encourage mass colonization with 160 to 640 acre land grants, the determination of the size of European farms lay more with geography and experimentation than with government planning. The failure of the wheat-and-sheep family farm made small farming a difficult venture until the success of coffee production just before World War I. Eventually cattle ranchers, some with large estates like those of Delamere and Cole, were able to deal with, but by no means overcome, the host of epizootic and enzootic diseases like East Coast fever, rinderpest, and foot-and-mouth disease. Other European farmers tried to meet expenses by growing maize for export, and vegetables and potatoes for the small internal market. The key aspect of government land policy was that during this period it leased or granted unoccupied land to Europeans who established farms of widely varying size and experimented with many crops; these farms were producing no more than 30 per cent[2] of Kenyan exports before World War I but eventually they came to dominate the monetary economy. Africans, on the other hand, were not yet hurt by land shortage and produced over 70 per cent of exports in 1912–13; later they were constrained increasingly by land shortage.

The dynamics of the labour market changed with the man-land ratio. Before World War I, Africans were not forced by land

---

[1] Harlow and Chilver, eds., *op. cit.*, pp. 227–8.   [2] *ibid.*, p. 243.

185

shortage to seek paid labour. The Europeans had serious labour problems because of their demands for help in establishing and operating their farms and because of competing demands by safaris, portage and government. Demand by Africans for material goods was small because of limited acquaintance with the money economy. At the prices offered, real supply and wishful demand were not in balance; so the Europeans looked to taxes and suasion to induce African labour. The 2 rupee hut tax of 1901 was raised to 3 rupees and supplemented by a poll tax of 3 rupees, but the labour-inducing consequences fell far short of the wishes of the settlers. The influence of indirect coercion through the chiefs, while impossible to verify, must have been important.

Thus by 1913 a great deal of experimentation had taken place. By 1914, 3·4 million acres had been alienated, much on 99 and 999 year leases.[1] Between 2 and 3 million acres were granted in freehold estates to about 200 individuals, with payment only of a fraction of survey costs. These settlers had overcome their initial trials and stood as a vested interest for a land and labour policy on the South African pattern. Their success attracted further settlers after the war and at that time the confrontation over policy led to more permanent policies.

In developing crop types, the government played a small role. The first agricultural experiments had been conducted in 1896, and in 1903 the newly formed Agricultural Department started an experimental farm near Nairobi. Potatoes, which had promised to do very well, proved to be a costly failure, partly due to marketing problems. Wheat imported in 1892 died out; more was brought in 1904, and efforts were begun to breed a type immune to the prevalent rusts and diseases. Not until after the First World War, however, was a satisfactory strain developed. Maize yields were disappointing at first, but by 1910 a hybrid called Kenya White was evolved that was remarkably free from disease, and production increased very rapidly. Wattle seed was introduced in 1901, and by 1908 the crop was providing substantial amounts of fuel for the railroad and a good supply of tannin as well. In 1907 sisal bulbils were imported in quantity. In 1912 the first decorticator was erected. By 1914 over 7,500 acres were planted. Coffee was started as early as 1896 by the White Fathers Mission, and although it developed a leaf disease, output was not significantly affected and the crop took hold.

The years 1910 to 1914 were good crop years. The drought was over; labour became more available both as a stronger government

[1] Norman Leys, *Kenya*, London, 1925, p. 114.

labour policy evolved and as Africans' demand for purchased goods increased; world demand for agricultural products was expanding. Rates on European-farm exports were lowered on the railroad to assure farmers that their crops would reach the market cheaply. A steady flow of settlers arrived in this period, many of them from the United Kingdom, and most brought far more capital than their predecessors. For these few years a boom atmosphere prevailed.

By 1914 the white economy was well established. In 1913 there were nearly 6,000 Europeans in the country, most of them on farms. Capital was flowing in. The chief crops, maize and livestock, had been identified, though exports were still tiny, even when compared with exports produced by African farmers along the lake. The labour problems seemed to have been solved, to the satisfaction of the Europeans though not of the Africans. Besides agriculture, industry was making progress. Flour mills, sawmills, a ginnery, brick and tile works, a bacon factory and several dairies were in operation. The growth of the white economy would be curtailed during the First World War, but would resume vigorously in the 1920s.

The year 1913 was prosperous for the Africans as well as for the whites. The opportunity to export was beginning to make itself felt, and the shortage of land in the reserves would not reveal itself until after the war. Grain and pulses, mostly maize, simsim, beans and peas, headed the list of exports for the year ending March 31, 1913, with a value of £131,258, more than four times the amount exported just three years before.[1] These were primarily from African farms and were not European produce. Likewise, the second item on the list, hides and skins valued at £87,673, was also mainly African produce; the same is true of the third item, copra valued at £31,956. European produce, coffee, fibres, potatoes, wheat, livestock and so forth all showed gains of two to four times over 1910, but they were still at pretty low levels. Total exports were £421,084 in 1913. Imports were valued at £1,808,343 for the same year, showing that the colony was far from self-supporting as yet.

Along the coast the Arabs were hard hit. With an end to slavery their plantations declined; they fell into debt and lost most of their land. Europeans took over most of the coastal plantation agriculture (rubber and sisal), although they, too, had a hard time at first. The coastal tribes never developed export crops on any large scale and soon became part of the labour supply to European plantations. Both cotton and sisal had been tried by the Africans and failed. At

[1] House of Commons, *Sessional Papers*, 1914–16, 'Statistical Tables Relating to the British Colonies . . .' (Cd. 7667).

Malindi, where a low quality maize was the staple crop, a better quality seed was introduced with noticeable improvement.

The tale would not be complete without mention of the Indian population. Without the nearly 32,000 coolies imported for railroad construction the railway would not have been possible. Of that number, nearly 7,000 decided to remain when their contracts were up.[1] It was suggested that Indian labour be used to develop the country agriculturally, but few Indians were interested, and there were vast problems of supervision, organization, and race relations. The greater part of the Indians who stayed became petty traders. Accustomed to a low standard of living and low profits, they were willing to go into new areas and open up small trading centres – first following the route of the railroad, but soon branching out in all directions. For all the problems of regulation, sanitation, and conflicts between Africans and Indians, the Indians did much to introduce currency and the habit of dealing with money to Africans. The fact that they made various goods available did much to loosen up the labour supply as Africans had more and more demand for money.[2]

Throughout the period prior to World War I, the transport infrastructure expanded to meet the increasing demands placed on it, and it was in this area that the greatest amount of public investment was concentrated. Transport capacity on Lake Victoria was expanded to provide access to the railroad for producers in Uganda and German East Africa. More than one-fourth of the 'up' traffic and one-third of the 'down' traffic of the railroad was handled by the steamer service on the lake.[3] Branch lines were connected to the Uganda railway, one to Lake Magadi finished in 1914, and one to Thika and Fort Hall in the direction of Mount Kenya.

The railroad turned a small profit in 1905, and the profits grew steadily until they reached £217,345 in the year ending March 31, 1914. These profits were made, however, with no provision for renewal of wasting assets, and no charge for interest on capital cost. What is more, the money accrued not to the railroad administration but to the treasury of the East Africa Protectorate. In effect the railway was used as a taxing machine. From 1895 to 1913, grants in aid to the Protectorate from the British Treasury totalled £2,843,383, and the British Treasury was insistent that all revenues

[1] Hill, *op. cit.*, p. 254.
[2] George Delf, *Asians in East Africa*, London, 1963, and L. W. Hollingsworth, *Asians of East Africa*, London, 1960.
[3] Hill, *op. cit.*, p. 305.

be used to balance the budget of the Protectorate so that the grants could be stopped. This policy kept the railway always short of money, and prevented a policy of low rail charges to encourage exports as much as possible. Rates were three times the equivalent rates in India.[1] This was partly due to the fact that the railroad was a hill railroad, climbing steep grades into the highlands, partly due to the fact that the seasons of heavy imports (which were twice the quantity of exports) were not the same as those of exports, so that trains ran empty in one direction, but mostly due to its function as a source of revenue. The policy was particularly unfair to producers outside of the protectorate who provided half of the real traffic, but received none of the profits while paying high rates. In 1911, 48 per cent of the railroad's earnings came from the East Africa Protectorate, 27 per cent from Uganda, and 23 per cent from German East Africa.[2] Another factor affecting the initial profitability of the railroad was that there was no surplus that the railway could tap immediately upon completion. All exports were new production of new crops on new land. Only about 3 per cent of administration expenditure went to roads and other forms of transport in this period. The motor car had made its entry, but was not yet of major importance.

IV. THE UGANDA PROTECTORATE 1903–1913

With the railroad in place, Uganda was ready to embark on development as well, but a very different development took place from that in the East Africa Protectorate. From the early endeavours to stimulate the supply of exports that Africans could easily produce or collect (ivory and rubber) developed a strong effort to promote the growing of cotton by Africans. The area was never really thought of as a 'white man's country' after the fashion of the East Africa Protectorate. The climate was not as pleasant and the land was more fully occupied by the indigenous population. The peace imposed by the British stopped the raiding for livestock and women. But the railroad opened new opportunities which the population was not slow to grasp. District officers made ceaseless efforts to impress the chiefs and people with the advantages of growing saleable products. Some cotton had been growing wild, and some spinning had been done by Africans, but no cotton had been cultivated. In 1903 the industrial missionary of the Church Missionary Society imported

[1] Hill, *op. cit.*, p. 306.   [2] *ibid.*, p. 309.

sixty-two bags of seeds of five varieties. This seed and Egyptian seed imported by the government was distributed to the chiefs. It was found that American Upland grew best, and subsequently this accounted for the bulk of the cotton grown. In 1904 seed was given to 27 or 28 growers of the Uganda Trading Company, and about 45 tons were harvested.[1] The next year nearly 500 cultivators applied for seed, and 300 tons of unginned cotton was expected. The initial pressures to get Africans to grow cotton soon became unnecessary as profits started rolling in.

In Buganda, near the lake, chiefs were given freehold ownership rights over large tracts of land where they had previously been only rulers and tax collectors. This was probably due to confusion of legal concepts, but it was also convenient for the British, since the creation of private ownership reinforced a ruling class through whom British administrators were working. Private ownership initially gave added incentives to chiefs to get their men growing cotton, and it was assumed at first that the chiefs 'would act as entrepreneurs and develop their estates after the manner of English landowners . . . the [cotton-growing] project was launched by means of written agreements between its authors, the British-owned Uganda Company, and certain prominent Baganda, the former undertaking to supply seed and instruction and to buy the crop, the latter to see that the seed was planted and the cotton in due course delivered to the Company. The chief beat the drum to assemble his people, and marked out plots by the roadside, and these were then cultivated more or less under his eye.'[2]

As it turned out, cotton cultivation did not develop on large African estates, and within a few years production was almost entirely done on small, scattered, peasant plots. C. C. Wrigley is of the view that the change was due to the attitude of the chiefs.[3] They tended to view land as a capital asset and not as a factor of production; instead of supervising labour on large estates they chose to sell or lease part of their land to dues-paying tenants. Interestingly enough, although the Baganda had been singled out by early explorers as the 'most civilized' or industrious group in East Africa, they did not move as rapidly with cotton as other tribal groups, even though they were the first to cultivate cotton. Up until 1910 they grew the bulk of the crop but the Eastern Province, once provided with transport and ginning facilities, had caught on to it,

[1] Hill, *op. cit.*, p. 325.   [3] *ibid.*, p. 34.
[2] Fallers, ed., *op. cit.*, p. 34

and by 1916 was producing three-quarters of the crop even though their soils were less suited to cotton cultivation.[1]

Two factors contributed to the difference in the speed with which cotton was developed in the two areas once transport facilities were available. In the Eastern Province, feudal dominion and other rights of chiefs were not transformed into or supplemented by legal ownership of land. 'Since the chiefs were unable to convert the land into cash by selling or leasing it, they had to make use of it in some other way, and many of them – particularly in Busoga – did so by the direct cultivation of cotton, converting their customary right to the services of the peasantry into a demand for agricultural labour for as many as fifty-two days in the year. This became a standard practice, not only in Busoga, but also in the "democratic" tribes of Bukedi, Teso, and Lango where the power of the chiefs had previously been very slight and where customary labour services had amounted at most to "a rudimentary form of boon-work".'[2] Thus there were strong pressures on the cultivators of the Eastern Province in addition to personal economic motives. The second factor in the difference was that the peasants of Buganda were in a stronger competitive position than those in the Eastern Province. Whereas peasants in the Eastern Province had few alternatives as a means of earning a living, Ganda peasants had opportunities in the urban areas of Kampala and Entebbe and landowners had to compete for peasants as a source of income. With other ways of earning money, the Baganda had less incentive to produce cotton.

The growth of the economy was remarkable. Cotton exports grew year by year as follows (in 400 lb. bales):

1904–05	54	1909–10	6,209
1905–06	241	1910–11	13,378
1906–07	980	1911–12	20,433
1907–08	3,973	1912–13	25,841
1908–09	3,945	1913–14	27,568

There was a crisis in 1907, due to deterioration of quality, for farmers had been producing their own seed. After 1908 strict regulations were introduced requiring that peasants obtain all their seed from government suppliers. Production was limited to one crop per year, though two might have been possible, and the plants had to be dug up yearly to prevent diseases and pests. Peasants were first instructed to plant on a communal system in which the inhabitants

[1] C. C. Wrigley, 'Buganda: An Outline Economic History', *Economic History Review*, August 1957.   [2] Fallers, ed., *op. cit.*, pp. 35–6.

of a village would join their plots in one area near the road, so as to facilitate instruction and supervision. The peasants objected to this method, preferring to have their plots in the immediate vicinity of their homes. Once they stopped producing their own seed there was less need for close supervision and peasants were allowed to plant where they wished. An advantage to the peasants' system was that insects and blights rarely appeared in small plots whereas they were quite a problem in concentrated areas of cultivation.[1] A typical farm might have up to 8 or 10 acres – about 3 acres of cotton, a few acres of plantains, and perhaps a little coffee or some other crop. Some land was left fallow. Africans could take up the farming of cotton quite easily as land was readily available to them. Since the growing of food, especially plantations, required little labour and most of it was done by the women, there was time for the men to take up the cultivation of economic crops as soon as the benefits became obvious. In 1909 Commissioner Hesketh Bell commented that the methods used by peasants were unbelievably bad and would have resulted in disaster in many another country: 'The simplest and roughest methods of cultivation have prevailed, and in many cases the plants have had to maintain an almost continuous struggle for existence. In spite of all these handicaps the yield has been fair and the profits derived from the cultivation have satisfied the peasant growers. With the adoption of reasonable cultural methods and by the help of competent instructors an immense improvement may be confidently expected.'[2]

Uganda was spared most of the problems caused by European settlers. In 1911 only 640 Europeans lived in Uganda. Of these, 203 were government officials, 183 were connected with the missions, 124 were women and children, and only 130 were engaged in private enterprise – and many of them not on farms.[3] According to Cyril Ehrlich, the primary reasons for the limited expansion of plantation and settler agriculture were: 'the greater attractions of British East Africa, to which applicants were referred; the attitudes of successive governors, whose personal influence on policy was inevitably very great; the surprising rapid success of cotton as a peasant crop; and perhaps, most important, the absence of a clearly defined land alienation law, offering favourable terms to planters'.[4] Adverse

[1] House of Commons, *Sessional Papers* 1909, 'Report on the Introduction and Establishment of the Cotton Industry in the Uganda Protectorate', by Hesketh Bell (Cd. 4910), p. 11. [2] *ibid.*, p. 10.

[3] H. B. Thomas and Robert Scott, *Uganda*, London, 1935, p. 359.

[4] Harlow and Chilver, eds., *op. cit.*, p. 410.

climate discouraged settlers. Governors were willing to try any system of production but would not act to the serious detriment of the native population which was already justifying such tolerance by rapid expansion of cotton cultivation. Despite Colonial Office restrictions on land leases (10,000 acres) and purchase (1,000 acres), Europeans managed to get much of the land that they desired.[1] Rather than governmental interference, the competition for labour from small-hold cotton and coffee and the decline in prices of coffee and rubber were the primary explanation for the failure of the plantation sector to thrive. However, this failure lies in the period after 1913. Until that time labour cost only 3 to 3·5 rupees per month[2] and prices of rubber, coffee, and cocoa allowed ample profit. By 1919, £500,000 was invested in rubber. Between 1911 and 1915, expatriate enterprise rose from 20 or 50 non-native estates with 2,000 acres to 135 estates with 21,675 acres under crops in 1915, primarily in Buganda. The transfer of land to alien enterprise had been slowed by the confused Buganda land settlement and had been forced to enter a money market through purchases from the Ganda chiefs as opposed to almost free grants in Kenya; but these factors explain far less than do comparative profitability calculations, particularly after World War I.

The 1910 boom produced little for export before 1914. Coffee has a three-year gestation period in Uganda and rubber seven years. Thus in 1914, European plantations produced 12,232 cwt. coffee worth £27,169 and about £3,000 in rubber. The figures greatly understate the apparent position of the expatriate planters in 1914, even though these planters did approximate a negligible position in the long run. Even at the 1920 high point of the settlers' fortunes in Uganda, the settlers held only 126,000 acres or 197 square miles as opposed to 3,000 square miles in Kenya, or, more relevantly, 38,000 acres under cultivation as opposed to 176,000 acres in Kenya.[3]

Cocoa, citronella, tobacco, rice, sisal, beeswax, and angora goats were experimented with in the search for African cash crops, but cotton was the overwhelming success. In 1904, £6 worth of cotton was exported. By 1908 the cotton industry was firmly established, forming the largest category of exports at £51,584. In the year ending March 31, 1913, cotton exports totalled £265,714; the next year, with an estimated 100,000 acres under cultivation, cotton exports totalled £317,687. Transportation was the chief bottleneck.

[1] C. C. Wrigley, *Crops and Wealth in Uganda*, Kampala, 1959, p. 28.
[2] *ibid.*, p. 29   [3] *ibid.*, pp. 33–4.

G   193

Commissioner Hesketh Bell wrote in 1908: 'Every peasant in the country appears to be willing to grow cotton on condition that he is not obliged to carry his crop on his head for more than two days' march. . . . The development of the industry on a great scale is only checked by lack of transport facilities from the interior to the lakeshore. . . . Every penny that could be spared from other services during the year was laid out on roads. The line of a main trunk highway connecting Lake Victoria with Lake Albert is surveyed and partly constructed.'[1] It was hoped to end porterage particularly because Africans had to prepare their land for food just at the time the cotton crop needed moving. Good metalled roads could be constructed cheaply due to an abundant supply of lateritic ironstone and a system of local labour instead of taxes, but the budget was too strained to allow as large a programme as was needed.

At first cotton-growing was a Ganda phenomenon. Their long and more penetrating contacts with European missionaries, soldiers, administrators, and traders, and their comparatively acquisitive nature allowed them to advance cotton cultivation rapidly. Also in their favour was the fact that 'in Buganda, a total crop failure is virtually inconceivable, and in the worst of seasons, even with the sketchiest of cultivation, the grower can be sure of a sizeable harvest. Thus the industry was here safe from the kind of setback which repeatedly befell it in Nyanza Province of Kenya, where, as an official commented sadly, the amount and timing of rainfall seemed to be almost never right.'[2]

After 1908, cotton progress was concentrated not in Buganda but in the Eastern Province where the work of European officials and Ganda agents was important in exerting suasion. By 1913–14, 4,000 tons of seed cotton was grown in Busoga, 3,600 in Bukedi, and 1,420 in Lango and 7,500 in Teso, much of the success being attributable to the introduction of the ox-drawn plough.[3] Elsewhere transport difficulties predominated and were usually reinforced by limited governmental development efforts. A. R. Dunbar[4] points out that some cotton, hides, skins, and salt were produced in Bunyoro with encouragement from the Mukama but that transport costs hindered major expansion. Areas like Bunyoro, Toro, and Ankole, like much of Northern Nigeria and the northern territories

[1] Hill, *op. cit.*, p. 326.
[2] Wrigley, *Crops and Wealth*, pp. 15–16.
[3] *ibid.*, p. 20.
[4] A. R. Dunbar, *A History of Bunyoro Kitara*, Nairobi, 1965, p. 115.

of Ghana, had to wait for the Ford lorry and roads to make export production feasible on any but a minimal scale.

Europeans and Asians ginned and marketed the cotton. Hand-gins were used until 1906, but they were prohibited because they gave a low-quality lint. The first power-driven gin was erected in Kampala in that year. By 1914 there were twenty ginneries in the country. For some years the crops were bought by itinerant buyers, but a system of open markets with fixed days was eventually established. Indians ran depots and stores, marketed other crops, and controlled much of the commerce of the country.

Government investment was mostly in the field of transportation, spurred by the need to facilitate the marketing of cotton. In addition to the road building, money was put into steamer and port facilities around Lakes Victoria, Albert and Kgyoga. As early as 1905 traffic demands were exceeding transport capacity on the lakes. There was a tenfold increase in traffic between 1905 and 1913 at Uganda ports, as producers responded to market opportunities afforded by the railway. By 1907, five steamships and one tug were making monthly rounds of Lake Victoria, including stops at the German ports of Shirati, Mwanza, and Bukoba. Three oil-burning ships were added by 1914. In 1911 construction was begun on the Busoga railway which connected Jinja to Namasgali, and a short spur from Kampala to Port Bell was built. With feeder roads, these promised to increase substantially the amount of land available for cotton production.

At the outbreak of World War I, Uganda, like the East Africa Protectorate, had made significant advances and had laid some of the basic groundwork for development. Resources were still severely limited; exports were still smaller than imports (£526,224 and £779,964 respectively), but the balance was improving. Production was better established than in the East Africa Protectorate, and Uganda had managed to avoid many of the problems encountered by her neighbour. The optimism which Uganda inspired was summed up beautifully by Winston Churchill a few years earlier when he said: 'Concentrate on Uganda. Nowhere else in Africa will a little money go so far. Nowhere else will the result be more brilliant, more substantial, or more rapidly realized. Cotton alone should make the fortune of Uganda. All the best qualities of cotton can be grown in the highest perfection. A hundred thousand intelligent landowners occupying 20,000 square miles of suitable land are eager to engage in the cultivation. An industrious and organized population offers the necessary labour.'[1]

[1] Winston Churchill, *My African Journey*, London, 1908, p. 209.

195

BIBLIOGRAPHY

Official Papers

Great Britain. House of Commons, *Sessional Papers*, 1905. 'Annual Statement of Trade of the United Kingdom with Foreign Countries and British Possessions for 1904, Vol. 2' (Cd. 2626).

——, *Sessional Papers*, 1900, 1901, 1902, 1904. 'Report by the Mombasa–Victoria (Uganda) Railway Committee on the Progress of the Works, . . .' (Cd. 355, Cd. 674, Cd. 1080, Cd. 1770 and 2164).

——, *Sessional Papers*, 1895. 'Report of the Committee Appointed to Consider the Question of Railway Communication with Uganda', August 1895 (7833).

——, *Sessional Papers*, 1909. 'Report on the Introduction and Establishment of the Cotton Industry in the Uganda Protectorate' by Hesketh Bell (Cd. 4910).

——, *Sessional Papers*, 1893–94. 'Report on Mombasa–Victoria Lake Railway Survey' (C. 7025).

——, *Sessional Papers*, 1912–13, 1914–16. 'Statistical Tables relating to British Colonies . . .', 1910 (Cd. 6400), 1912 (Cd. 7667).

Books

Delf, George, *Asians in East Africa*, London, 1963.

Dunbar, A. R., *A History of Bunyoro-Kitara*, Nairobi, 1965.

Fallers, L. A., ed., *The King's Men*, London, 1964

Fearn, Hugh, *An African Economy: A Study of the Economic Development of Nyanza Province of Kenya, 1903–1953*, London, 1961

Harlow, Vincent, and Chilver, E. M., eds. *History of East Africa*. Vol. 2, London, 1965.

Hill, M. F., *Permanent Way*, Nairobi, 1949.

Huxley, Elspeth, *White Man's Country*, London, 1935.

Johnston, Harry, *The Uganda Protectorate*, New York, 1902.

Leys, Norman, *Kenya*, London, 1925·

Mungeam, G. H., *British Rule in Kenya, 1895–1912*, Oxford, 1966.

Pim, A. W., *The Financial and Economic History of the African Tropical Territories*, Oxford, 1940.

Robinson, Ronald, and Gallagher, John, *Africa and the Victorians*, London, 1961.

Rotberg, R. I., *A Political History of Tropical Africa*, New York, 1965.

Thomas, H. B., and Scott, Robert, *Uganda*, London, 1935.

Woolf, Leonard, *Empire and Commerce in Africa*, New York, 1920.

Wrigley, C. C., *Crops and Wealth in Uganda: A Short Agrarian History*, Kampala, 1959.

Articles

Ehrlich, Cyril, 'Cotton and the Uganda Economy, 1903–1909', *The Uganda Journal*, September 1957.

Ehrlich, Cyril, 'The Economy of Buganda, 1893–1903', *The Uganda Journal*, March 1956.

Ingham, Kenneth, 'Some Aspects of the History of Buganda', *The Uganda Journal*, March 1956.

Wrigley, C. C., 'Buganda: An Outline Economic History', *Economic History Review*, August 1957.

Chapter 8

EGYPT

by Russell Stone

The modernization of Western Europe touched Egypt well before
it reached the other countries dealt with in this book. The brief
occupation by Napoleon (1798–1801) created a vacuum which was
soon filled by the dynamic and innovative leadership of Mohammed
Ali (in power 1805–49) and his son Ibrahim Pasha. Their actions
included sweeping reforms, large-scale investment, and the founding
of quite 'modern' economic institutions. The reforms affecting rural
peasant life included the beginnings of a change from feudal and
collective land holdings to individual ownership, extension of
cultivated land, extension of irrigation on cultivated land (allowing
double cropping), and most significant of all, introduction of long-
staple cotton as a peasant-grown cash crop in 1821. Long-staple
cotton was later to become Egypt's economic backbone, indeed
lifeline, and it is also important as the medium through which
peasants were first brought into a cash economy (in theory; in fact,
cotton was paid as a tax, and little money actually reached the
peasants).

Transportation and communications were also improved during
Mohammed Ali's reign, although the stress was still on water
transport. The port of Alexandria was improved and linked to the
Nile by a new canal. A well-organized army and an efficient, highly
centralized bureaucracy, for tax collection, give evidence that
organizational and managerial ability were also not lacking in
Mohammed Ali's time. More significant of all, however, was the
industrial development initiated by Ali. While it is true that most of
the factories founded were intended to supply the needs of the army,
and little else, the fact remains that in the early part of the nineteenth
century a great deal of industry was operative in Egypt, much of it
heavy industry. Unfortunately all traces of these industries died
with Mohammed Ali; this was a 'big push' that failed.

The reaction to Mohammed Ali was a return to a completely
agricultural economy. From the time of his death (1849) until the
British occupation (1882), the economic history of Egypt can be

summed up in three topics. First, work continued in improving the system of irrigation. Second, transportation and communications were greatly improved. As in other parts of the world, this period saw the laying of railroads. In the case of Egypt, the first rail line was introduced in 1853, and by 1880 there were almost 1,000 miles of railway, which is a sizeable amount when one considers that south from the end of the Delta, most of Egypt's population is within walking distance of the Nile, which the railroads follow. The railroad system was (and remains today) oriented towards moving goods and people to the Mediterranean (and later, Red Sea) seaports. Overland rail ties to other countries came only at a later date, lasted for a brief period, and were never a serious means of transportation of export commodities.

Third, a rapid accumulation of public debt took place. The Khedive took his first sizeable foreign loan in 1858, and by 1876 government income was insufficient to pay the service charges on a debt which had grown to £98 million. Egypt was, in a very real sense, bankrupt at the beginning of our period.

As a result of the bankruptcy, the *Caisse de la Dette Publique* was organized. Growing from an Anglo-French advisory committee, this body had members from England, France, Austria, Italy, Russia, and Germany, who represented the private financial interests of Egypt's creditors. The *Caisse* had control of certain taxes and other sources of government income, which totalled over half of all revenue during the period 1880–90, and which was devoted to ensuring that interest on the debt was paid. After 1886 a surplus accumulated, which was used to provide a reserve fund for government expenditure, and to amortize the loans. The *Caisse's* influence in Egyptian financial affairs began to recede after 1890, as the relative importance of the taxes it received declined. Its influence died out in 1904, following the Anglo-French Accord which gave the British greatly increased power and freedom relative to the other foreign powers in Egypt. From that time the *Caisse* was simply the fund which collected and paid debt charges for the government.[1]

Political action accompanied the formation of the *Caisse*. The principal debtors, England and France, thought it important that Egypt's governmental and financial affairs be guided beyond the powers of the *Caisse*. A system of Dual Control, whereby British and French advisers were present and influential in Egyptian

[1] R. L. Tignor, *Modernisation and British Colonial Rule in Egypt*, Princeton, 1966, p. 214. I am much indebted to Professor Tignor for his advice in the early stages of preparing this chapter.

internal affairs, was begun. Following a stormy and brief history, this system was replaced in 1882 by the British occupation. From that time until World War I, the virtual ruler of Egypt was the British High Commissioner. The post was filled for most of the period – that is, until 1907 – by Evelyn Baring, Lord Cromer. Much of the economic and administrative advance of Egypt during this period was due to Cromer's leadership and personal activity. However, the fact of missed economic opportunities has also been attributed to Cromer's laissez-faire, liberal economic outlook and his primary, if not sole interest in maintaining Egypt's solvency so the debt could be repaid as quickly as possible. There is also some evidence that Cromer was reluctant to allow Egyptian competition with British home industry, but this seems doubtful.[1]

I. THE DEBT AND THE BRITISH OCCUPATION

Among the countries included in this volume, Egypt is unique in terms of the magnitude of its national debt. Throughout the following analysis it should be borne in mind that the debt represented a chain which weighed the country down through any attempts at economic development. Although the chain became worn down and lightened over time, the debt was a constant drag on government finance and a drain on foreign-exchange balances throughout the period of analysis. Taxes were higher than would otherwise have been necessary, and the government did not have complete control over how its revenues were to be spent. Thus both private and public sources of potential investment were limited.

The debt had not reached its maximum at the beginning of the period. The government of Egypt was on the border of insolvency until almost 1890. In the decade 1880–90, four additional loans were taken, and the debt reached a maximum of £106·8 million in 1890. At the eve of World War I, the debt was still £94·2 million. Annual interest payments on the debt were reduced slightly during the period, from a maximum of £4·5 million in 1885 (46 per cent of ordinary government revenue), to £3·9 million in 1913 (23 per cent of ordinary government revenue). Other drains on ordinary government revenue included military spending, to which an almost constant proportion of government income was devoted, and the anachronous payment of a fixed tribute to the Ottoman Porte! Over the whole period of 1880–1913, expenses of maintaining the army amounted to 5·9 per cent of ordinary government revenue, and tribute pay-

[1] See below, pp. 211–2

ments totalled 5·5 per cent. Thus these three drains on government revenue were a serious barrier to potential economic development. Together they claimed over half the budget in 1880 (52 per cent), and by 1913 they still took up almost one-third of available government funds (33 per cent).[1] Details are shown in Table 8.1.

TABLE 8.1: *Government Revenue and 'Non-productive' Expenses*

	Ordinary government revenue	'Non-productive' regular government expenses in £E thousands			
		Total	Debt payments	Army	Tribute
1880	8,998	4,651	3,529	443	679
		(52%)	(39%)	(6%)	(8%)
1890	10,237	5,415	4,228	522	665
		(53%)	(41%)	(5%)	(6%)
1900	11,447	5,147	3,675	807	665
		(45%)	(32%)	(7%)	(6%)
1910	15,966	5,596	3,922	1,009	665
		(35%)	(25%)	(6%)	(4%)
1913	17,369	5,716	3,925	1,126	665
		(33%)	(23%)	(6%)	(4%)

Source: Egypt, *Annuaire Statistique*, 1914, pp. 406, 418.

It is necessary, however, to point out that a part of the money borrowed in the original debt was put to constructive use. From 1850 to 1880, Egypt's irrigation system was expanded, increasing the total number of feddans[2] under cultivation from about 4·2 million in 1852 to about 4·7 million in 1880.[3] By 1880, almost 1,000 miles of railway were in operation. Only 450 additional miles of track were added during our period of analysis, but at this point Egypt did have adequate rail communications, considering that most of the pale of settlement is virtually within walking distance of the Nile (and the railway) south of the delta. Telegraphic communications were also established, and some loans were used to finance Egypt's share of the construction of the Suez Canal, completed in 1869. As the Khedive's shares in the canal were later sold abroad at a drastically discounted rate, the canal was not a significant economic asset to

[1] Egypt, Ministry of Finance, *Annuaire Statistique*, 1914, pp. 406, 409, 418 and 489–90.
[2] feddan = 1·038 acres.
[3] A. E. Crouchley, *The Economic Development of Modern Egypt*, London, 1938, p. 259.

Egypt during this period of time. It was, however, a serious political liability. Thus, although much of the debt was the result of the Khedive's personal extravagance, some of the money received on loan was used to build a foundation for potential economic growth in the future.

This foundation was built upon by the British administration, but at a slow rate. The early period of the occupation was devoted mainly to political matters, and to the payment of debt charges. Although the preoccupation with political matters characterized the occupation as a whole, after 1888 attention was devoted to the economy as well. Railroad connections to various parts of the country were filled in to make a complete network, and port facilities were improved. Most economic development projects carried on by the government were largely limited to the agricultural sector, where irrigation improvements allowed extension of cultivated area and intensification of cultivation on already worked land, and additional rail lines and spurs facilitated faster marketing of agricultural products.

The British presence was responsible for a number of other changes which were relevant to Egypt's potential for economic development. Reforms in the administrative departments of the government were undertaken, beginning with the finance ministry, and working through the other ministries which were operating. The reforms amounted to cleaning out redundant personnel and positions, and reorganizing the ministries along lines which would assure the maximum of rationality and efficiency possible in a Victorian-model government. While the reforms did not reach out to administrative levels below the central government, they did allow the occupying power to increase its knowledge and control of the country. Also, the potential to initiate change was less likely to be hampered by unfathomable bureaucratic structures. Over time, of course, the number of sinecures again rose, but this time they tended to be filled more and more by British personnel. This became the subject of considerable nationalist agitation. While the potential for a streamlined administrative bureaucracy did not last for long, one lasting effect of the administrative reforms was the collection and publication of reasonably reliable statistics from 1909 on, based on series stretching back, in some cases, to 1880 and covering many aspects of the society.[1]

Although the British administration was faced with the task of maximizing revenue from taxes, it realized that the existing system

[1] These appear in the *Egyptian Statistical Yearbook*, or *Annuaire Statistique*, used as a primary reference for this paper.

of taxation in 1880 was inadequate. This consisted of myriad small taxes in addition to basic land and poll taxes. The small taxes were very costly to administer, and the income from them was negligible. They were abolished early in the British occupation, along with the poll tax. Collection of taxes had previously been carried out at irregular intervals and tax rates had fluctuated unpredictably. Predictability was restored to both the regularity and the stability of tax rates and collection. Tax arrears were wiped out, and as has been suggested, taxes were brought into line with ability to pay.[1] At the beginning of the period, the major source of income was a direct land tax (see Table 8.2 below). This tax was administered inflexibly.

TABLE 8.2: *Government Revenue from Taxes*

(£E thousands)

	Total tax income	Land tax	Customs duties	Special tobacco tax	Other
1881	7,383	4,881	662	97	1,743
		(66%)	(9%)	(1%)	(24%)
1891	8,366	4,994	809	829	1,743
		(59%)	(10%)	(10%)	(21%)
1901	9,190	4,591	1,342	1,221	2,036
		(50%)	(15%)	(13%)	(22%)
1913	11,530	5,041	2,134	1,720	2,635
		(43%)	(18%)	(15%)	(23%)

Source: Egypt, *Annuaire Statistique*, 1914, pp. 410–11.

In fact, annual totals of land tax income barely increased from 1880 to 1913, because land-tax rates were lowered as fast as cultivated area increased. Two other taxes grew steadily in importance during the period of analysis, customs duties and the special tax on tobacco. Both of these are highly flexible taxes, and they grew quickly as incomes of the upper classes rose. The former multiplied $3\frac{1}{2}$ times, and the latter 17 times during the period of analysis. These three taxes constituted over 75 per cent of government income from taxes in both 1881 and 1913, although the increase in tax income from £E7·4 million to £E11·5 million[2] is explained entirely by the increase in the latter two taxes. The interesting question of whether government income from taxes rose more quickly than national

[1] Tignor, *op. cit.*, p. 109.
[2] £E1 = £1 0s. 6¼d. sterling, and the exchange rate remained constant throughout the period 1880–1913.

income is, unfortunately, not answerable because there is no way of estimating national income in this period from available sources.

The labour assessment or *corvée* was also discontinued during this period. It was gradually reduced after 1885 and cancelled altogether in 1889, except for short-term drafts necessary for flood control.[1]

The rule of law and civil order were also improved during this period. It was evident that traditional Islamic law had become inadequate in coping with all aspects of behaviour in society, and the necessity of improving the laws and the courts was obvious. Accordingly, changes in criminal law and the introduction of Western legal codes and court systems occurred during the British occupation. Although the problem was not settled adequately, the beginnings of legal reform can be found in this period. In the area of law enforcement, chaos was reduced to inadequacy. While the armies, both Egyptian and British, were ultimately responsible for exercising power, most of their activities were purely military or political in nature. Law enforcement on the local level had previously been the responsibility of each village leader, and the system was varied and unco-ordinated. After the reorganization of the Ministry of Interior in 1895, local constables were appointed in each village where they did not previously exist, and they were made responsible to regional law enforcement officers. Again, these changes were just a beginning and not a major reform.

A final general effect of the British occupation on Egyptian society which is relevant to economic development can be expressed as the 'demonstration effect'. The term refers to the influence upon the demands, aspirations, and ways of life of some Egyptians which came about by virtue of their contact with British officials and other Europeans. In the case of Egypt this demonstration effect operated largely in the cities, where Egyptians were introduced to European goods, ways of life, and values. This increased the demand for manufactured goods, and therefore created opportunity for some industrialization. This opportunity, as we shall see, was largely missed. It is ironical, and rather unfortunate, that the lessons of European-style aspirations were learned better than the lessons of economic development.

II. ECONOMIC GROWTH, 1880–1913

Irrigation. During our period Egypt was almost entirely an agricultural country, and the main constraint on its growth was irrigated

[1] Tignor, *op. cit.*, p. 122.

land. Major advances in the irrigation system were accomplished. Three aspects of irrigation improvement are worthy of mention, building of dams, maintenance and augmentation of water distribution (canals, pumps, etc.), and engineering and administration of irrigation works.

Two major dams, and several minor barrages and weirs were put into service. The first dam, consisting of two sections, controlled the waters at the head of the Delta. Its construction was completed in 1862, with part of that small portion of the borrowed funds leading to Egypt's bankruptcy that was put to constructive use. The first test of the dam, however, showed that there were serious structural weaknesses, and the whole project was abandoned until 1884, when a subsequent test indicated that, with repairs, the dam could be used. The repairs were effected during the period 1887–90 by British engineers employed as irrigation inspectors by the Ministry of Public Works. The money was obtained from two sources: the 1885 loan taken by the Egyptian government and the reserve fund of the *Caisse de la Dette*. Further repairs were made in 1896 at government expense. A second major dam at Aswan was built during this period, on the initiative of Lord Cromer and his engineer-advisors. The Aswan Dam, completed in 1902, was financed by a loan from a private European banker, Ernest Cassel, to the Egyptian government, with supplementary funds from the reserve of the *Caisse*. This dam was subsequently heightened during the period 1907–12 to increase its capacity. In addition, several smaller barrages were put across the Nile to further even out the seasonal variations in river level and permit perennial irrigation projects at intermediate points along the course of the river and in the delta. Three of these were located at Assiut, Esna, and Zifta.

In addition to the dams themselves, much time and money was devoted to maintaining, improving, and extending the system of irrigation canals and ditches. Although much of this work had been done in an earlier period, it was done poorly and canals had silted up and been dropped from use. Re-dredging, realignment, and unification of the canal system and the methods of water allocation and control occupied the attention of the irrigation advisors and absorbed the irrigation budget of the government throughout the period. Government allocation of funds to irrigation was relatively liberal throughout the period, averaging 8 per cent of regular government revenue during the period 1882–1902.

The Ministry of Public Works, which was responsible for irrigation, was one of the first to be reorganized under Cromer's govern-

205

ment. It employed a battery of British irrigation engineers who had been trained in India. The strength of this ministry, based on a mutal interest in irrigation on the part of British and Egyptian officials, explains in large part why irrigation improvement can be pointed to as one of the major accomplishments relevant to economic growth which took place during the period of analysis.

The outcome of this work was a 11 per cent increase in cultivated area, and, more important, a 61 per cent increase in cropped area (see Table 8.4 below). This was achieved by perennial irrigation, making possible two crops per year. Although the idea of perennial irrigation was first introduced to Egypt under the reign of Moham-med Ali, the statistics for 1877 show the cropped area only slightly greater than the cultivated. In contrast, by the close of our period over 70 per cent of all agricultural land was under perennial irriga-tion.

Population and the land. Despite this enormous investment, the race between land and population was won by population even before our period ended.

The rate of growth of population cannot be established precisely, especially before 1900. Table 8.3 shows the results of the Censuses, but

TABLE 8.3: *Population*

(in thousands)

		Growth % p.a.
1882	6,804	
1897	9,715	2·4
1907	11,287	1·5
1917	12,751	1·2

the figures are not reliable. The 1882 Census is particularly bad, since it was taken in a year of turmoil. It is not impossible that the death rate increased as irrigation spread, but it is highly unlikely that the rate of growth exceeded 1·5 per cent in the last quarter of the nineteenth century. The 1907 Census is considered to be very good, and can be used as a benchmark for projecting the population backwards.

With the spread of irrigation, double cropping increased, so the acreage cropped grew faster than the acreage cultivated. Between 1877 and 1897 the acreage cropped grew at an average rate of 1·8 per cent per annum. This is considerably faster than any likely increase in the population, and therefore indicates an increase in

206

acreage per head. The main factor in this was the completion of the Delta Barrage in 1890 which raised the level of the river and so increased the area that could be reached for double cropping. However, by the end of the century, population growth had caught up with acreage expansion. The growth rate of cropped land between

TABLE 8.4: *Area Under Crops*

(in thousands of feddan)

	Cultivated	Cropped
1877	4,743	4,762
1897	5,088	6,848
1906	5,403	7,662
1916	5,319	7,686

Source: Crouchley, *op. cit.*, p. 259.

1897 and 1906 was only 1·3 per cent, as against a population growth rate which was at least 1·3, and which the census puts at 1·5. Thereafter cropped acreage ceased to grow almost entirely and acres per head fell steadily – the ratio continued to fall steadily for several decades.

This change is clearly revealed in output. The average annual production of cotton rose by 100 per cent over the ten year period 1885–9 to 1895–9, but only by 22 per cent over the next fifteen years to 1910–14,[1] although the price of cotton was falling sharply in the first period, and rising sharply in the second. The change can also be seen in the trade in cereals, for which annual averages moved as follows (in £E thousands):

TABLE 8.5: *Trade in Cereals, Five Year Averages*

	Imports	Exports	Net exports
		(£E thousands)	
1885–9	770	964	+194
1895–9	1,112	947	−165
1905–9	3,261	760	−2,501

Source: Annuaire Statistique, 1914, pp. 303–5. The category is 'cereals, vegetables, flour and other vegetable products', excluding cottonseed and fibres.

Taking prices into account, one may deduce that the volume of exports increased slightly in the first decade, then fell sharply after 1900. Imports also accelerated markedly after 1900, as a growing population was fed increasingly with imported food.

Thus the pattern of the Egyptian economy is one of swift agri-

[1] Computed from Crouchley, *op. cit.*, pp. 263–4.

cultural growth between 1880 and 1900, followed by deceleration with water as the decisive growth factor, and population pressure effecting the deceleration.

Faced with declining land per head the community had four options. The first, which was impractical at this time, was to reduce its birthrate. The second was to use land more intensively, raising its yields per acre. The third option was to switch land to more profitable crops. And the fourth was to develop non-agricultural ways of earning a living. Egypt adopted the third (more profitable crops), but none of the other three options.

If the official statistics are to be believed, the yield of the chief export crop, cotton, actually fell after 1900; specifically from 5·46 kantars[1] per feddan in 1895–9 to 4·16 kantars in 1909–13. Previously yields per feddan had risen substantially; according to Crouchley, had doubled in the preceding fifteen years;[2] more water per acre and wider use of fertilizers would certainly have had some such effect. It is also not difficult to believe that the yield of cotton fell somewhat after 1900, since the acreage increase may have involved lands less suitable for cotton. But the statistics probably exaggerate what actually happened.

According to the statistics, there was a very large increase in the proportion of the crop acreage devoted to cotton. Between 1897 and 1906 the total area cropped increased at an average rate of 91,500 feddans per year (see Table 8.4). Using five-year averages centred on those years, the cotton area increased at an average rate of 51,200 feddans per year. This gives a marginal rate of 0·56, whereas in 1897 cotton occupied only 16 per cent of the cropped area. From 1895–9 to 1910–14 production of cotton increased by only 23 per cent, whereas the crop area in cotton is shown as increasing by 56 per cent. The most likely explanation of these implausible results is that the official figures underestimate the acreage cropped in cotton in 1895–9, thereby giving too big an increase in yields per feddans over the preceding twenty years, and too big a fall over the next twenty.

Nevertheless, it may be accepted that from 1900 Egypt faced a crisis in which population was growing faster than acreage cropped; that the main reaction was to increase the percentage in cotton; and that this either checked the growth of yields per acre, or caused an actual fall. This switch to cotton was helped by the sharp rise in the price of cotton after 1895. The price of cotton was one of those

[1] One kantar = 99·05 lbs.
[2] *op. cit.*, pp. 263–4, for all cotton statistics computations.

which had fallen most during the great 'Kondratieff' depression.[1] The c.i.f. London price of American middling had fallen 34 per cent from 1880 to 1895; it now rose 88 per cent to 1913. This rise in price also more than offset the deceleration in the growth of output. The value of cotton exports, which had risen only 28 per cent between 1885–9 and 1895–9, rose by 103 per cent in the next ten-year period ending 1905–9 (see Table 8.6).

TABLE 8.6: *Exports, Five Year Averages*

(£E thousands)

	Cotton	Cottonseed	Cereals*	Other	Total
1885–9	7,548	1,352	964	1,455	11,319
1890–4	8,561	1,629	1,524	1,366	13,080
1895–9	9,683	1,421	947	1,460	13,511
1900–4	14,228	1,766	794	1,807	18,595
1905–9	19,700	2,271	760	1,799	24,530
1910–14	23,788	2,299	1,745	2,205	30,037

* 'Cereals, flour and agricultural produce.'
Source: Mead,[2] p. 343.

Thus the crisis to which Egypt was moving was masked. Thanks to improved terms of trade the country was more prosperous after 1900 than in the twenty years before, although real output per man was probably about constant, and may even have been falling slightly.

Land tenure. The extent of the switch to cotton at this time was governed by the distribution of land as well as by prices and by technical possibilities

Land ownership fell into two rough categories, by size of unit owned. On the one hand, many peasants owned the land they worked. Thus there were large numbers of ownership units in the 1 to 3 feddan range. On the other hand, there were large units of land, either owned communally by villages, or pledged to the support of mosques, schools, and other religious institutions, or owned by absentee landlords or land companies or foreigners. The royal family owned large estates as well, although some of these were broken up and sold to help pay the debt. In almost all cases, however, the land was divided into small plots which were worked by individual families. In cases of absentee landlordship, the system

[1] See Chapter 2.

[2] D. C. Mead, *Growth and Structural Change in the Egyptian Economy,* Homewood, Ill, 1967.

was typically one of share-cropping. In the case of village-owned land, plots were assigned to each family, and reassigned periodically to even out inequalities in location, fertility, access to water, etc. This system died out during our period of analysis[1] and private ownership of land became the universal pattern.

During the period of analysis cultivated area was extended by 576,000 feddans (see Table 8.4). The only category of landowners which increased in number during this time was those owning less than 5 feddans. Thus, through the period the number of peasants who owned the land they worked increased.[2] This does not mean, however, that the peasants acquired ownership of newly-opened and irrigated land. In fact, the converse appears to be true. The new ands were allocated to large landowners. The peasants simply acquired the land that they were previously working as share-croppers. One outcome of this process was the increase in rural debt, a type of debt which tended to spiral.[3] Another reason for the growth in number of small landholders was the Islamic inheritance law, under which all sons received equal shares of their father's land, causing fragmentation of holdings.

While cotton was the main cash crop grown, it was never grown on the same plot of land more than once every two years. There are two reasons for this. First, although fertilizers began to be used more widely during this period, there was widespread belief that only crop rotation would maintain the fertility of the soil. With the introduction of perennial irrigation, a two-year cycle of four crops became widely utilized. Some larger units followed a formerly used three-year cycle of five crops and one fallow period. In each case only one of the crops in the cycle was cotton. Cotton could have been grown more frequently, but it was believed, although never adequately proven, that even with fertilization more frequent cropping of cotton would deplete the soil fertility. The second reason why cotton was not grown more frequently was that it was considered by the peasants to be a supplement to their subsistence. The first consideration was to grow enough food and animal feed.[4] The cotton was a supplement used to pay taxes (in case of ownership) or rent, and to buy the few necessities which the peasant did not produce for himself. Personal debts, which increased greatly during this period, were also repaid out of cotton earnings . . . when yields permitted.

[1] Tignor, *op. cit.*, p. 247.
[2] G. Baer, *A History of Land Ownership in Modern Egypt, 1800–1950*, London, 1962, pp. 64–9.
[3] *ibid.*, p. 39.   [4] C. H. Brown, *Egyptian Cotton*, London, 1953, pp. 5–14.

Thus the system was one which set limits on how much cotton would be produced. Nowhere is there evidence that the possibility of replacing subsistence agriculture with cash crops was seriously considered. Even in the case of large landowners who hired workers to cultivate their cotton crops (about 70 per cent of the cotton was grown on large estates),[1] the lands were rented out in small plots for the other three cropping periods in the cycle.[2] The area in cotton rose to about the 25 per cent consistent with the rotational system, and did not pass this limit. Failure to recognize the potential for larger-scale production of cotton, replacing food production, was one aspect of the 'missed opportunities' for economic development which characterize Egypt during this period.

Industrialization. Little headway was made in this sector. Very few industrial enterprises existed, and the majority were small craft operations, typically employing less than ten workers. According to the Census of Population, the number of persons engaged in manufacturing rose from 281,000 in 1907 to 361,000 in 1917 – the latter figure being about 8 per cent of the Census figure for the active population, and including the handicraft workers. This growth rate, 2·5 per cent per annum, was relatively high, whether in comparison with the total population growth rate of 1·2 per cent per annum, or by comparison with contemporary Western Europe; but the smallness of the absolute figure indicates how little had been achieved in this sector before the outbreak of World War I.

The outstanding opportunity which was missed was cotton manufacturing. Cotton textiles were the largest import, amounting to about 30 per cent of all imports. Moreover, these imports were growing swiftly. In terms of value, imports of textiles increased at an average annual rate of 4·0 per cent per annum between 1885–9 and 1909–13.

The reason usually given for the failure of Egypt to develop local industries during this period is the policy of the British administration. It is true that the government was unwilling to protect local industry. From 1901, an excise tax of 8 per cent, equal to the current customs duties, was levied on most domestically-produced articles which were sold locally. The move followed on a scheme by some British businessmen to found a large-scale textile industry in Egypt,[3] and some interpreters have imputed Cromer's intention to protect British home industrial interests. In fact, what he seems to have been

---

[1] Tignor, *op. cit.*, p. 234.   [2] Brown, *op. cit.*, pp. 11–13.
[3] Tignor, *op. cit.*, p. 364.

protecting was the government income from customs duties, an income which was necessary to meet government financial obligations.

It seems that there was some degree of threatened administrative deterrence of attempts at industrialization, judging from the tone of some of Cromer's reports. How strong this opposition was is not exactly clear. Actual action was limited to the customs tariffs placed against all imports, including coal, building materials, and other commodities which can be considered necessary factors of production for any local industry. The most recent analysis of Cromer's policy on this issue minimizes the importance of government discouragement of industrial development.[1] Also, from an economic point of view, the potential which Egypt possessed for development of industry far exceeded any administrative deterrents which might have existed. This potential lay mainly in the textile industry, for reasons mentioned above. In textiles, Egypt was the source of the raw material. Thus, given costs of production equal with England's, lower transportation costs in both directions would give Egyptian production a competitive advantage. Also, there is no reason why costs of production should be as high as England's. Labour should have been available for work at fairly low rates, had the opportunity for employment existed, and had the effort to train workers to competitive standards been made. Neither large capital investments nor large-scale factories were necessary, despite the fact that they were evolving in Lancashire. Thus capital requirements and economies of scale did not constitute competitive advantages for English over Egyptian textile industry. There is every reason to believe that indigenous industry in Egypt could have been successful in competing with British textiles, both in the Egyptian market and in foreign markets. This idea is supported by the experience with Indian textiles.

To what, then can the failure to begin textile industries be attributed? One answer is that Egyptians themselves did not recognize the potential for new industrial investment in their own country. The predominant pattern of investment and entrepreneurship in Egypt during this period was one of foreign capital invested in companies managed by foreigners. Rich Egyptians invested in these same companies, but were not active in their management. There

[1] See E. R. J. Owen, 'Lord Cromer and the Development of Egyptian Industry, 1883–1907', *Middle East Studies*, July 1966. The opposite view is taken by C. Issawi, *Egypt at Mid-Century*, London, 1954, p. 37; and by T. Rothstein, *Egypt's Ruin*, London, 1910, pp. 288–309.

were very few all-Egyptian companies with Egyptian entrepreneurs. For instance, in 1914 only 8 per cent of all money invested in joint-stock companies was in operations controlled by Egyptians.[1] Thus, most potential Egyptian industrialists of this period prefered to subordinate their capital to foreign control, and to avoid the risk and responsibility of new forms of independent investment.

In addition, it is clear that the government was able to influence foreigners more easily than native Egyptians, both because it had to grant concessions for foreign investments, and because foreign investors were interested in complementing, not in competing with the industries in their home countries. Also, they were interested in large, short-term profits. This meant a tendency to invest in land and housing speculation or in the purchase of raw materials (cotton), rather than in the production of finished products. If the trend had been different, the British administration in Egypt, in addition, could have discouraged British investors from competing with the British textile industries.

It is not clear, however, that the government would have tried to interfere with attempts by native Egyptians – or even by foreigners who were permanent residents of Egypt – to found industries. Official statements and policies of the administration were neutral, discouraging protection but not initiative. Informal coercion and pressure could not have been exercised so easily by the administration over natives as over foreigners.

The answer to the failure to invest in industry seems rather to lie in lack of imagination and initiative on the part of the rich Egyptians. They tended to spend their money on luxuries, which were all imported either because demand was too small to justify the setting up of local production of luxury goods, or because the desire to consume luxury goods exceeded the desire to produce them. They also tried to increase their land holdings (often the source of their wealth to begin with), and invested in existing, European-run companies. During this period, either the Egyptian upper classes failed to realize that their country had a strong potential for industrial development in textiles, or else they simply lacked the ambition and initiative to strike out in this new line of endeavour.

Regardless of the reasons for the failure to industrialize, the point remains that there was a significant and unfortunate 'missed opportunity' for development. While the period 1880–1913 may be characterized as one during which the infrastructure and other elements of the preconditions for development were being prepared,

[1] Crouchley, *op. cit.*, p. 273.

it must also be characterized as one in which the possibility for industrial development was overlooked.

Foreign investments in Egypt. A great deal of private foreign capital was invested in Egypt, particularly after the turn of the century when bankruptcy was no longer a serious threat. By 1914 there was more than £E100 million of paid-up stock in joint stock companies, of which £E92 million was in companies controlled by foreign investors. The value of stock which was actually held in Europe was somewhat less, about £E71 million.[1] While much of this foreign capital in joint stock companies represented reinvested dividends (dividends in the latter part of our period of analysis averaged around 9 per cent per year), foreign domination of joint stock companies was very strong. It has been estimated[2] that foreign-owned land, private loans, and private investment brought the total of private foreign investment in Egypt up to £E200 million by 1914. This was in addition to the public debt, £E94 million in 1913, of which about £E86 million was held in Europe, and the Suez Canal shares, valued at £E14·2 million, all held abroad. Not only were the amounts of foreign investment quite large (over £E300 million) but the proportion of total investment which was European was an overwhelming 85 per cent or more.

The composition of the Egyptian economy explains the pattern of foreign investment during this period. In 1914, over 72 per cent of all investment in foreign-controlled joint-stock companies was in mortgage and land companies. More was invested in transportation and other forms of infrastructure, and very little was in manufacturing industry. Most of the foreign companies operated under special concessions granted by the government, a part of the broader capitulations system which governed the personal status of foreigners in Egypt. Thus the government was able to influence, to some extent, how foreign funds would be invested. There is no evidence, however, that much influence was necessary. The investment went where the returns were highest, namely operations tied to the cotton crop (transportation, canals, irrigation), and land speculation. The latter was fruitful because of earlier efforts to extend the margin of agriculture, and because of the mounting pressure of population on the land.

Private domestic (Egyptian) investment followed one of two patterns. Either it was channelled into relatively small Egyptian-owned companies, or it went into minority shares in the larger, European-controlled companies, as mentioned above. This capital

[1] Crouchley, *op. cit.*, p. 273.   [2] Tignor, *op. cit.*, p. 361.

could have been invested relatively free from British administrative influence. This did not occur, however, and it is another aspect of the 'missed opportunities' for industrial development.

Despite the unfortunate direction which most of the private foreign investment took in Egypt during this period, the fact remains that much of the profit was reinvested in the country, and along with speculation came investments which did contribute to Egypt's potential for economic development.

III. GROWTH FACTORS

We have dealt with the major elements accounting for economic growth before World War I, especially transportation, irrigation and foreign investment. In this section we note briefly two other elements which were still minor in 1913, but which had their beginnings in our period, and would become more important later. These are the emergence of domestic financial institutions, and the build-up of education.

Financial institutions. Prior to our period, all the banks operating in Egypt were foreign institutions. However, in the period 1880–1913, three of the four new banks which began operations in Egypt had their head offices in Cairo. However, all except one, the National Bank of Egypt founded in 1898, were based on foreign capital. The National Bank of Egypt, managed by British advisors, was set up to serve as a central bank. Although it began by carrying on conventional commercial transactions, it also issued paper currency which slowly replaced both Egyptian and foreign coins in circulation. Until the turn of the century, all the banks in operation concentrated on short-term lending, in large amounts and mainly to commercial interests and large land companies. Thus they were of little use to the majority of native Egyptians.

This situation began to change at the turn of the century, with the founding of the Post Office Savings Banks. This service of the post offices was intended to introduce the idea and provide the opportunity for saving to all the people of the country. From a slow start of 6,740 depositors in 1901,[1] the system grew to 282,401 depositors in 1,929 branches throughout the country in 1913.[2] In 1913, a special department was begun, called the Rural Savings Banks, which was even more specialized in trying to introduce banking to the peasants. The postal carriers were authorized to act as bank tellers on the spot. It is clear that this operation was important

[1] *Annuaire Statistique*, 1909, p. 125.　　　　[2] *idem*, 1914, pp. 538–44.

for introducing all segments of the Egyptian population to the idea of financial institutions and savings.

In 1902 the Agricultural Bank of Egypt was founded. Its purpose was to provide long-term, relatively low interest loans in small amounts to peasants. Its ten-year life was a rocky one, and it cannot be considered a success in terms of remaining solvent, much less making a profit. However, it was the first lending institution which was conceived with the economic interests of the majority of native Egyptians in mind; it did put some money into the hands of very small landowners, and it apparently succeeded in driving out the private money-lenders from the villages, where they had previously charged usurious rates.[1]

Most important, it helped in the task of educating the peasants in the use of a system of currency and a modern banking system. The lesson was undoubtedly useful in beginning to change attitudes toward the possibility of economic development, and it may explain the success of banks which were started after World War I.

Education. Achievements in education were not impressive during this period. Failure to devote more attention and funds to the question of education has been one of the main criticisms of the British occupation of Egypt. Statistics are scarce, and likely inaccurate even in comparison with other statistics for Egypt during this period. However, there were apparently 4,817 schools of all types (public, private, all levels, all languages) in 1879.[2] Government statistics show this number had increased only to 5,229 in 1913.[3] These figures included a majority of *kuttabs*, traditional primary schools in which only the Koran was taught, by rote. The contribution these made to potential for economic development was minimal. The statistics for all other kinds of schools (public, private, all levels, all languages) are given in Table 8.7. Government interest in improving the schools did not come until fairly late in the period. This is evident by the increased number of schools after 1900. Also, after the turn of the century more attention was paid to the improvement and co-ordination of curricula.

Thus, some foundations for future advance were laid during this time. Before 1902 government spending on education never exceeded 1·0 per cent of the current budget. Thereafter it rose to 3·2 per cent, still low but nevertheless rising.[4] In 1880 the *Ecole Normale* for the

[1] Aukland Colvin, *The Making of Modern Egypt*, New York, 1906.

[2] See Z. Y. Hershlag, *Introduction to the Modern Economic History of the Middle East*, Leiden, 1964, p. 107.

[3] *Annuaire Statistique*, 1914, pp. 75–6.   [4] Tignor, *op. cit.*, p. 346.

training of teachers was begun. Special schools for advanced training in technical subjects such as medicine, law, engineering, agriculture, and veterinary medicine which were founded earlier in the nineteenth century, continued to operate, and their enrolments gradually grew. Most graduates tended to enter the civil service, but in positions

TABLE 8.7: *Number of Schools 1880–1913*

(exclusive of *kuttabs*)

1880	114
1890	241
1900	465
1907	735
1913	1,135

Sources: Egypt, *Annuaire Statistique*, 1909, p. 194, and 1914, pp. 75–6.

subordinate to British administrators and advisors. A few students began to study abroad, in Europe. In 1882, the government sent 38 students abroad on stipends, and another nine were sent to study by their families.[1] In the period 1907–10, 59 students were sent abroad at government expense.[2] Apparently about two-thirds of them studied the humanities, however, rather than engineering or other technical subjects which are more pertinent to the needs of economic development. The Egyptian University was founded in 1908. The university had a secular curriculum, in contrast to the traditional religious teaching at Al Azhar, the seat of Islamic higher education since the Middle Ages. Although two-thirds of Egyptian students abroad pursued a humanistic curriculum by choice, those at home had no real option, since the Egyptian University offered no technical training. In the first term, the courses taught were Muslim civilization, ancient civilization, history, geography, and English and French literature.[3] Although enrolment exceeded expectations, the university did not tend to meet the country's needs for economic development until a later period. The humanistic tendency probably helps to explain why the early graduates were much more effective as political and nationalist leaders of their country in the twenties and thirties of this century than they were as economic developers. During this period, education for girls also began to become an accepted practice. This initiated the movement for female equality and freedom

[1] J. Heyworth-Dunne, *An Introduction to the History of Education in Modern Egypt*, London, 1938, p. 436.

[2] Tignor, *op. cit.*, p. 388.

[3] M. K. Harby and el-S. M. el-Azzawi, *Education in Egypt in the Twentieth Century*, Cairo, 1960, p. 15.

which remains an important issue in Egypt and other countries of the Near East.

Thus, our period of analysis saw the beginnings of ongoing Western-style education. The first steps were weak ones, but then the needs for educated people are not that great in the early stages of economic development. However, the needs which do exist lie in the spheres of engineering, technology, and teacher training, rather than in humanistic studies and educational requisites for obtaining civil service appointments. The latter patterns were more predominant in Egypt, and they harmed her potential for economic development. In later years, Egypt's national struggle for independence was limited almost entirely to the political sphere, to the exclusion of serious attempts at economic and, particularly, industrial advance. There is reason to believe that the pattern of education during the period of our analysis is in part responsible for the kinds of activities undertaken by the Egyptian leading classes in later years. Thus the basis for future political action finds its roots in the education system and subjects taught prior to World War I.

IV. CONCLUSION

Our period begins hopefully. The irrigated acreage extends faster than the population, and output per head is substantially increased. Some of this is lost in adverse terms of trade for cotton, nevertheless there is a substantial net gain per head. Simultaneously Egyptian administration is streamlined, albeit under foreign domination.

The great challenge comes after 1900, when population catches up with acreage, and further progress requires either more intensive use of resources or the creation of alternative ways of making a living. Neither of these opportunities is seized. Agricultural output per head is constant or declining, and the industrial opportunity is neglected. The crisis is masked up to 1913 by a sharp improvement in the terms of trade, but thereafter the country's output per head falls significantly.

Egyptian historians blame Lord Cromer for not interesting himself sufficiently in industrialization, if not actually preventing it. This we have seen is too narrow a view. If Egyptian or foreign capitalists had been inclined to create a cotton-manufacturing industry they could have done so. The essential cause of failure is that Egypt had in 1880 no native entrepreneurial class, and, unlike India or Brazil or Colombia, had failed to produce one even by 1913. This resulted more from the ways of life and thought of the Egyptian upper classes than from the potential hostility of Lord Cromer.

218

BIBLIOGRAPHY

Official Papers

Egypt. Ministère des Finances. Direction de la Statistique, *Annuaire Statistique*, 1909, 1914. Cairo.

——. Ministry of Finance. Statistical Department *Industrial and Commercial Census, 1947*. Cairo, 1955.

Great Britain. House of Commons, *Sessional Papers*, 1890–91, 1901, 1912–13, 1914. 'Statistical Abstract for the Principal and Other Foreign Countries . . .' (C. 6285, Cd. 486, Cd. 6099, Cd. 7525).

Books

Arminjon, Pierre, *La Situation Economique et Financière de l'Egypte*, Paris, 1911.

Baer, Gabriel, *A History of Land Ownership in Modern Egypt, 1800–1950*, London, 1962.

Brown, C. H., *Egyptian Cotton*, London, 1953.

Cleland, Wendell, *The Population Problem in Egypt*, Ph.D. thesis, Columbia University, New York, 1936.

Colvin, Aukland, *The Making of Modern Egypt*, New York, 1906.

Cromer, E. B., *Modern Egypt*, 2 volumes, New York, 1908.

Crouchley, A. E., *The Economic Development of Modern Egypt*, London, 1938.

Cunningham, Alfred, *Today in Egypt*, London, 1912.

Eman, André, *L'Industrie du Coton en Egypte*, Cairo, 1943.

Feis, H., *Europe, the World's Banker, 1870–1914*, New Haven, 1930.

Hansen, Bent and Marzouk, G. A.. *Development and Economic Policy in the U.A.R.* Amsterdam, 1965.

Harby, M. K. and el-Azzawi, el-S. M., *Education in Egypt in the Twentieth Century*, Cairo, 1960.

Hershlag, Z. Y., *Introduction to the Modern Economic History of the Middle East*, Leiden, 1964.

Heyworth-Dunne, J., *An Introduction to the History of Education in Modern Egypt*, London, 1939.

Holt, P. M., ed., *Political and Social Change in Modern Egypt*, London, 1968.

Issawi, Charles, ed., *The Economic History of the Middle East, 1880–1914*, Chicago, 1966.

——, *Egypt at Mid-century*, London, 1954.

——, *Egypt in Revolution*, London, 1963.

Little, Tom, *Egypt*, London, 1958.

Lloyd, G. A., *Egypt since Cromer*, Vol. I, London, 1933.

MacKenzie, N. F., *Notes on Irrigation Works*, New York, 1910.

Marlowe, J., *Anglo-Egyptian Relations, 1880–1953*, London, 1954.

Mead, D. C., *Growth and Structural Change in the Egyptian Economy*, Homewood, Ill., 1967.

219

O'Brien, P. K., *The Revolution in Egypt's Economic System*, London, 1966.
Rifaat, M. A., *The Awakening of Modern Egypt*, London, 1947.
——, *The Monetary System of Egypt*, London, 1935.
Rothstein, T., *Egypt's Ruin*, London, 1910.
Tignor, R. L., *Modernization and British Colonial Rule in Egypt, 1882–1914*, Princeton, 1966.

Articles

Anonymous, 'Construction, Development and Organization of the Egyptian State Railways, Telegraphs and Telephones System', *L'Egypte Contemporaine*, January 1933.
Baster, A. S. J., 'Origins of British Banking Expansion in the Near East', *Economic History Review*, October 1934.
Bresciani-Turroni, Constantino, 'Egypt's Balance of Trade', *Journal of Political Economy*, June 1934.
Craig, J. I., 'Distribution of Landed Property in Egypt', *L'Egypt Contemporaine*, January 1913.
——, 'Notes on the Cotton Statistics in Egypt', *L'Egypt Contemporaine*, March 1911.
——, 'Statistics on the Yield of Cotton', *L'Egypt Contemporaine*, November 1911.
Crouchley, A. E., 'A Century of Economic Development, 1837–1937', *L'Egypte Contemporaine*, February–March 1939.
——, 'The Visible Balance of Trade since 1884', *L'Egypte Contemporaine*, March–April 1935.
Issa, M. K., 'The Economic Factor behind the British Occupation of Egypt in 1882', *L'Egypte Contemporaine*, October 1964.
Scott-Moncrieff, C. C., 'Irrigation in Egypt', *The Nineteenth Century*, Vol. 17, 1885.
Owen, E. R. J., 'Lord Cromer and the Development of Egyptian Industry, 1883–1907', *Middle Eastern Studies*, July 1966.
Todd, J. A., 'The Market for Egyptian Cotton in 1909–1910', *L'Egypte Contemporaine*, January 1911.

Chapter 9

CEYLON

by J. Edwin Craig, Jr.

The years 1880 and 1913 delineate a period of remarkable progress in the island economy of Ceylon. The dollar value of exports grew at an average annual rate of 5·4 per cent. Besides, the economy became highly diversified. In 1880 one crop, coffee, accounted for 60 per cent of all exports. This crop had virtually disappeared by 1913 when, as Table 9.1 shows, three different crops had attained significance, tea with 35 per cent of exports, rubber with 26 per cent and coconut products with 20 per cent. The island had spent heavily on infrastructure, and probably had the highest *per capita* output in all the Far East, excluding Japan.

Yet in a sense this was not one economy, but several. The richest part was the European plantation economy, which had opened up lands hitherto unoccupied, and imported labour from India with which to cultivate them. At the other end of the spectrum were the subsistence farmers growing rice, and hardly affected by the planta-

TABLE 9.1: *Exports from Ceylon,* 1913*

(Rs. million)

Tea	88
Rubber	61
Copra	21
Coconut oil	17
Desiccated coconut	8
Other	38
	233

* Ceylon is well covered by statistics, in Censuses, Trade Reports, Blue Books, Annual Reports, etc. There is a fine collection in Donald R. Snodgrass, *Ceylon: An Export Economy in Transition*, Homewood, Ill., 1966, which is the source of all statistics quoted in this paper unless otherwise stated.

tion economy, which imported its own rice as well as its own labourers. Yet Ceylon was not wholly a dual economy since there were two intermediate groups, having in common with the European

221

planters that they also grew the 'plantation' crops for export. One was a group of Ceylonese planters, growing such crops on fairly large estates of their own; and the other a group of very small farmers doing the same, especially in rubber and coconuts. The spillover of plantation experience to these two groups is notable because it seems to have gone farther than in the Philippines, in Java, or elsewhere in the Far East.

In what follows we shall first trace the history of the adoption of the plantation crops in the island, and then try to estimate the impact on the three groups of Ceylonese farmers.

I. THE PLANTATION CROPS

The plantation system was introduced by the British in the 1820s. The Portuguese, and then the Dutch, had occupied the island for two and a half centuries without developing a technique for the systematic exploitation of the island's agricultural wealth. Arriving in 1580 in time to take advantage of the break-up of the old Sinhalese feudal kingdoms, the Portuguese did little more than open up the western maritime provinces and the Jaffna peninsula in the north to Western culture and Christianity. The Dutch, who drove out the Portuguese in 1658, made a somewhat more permanent impression on the island. Although the main interests of the Dutch government were the exploitation of the cinnamon forests and pearl fisheries and the maintenance of the capital, Colombo, as a trading station, Dutch settlers arrived in sufficient numbers to attempt a limited modernization and expansion of the agricultural sector. Contemporary accounts reveal that attempts were made to introduce pepper, coffee, and sugar cane, and that coconut acreage was greatly expanded. Further, seeking to reduce Ceylonese dependence on rice imports from southern India and Indonesia, the Dutch introduced slave labour to resettle and cultivate rice fields and to rebuild irrigation dikes ruined by the Portuguese wars. These efforts necessitated the co-operation of the local Sinhalese chieftains and thus led to the creation of the Sinhalese middle class, the Mudaliyars, who would continue to play an important role in modernization under British rule. A final accomplishment of the Dutch was the virtual destruction of Kandy, the last of the Sinhalese kingdoms, by devastating wars accompanied by economic blockade. Since Kandy occupied the central highlands where the great plantation crops of coffee and tea could be grown, the Dutch in effect prepared the fertile soil for the implanting of the British plantation system.

222

The British: conquest, colonization, and coffee. When the British arrived to stay in 1796, the Ceylonese economy could be almost fully described as based on subsistence agriculture, exploitation of the rain forests, and smallholdings of coconuts. In the first thirty years of their occupation, the British did not substantially alter this description, although during these years they laid the ground work for extremely rapid change after 1830. From the very beginning, Ceylon was much more valuable to the British than it had ever been to either the Dutch or the Portuguese. The island was viewed as a major link binding India and the British possessions in the East into a single empire. Thus its harbours must be developed and the island must rest firmly under British domination; the British could not settle for the tribute-paying status of Kandy that the Dutch and Portuguese had agreed to.

The Kandyan rebellion of 1815 forced the British to recognize the wisdom of the old Kandyan proverb that Kandy would never be conquered until an invader drove a road from the highlands to the sea. By the mid-1820s there existed military roads linking Kandy with the western port of Colombo and eastern port of Trincomalie. This was a notable accomplishment given the fact that, prior to the British activity, roads in Kandy were virtually non-existent. During the next twenty-five years the majority of total public expenditures went to the construction and maintenance of a network of roads – most of them toll – extending throughout the western maritime provinces with major branches into the highlands and the northern, eastern, and southern provinces. By 1841 the roads were being metalled for greater durability. Most of these early roads were built by compulsory labour, a practice sanctioned by tradition which required a period of annual service of natives holding lands in service tenure.

While tightening their hold on the island by improving communications, the British set about establishing an efficient system of administration. In accomplishing this end, they eventually welcomed the assistance of the Mudaliyars, the Ceylonese Moors, and the remaining Dutch burghers. It should be noted that in the process of early British colonization, several low-country Sinhalese fortunes were made in Kandy and outlying provinces on government timber, road construction, and rent collection contracts. British colonization was not merely an administrative veneer, but rather rested heavily on the active assistance of native Sinhalese and thus provided a natural inroad for modernizing influences on traditional village life.

But to speak of British colonial policy for Ceylon in terms of

223

administrative techniques and public expenditures is to miss the point; for the story of coffee in Ceylon is the story of early British colonization of Ceylon. Before the emergence of coffee, the British exhibited no clear intentions as to what they planned to do with the island, other than to develop its harbours. Once coffee arrived and was shown to be profitable, all other policies became subordinate to a single overriding interest – the welfare of the coffee estate system.

Coffee was first planted by the British in Ceylon in 1824. The plant had been introduced by the Dutch, but the failure of these invaders to gain control of Kandy had made the profitable growth of coffee impossible. The plant thrives only at elevations between 1,500 feet (above sea level) and 4,500 feet; only the central highlands occupied by Kandy contained large areas of unoccupied territory satisfying this requirement, the coastal plains being unsuitable because of excessive rainfall and too high temperatures.

The expansion of the coffee industry in Ceylon fits very nicely into the standard format for the development of monoculture in a tropical country: large homogeneous areas of unclaimed or seized land highly suited to the crop's cultivation are available; Europeans after a time discover the profitability of the crop; the colonial government makes the land available and provides the necessary roads; the crop 'catches on', leading to wildfire expansion to gain a share in its profitability; eventually the entire homogeneous area (barring price declines) is planted in the single crop. This is indeed the story of coffee in Ceylon, but a few details are relevant to events in our period of consideration, 1880–1913.

One is the failure of native Sinhalese to gain control of the highland plantations. When the British conquered the kingdom of Kandy, they declared all lands for which no clear property title existed to be crown lands. As a result of the feudal traditions and the confusion of the Dutch retreat, practically all of Kandy passed into the crown's hand, to be disposed of at will. After Kandy was secured and the roads built, the crown lands were made available at 5 shillings per acre, virtually a giveaway price, especially given the increasingly obvious high profitability of coffee. The curious part of this method of disposal is that so few of the lands passed into the hands of the native Sinhalese. In the early years of coffee, money could not have been a serious handicap, for at 5 shillings per acre, there must have been many Sinhalese entrepreneurs (even villagers) able to finance large purchases. Further, the agricultural technicalities did not require the existence of large plantations, since economies of scale in coffee production are inconsequential. Yet most of the Kandy lands passed into large plantation holdings. The explanation of the early appearance of the plantation system must be that the British administration followed a definite land policy of preferential treatment for Europeans, particularly those in the government service. The fact that most administrative officials did in fact secure large holdings in the 1820s and 1830s substantiates this thesis. Only after the wildfire expansion of coffee had begun in the 1830s and produced extensive speculation in land could money have been a serious impediment to native participation in the crown-lands market.

A second point to be made is that very little foreign capital was involved in the development of the coffee plantation system. British investors were capital-shy throughout the coffee era. Although very little capital was required for the establishment of a coffee plantation – labour was hired cheaply to clear the land; the plant required little care during the gestation period; only seasonal labour was necessary for harvesting – that which was needed was supplied out of the savings of workers in the government service. The costs (greatly reduced by the use of compulsory labour) of road construction and maintenance were paid for out of tolls and taxes on the gains from exports.

Thirdly we must note the failure of the Sinhalese peasantry to participate in the plantation economy once the land had been cleared and planted in coffee. The refusal of the Sinhalese to work on the plantations forced the plantation owners to import Tamil labourers, the 'South Indian coolie'[1] from southern India, starting in 1828. The importation of Tamil labourers remained the major source of plantation labour in a labour-scarce island throughout the pre-World War I era. The reasons for the disinclinations of Sinhalese to work on the plantations are many, probably the most important of which was the harshness of estate life compared with the relative ease of village life. Although village agriculture was very definitely subsistent, there was only occasional danger of starvation provided a minimal effort was made to tap the riches of the rain forests. In contrast, estate wages were extremely low, living conditions were dismally bad (there exist records of as many as 16 coolies living in a 10-foot square room), and plantation managers were often quite cruel. In sum, the small financial gain offered by plantation owners simply could not compensate for the relative ease and freedom of village life. The British were not the first to encounter this problem: the kings of ancient Ceylon also had had to import

[1] 'Coolie' was the Indian word for a labourer on daily wages.

H   225

Indian labour to harvest the cinnamon crop (a very nasty job) in the forests.

We must not give all credit to Sinhalese dislike for hard work and low wages, for there was also very definitely at least one pressing economic factor contributing to the reluctance to join plantation labourers. That factor consists of the traditional scarcity of labour (tropical diseases and constant warfare had established this) in a highly labour-intensive agricultural economy. Paddy (rice) production, the source of the bulk of the Ceylonese diet, requires large labour inputs virtually year round; further, most villagers had small gardens of jungle crops – coconut, cocoa, coffee – requiring intermittent attention. Thus a family could ill afford to have part of its work force earning a pittance on a plantation when the missing pair of hands could well be used in the harvesting of paddy or the cultivation and harvesting of its own coffee plants.

Finally, we should take note of the fairly extensive independent participation of the Sinhalese peasantry in the coffee industry. The cultivation of coffee was so simple as to make anyone holding a few square feet of extra land in the cooler parts of the western provinces a viable coffee producer. Evidently most Sinhalese took advantage of this natural blessing, so much so that at the height of the coffee era, approximately one-fourth of all coffee exports were produced on smallholdings. But peasant participation was not limited to primary production. Before the construction of the railroads, planters were dependent on native-owned bullock carts to haul coffee to Colombo and to bring supplies, particularly rice, to Kandy. Once the railroads were in use, native Sinhalese were employed to run them. Thus the village peasantry probably was quite active in the ancillary services necessary for the coffee industry. Much of this labour was undoubtedly casual, but it was significant in that it established additional connections between the plantation economy and village life.

These, then, are the essentials of the story of coffee in Ceylon. The first boom period came to an end in the late 1840s when prices fell and speculation in land collapsed. This setback, however, was only temporary and was followed by the great coffee era of the 1850s and 1860s. Further expansion of production was spurred by the construction of the Colombo–Kandy railroad between 1863 and 1867. The demise of coffee resulted from the appearance and rapid spread of the leaf disease *hemalia vextatrix*. Under the attack of the disease coffee production began to decline rapidly after 1870 and only an accompanying rise in price and increase in acreage planted

226

prevented a fall in the total value of the export crop. After 1880 the ravages of the disease were such that the value of annual coffee exports entered a stage of final decline, and by 1886 the coffee industry in Ceylon was, for all practical purposes, dead.

Thus our period of study 1880–1913 begins in a year of depression and in a decade of transition. If coffee was the immediate cause of a bankrupt island economy in 1880, its long-run legacy was not one of bankruptcy. Rather, coffee established a money economy in the island and brought prosperity to native islanders involved in the trade. In addition, it opened up the central highlands and left behind vast acreages of cleared lands. If in 1880 the originator of the plantation system was dead, the system itself was not. In 1880 the modern sector of Ceylon was a plantation system in search of a crop.[1]

After coffee, a search for a crop. The first contender for the position formerly held by coffee was cinchona, a jungle tree long known in Ceylon. (When dried, the bark of the cinchona tree yields the alkaloid, quinine.) In 1872 there were only 500 acres of cinchona in Ceylon, but the profitability of the bark product and the rapid demise of coffee caused an expansion of acreage to 65,000 acres in 1883. The quantity of exports grew from 1·2 million pounds in 1880 to 15·4 million pounds in 1886. The potential of cinchona as a major plantation crop, however, was severely limited by the fact that the plant grows best at altitudes above 4,000 feet, higher than most of the coffee estates. Further, the demand for quinine, a medicinal product, was apparently highly inelastic, and the enormous increases of production in Ceylon were more than matched by heavy increases in exports from Java. Thus after 1880 prices fell rapidly, from twelve shillings per ounce to one shilling in 1886. To complicate the matter, Ceylonese production was hampered by the attacks of a canker disease. Apparently world production remained at high levels, for the price of cinchona hovered around one shilling per ounce throughout the 1890s. As a result Ceylonese planters turned to more profitable crops, and by 1906, no more than 450 acres were planted in cinchona.

A similar effort was made for the production of cocoa after 1875. Cocoa was never an important crop, primarily because temperature requirements limited its growth to land areas between 500 and 2,000 feet above sea level. Further, the tree requires much shade

[1] Excellent surveys of the history of Ceylon prior to 1880 may be found in S. Arasaratnam, *Ceylon*, Englewood Cliffs, NJ, 1964, and E. F. C. Ludowyk, *The Story of Ceylon*, London, 1962.

227

and protection from wind, neither of which could be provided on the cleared plantation lands without planting other trees. Also, after harvesting and fermentation, the cocoa berry requires drying in the sun; artificial heat generally yields less satisfactory results. This last requirement produced a major problem for cocoa production in rainy Ceylon. Given such a combination of factors, it is not surprising that cocoa failed to catch on as a plantation crop and that by 1904 cocoa acreage amounted to only 470 acres.

The rise of tea. The period 1880–1913 in Ceylonese economic development was clearly dominated by the tea industry, yet in 1880 few persons familiar with the island economy would have ventured that this would necessarily be the case. The tea bush had been introduced into the island in the 1860s, but the profitability of coffee had prevented any serious production of tea. When coffee began its rapid decline, planters were slow to turn to tea because of the initial high profitability of cinchona, which, lacking the long (three to six years) gestation period of the tea bush, offered a faster return on investment. Further, because tea necessitated the construction of a factory on the estate for the processing of the tea leaves, the product required large capital outlays at a time when most planters had been ruined by coffee and were unable to obtain credit.

In spite of these early obstacles the tea industry soon achieved dominance, primarily for two reasons. One, the plant was, if anything, more suited to the homogeneous estate system than even coffee had been, and greatly more so than any alternative crop. Tea could be grown at a greater range of altitudes – 2,500 to 6,000 feet, with the best above 4,000 feet – than could coffee, and the heavy tropical rainfall, which had constantly endangered the coffee crop in the drying stages, actually increased the productivity of the tea bush. And two, the rising demand of the British Victorian working class for a strong stimulating but non-alcoholic beverage had forced the price of the black tea of India and Ceylon upwards around 1880. As a result, extremely large profits could be obtained once development costs were ended.

The growth of the Ceylonese tea industry between 1882 and 1914 is documented in Table 9.2. After 1882 acreage, quantity produced, and total value of exports of tea increased rapidly; by 1890 the value of tea exports was greater by far than any other export crop. The value of tea exports continued to increase up until 1897, with an average of 20,000 acres being added to production each year.

A few comments should be made on the nature of the tea industry

228

TABLE 9.2: *The Ceylonese Tea Industry, 1882–1914*

Year	Quantity (million lb.)	Acres	Unit values (Rs.)	Total value (Rs. thousand)
1882	1	15	0·85	592
1885	4	121	0·71	2,482
1890	46	236	0·50	22,900
1895	99	323	0·50	49,291
1897	114	405	0·41	46,931
1900	149	405	0·36	47,611
1905	142	458	0·42	59,564
1907	180	438	0·42	74,635
1910	184	581	0·46	84,137
1914	194	487	0·46	89,726

Sources:
Snodgrass, *op. cit.*, Table A–52, Appendix.
S. Rajaratnam, 'The Growth of Plantation Agriculture in Ceylon 1866–1931', *The Ceylon Journal of Historical and Social Studies*, Vol. IV, Jan.–June 1961, pp. 6–7, Ceylon.
Registrar General's Department, *The Ceylon Blue Book*, various years.

in Ceylon. Tea differed substantially from coffee in that there existed definite economies of scale in tea production and processing, a factor which tended to encourage large-scale operations for efficient production. The most important economies of scale were encountered in the processing stage, where large factories involving substantial capital outlays were required for fermentation, drying, and packing. Further, since flushing (picking the tea leaves) is done year round in Ceylon, a steady well-organized labour force was necessary, which in turn made the presence of good managers more important than had been the case with coffee. At the same time, the efficient use of managerial talent certainly introduced further economies in large-scale operation. Thus, in contrast with the situation of coffee, tea was most successfully grown on large-scale plantations. (Nowadays small growers sell their leaves to central factories, but this was rare in the nineteenth century.)

An additional point of interest is the refusal of the Sinhalese peasantry to work for wages on tea plantations in substantial numbers. Their unwillingness to work on the estates was based on the same factors that had caused them to refuse employment on the coffee plantations. If anything, conditions on the tea estates made the decision to shun estate employment more rational than had been the decision with respect to coffee. Whereas coffee production required only seasonal labour, tea production was a year round process, involving a great deal of backbreaking work for very low wages. Once a peasant accepted employment on a tea estate, his pair of hands could under no conditions be made available to assist in the paddy harvest. Thus the importation of Tamil workers from southern India remained a prominent feature of the estate sector throughout the tea era, and the net immigration figures for the years 1887–97 averaged higher (31·2 thousand annually) than they had for any comparable period in the coffee era. Out of the 465,000 plantation labourers in 1911, the number of East Indian Tamils was 366,000. Out of the total population of 4,106,000, East Indian Tamils were 531,000.

But in contrast with the case of coffee, the native Sinhalese also failed to establish any significant amount of smallholdings of tea. The major reason for this lay in the economies of scale present in tea production. In addition, tea is not a plant easily adapted to garden cultivation, which the peasants always of necessity regarded as secondary to paddy production. Unlike the other garden crops of coffee, coconut, cocoa, etc., tea could not be grown virtually wild, but rather required frequent cultivation and constant flushing if the product were to be fit for the market. And, if a peasant found the time to care for his tea bushes properly, he then had to share the profits with the owner of the tea factory which could process his harvest. It is not surprising, therefore, that native smallholdings of tea never made a significant contribution to tea exports.

Table 9.2 indicates that, although the value of tea exports increased until 1897, the price of tea was actually falling from 1882 onwards. The fall in tea prices between 1882 and 1900 was a part of a general fall in prices resulting from the world-wide depression of the 1890s. In the case of tea the price fall reflected also the declining rate of increase in *per capita* consumption of tea in the United Kingdom (the recipient of most of Ceylon's exports) accompanying the general depression. At the same time the price decline was accelerated by the rapid increase of tea production outside of Ceylon. Ceylonese planters were able to maintain profits between 1885 and 1897 because of two factors: the initial difference in the early 1880s between the selling price of tea (1s 3d per pound) and the average cost of production (6d per pound) had been so large as to permit substantial price declines without profits turning into losses; also at the same time that the London price of tea was declining in terms of pounds sterling, the Indian rupee (the currency of Ceylon) was undergoing depreciation, which acted to cushion the fall of price in rupees, without an equivalent rise in rupee costs. (The value of the rupee fell from 2s 0d in the mid-seventies to 1s 4d in the early nineties; it was eventually pegged at 1s 4d in 1898.)

In spite of forces supporting the continued profitability of the tea industry, the sustained price declines were producing an increasing number of bankruptcies by 1893. The crisis atmosphere deepened steadily until in 1897 the planting of new acreages ceased altogether. Prices continued to fall until their turning point was reached in 1905, and since the rupee was stabilized in 1898, the adverse effect on profits could not be escaped. The Ceylonese planters at first resorted to the production of a poorer quality of tea (due to over-flushing) in order to increase output, only to find that the lower quality teas suffered most severely from price declines.

Supplementing declining tea profits: rubber. The upshot of this combination of events was that after 1897 increasing portions of the most recently developed tea acreage fell under the shadow of the productive margin, and planters began to look for an alternative crop. One possible selection was the rubber tree, which had been introduced into the island in 1877 but had remained the property of the smallholders. The decline in tea prices was accompanied by a rise in rubber prices, with the result that acreage planted in rubber trees increased rapidly after 1900; the cultivated acreage grew from 1,000 hectares in 1900 to 94,000 hectares in 1913.

Rubber could be grown only in the low country (not higher than 2,500 feet) of the central, western and southern regions of Ceylon, so that it could never have taken over the plantation lands of the up country. It required very little capital and although there were some advantages to plantation production – mainly superior tapping and processing techniques – the tree was about equally well suited to smallholder production. Thus from the beginning, rubber production was initiated not to take the place of tea, but rather to provide a supplementary source of income and to serve as an outlet for investment for native and plantation earnings in other sectors. Very little foreign capital was needed or involved in the development of the Ceylonese rubber industry. Rather, the major participants in the rubber plantings were the tea companies and the new Sinhalese capitalist class which had arisen from the coffee smallholdings and the provision of services to the tea industry.

Smallholders took to rubber planting from the beginning, and had perhaps 20 per cent of the acreage in 1913. Tremendous difficulties were encountered in finding the species of the rubber tree most suited to Ceylon and then in discovering the proper technique of tapping the trees. The latter was not accomplished until 1897 and was not paying off in increased yields until around 1905. Once the technical difficulties were solved, there remained the problem of convincing the peasants of the wisdom of applying the new techniques. Officials of the Royal Gardens were never completely successful in this endeavour, and throughout the period under consideration, mismanagement of peasant trees was extensive. Numerous observers relate how a visitor could denote boundaries between estates and peasant holdings by the difference in the care in tapping.

Unlike the other plantation crops, rubber was able to attract native labour. This was possible because the work was intermittent and not very difficult; most of the tapping was done by women; and the workday lasted only from seven in the morning until noon, leaving sufficient time for the performance of domestic duties. The smallholdings themselves provided an important source of village labour employment. In the rubber areas each village had one or several small processing centres where the fresh latex was rolled into sheets in hand-operated presses and then smoked. The owner of these rubber sheets or cakes then took the rubber to town himself to sell or sold it to a local rubber dealer, who was as likely as not a Ceylonese Moor. The village processing was crudely done, so that prices were generally lower for smallholdings production.

The net effect of the introduction of rubber production was to bring large parts of the traditional sector in the western, central, and southern provinces of Ceylon into the export economy. It increased the strength of the Sinhalese middle class and greatly expanded the opportunities for desirable wage employment for the village peasants. Further, the care and harvesting of the rubber tree is such as to enable fairly wide variation in output from year to year and the use of temporary local labour without any harmful effects on future production. Thus the supply of rubber could be quite elastic, something which the technicalities of production prohibited for tea, which must be flushed regardless of price in order to maintain the quality of future production. Because owners of rubber trees could cut back production should the price of rubber fall, they could exercise more control over price (assuming planters outside Ceylon also reduced production) than could the tea planters or the coffee planters.

Coconuts. A second crop of increasing importance was the coconut. The coconut had, of course, been known in Ceylon at least since ancient times, and as the multifarious 'tree of life' had long been the favourite producer of the village gardens. The coconut is a coastal tree in Ceylon, growing up to 2,500 feet, producing five years after planting and having a productive life of up to seventy years.

Dr Snodgrass estimates that there were already 200,000 hectares under this crop in 1871, growing to 384,000 hectares in 1913. At first it was essentially a peasant crop, since there are no economies of scale in cultivation, and it is easy to sell part of the crop to central factories for processing. Middle-class Sinhalese also held some plantations. Their interest in coconuts quickened as tea prices fell; the swift growth of coconut acreage dates to the middle eighties. The expatriate tea companies became interested in the middle nineties, and were planting coconuts by the end of the century. However, tea was a highland crop and coconut a lowland crop, so they were not alternative users of the same land. The investment of expatriate companies in coconuts was never as high as 5 per cent of the total coconut acreage.

Exports of coconut products rose from 10·7 per cent of total exports in 1891 to 14·0 per cent in 1900 and 19·6 per cent in 1913. In contrast with tea, prices were well maintained. Coconut oil, having held at Rs. 12·5 per cwt. for over two decades began to escalate in price up to Rs. 15·6 in 1893, dropping to Rs. 13 for 1897 and 1898, and then climbing up to Rs. 18 in 1902; copra climbed from a long-time price of Rs. 8 per cwt. to Rs. 13 in 1891, dropping back briefly to Rs. 9·7 in the last four years of the decade, then starting a climb to Rs. 13·8 in 1907 and on up to Rs. 18 in 1913; only desiccated coconut experienced a noticeable price decline in the 1890s, but as a new export product its share was very small and apparently continued to be very profitable throughout the period, as evidenced by the uninterrupted increase in exports from 16,000 cwt. in 1892 to 293,000 cwt. in 1902 (at no time did the total value of desiccated coconut exports fall prior to 1902).

The major increase in acreage after 1900 occurred in the north-western, western, and southern provinces, in the Jaffna peninsula, and along the coast of the eastern province. Apparently, though, most of the coconut production was concentrated in the western maritime provinces, where rainfall is most abundant and where contact with the plantation sector was closest and of longest duration. Significantly, this same statement applies generally to the locational characteristics of the rubber industry. Further, like rubber the technicalities of coconut production made for a highly elastic supply and thus for greater control over price fluctuations.

In at least one respect the depression of the 1890s performed a beneficial service for the island economy of Ceylon: it distracted the

233

attention of investors from tea and its ancillary services long enough for the profitability of rubber and coconut products to be demonstrated. Thus, when tea prices began to rise again in the first decade of this century, and dormant acreage was returned to production, there was no noticeable effect on the growth of production of rubber or coconuts. Of course, for technical reasons neither of these crops was competing with tea for land, but certainly they competed for local capital and for some types of labour.

The revival of tea. The price increases for tea after 1905 were a part of the general pre-war upward movement of commodity prices. They were also caused partly by a change-over to production of a finer quality tea on the Ceylonese estates. The latter was accomplished when Ceylonese tea producers recognized that overproduction had contributed to the problems of the depression years and consequently returned to finer flushing of the tea bush, a procedure which produced a higher quality tea and, with decreased acreage, less output.

A further post-depression development relates to the ownership and organization of the estates after 1900. Before the stagnation of the tea industry in the late 1890s, individual estate ownership had been quite common, if not the rule. Recovery from the slump at the turn of the century involved significant mechanization of the tea factories as well as better management of production to improve the quality of tea. The combination of accumulated individual misfortunes accompanying the slump and the large capital requirements needed for recovery greatly facilitated the reorganization of estates into the company form of ownership and management. The company proved to be an efficient means of organizing production, so that by the end of World War I the number of individual estate proprietors had become quite small. Thus the plantation sector had by 1914 advanced not only in terms of expanding output, but also in terms of industrial organization.[1]

II. THE DRY ZONE

The plantation crops were concentrated in the 'wet zone' of Ceylon; especially tea and rubber (coconuts were spread more widely). The core of this zone is the western and central provinces of the island,

[1] For a more complete account of the development of the estate economy, see S. Rajaratnam, *op. cit.*, and, 'The Ceylon Tea Industry 1886–1931', *Ceylon Journal of Historical and Social Studies* (July–December, 1961), pp. 169–202.

where rain falls throughout the year. Elsewhere rain falls only for three months of the year, and though the fall is normally heavy, the area is known as the dry zone because full utilization of water requires conservation and irrigation facilities.

In the introduction to this paper, Ceylonese agriculture was divided into four sectors: the expatriate planters, the Ceylonese planters, the mixed-economy peasants, and the subsistence farmers. The first three were almost exclusively in the wet zone, apart from peasants with coconuts in the dry zone. The wet zone also had some pure subsistence farmers, but most of these were in the dry zone. According to the Census of 1911, the number of paddy farmers in the western and central districts was 154,000, compared with 301,000 in the rest of the island. In this section we shall consider the economy of the dry zone; in the next section we shall return to the two intermediate groups in the wet zone.

The dry zone itself has to be considered in two separate parts. On the one hand there is the Jaffna peninsula and the mainland area surrounding it in the north. On the other there is the rest of the dry zone, the north-west and north-east, the eastern and south-eastern and parts of the southern provinces. The distinction between the two regions is both geographical and historical. Jaffna, unlike the rest of Ceylon, was inhabited by Hindu Tamils who had settled in the area following one or several of the ancient Indian invasions of the island; the other part of the dry zone was inhabited by Buddhist Sinhalese peasants, with large scatterings of Moors, Malays, and small groups of aboriginal Veddahs. Also, unlike the rest of the island, the Jaffna peninsula rests on a base of solid rock which traps water and thus makes irrigation by wells possible. The completely porous soil of the remainder of the island makes well-irrigation impossible. These two factors make the two areas quite distinct, and we shall consequently deal with them separately.

The rice economy. When one looks at the dry zone (excluding Jaffna), at what it once had been and what it apparently was capable of becoming again, one must immediately ask why it did not develop more rapidly between 1880 and 1913. For the north and north central parts of the dry zone had been the centre and the controlling power in the ancient Sinhalese civilization; they had been the granary of the island, producing most of the paddy used to feed the Sinhalese population. This had been accomplished by constructing an elaborate irrigation system of great bunds or dams (some six miles long), tanks for holding the water, and connecting canals extending as much as 55 miles. This system caught the rainfall in the three-month rainy season, conserved it and redistributed it as needed to the rice fields.

The savage Sinhalese civil wars, the Tamil invasions between AD 700 and 1300, the onslaught of the Portuguese and Dutch, and the widespread prevalence of malaria had reduced the ancient irrigation system to ruin by the time of the arrival of the British. By the beginning of the nineteenth century Ceylon was already importing considerable quantities of rice.

The arrival of the British and the creation of the plantation system should have given an impetus to increased rice production. The island had ceased to be capable of feeding itself primarily because centuries of political instability had destroyed its production system; now a central government unquestionably capable of maintaining stability was firmly established. In addition, by importing twenty to forty thousand Indian Tamils annually for work on the estates, the British threatened to increase dependence on foreign sources for food unless something were done to increase domestic production. Here was an opportunity for peasant entry into the money economy which involved no submission to plantation managers nor work any more difficult than that traditionally associated with paddy production. The surprising fact is that the peasants did not take significant advantage of the increased demand for rice. Just as the estate owners had to import their labour, so they had to import most of the rice to feed it. No single factor accounts for this circumstance; rather it was the result of numerous conditions and events. We shall attempt to piece the story together in what follows.

A major factor involves the reconstruction and maintenance of the ancient irrigation system. In the first place, it is probably a mistake to believe that all that was needed to make the dry zone capable of feeding the island was to effect a complete restoration of the ancient irrigation system. The irrigation system had been constructed over a period of several centuries, usually between wars in which large parts of the existing constructions were destroyed or filled with silt. Thus at no time were the 10,000 to 11,000 tanks, which lay in ruins in the nineteenth century, in simultaneous operation and, given the labour required for their maintenance, it is doubtful that the always scarce labour supply of Ceylon could have maintained them in any event. The irrigation system as it existed at various times in the ancient period was undoubtedly efficient and probably was in fact capable of feeding the smaller native population. Whether it would have been efficient if it had been reconstructed in its entirety and whether it could have fed the larger and growing population of the nineteenth century is another matter. (There may be some question as to whether the nineteenth century population of Ceylon was in fact larger than that of ancient Ceylon. There is no proof of the matter, but the cessation of the fratricidal wars and Indian invasions, the importation of the Indian Tamils, and the slight improvement in health conditions under the British would lead one to believe that the nineteenth-century population was larger.) This point must be raised in view of numerous complaints of British neglect of the irrigation system.

Even with this point in view, the British almost certainly devoted less attention to the irrigation system than they should have. The irrigation system was by nature something of the classic public good: if its services were provided to one peasant in an area, they were provided to all (gravity and the liquidity of water guarantee this). Like all public goods, because individual disincentives to pay for the service when it would be provided regardless of payment tend to produce underprovision of the service or no provision at all, the ancient irrigation system had been constructed and maintained under the strict supervision of the central government. Thus the breakdown of the central government had been as much responsible for the ruin of the system as had the devastation of the wars. Peasants broke the bunds wherever they pleased to water a random field; the large tanks silted up where no single village controlled the water flowing from them: and great stretches of the bunds were washed away by the torrential tropical rains, again with no efforts made at repair unless possibly a single village controlled the water services of the affected tanks.

In the early period of colonization, the British actually worsened the prospects of revitalizing the dry zone by abolishing in 1832 the village compulsory-service system and substituting for it a grain tax. The compulsory service owed by each villager had been under the control of the village councils, which had more or less successfully marshalled it to maintain the tanks directly servicing the particular village. The abolition of the compulsory service effectively destroyed the village councils' power, and henceforth there existed no agency for even the most minimal maintenance of local tanks, much less tanks serving more than a single village. Further, the British failed to provide any public funds for irrigation maintenance to replace the lost payment-in-kind provided by the traditional service system. The two decades under this situation must have been particularly difficult ones for agricultural activity in the dry zone.

By 1856, however, Europeans were frequently decrying the lost

237

potential of the dry zone as a food centre for the estate system, and in that year an irrigation ordinance was passed restoring local authority to exact village services on the bunds and canals and providing 78,000 pounds sterling for restoration purposes. This fund was used between 1856 and 1858 to effect extensive restoration of the irrigation system in the eastern and southern provinces. At the same time, the roads being built by the colonial government further spurred greater rice production by making it possible for farmers to transport their produce to the estate region. Following these improvements, government officials were pleased to report rapid expansion of rice production in the affected regions.

Expenditures on irrigation following the 1856–58 programme were apparently small, and not until 1873 was another major irrigation programme initiated. This programme, concentrated on the vast network of the northern provinces, lasted until the decline of coffee around 1880, and, complemented with reconstruction of roads and the arrival of the railroad, led to a major expansion of rice production, as much as fivefold according to the British governor of the island. After the early 1880s, expenditures virtually ceased until the tea estates became profitable. From the mid-1880s until 1905, however, the government expressed a continuing interest in improving irrigation, although expenditures never amounted to more than 1·5 per cent of government revenues, and varied widely with the prosperity of the export trade. Thus expenditures amounted to 455,000 rupees in 1890, 214,000 rupees in 1895, and 838,000 rupees in 1910. The establishment of a separate Irrigation Department in 1900 seemed to indicate the greater interest of the government in irrigation projects, but this action was followed in 1905 by the cessation of all new projects, the consensus within the administration being that more irrigated lands had already been supplied than were needed. In view of the 350,000 metric tons of rice imported in that year, presumably the real meaning of that decision was that the total irrigated lands already supplied were more than could be used efficiently. Thus the estates continued to import rice, the figure reaching 400,000 metric tons in 1913.

But why did the irrigation projects yield such poor results? Certainly a major problem lay in the character of the projects themselves. The torrential rains of the tropical island are easily capable of breaking a bund which is not subjected to constant maintenance; tanks also quickly silt up unless clearing crews are kept at work practically year round. Yet the British programme of expenditures, as small as it was, varied enormously in size and

238

direction from year to year. In some years 200,000 rupees might be spent on a project in the north; the project might or might not be completed, and for the next five years all of the irrigation funds (if any existed) would be devoted to projects in the south or east. This same problem was characteristic of road construction in the dry zone. Roads were laboriously built, then left untended for long periods and eventually virtually washed away by the tropical rains. After the first great period of road-building, the governors' reports talk much more of reconstruction than of new construction. Finally, the irrigation system, to be properly run, required at the very least some regional administration. Under the British, very little machinery existed to co-ordinate the village programmes, and regional control was minimal. Thus the colonial administration's irrigation programmes lacked consistency and were both too small and too variable to augment rice production steadily. The same, of course, was true of the complementary road programmes for the dry zone.

The slowness of agricultural progress in the dry zone, however, was not due entirely to inadequate public works programmes. The peasants' methods of cultivation were extremely conservative, so that it is doubtful that they made efficient use of the water provided them. The soil of much of Ceylon has suffered severe leaching, and needs mineral supplementation, yet the peasants seldom used manures. Crop rotation was virtually non-existent and, owing to the scarcity of labour and a long tradition, the natives sowed the rice seed by broadcasting rather than by using the more productive technique of transplanting. The prevalence of broadcasting was due at least partly to the lack of an assured and regulated supply of water, but we must not underestimate the force of tradition in this matter: in the years after World War II when water has been available on a regular basis in many areas, the farmers have stubbornly held on to the tradition of broadcasting.

Another factor contributing to the failure of extensive revitalization of the dry zone was the widespread prevalence of malaria in the area. The irrigation tanks were natural breeding grounds for the disease-carrying mosquito, and there exists considerable evidence that malaria had contributed heavily to the breakdown of the ancient Sinhalese civilization in the northern provinces. In the period under consideration here, there were no effective techniques for preventing malaria, so that the disease was undoubtedly a constant drain on an agricultural system requiring large quantities of labour.

A final factor of great importance in explaining the peasants' failure to supply the food inputs needed for the estates relates to custom. The estate workers were, of course, Indian Tamils who were accustomed to parboiled Indian rice. According to contemporary accounts, the Tamil coolies refused to touch the Sinhalese country rice, saying that it gave them indigestion. This cannot be pushed too far, since we know that most rice imports eventually came from Burma, not from India. However, the cleaned rice of even quality from Burma must also have contrasted with the country rice of very uneven quality produced in Ceylon.

In summary, a combination of cultural, governmental, and agricultural factors combined to hinder the redevelopment of the dry zone as the granary of the island. Ceylonese rice productivity remained quite low: a 1930–1 to 1934–5 survey[1] revealed that of the Asian monsoon countries, Ceylon had the lowest rice productivity per acre. The rice-growing regions of greatest potential were furthest from the modernizing influences of the western and central provinces; greater productivity probably could have been achieved in the latter provinces (and apparently was), but here rice competed directly with the export crops for labour and there could be little question as to which was more profitable. The extreme variability of road conditions in the dry zone made marketing an additional hazard even when surplus rice was produced. Thus, the Sinhalese country rice was inefficiently produced, varied in quality, was not always available, and was inefficiently marketed. In contrast, Burmese rice was cheap and its quality uniform; it could be obtained throughout Ceylon through highly organized and efficient trade channels. The preference of the estates, then, for imported rice was entirely rational.

The question must still be answered, if irrigation was a serious problem, why was dry rice not grown instead of the wet varieties? An important explanatory factor is the poverty of the soil of the dry zone of Ceylon. The jungle land, which was cleared by the customary method of felling trees and burning, could be relied upon for no more than one to three crops. After this the land was abandoned and was not eligible for slash-and-burn clearing for at least another decade.[2] Lacking domestic animals and large quantities of surplus land for the growth of leguminous plants, the Sinhalese peasants would have had to purchase most of the manures (as did the estates). There was also the conservatism of the peasantry which

---

[1] V. D. Wickizer and M. K. Bennett, *The Rice Economy of Monsoon Asia*, Stanford, 1941, p. 61.

[2] J. C. Willis (*Agriculture in the Tropics*, Cambridge, 1909, p. 2) estimates the period of abandonment and re-growth at 8 to 50 years. Wickizer and Bennett (pp. 12–13) suggest a period of two decades.

could have been overcome only with a great deal of effort. Botanists in the Royal Gardens had repeatedly shown that maize and sorghum could be grown in the dry zone, with adequate manuring. But lacking the support of the government, they were unable to introduce the plants to any considerable extent. (Agriculturists were still trying to popularize these crops after World War II, without much success in overcoming peasant conservatism.) The same would have been the case with dry rice in the nineteenth century. In addition, the Tamil cultural factor would have been another obstacle: if the Tamils were extremely prejudiced toward one of two strains of wet rice, then they would undoubtedly be just as decided in their choice between dry and wet rice.

Even had an enterprising Sinhalese or European entrepreneur appeared on the scene to win his fortune in the development of a rice empire – wet or dry – the obstacles would have been enormous: no great open (and cheap) land areas would have been available, since, unlike the central highlands, the treasured ricelands had remained in service tenure; for wet rice, large expenditures on irrigation works would be necessary; for both wet and particularly dry rice, great quantities of expensive manures would have to be imported; and quite likely, for either crop, a labour force would have to be imported, since natives would be involved enough in their own production. Little wonder, then, that the island economy decided that it was cheaper to import rice than to buy manures and labour and grow it at home. Undoubtedly, the early European influence, with its major emphasis on the production of coffee, tea, and rubber, tended to give too little attention to the extension of paddy acreage and to productivity improvements. On balance, however, from the viewpoint of the short run, this economic decision is quite understandable.

We should not conclude that because the dry zone failed to regain its ancient status as the granary of the island that it also failed to make economic progress between 1880 and 1913. The construction of the roads connecting the various parts of the dry zone with the western provinces undoubtedly increased commerce and greatly facilitated the movements of the peasants' jungle garden harvest – coconuts, cocoa, cinnamon – to the export markets. If the irrigation works were inadequate to the total needs of the island, they undoubtedly extended the paddy acreage under cultivation and probably increased productivity as well. Certainly life went on much as it had been before the coming of the British, but important changes whose full effect was not yet evident were present: for the first time in centuries there was a central government to oversee reconstruction of the bunds and canals; roads appeared where none had passed before; schools were established in regions long since stripped of an ancient civilization; railroads provided easy connections with once inaccessible parts of the island. And if the increase in cultivated acreage (approximately 17 per cent) during the 39-year period was small, it was, nevertheless, an *increase*, which probably had not been the case for any comparable period in the four or more centuries preceding.

The Jaffna peninsula. Turning very briefly to developments in the Jaffna peninsula, we find a story different only in its details. The Jaffna peninsula was in 1880 a much more highly developed region than was the rest of the dry zone. It was occupied by Hindu Tamils from southern India, an enterprising group, evidently less tradition-bound than were the Sinhalese peasantry. The Jaffna Tamils also maintained close contacts with their Indian neighbours across the narrow straits, being closer culturally to India than to southern Ceylon. Although it benefited from the roads constructed by the colonial government and from government schools established in the area, whatever progress Jaffna made in this period was probably influenced as much by modernizing influences coming from southern India as by those coming from southern Ceylon.

Unlike the rest of the island, the Jaffna peninsula was densely inhabited and there was practised there a well-developed, intensive agriculture. The limestone bed on which the peninsula rests made possible well-irrigation, and, again unlike the rest of the dry zone, the Tamil peasants by tradition practised extensive manuring, using both leguminous 'green' manures and the foliage of the tulip tree. A dependable water supply and heavy manuring made for greater yields than were present in the rest of the dry zone. The Tamil peasants also grew tobacco on small plots and sold it to traders in southern India. The tobacco was of a coarse variety unfit for export to Europe, but provided an additional money crop for the Jaffna villagers. Tobacco could probably have been grown in other parts of the dry zone, but lack of heavy manuring and inaccessibility to the markets of southern India probably restricted its cultivation.

Life in Jaffna differed only in degree from life in the rest of the dry zone. As in all of the peasant economy, the inhabitants cultivated mixed gardens of everything from coconuts and mangoes to tobacco and yams on lands too high to be reached by irrigation. Yet, with more money crops available (tobacco, fishing), a steady water supply, a perhaps more vigorous culture (at any rate, a people

242

certainly less inervated by malaria), life in the Jaffna peninsula moved at a considerably faster pace than was true in the rest of the dry zone.

III. FOUNDATIONS OF DEVELOPMENT

The expatriate plantation sector grew rapidly and created great wealth. Much of this was withheld from the Ceylonese; wages went to labourers from India; salaries were paid to European managers and profits went home to shareholders in England. In this section we are concerned with the impact of this expatriate development on the indigenous economy. We shall examine this impact under four headings: the rise of a Ceylonese planter class, peasant production of export crops, industrialization, and the development of infrastructure.

Ceylonese plantations. An upper class of substantial landowners had existed long before the British arrived, but they had lived more by renting land than by cultivating it. The rise of the coffee industry converted several of these into planters. At the same time the prosperity in coffee expanded the urban middle class, trading, civil servant and professional, and some of the savings of this class went also into starting and owning coffee plantations. Tea was a more difficult crop than coffee, since success required more meticulous management; nevertheless a few Ceylonese went into tea. The big boosts to Ceylonese planting, however, came from coconuts and rubber, the first from the 1880s on, and the second from the turn of the century. Coconuts were especially attractive.

Relevant statistics are scarce. The 1911 Census gives the number of 'owners, managers and superior staff' on plantations as 93,000. Of these only 1,600 were Europeans. The remaining 92,300 were distributed as follows:

Coconut plantations	74,700
Tobacco	7,400
Other	10,200
	92,300

In addition, 22,400 persons were engaged in planting vegetables, fruit and flowers, of whom perhaps a half were in a substantial way of business (in terms of income rather than of acreage). The 'managers and superior staff' were not all on Ceylonese estates, but only the

243

category 'other' includes any significant number who were on European estates. This 100,000 men and women planting or managing is a very substantial number when compared with the number of paddy farmers (some of whom also grew export crops), which was only 454,000.

Ceylon seems to have gone further than any other South Asian country – certainly than India, the Philippines or Indonesia – in producing a middle class of indigenous agriculturalists. This element was important not only because of the wealth it produced for itself, but also because of its impact on the rest of the economy. Unlike the expatriate planters and managers, it spent and invested its earnings in Ceylon. Its young people were likely to receive a secondary education, and could therefore be recruited by the rest of the economy for supervisory and higher posts. Possibly some of its savings also flowed into commerce and manufacturing industry, or other entrepreneurial avenues. The emergence of this kind of indigenous middle class is one of the foundations for further progress, both economic and political.

Peasant exports. Relevant figures are again conjectural. Dr Snodgrass estimates that, in 1911, smallholders had about 10 per cent of the acreage in tea, 20 per cent in rubber, and 60 per cent in coconuts. This comes to 701,000 acres, compared with only 645,000 acres in paddy – but the distinction between acreage in coconuts and other acreage is probably somewhat vague. Using plantation figures to translate these acreages into numbers of persons engaged gives about 41,000 for tea, 10,000 for rubber, and 156,000 for coconuts. Whatever further glosses one may put on these figures, they are still quite considerable when compared with the 454,000 paddy farmers. Indeed, separate figures for the wet zone, if they existed, would probably show that two-thirds of the small farmers had some land planted in one or more of the export crops.

The small farmers of the wet zone were therefore much richer than those of the dry zone – one finds this everywhere in the tropics. The dry zone could have done better for itself; other dry zones elsewhere were doing quite well out of cotton, tobacco, or peanuts at this period, even without irrigation. As is usual, where the opportunities for wealth are greater, people also tend to show greater initiative; this element cannot be omitted when one tries to understand why the dry zone – containing half of the population – did not make a better showing.

Industrialization. Some of the wealth generated by exports spilled

244

over into industry. The Census of 1911 classified 9·8 per cent of the active population as being engaged in mining, manufacturing, gas, electricity and water supply. (This classification understates the percentage by modern standards, since inclusion of many housewives in agriculture has inflated the active population.) The numbers had grown considerably since the Census of 1881, as is shown in Table 9.3.

TABLE 9.3: *Industrial Employment*
(thousands)

	1881	1911
Mining, quarrying	2·6	16·8
Food, beverages, tobacco	16·7	22·9
Textiles, clothing	10·5	47·8
Wood products	35·5	50·2
Non-metallic minerals	8·3	7·3
Metal products	5·3	10·6
Other manufacturing	10·1	12·5
Utilities	—	1·7
	89·0	169·8

The overall rate of growth of employment in manufacturing was high (2·8 per cent per annum), whether we compare it with the international standards of the time or with the growth rate of total population (1·3 per cent per annum). The textile industry clearly took off in this period.

Government. Finally we come to the role of the government, whose revenues swelled enormously between 1880 and 1913. (See Table 9.4.) Most of its activities have already been referred to in the preceding sections of this paper, so this survey will be in summary form. Two facts dominate: the government was the property

TABLE 9.4: *Population, Revenue and Expenditure, 1881–1911*

	Population* (thousands)	Revenue (Rs. thousand)	Expenditure (Rs. thousand)
1881	2,760	13,686	13,979
1891	3,008	17,963	16,772
1901	3,571	26,437	29,217
1911	4,106	65,613	58,954

* Excluding military and shipping personnel.
Source: The Ceylon Blue Book, 1936, p. vi.

of the export sector, and most of its activites were designed to benefit that sector; the revenues of the government were derived almost solely from export income, with the result that government revenues and expenditures varied with the fortunes of the estate and smallholdings exports in the world market.

The Public Works Department spent a considerable part of the central government's revenues. Public works expenditures were devoted to a variety of projects, roads, bridges, public buildings, hospitals, harbours, drainage and irrigation, coolie lines[1] and school buildings; but in a given year, most were used for road and bridge construction and maintenance. The road system was, of course, designed to serve the estates; however, it simultaneously opened up large areas of the traditional sector.

The roads greatly facilitated the estate commerce, but in the tropical climate of Ceylon their services were undependable, even when metalled, during the monsoon seasons. Under the onslaught of the tropical rains and traffic of heavily loaded bullock-carts, roads turned to mud, and the prices of rice and manures for the estates fluctuated violently, depending on the conditions of the roads. Thus the construction of the railways was an essential element in the development of the modern sector. After the failure of private attempts at construction, the colonial government undertook the first project in 1863, completing the line to Kandy in 1867. Henceforth the government built, operated, and owned all rail lines, using compulsory labour and Indian Tamil workers in the construction process. The railroads proved to be a profitable enterprise and remained a major source of revenues throughout the 1880–1913 period.

Other government activities directly related to the welfare of the estate sector were the construction of the breakwater for the Colombo harbour in the 1870s and the provision of support for the importation of the Indian Tamils. The latter involved establishment of a system for inspecting the treatment of the coolies en route to the highlands and on the plantations. Eventually the government established Tamil schools on the estates as well.

The government also contributed to the significant strides of education in the period under consideration. In 1885 the administration established a policy of concentrating its direct expenditures on the native vernacular schools (called government schools), leaving education in English almost entirely to the aided or unaided mis-

[1] Housing for the 'coolie' (a coolie line) was usually a barracks-type building on one floor, subdivided into cubicles of 10 or 12 square feet.

sionary schools. The development of these three types of institutions is shown in Table 9.5. The enrolment of 1910 is 31 per cent of the population aged 5 to 14, which was a relatively high figure in those days.

TABLE 9.5: *Education in Ceylon, 1890–1910*

	Government		Aided		Unaided		Total	
	schools	Pupils	schools	Pupils	schools	Pupils	schools	Pupils
1890	436	40,290	984	73,698	2,617	32,464	4,037	146,452
1900	500	48,642	1,328	120,751	2,089	38,881	3,917	208,274
1910	759	96,600	1,910	203,020	1,546	36,754	4,215	336,374

Source: L. A. Mills, *Ceylon Under British Rule, 1795–1932*, London, 1933.

The active role of the government is reflected in Table 9.5 in the greatly reduced number of unaided schools and the increased number in the other two categories. The aided English schools grew most rapidly, largely due to the job-value of being able to speak English. Most of the aided schools were located in the coastal provinces and larger towns, so that government schools were established largely in the rural areas of the interior. All vernacular education was free; fees were charged in the English schools. The system was strengthened in 1907 when the administration gave local authorities the power to impose compulsory vernacular education in the towns and rural areas. Although no university was established during the period, the Government Technical College was founded in 1893 and strengthened the work of the island's medical and law schools. Under the influence of this varied educational programme, literacy rates (according to census figures) showed substantial improvements between 1880 and 1913. In 1911, 40·4 per cent of all males were literate, compared with 24·6 per cent for 1881. The corresponding figures for females are 10·6 per cent versus 2·5 per cent. In addition, by 1911, 3·3 per cent of all males and 1·2 per cent of all females were literate in English.

The government made a few tentative moves in the direction of improved health services. The widespread prevalence of tropical diseases – malaria, hookworm – aggravated by insanitary living conditions and large bodies of still water (in the dry zone) made the health problem a severe one. The establishment of the Colombo Medical College in 1870 helped increase the number of medical officers in the island to 134 in 1903, and numerous hospitals were constructed in the thirty-year period. However, the evidence available (the high death rates remained unchanged) suggests that not much real progress was made in the area of public health before 1915. An example of the slow pace of advances is that an effective system of drainage and sewage disposal for Colombo was begun only in 1903 and not completed until 1924.

Conclusion. Ceylon confutes the stereotype of the plantation economy as one which benefits only expatriate shareholders, while doing nothing to prepare the indigenous economy for growth. This can be the situation, but it was not so in Ceylon, partly because the Ceylonese, too, took up the export crops, and partly because public revenues were raised and used to provide infrastructure and education. Half of the population, living in the dry zone, was making little progress, and another 9 per cent, the immigrant labourers on the plantations, were living a life for which all that one could say was that it was better than what they had left behind in India. But a sound foundation for growth was being laid in the indigenous economy, which would have led to self-sustaining growth if the great war had not plunged tropical trade into a thirty-year depression. The most troublesome aspect of the plantation economy turned out in the end to be the racial mélange it produced, whose conflicts have intensified with time to the point where they threaten to tear the country apart. This is, alas, a twentieth century heartache which Ceylone shares with many other tropical (and temperate) countries.

BIBLIOGRAPHY

Official paper

Ceylon. Registrar General's Department, *The Ceylon Blue Book*, yearly beginning 1891. Colombo.

Books

Arasaratnam, Sinnappah, *Ceylon*, Englewood Cliffs, NJ, 1964.

Bingham, P. M., *History of the Public Works Department, Ceylon, 1796–1913*, Colombo, 1912.

International Bank for Reconstruction and Development, *The Economic Development of Ceylon*. Balimore, 1953.

Ludowyk, E. F. C., *The Story of Ceylon*, London, 1962.

Mills, L. A., *Ceylon under British Rule, 1795–1932*, London, 1933.

Snodgrass, D. R., *Ceylon: An Export Economy in Transition*, Homewood, Ill., 1966.

Wickizer, V. D., and Bennett, M. K., *The Rice Economy of Monsoon Asia*, Stanford, 1941.

Willis, J. C., *Agriculture in the Tropics*, Cambridge, 1909.

Articles

Rajaratnam, S., 'The Ceylon Tea Industry, 1886–1931', *Ceylon Journal of Historical and Social Studies*, July–December 1961.

——, 'The Growth of Plantation Agriculture in Ceylon, 1886–1931', *Ceylon Journal of Historical and Social Studies*, January–June 1961.

Vandendriesen, I. H., 'Some Trends in the Economic History of Ceylon in the "Modern" Period', *Ceylon Journal of Historical and Social Studies*, January–June 1960.

249

Chapter 10

INDONESIA

by Robert J. Van Leeuwen

I. HISTORICAL BACKGROUND

When Dutch ships first dropped anchor in Indonesian waters in June 1596, their occupants had travelled half way around the world not 'to collect butterflies', but instead 'to obtain much desired commodities for which that remote region was famous or for the production of which it was reputed to be suitable'.[1] For almost a century the Dutch imagination had been tickled by tales of the fabulous wealth of the Spice Islands, from which the return of a single ship loaded with pepper, cloves, nutmeg, mace, and cinnamon meant a fortune to its owner. The mercantilist dream survived more or less intact until the late nineteenth century; during its life it served the economic interests of the Netherlands exceedingly well.

At first the Dutch encounter with the Indonesian rulers evinced an aura of diplomatic cordiality, and the first treaty concluded with the sultan of Bantam (West Java) expressed the latter's confidence in the continuance of this atmosphere. It was not long, however, before hostilities broke out between the four ships of this first Dutch expedition to Indonesia and the coastal principalities which lay along their way. Henceforward the history of the Dutch in the East Indies was inexorably shaped by the combination of their economic interest, political skill and relatively advanced military technology.

The European explorers and traders of the sixteenth century had little reason to consider themselves generally superior to the Indonesians. The Indonesian principalities of the sixteenth century, in fact, 'had gunpowder, and their navigation techniques, modes of land and water transport and techniques of manufacture and agriculture were not markedly inferior to those of Europe'.[2] International trade, too, was highly developed in the Indonesian archipelago, and

[1] J. H. Boeke, *The Evolution of the Netherlands Indies Economy*, New York, 1946, p. 1.
[2] Benjamin Higgins, 'Western Enterprise and the Economic Development of Southeast Asia: A Review Article', *Pacific Affairs*, Vol. XIII, March 1958, p. 76.

when those first Dutch sailors arrived in Bantam, 'there came such a multitude of Javanese and other nations as Turks, Chinese, Bengali, Arabs, Persians, Gujarati, and others that one could hardly move'.[1] Among the products traded at that time were pepper, spices, Indian textiles, Chinese porcelain and silk, gold, silver, precious woods, tin and rice.

Dutch influence, however, spread rapidly through the archipelago during the seventeenth century; in port after port, Dutch naval power and political skill wrested trade monopolies from Indonesian rulers and the Portuguese. Later these monopolies were to be converted into compulsory tributes. This rapid spread of Dutch influence occurred under the aegis of the United East India Company, which was organized in 1602 as a union of the various independent companies engaged in trade with the Far East. From its inception the UEIC was closely linked to the Dutch government, being in effect the latter's extension in Asia, with full powers 'to make alliances with native princes, to appoint governors, and to employ troops'.[2] During the course of the century the Company adroitly furthered its interests by making use of conflicts and rivalries within the archipelago. Simultaneously, its economic orientation was changing. The spice trade was in decline and intra-Asian trade was becoming less profitable, while the prices for Asian goods in European markets were rising. Consequently, the Dutch economic interest turned from trade *per se* to production for export, for the most part to Europe. It never really shifted again.

The eighteenth century saw the introduction of the coffee tree to Java as well as the introduction and florescence of the system under which the UEIC exacted native-grown produce from the Indonesian rulers as tribute. Coffee, sugar, and pepper were the most important sources of profits for the Company during this era. It is extremely interesting to note that the native aristocracy reacted with speed to the introduction of the coffee plant, and between 1711 and 1720 the supply of coffee to the Company's storehouses rose a hundredfold. Worried that the growing wealth of the Javanese aristocrats might make them more difficult to control, the directors of the Company soon moved to lower the price of coffee arbitrarily in Batavia (today Djakarta) and to restrict the planting of coffee. By the end of the eighteenth century coffee had become the principal source of the Company's profits.

[1] J. C. van Leur, *Indonesian Trade and Society*, The Hague, 1955, p. 162.
[2] G. C. Allen and A. G. Donnithorne, *Western Enterprise in Indonesia and Malaya*, London, 1957, p. 18.

Towards the end of the eighteenth century the United East India Company was in serious financial trouble. The involvement of the Netherlands in the Franco–British–American war led the British to blockade the Dutch ports so as to sever all direct communications with the Indies. At the same time, the Company's directors in Holland stuck by the principle of excluding foreign traders from Indonesian ports. Already plagued by speculation on the part of its poorly paid employees and piracy in the seas of the archipelago, the Company accumulated large stocks of tropical products which could not be sold. By 1780 it was bankrupt and in 1796 the Dutch government took over its administration. The Company's charter expired on December 31, 1799, and was not renewed. Thus, for the meagre sum of $54 million,[1] the Dutch State acquired the foundations of a colonial empire built by merchants, civil servants, soldiers and explorers in the course of two centuries.

Throughout the greater part of the nineteenth century Dutch colonial policy was based primarily on the principle that the colonies were to be governed in such a way as to maximize economic benefits to the home country. The Culture System,[2] in effect between 1830 and 1870, had embodied this principle to a 't'. This system was introduced in the early thirties by Governor-General van de Bosch, who had arrived in the Indies with instructions 'to raise the production on Java of products suitable for the European market to at least 5 guilders per head'.[3] Its motivation, not surprisingly, was the hollow ring of the Dutch treasury during and after the war with Belgium. 'Under its aegis, virtually every crop which at the time might conceivably be grown with profit was attempted: indigo, sugar, coffee, tea, tobacco, pepper, cinchona, cinnamon, cotton, silk and cocheneale.'[4] The most successful of these was coffee, which accounted for more than three-fourths of the System's profits over its lifetime.[5] These crops were extracted from the native economy by the requirement that native cultivators set aside one-fifth of their lands for their cultivation. In theory, they were to have been compensated for this compulsory production by a reduction in the traditionally paid land rent and the sale of their produce to the

[1] 134 million guilders, at the rate of us $1 = f2.5.
[2] The Dutch term *cultuurstelsel* literally means 'cultivation system', but the name 'culture system' is more widely used.
[3] H. T. Colenbrander, *Koloniale Geschiedenis*, Vol. III, The Hague, 1926, p. 36.
[4] Clifford Geertz, *Agricultural Involution*, Berkeley, 1963, p. 54
[5] J. A. M. Caldwell, 'Indonesian Export and Production from the Decline of the Culture System to the First World War', in *The Economic Development of Southeast Asia*, edited by C. D. Cowan, New York and London, 1964, p. 81.

government. In addition, the government demanded labour services,[1] 'cast in the mould of the traditional *corvée* powers of the indigenous aristocracy',[2] which is utilized to build the requisite transportation and irrigation systems and to operate the processing factories.

Much has been written about the effects of the Culture System on Indonesian society. One thing is certain: the Indonesian cultivator was more often than not the victim of flagrant inequities. The limit on the amount of village land which could be set aside for compulsory cultivation appears often to have yielded to the demands of economic expediency, especially in the case of sugar production.[3] Land rent continued to be levied, while the wages for compulsory labour were kept low. Peasants were often required to spend months working far from their native village, during which time they had to provide their own food. It is not surprising, therefore, that rice production fell significantly while the price of rice rose sharply. Serious famines broke out in the 1840s and 1850s in three areas on Java.

By the middle of the nineteenth century both the inequities and the economic worth of the Culture System were debated heatedly throughout Dutch government circles. Its success as an economic enterprise was not easily assailed: in the forty-odd years after 1830 the Dutch treasury drew some $330 million from the Indies.[4] During the 1850s, however, many Dutchmen were asking with Baron van Höevell, a Member of Parliament, 'What have you done to promote the material and moral happiness of the Indonesian people?'[5] In 1860 public opinion in Holland was aroused by the publication of *Max Havelaar*,[6] a scathing criticism of colonial policies and practices. Meanwhile, Dutch Liberals, who sought to replace government with private enterprise, were gaining ground. In 1863 all government commercial activity in agriculture ceased except in sugar and coffee. In 1864 the administration of the colonies was brought under the control of Parliament. The end came in 1870 when a new

[1] The so-called *heerendiensten*.

[2] Geertz, *op. cit.*, p. 63.

[3] For two perspectives on the effects of the Culture System, see D. H. Burger, *De Ontsluiting van Java's Binnenland voor het Wereldverkeer*, Wageningen, 1939, pp. 117–60, and Colenbrander, *op. cit.*, pp. 37–42.

[4] 823 million guilders; the exchange rate used is US $1 = f2·5.

[5] Colenbrander, *op. cit.*, p. 47.

[6] E. D. Dekker (pseudonym Multatuli), *Max Havelaar; or the Coffee Auctions of the Dutch Trading Company* (reprinted, New York, 1967). A partly auto-biographical novel about a Dutch civil servant named Max Havelaar in the Indies and his unsuccessful attempt to protect Indonesian villagers from exploitation by their native regents.

Agrarian Law prohibited the sale of Indonesian land to non-Indonesians, while opening the door to private individuals and concerns by claiming as government domain all uncultivated land, permitting this land to be leased to private enterprise for periods of seventy-five years. At the same time, the Sugar Law limited the government's role in the sugar industry to the growing of cane, and provided for the gradual shrinkage of this function and its elimination by 1891.[1] The Dutch Liberals had won, and the period from 1870 to 1900 is generally referred to as the Liberal Period in Indonesian history.

Thus the thirty-odd years between 1880 and the First World War witnessed a large flow of private Dutch capital and entrepreneurship to the Indies. The laws that spelled the end of the Culture System had opened the door to private enterprise. Geography and technology opened it still wider. The opening of the Suez Canal in 1869 had drastically cut the distance between the Netherlands and its Asian colony, and brought a rapidly growing number of European families to the Indies. The development of steamship transportation brought Europe even closer to Asia. These factors, of course, inevitably reduced the share of the colonial government in export production. Between 1880 and 1913 it fell from 21 per cent to 8 per cent (see Table 10.2).

The period was not only one of economic transformation, it was marked also by a revolution in political thought. The Liberal colonial policy, in effect roughly between 1870 and 1900, did not question the principle that the Indies were to be governed for the benefit of the Netherlands. It was based on the belief that private enterprise would increase both Dutch government profits (in duties and taxes) and native welfare. Thus the end of the Culture System is not to be equated with a turn to the politics of humanitarianism, although humanitarian considerations did have an important role to play.

The real revolution in political thought occurred only at the turn of the century. Its expression was the 'Ethical Policy', which embodied the radical idea that the Indies were to be governed for the Indonesians. Although the Ethical Policy was often slow to translate good intentions into tangible results, it was an important spur to the modernizing influence of economic expansion. Its most important effect was a growing concern with native education, which had existed only in token form before 1900. The small but

[1] See H. C. Prinsen Geerligs, 'Rietsuiker', in K. W. van Gorkom, *Oost-Indische Cultures*, republished and edited by H. C. Prinsen Geerligs, Amsterdam, 1919, Vol. 2, p. 125.

growing educated Indonesian élite became the core of a new nationalist awakening, and in 1908 the *Budi Otomo* (High Endeavour) society was formed with the, at first non-political, purpose of promoting popular education in Indonesia. The Ethical Policy also spurred efforts to safeguard native institutions, to protect Indonesian peasants from the usury of (mostly Chinese) moneylenders, and to guarantee Indonesians a limited right to enter politics.

It is tempting, in the face of the many documented changes taking place in the period under consideration, to overstate the case. After all, the written history of the Indonesian archipelago after about 1600 has been concerned largely with the story of European settlement in the region. Owing to this historical bias, it is easy but erroneous to equate the rate of change of European society in the Indies with that of Indonesian society. In fact, their rates of change differed drastically. Clearly the rapid growth of Dutch emigration to the Indies and of a private plantation economy there during the period had important implications for certain segments of Indonesian society. But large segments were left virtually unaffected as well. In general, the Dutch influence was most pervasive on Java and decreased in proportion to the distance from that island.

In fact, the consolidation of Dutch rule in the archipelago was not accomplished until about 1915. The UEIC's aims had always been more mercantile than territorial, and its dominion had extended only over 'a series of settlements, factories, and forts'.[1] After 1750 the Dutch presence became more territorially oriented, but for more than a century Dutch rule on Java was indirect in the extreme. With the Liberal period 1870 came a shift of power from the Indonesian regents to the Dutch civil service, and by the turn of the century the Dutch exercised *de facto* sovereignty over Java, with the exception of four relatively small principalities.

In the Outer Islands, however, the extension of Dutch rule was a far more arduous process. The nineteenth century is stained with a number of bloody wars and punitive actions in Bali, Lombok, Sumatra, and elsewhere. Between 1890 and 1910 alone the colonial army lost almost 8,000 troops and officers, not including forced labourers.[2] Most important to the economic development of Sumatra was the war with the Sultanate of Achin (in North Sumatra) which raged from 1873 until about 1915. Only after 1904, when the colonial army under General van Heutsz broke the bulk of Achinese resis-

---

[1] Robert Nieuwenhuijs, *Tempo Doeloe: Fotografische Documenten uit het Oude Indie, 1870–1914*, Amsterdam, 1961, pp. 99.

[2] *ibid.*, p. 67.

tance, could Sumatra's exports and infrastructure grow more freely in response to world demand.

It would be misleading, therefore, to rate the period between 1880 and the First World War as the economic 'take-off' of Indonesia on the basis of aggregate production and trade statistics. It is essential to delineate carefully the sources of the rapid growth in production and trade, which lie largely in the European and Chinese segments of the colonial society, and to determine their effects on the native economy. Within the native economy, in turn, it is essential to distinguish between Java and the Outer Islands and between the characteristics of the various crops and regions in each. If generalizations about the period must be made, however, it may be said that technological, economic, and political developments rapidly began to multiply the number and kinds of 'poles of modernization' throughout Indonesian society.

II. ECONOMIC GROWTH: THE EVIDENCE

In 1880 the world stage was set for the rapid expansion of Indonesia's export production. The Suez Canal had significantly lowered transportation costs from the East Indies to Europe, and the development of steamship transport further accelerated this trend. The new route from Europe to East Asia through the Suez Canal cut the distance between the English Channel and the southern tip of Ceylon by almost one-half and was more than five weeks faster than the old sailing route around the Cape of Good Hope. Between 1875 and 1900 the number of European sailing ships arriving in Djakarta fell by a factor of nine while steamship arrivals more than tripled.[1] At the same time, the rapid industrial growth of Western Europe, the United States, and Japan during the last quarter of the nineteenth century buoyed up the demand for raw materials as well as consumption goods from the tropics.

How did producers and traders in the East Indies respond to these new opportunities for export production? The aggregate statistics for the period 1880–1913 show a rapid growth and diversification of exports. Table 10.1 gives an overview of the trends in the Indies' foreign trade between 1881 and 1915. Growth is relatively slow up to 1900, not only because of falling prices. Thereafter exports leap upwards, in volume as well as in prices. Indonesia, like the rest

[1] J. S. Furnivall, *Netherlands India, A Study of Plural Economy*, Cambridge, 1939, p. 206.

of the tropical world, was more prosperous after 1900 than before, on account of the rapid increase in export prices.[1]

TABLE 10.1: *Average Yearly Imports, Exports, and Export Surplus, 1881–1915*

(US $ million)*

Period	Imports	Exports	Export surplus
1881–5	56·8	75·6	18·8
1886–90	52·0	74·0	22·0
1891–5	64·8	82·4	17·6
1896–1900	68·0	90·8	22·8
1901–05	78·8	110·0	31·2
1906–10	103·2	165·6	62·4
1911–15	162·8	257·2	94·0

* At the exchange rate of 1 guilder = US $0·40.
Source: W. F. Wertheim, *Indonesian Society in Transition*, The Hague, 1964, p. 101.

Rapid export diversification also occurred during the period. The number of export categories recorded rose from 115 in 1865 to 239 in 1905.[2] The composition of exports is shown in Table 10.2. In agriculture the pace was set by sugar and tobacco, later by rubber and copra; in mining, by tin and oil. The production of sugar, largely on Java, more than doubled between 1870 and 1885, rising from about 153,000 metric tons to some 380,000 tons. The following fifteen years saw it double once again to reach a level of 744,000 metric tons in 1900. By 1912 production had again early doubled, at 1,465,000 metric tons. Rapid spurts in productivity lay at the heart of this growth of production. Between 1870 and 1913 the area planted with sugar on Java increased almost fourfold, while total production grew almost tenfold.[3] Necessity was, in the case of Javanese sugar, very much the mother of invention. The crises in world sugar prices of 1884 and 1895, and the destruction wrought by the *sereh*-disease forced the sugar plantations to seek new ways of keeping themselves from bankruptcy. One of these ways proved to be the establishment of experimental stations where all that was known about the cultivation of sugar cane was collected and distilled into useful new techniques. Planters of other crops later followed the successful example of the sugar industry and the

[1] See Chapter 2 above.   [2] Caldwell, *op. cit.*, p. 91.
[3] See G. F. E. Gonggrijp, *Schets ener Economische Geschiedenis van Indonesië*, Haarlem, 1957, p. 170.

I

TABLE 10.2: *Value of Principal Exports, Indonesia*

(us $ thousand)

	1880	1890	1900	1913
Sugar: Java	19,555	20,596	2 9,464	62,644
Outer Islands	2	..	..	..
Tobacco: Java	3,804	6,679	7,384	8,553
Outer Islands	2,496	6,258	5,452	28,316
Copra: Java	..	154	2,080	7,599
Outer Islands	..	664	2,044	14,418
Rubber: Java	10	16	27	3,552
Outer Islands	63	104	148	5,999
Coffee: Java	19,610	10,984	10,718	7,074
Outer Islands	4,342	3,641	3,128	2,091
Tea: Java	705	898	1,678	8,617
Outer Islands	..	..	1	..
Cassava: Java	..	..	234	3,599
Outer Islands	..	..	..	41
Petroleum: Java	..	..	..	452
Outer Islands	..	2	1,837	44,899
Tin: Java	..	..	..	..
Outer Islands	3,823	3,691	9,667	14,678
Total	70,000	70,000	103,200	268,400
Private	55,200*	63,200	92,000	245,600
Java	38,000*	43,600	62,800	126,800
Outer Islands	16,800	19,600	29,200	118,800
Government	14,800	6,800	11,200	22,800

* The total of private exports from Java in 1880 is an understatement of the sum of the commodities shown separately, but the table is internally consistent. *Source:* Furnivall, *op. cit.*, pp. 336–7.

experimental stations became an important feature of the Indonesian agricultural landscape.

Another development of great importance to the sugar industry on Java was the Brussels Convention of 1903, an agreement among European governments to stop the provision of export subsidies to their domestic beet sugar producers.[1] Sugar prices at last began to rise, and production raced ahead. Rapid productivity growth was also important in the case of cinchona, the quinine standard of the bark increasing almost threefold between 1884 and 1916. This product became an important export after 1880, when production was about 81 metric tons. By 1913, however, production was up to

[1] See Chapter 2 above.

about 7,500 metric tons, and by 1930 Indonesia supplied 97 per cent of world production.[1] Cinchona was produced almost exclusively on Java.

An event of particular economic significance for Indonesia was the introduction of the Brazilian rubber tree in 1883. Small quantities of relatively low-quality rubber had been produced on Java and Sumatra before that date, but the commercial production of rubber could become important only after the introduction of the 'superior brand'. The data on rubber production before the turn of the century are not very reliable, but it appears that the value of rubber exports more than doubled between 1880 and 1900. After 1900 the world market for rubber expanded rapidly owing to the growing use of the automobile, and before long rubber had moved to the forefront among Indonesia's exports. In 1910 the world market price of rubber reached its peak for the period and between 1900 and 1913 the value of Indonesia's rubber exports grew by a factor of 54. The greater part of these exports originated on Sumatra and Borneo (now Kalimantan), where land was relatively plentiful and native farmers took quickly to the growing of rubber trees.

The industrial growth of the Western nations during the period created a dynamic world market for minerals. Tin mining had been a profitable Netherlands government enterprise throughout the nineteenth century. Advances in mining technology had more than doubled the output of the mines, concentrated on the two small islands of Banka and Billiton, between 1811 and 1870. Thereafter output increased rapidly, reaching 12,600 metric tons in 1890 and 21,200 metric tons in 1913. This rapid spurt in tin production after 1890 was stimulated by a doubling in its world price between 1895 and 1900.

The largest new source of wealth that began to be tapped in the two decades before 1900, however, was oil. Serious interest in the exploitation of Indonesia's oil resources did not develop until after 1885, but the early efforts of small companies soon proved the profitability of oil production. The year 1890 saw the establishment of the famous Royal Dutch Oil Company, and by 1899 the interest of international business in the country's oil resources had induced the Dutch government to promulgate a new mining law which decreed 'that the government of Batavia should reserve certain oil fields for government exploitation'.[2] Oil production, in the mean-time, had risen from 300 metric tons in 1889 to some 363,000 tons

[1] Caldwell, op. cit., pp. 85–6.
[2] B. H. M. Vlekke, Nusantara: a History of Indonesia, Chicago, 1960, p. 297.

in 1900. The discovery of large oil fields in Indonesia was particularly fortunate in view of the general scarcity of oil in eastern Asia, and its importance today is underwritten by the international scramble for exploitation rights facing the Indonesian government.

In this period one major industry declined, viz. coffee. Government production was phased out, from around 53,000 metric tons yearly in 1882/6 to 21,000 in 1892/6 and 3,000 in 1906/11.[1] Private production did not make up the difference. It rose up to the middle 1890's, averaging around 25,000 tons per year,[2] but was then checked both by declining prices, and also by the spread of disease among the coffee trees. In addition, 'with the shedding of forced deliveries, there were fewer areas which could not be more profitably used for some other crop. . . . Growers . . . frequently combined their coffee cultivation with the cultivation of some other crop, such as rubber'.[3] This was the one dark spot in the agriculture of this period.

The growth of exports was accompanied by a rapid growth of imports, though the pace was slower. The composition of imports in this period, shown in Table 10.3, reveals important structural changes in the Indonesian economy.

TABLE 10.3: *Imports of Private Merchandise*

(US $ thousand)

	1880	1885	1890	1895	1900	1913
Rice and paddy						
Java	6,579	995	1,842	3,018	3,778	11,370
Outer Islands	3,069	1,352	3,028	2,848	3,230	10,911
Cotton goods						
Java	11,408	11,512	10,252	11,810	11,575	29,533
Outer Islands	2,326	2,962	4,033	2,188	2,723	8,956
Fertilizer	202	134	847	1,128	2,180	4,248
Machinery and tools	1,232	1,336	1,449	1,534	4,522	13,154
Iron and steel	1,016	1,150	1,502	1,708	4,005	14,162
Total	58,088	47,661	56,529	58,070	70,431	175,161

Source: Furnivall, *op. cit.*, pp. 207, 329.

Imports of rice and paddy had been minimal in the mid-nineteenth century. As the population of Java and Sumatra grew rapidly, however, especially with the inflow of foreign labour to work on the plantations, and as more and more land was devoted to the

---

[1] Z. Kamerling, 'Koffie'; see Gorkom, *op. cit.*, p. 241.
[2] *ibid.*, p. 255.   [3] Caldwell, *op. cit.*, p. 83.

production of non-food crops for export, it became necessary to import growing quantities of rice. Rice imports per year surpassed the million guilder (US $400,000 at the rate of 1 guilder = 0·40 US dollars) mark early in the 1870s, and doubled between 1880 and 1913, reaching a level of about US $22 million in the last year.

Imports of cotton goods remained approximately constant in the twenty years before 1900, but tripled in the next thirteen. It would be tempting to relate this spurt in imports after 1900 with the beginning of the Ethical Policy, a fall in the mortality rate and a rapid increase in population growth. The statistics, however, do not bear this out: the rate of native population growth actually fell sharply between 1890 and 1900, and remained low through 1913 (see Table 10.4). The truth is simply that Indonesia, like the rest of the tropical world, was more prosperous after 1900 than before, because of the rapid increase in export prices.[1]

TABLE 10.4: *Average Yearly Percentage Rates of Growth of Population, Java and Madura*

Category	1880–1890	1890–1900	1900–1905	1905–1913
European	3·06	3·06	0·78	5·63
Foreign Oriental	1·66	1·39	1·16	1·85
Native	1·91	1·82	0·98	0·96
Total	1·91	1·82	0·98	1·08

Source: Calculated from Furnivall, *op. cit.*, p. 347.

The rapid growth of consumer imports during the period was accompanied by an equally spectacular growth in imports of capital goods. Between 1880 and 1913 imports of fertilizer rose by a factor of 23, of machinery and tools by a factor of 11, and of iron and steel by a factor of 14. The rapid growth of these imports was clearly the result of the stepped-up economic activity in the relatively capital-intensive European sector of the Indies' economy.

III. FACTORS IN DEVELOPMENT

On the surface, then, it appears that the Dutch East Indies responded vigorously to the new opportunities afforded by a growing and changing world market between 1880 and the First World War. The aggregate statistics of production and export, however, throw little light on the economic, social, and political developments that

[1] See Chapter 2, page 50.

determined the precise nature of the response. Without an analysis of these developments there can be little understanding of Indonesia's response and its implications for the years that followed. In this section we pay special attention to infrastructure, the roles of the Chinese, Dutch immigration, financial institutions, land tenure, and labour.

Infrastructure. The rapid growth of Indonesia's export production required the construction of transport and communications facilities at a commensurate pace. Between 1880 and 1900, the colonial government spent approximately US $100 million on railroads, irrigation, and harbours.[1] The years between 1880 and the First World War saw railway mileage on Java and Sumatra multiply almost twenty-one times, in response to the needs of the growing European plantation economy (see Table 10.5). Nevertheless, at the end of this period, Indonesia had only some 3,400 miles of railway and tramway, little more than the span of the archipelago. Most of the lines, along with most of almost everything else, were concentrated on Java. As Sumatra's economic importance grew with the production of tobacco, rubber, copra, coal, and oil, however, the

TABLE 10.5: *The Growth of Communications by Rail, 1873–1913*

(miles)

	Railways				Tramways		
	State		Private		State	Private	
Year	Java	Sum.	Java	Sum.	Sum.	Java	Total
1873	—	—	162	—	—	—	162
1891	586	87	162	64	24	148	1,071
1900	1,025	130	162	64	48	822	2,251
1913	1,381	152	128	57	288	1,362	3,368

Source: Furnivall, *op. cit.*, p. 329.

island began to attract its share of new transport and communications facilities. An indirect index of its economic development, therefore, is given by the fall in Java's share in total railway and tramway mileage from 100 per cent in 1873 to 85 per cent in 1913. The growth of roadbed was extremely lopsided: 'apart from a short line in Celebes and a few light railways that served forestry and other large-scale undertakings, there was no railway construction in the rest of the Outer Provinces'.[2]

[1] Caldwell, *op. cit.*, p. 75.
[2] Allen and Donnithorne, *op. cit.*, p. 227.

Private capital flowed predominantly into tramway construction between 1880 and 1913, while the government took the initiative in the construction of the main railways. Both railways and the tramways, of course, were indispensable to the ability of European-owned and managed plantations in the Indies to produce competitively for the world market. The surge of private economic activity during the period is reflected in the fact that the government's share in rail transport declined from 65 per cent in 1891 to 54 per cent in 1913.

By 1880 road construction in the Indies had still been confined almost entirely to Java. This was not unnatural, since Sumatra and the other Outer Islands did not begin to gain importance as producers for export until the last quarter of the nineteenth century. The Culture System, confined to Java, had required the large-scale construction of roads to transport produce to the coast. Until 1851 these roads had been built exclusively by compulsory labour. In that year, after it was discovered that paid labour performed more efficiently, 'orders were given for all government buildings to be constructed with paid labour'.[1] Compulsory labour (*heerendiensten*), however, continued to be used until the First World War and was not abolished in most areas on Java until 1916.[2] Road construction in the Outer Islands did not gain momentum until the war with the Sultanate of Achin in North Sumatra came to an end in 1904. After that year, 'zealous officers pushed on road building with such energy that the burdens imposed on the people led to serious outbreaks which had to be suppressed by force'.[3]

One important effect of improved road and rail transportation in Indonesia was reflected in the convergence of food prices in different parts of Java. In 1861 rice sold for about thirteen times as much in Semarange (central Java) as in the Preanger (west Java). In 1901, when rice was in short supply, the largest price differential on Java was only 62·5 per cent![4]

The latter part of the nineteenth century was a time of rapid progress in telegraph and telephone communications. The first telegraph service in the Indies was opened in 1856, and by 1880 telegrams could be sent to Europe. The first private telephone company was founded in 1882, and sixteen years later there were thirty-five such companies. In the Dutch spirit of order and punctuality, the government took over the telephone companies in 1898. Postal communications, meanwhile had not stagnated. Inland and foreign mail services were established in the 1860s and were

[1] Furnivall, *op. cit.*, p. 184.   [2] Gonggrijp, *op. cit.*, p. 184.
[3] Furnivall, *op. cit.*, p. 330.   [4] Colenbrander, *op. cit.*, p. 85.

expedited by the growth in the number of steamships after the opening of the Suez Canal.

In Indonesia, the growth of steamship transport and communications in the 1870s and 1880s was dominated by the British. The famous Dutch K.P.M. (Koninklijke Paketvaart Maatschappij) steamship company was not founded until 1888, and Dutch steamship transport did not become a serious affair until the twentieth century. Inevitably, the rapidly expanding plantation economy and the growth of steamship transport through the Suez Canal created a strong demand for new and better harbours: 'When the opening of the Suez Canal inspired Prince Henry with the vision of a modern fleet, he urged on the . . . Government the need of better dock facilities.'[1] Consequently, the construction of a new harbour at Batavia, begun in the 1870s, was completed in 1893. Railroad construction to the coast of south central Java induced the building of a harour at Tjilatjap in the 1880s. And the 1890s saw the construction of harbours to serve the tobacco and coal regions of Sumatra.

As was the case with roads, Java inherited significant irrigation facilities from the days of the Culture System, when water was required to grow the export crops. Compulsory labour was freely used in the construction of irrigation works at that time, even if its efficiency was impaired by practices caricatured in the case of 'a Resident who constructed a dam across a river by requiring every one liable to service in the Residency to throw down one stone'.[2] The importance of the sugar plantations as well as the necessity-induced expansion of wet rice cultivation on Java between 1880 and 1913 provided the thrust for a continued growth in irrigation facilities. Between 1885 and 1900 the average annual increase in irrigated land on Java was almost 4,700 hectares. Between 1900 and 1915, under the impetus of Ethical Policy funds, this figure rose to more than 23,000 hectares.[3] A separate Irrigation Department was formed in 1889. Between 1900 and 1910 the government spent about US $7·6 million on irrigation in the Indies; between 1910 and 1920 about US $23·2 million.[4] Irrigation facilities were, of course, scarce on Sumatra, due to a lack of Dutch interest in the first two-thirds of the nineteenth century and to the fact that its economic development rested largely on the cultivation of unirrigated export crops such as tobacco and rubber.

---

[1] Furnivall, *op. cit.*, p. 207.   [2] *ibid.*, p. 184.
[3] Calculated from *ibid.*, p. 324.
[4] See J. Th. Metzelaar, 'Irrigatie', in C. J. J. van Hall and C. Van de Koppel, eds., *De Landbouw in den Indischen Archipel,* The Hague, 1946–50, Vol. 1, p. 230.

The sizeable investments in roads, railways and tramways, harbours, and telegraph, telephone, and postal communications, as well as the growing importance of steamer traffic in the 1880–1913 period opened the way to a rapidly swelling flow of produce from the hinterlands to the coastal towns. The channels through which this flow finally reached the harbours were predominantly Chinese

The role of the Chinese. The Chinese, of course, had been the trading class of the Indonesian archipelago for centuries. As early as the beginning of the seventeenth century, Jan Pieterszoon Coen, the famous fourth Governor-General of the Indies, had urged that 'retail trade should be left to the Chinese ("retailers who in this connection, and even as merchants, far exceed ours in ability")'.[1] About two centuries later Raffles referred to the Chinese as 'the agents of the Dutch', who 'have almost an uncontrolled command of the Javanese market for foreign commodities'.[2] Expanding on this theme, he wrote: 'Almost all the inland commerce . . . is under the direction of the Chinese, who possessing considerable capital, and frequently speculating on a very extensive scale, engross the greater part of the wholesale trade, buy up the principal articles of export from the native grower, convey them to the maritime capitals and in return supply the interior with salt and with the principal articles imported from . . . foreign countries. Coasting trade is carried on in vessels belonging chiefly to Chinese, Arabs, and Bugis'.[3]

During the two centuries of the UEIC in the archipelago, the Chinese penetrated the hinterlands of Java and, to a lesser extent, those of the Outer Islands, and gained the virtually uncontested dominance of trade with the natives, who were left with a minor role in petty domestic retail trade. Inevitably, the Chinese dominance of trade was furthered and complemented by their virtual monopoly of credit to the native producers. Thus Chinese continued in their dual function of traders and moneylenders throughout the nineteenth century and are today still engaged predominantly in these activities.

The economic activities of the Chinese in the Indies did not fail to arouse antagonism, among the Indonesians as well as the Dutch. Two legal developments deserve mention in this regard. One is the system of passports and quarters. The passports system, requiring special

[1] H. T. Colenbrander, *Jan Pietersz. Coen: Bescheiden omtrent zijn Bedrijf in Indië*, The Hague, 1948, Vol. 2, p. 181.
[2] T. S. Raffles, *A History of Java*, London, 1817, Vol. 1, p. 224.
[3] *ibid.*, pp. 199–201.

permits for travel in the hinterland, had been established by the UEIC by the end of the seventeenth century, mainly as a device to maintain order. The enforcement of these travel restrictions, however, was so deficient as to render them 'worthless as a means of preventing the spreading of the Chinese over the interior of the country'.[1] These regulations were relaxed after 1904, and abolished for Java and Madura in 1914, for the Outer Islands in 1918. The quarter system was instituted after the Chinese rebellion in Batavia of 1740, and required the Chinese to live in separate quarters. This system, too, 'was never rigorously applied',[2] and was abolished for Java in 1919. Nevertheless, 'the permit-and-quarter system may be mentioned as one of the principal causes of the non-development of Chinese small-scale farming in Java'.[3] Another important constraint on the economic dominance of the Chinese in the hinterlands was the agrarian legislation of 1870, which forbade the alienation of native lands. The Irrawaddy Delta in Burma provides an illustration of what might have happened on Java in the absence of this legislation.

Dutch welfare surveys after 1900, under the impetus of the Ethical Policy, tended to place a good deal of the blame for the economic stagnation of the Javanese on the activities of Chinese moneylenders who 'managed to get the cultivators in their power, . . . encouraged opium-smoking and gambling . . . and as middlemen . . . shut off the native from industry and commerce, and restricted him to agriculture'.[4]

Dutch immigration. Transportation, communications, and the Chinese thus were among the factors which made possible Indonesia's response to a dynamic world market for tropical products. The protagonists on the economic scene, however, were the swarms of Dutch entrepreneurs who came to the Indies in the last quarter of the nineteenth century.

Before 1870, Indonesia had never offered an attractive prospect to the Dutch entrepreneur. Export production was securely in government hands, and the native market was far from promising. In addition, life in the Indies was regarded by many as a form of exile in a hot, hardship-ridden, strange, faraway place, fit only for those who could not build a comfortable niche in Dutch society. In the 1830s, the Dutch 'could not be beaten out of their homes with

---

[1] B. J. Cator, *The Economic Position of the Chinese in the Netherlands Indies*, Oxford, 1936, p. 33.
[2] *ibid.*, p. 18.   [3] *ibid.*, p. 35.   [4] Furnivall, *op. cit.*, p. 397.

sticks',[1] and in 1852, out of a total European civil population in the Indies of more than 22,000 'the number of non-officials was less than a thousand, possibly no more than six hundred'.[2]

After 1870, all this began to change rapidly. The Suez Canal and the steamship drew the Indies closer to the home country, and the Agrarian Law of 1870 'opened Java to private capital'.[3] The Culture System was no more, and private enterprise was to take its place. The Indies, in fact, became a new land of promise not dissimilar to the United States and Australia. The results of the change in the character of life in the Indies are reflected in Table 10.6.

TABLE 10.6: *Population of Java and Madura, 1880–1913*

(thousands)

Year	Europeans	Foreign Orientals	Natives	Total
1880	33·7	219	19,540	19,794
1890	45·9	259	23,609	23,914
1900	62·4	298	28,384	28,746
1905	64·9	317	29,715	30,098
1913*	102·2	369	32,215	32,688

* Interpolated between 1905 and 1920.
Source: Furnivall, *op. cit.,* p. 347.

As the table indicates, the European population in the Indies grew at a rate far higher than the native population. By 1913 it had more than tripled its size in 1880, while the native population had grown by only 65 per cent. The number of foreign orientals (mainly Chinese) in Indonesia had increased slightly more, 68 per cent over the period. It should be noted, however, that the percentage of Europeans in the total population of Java and Madura in 1880 was a mere 0·2 per cent. In 1913 it was no more than 0·3 per cent. The percentage of Europeans and foreign orientals taken together grew from 1·3 per cent in 1880 to 1·4 per cent in 1913.

If the number of Europeans in the Indies during the period seems at first glance incongruous with the political and economic power which they wielded, it must be remembered that most of this power was concentrated on Java, and that governmental authority was exercised through indirect rule. The economic influence of the European minority in the Indies was always strongest on Java, where

[1] W. M. F. Mansvelt, *Geschiedenis van de Nederlandsche Handel-Maatschappij,* Haarlem, 1924, Vol. 2, p. 9.
[2] Furnivall, *op. cit.,* p. 212. [3] Nieuwenhuijs, *op. cit.,* p. 49.

267

the Culture System, land shortage, and the concentration of European-run plantations discouraged native commercial production. In a parallel fashion, the machinery of Dutch rule was concentrated on Java. In addition, indirect rule was extremely labour-saving with respect to European civil servants. In 1900 some 5,300 Europeans constituted the apex of the civil service on Java and Madura, resting on a base of about 24,000 native civil servants, ranging from regents to clerks and guards.[1] In effect, Dutch rule had made use of the Indonesian aristocracy as a colonial civil service.

Financial institutions. The rapid growth of the European population in the Indies during the period was accompanied by a spurt in private lending. Before 1860, the flow of private capital to the Indies had been a mere trickle. Between 1860 and 1880, however, a number of banks and trading companies were founded 'with the purpose of purveying the necessary capital to private agricultural enterprises'.[2]

In the period from 1880 to the First World War these institutions continued to meet the demand for capital created by a rapidly growing European plantation economy in the Indies. Thus the paid-up capital in Dutch institutions financing agricultural enterprises in Indonesia almost doubled between 1900 and 1915, rising from about US $29 million to some US $56 million.[3] At the same time, total outstanding direct investments in Indonesia are estimated to have risen from US $300 million in 1900 to US $675 million in 1914; *rentier* investments, mainly in government securities, are estimated to have risen from US $18 million in 1900 to US $68 million in 1914.[4]

On Java, the sugar crisis of 1883–4 proved disastrous to many financing institutions in the Netherlands, and thereby set the stage for the rapid growth of their direct control and ownership of plantations in the Indies. Thus the agricultural commitments of the specialized Dutch 'cultivation banks' (*cultuurbanken*) in Indonesia 'rose from 37 million florins (US $15 million) in 1888 to over 70 million florins (US $28 million) in 1912'.[5] At the same time, these banks became 'increasingly concerned with investment rather than with lending operations. In 1912 they supported 103 sugar factories and 42 other agricultural undertakings, apart from those which they administered but did not finance. Of this total of 145, 42 undertakings were wholly owned by the banks and 27 were partially owned by them'.[6]

---

[1] Colenbrander, *Koloniale Geschiedenis*, pp. 82–3.
[2] Vlekke, *op. cit.*, p. 290.
[3] See Furnivall, *op. cit.*, p. 335.
[4] See Allen and Donnithorne, *op. cit.*, p. 288.
[5] *ibid.*, p. 192.   [6] *ibid.*, p. 192.

The sugar crisis also brought about a shift from personal to corporate enterprise in the Indies, which was an important catalyst to the flow of capital and entrepreneurship into the archipelago.[1]

Land tenure. The European plantation economy could not have grown as fast as it did in the Indies without the availability of land and labour. In this respect, great differences exist between Java and the Outer Islands. In the former, labour was relatively plentiful while land was scarce; in the latter the reverse held true. This contrast in the supply of land and labour inputs between Java and the Outer Islands had far-reaching implications for the types of crops cultivated on each, and the extent to which natives took part in export production on an independent basis. Thus the foundations for future economic growth were distributed very evenly throughout the Indies.

The structure of land ownership, tenure, and use in the Indies in the period under consideration is extremely varied and complex. This is due in large part to the superimposition of Western legal concepts on a system of native customs regarding the use and ownership of land. This superimposition did not present serious problems to the colonial government until the 1860s when private enterprise began to replace the Culture System. Until that time, the Dutch government had settled questions of land use mainly by its authority, duly supported by force. With the growth of the private plantation sector in the Indies, however, the government had to respond to the need for a clear, workable system of land use.

The Agrarian Law of 1870 embodied its dual response. On the one hand the new law sought to 'continue to protect native rights on the land, on the other hand to provide private agriculture . . . with a more solid basis'.[2] Its most important provision stated that all lands for which ownership could not be proved by others were government domain. Since this provision alone could technically have erased most native claims to land, a distinction was later drawn between 'free' and 'unfree' domains. 'Unfree' domains were all lands to which individual or communal native claims existed; 'free' domains were the remainder. In effect, the distinction was drawn between lands cultivated or occupied by natives and uncultivated but cultivable 'waste' lands. It was on the latter that the Western plantation economy, with the major exception of sugar plantations, flourished after 1870. All land in the 'free' category

[1] See Nieuwenhuijs, *op. cit.*, p. 7.
[2] A. D.A . de Kat Angelino, *Staatkundig Beleid en Bestuurszorg in Neder-landsch-Indië*, The Hague, 1930, Vol. 2, p. 507.

could henceforth be allocated by the government to one of three classes. Small pieces, not in excess of about seven hectares, could be allocated to the expansion of cities and villages, or to industrial uses. Since the sale of larger pieces of land was forbidden by law, the formation of new private farms became impossible. The second class consisted of land to be used for barns, warehouses and rail transport. The most important class, however, was land for leasing to private persons, known as *erfpacht* lands.

While the Agrarian Law protected native landowners and users by prohibiting the sale of land by Indonesians to foreigners, it opened the door to Dutch private agriculture by permitting the lease of 'free' domains on the basis of *erfpacht*, 'that is to say . . . on heritable lease from the government'.[1] The duration of such a lease was seventy-five years, almost four times the maximum length of govenment leases in earlier years. It is hardly surprising, therefore, that 'there was a sharp increase in the area held on *erfpacht* after 1870, especially in the Outer Provinces where the amount of 'free' land was greater than in densely settled Java'.[2] With the passage of the Agrarian Law a major step had been taken to assure private planters an adequate and stable supply of land. Most of the native cultivated lands on Java were lowlands used for wet rice cultivation. Thus the perennial crop plantations rapidly crept up Java's hillsides and spilled on to the highlands, while the annuals, the most important of which was sugar, were planted on native irrigated lands in rotation with the rice crops.

This system of interphasing sugar and rice production on the same village lands deserves mention, since on the one hand it is an example of the way in which both food and commercial non-food crops can be produced where land is very scarce, and on the other it constitutes an important reason for Java's history of food shortage. The system in the 1870s as a result of the scarcity of land suitable for originated sugar cane, and the gradual transition from a government-dominated to a private Dutch sugar industry in the Indies. The private concern would contract a lease of some twenty-one years with a village. It would then plant one-third of the village *sawah* (irrigated land) in cane. The cane would grow and be cut on this land over about eighteen months. At the end of this period the land was returned to its holders and another third of the village lands would be planted with cane. However, since new cane was usually planted before the old was cut, an average of *one-half*, not one-third, of the village lands would be used in the production of sugar (since

---

[1] Allen and Donnithorne, *op. cit.*, p. 68.   [2] *ibid.*, pp. 68–9.

the portion of village land in sugar would vary from one-third to two-thirds). It took three years for one cycle to be completed[1] and seven cycles could take place during a single lease.[2]

In practice, this system actually reduced the amount of land cultivated in rice. During the period of the Culture System, villages in districts suitable for the growing of sugar cane put one-third of their arable land at the disposal of the government, and not all of this land was necessarily used for the growing of cane. So the period of Liberalism (1870–1900) saw a greater pressure on land suitable for the production of rice in Java than the period of the Culture System!

A Sugar Law accompanied the Agrarian Law of 1870, and *de jure* put an end to all government enterprises in the cultivation and processing of sugar. In effect, however, the transition from forced sugar cultivation to free enterprise took place over more than a decade. The curious fact is that during this transition period native peasants received more in compensation for the use of their land, where they ceded this land on government authority under the pre-1870 system, than they did for freely rented land.[3] What, then, was the incentive to rent land? The answer lies partly in the widespread use by Dutch planters of advance payments as a means to secure an adequate supply of land at a relatively low cost. Apparently, peasants were easily persuaded by the size of lump payments, often between three and five years' rent,[4] to cede their land to the planters on a seasonal basis. In addition, since the same people whose land was rented to the sugar companies often provided the labour to grow and process the crop, they may have been better off. On the Outer Islands, of course, the relative abundance of land rendered such arrangements superfluous.

Labour. In the period between 1880 and the First World War, the distribution of labour in the Indies stood in marked contrast to that of free land. In densely populated Java, labour was not difficult for the planters to obtain, especially on a seasonal basis. On Sumatra and the other Outer Islands, however, labour was scarce and plantations and mines were usually worked with immigrant Chinese labour, both free and indentured.

Immigrant Chinese labour was used in significant quantities on

---

[1] With an average of one-half of the village lands in sugar at any one time, and the passage of 18 months between the planting and cutting of cane, one cycle took 36 (twice 18) months.

[2] See Geertz, *op. cit.*, pp. 86–7.

[3] Gonggrijp, *op. cit.*, p. 183.   [4] *ibid.*

the plantations of Sumatra and in the tin-mines of Banka, Billiton, and Singkep. The history of this labour is, not surprisingly, cluttered with abuses and incidents of maltreatment. In the 1870s, the initiative to protect the immigrant Chinese labourer from abuses came from the British authorities in Singapore and Penang, important recruiting grounds, rather than from the colonial government itself.

Measures taken by the Dutch government to protect the rights and welfare of immigrant labour do not exactly spell a history of muck-raking. It is true that an end was put to outright slavery in 1860, but the growing numbers of Dutch planters in the Indies put strong pressures on the government to cede to their demands for greater legal control over labour. Thus in 1873 foreign labourers in Deli (East Sumatra) became subjects of the Dutch government rather than of the sultan, enabling planters to control their labour supply through legal means. In 1880 the Coolie Ordinanace was applied to East Sumatra, later to other regions. This Ordinance included a penal sanction in cases of breach of contract, in effect an easy means for planters to retain and strengthen their hold in the labour supply. The system of penal sanctions, although constantly under attack in Holland in the twentieth century, was not finally abolished until 1942, under the combined pressures of 'the democratic ideal, the "ethical" colonial policy, and, above all, international interests'.[1] Under the aegis of the Ethical Policy after the turn of the century the first Inspector of Labour 'was appointed in 1904 for the East Coast of Sumatra, and in 1908 he was charged with the supervision of recruiting and the general working of the Coolie Ordinances'.[2] Clearly, however, the moral considerations of the Ethical Policy were not sufficiently compelling to move the colonial government to take a stand against the planters on the labour issue.

IV. THE INDIGENOUS ECONOMY

The aspects of economic change discussed above are largely confined to the spheres of the colonial government and the European plantation economy. Today the problems of economic development are those of an Indonesian government and a native Indonesian economy. It is extremely important, therefore, to consider the effects of Western government and enterprise on the Indonesian economy during our period. What were the foundations of later economic

[1] J. H. Boeke, *Economics and Economic Policy of Dual Societies*, New York, 1953, p. 156.
[2] Furnivall, *op. cit.*, p. 355.

development established during the period, and where were they laid?

As Table 10.7 indicates, the Indonesian share of total agricultural exports rose from a tenth in 1898 to a quarter in 1913. The increasing weight of Indonesian export production derived mainly from spurts in the cultivation of coconut palms and rubber trees in the Outer Islands, and tea, tobacco, and sugar on Java. Of these, copra was almost exclusively an Indonesian product (by 1931, 95 per cent of the Indies' total production was still Indonesian).[1] Indonesian production of tea rose from 37 metric tons in 1880 (1·5 per cent of the total) to 2,325 tons in 1910 (15 per cent of the total).[2] On Java, the area planted with tobacco by Indonesians rose from about 65,000 hectares in 1885 to almost 160,000 in 1914.[3] On the same island, Indonesians planted twice as much land with sugar in 1900 (124,000 hectares) as in 1890 (63,000 hectares).[4]

How was the Indonesian response to buoyant world markets distributed? Table 10.7 clearly spells out the difference in this respect between Java and the Outer Islands.

TABLE 10.7: *Exports of Agricultural Commodities*

(US $ million)

Year	Java and Madura			Outer Islands			Total		
	(*)	(†)	(‡)	(*)	(†)	(‡)	(*)	(†)	(‡)
1898	48	2	4·2	13	4	31·7	61	6	10·1
1902	54	5	9·6	19	10	51·3	73	15	20·3
1913	110	17	15·5	50	22	42·3	260	39	24·5

(*) Total value.
(†) Value of Indonesian share.
(‡) Percentage of Indonesian share.
Source: Furnivall, *op. cit.*, p. 320.

Whereas on Java and Madura in 1913 less than one-sixth of the value of agricultural exports was produced by Indonesians, the corresponding figure for the Outer Islands is more than two-fifths.

Moreover, the Outer Islands were now developing faster than Java. Whereas the value of nine leading exports from Java rose by a factor of about 5·5 between 1870 and 1930, the corresponding figure for the Outer Islands is about 37.[5] It is clear, therefore, that while Java's export production grew at a non-spectacular pace, a kind of economic 'take-off' gathered momentum in the Outer

[1] Caldwell, *op. cit.*, p. 89.   [2] *ibid.*, p. 93.
[3] *ibid.*   [4] *ibid.*, p. 94.   [5] Geertz, *op. cit.*, p. 104.

Islands, fed increasingly by Indonesian commercial production. This trend has continued since the turn of the century to the point where almost all foreign exchange earned by Indonesia today derives from a consistent Outer Islands trade surplus. Overpopulated Java, in contrast, is a net consumer of this same foreign exchange in duties and taxes. This disparity in earnings and consumption has considerably increased political tensions between Java and the Outer Islands since independence.

What factors account for this trend? In capsule form, the relatively slow growth of Java's agricultural exports was due to a shortage of suitable land. The possibilities of expanding the area under wet-rice and sugar cultivation (they were often grown on the same land in cycles) were extremely limited. Aside from increases in productivity in these crops, therefore, and the conversion of rice land to sugar cane, increased export production had to come from the 'free' *erfpacht* lands.

The Agrarian Law of 1870 had permitted the lease of *erfpacht* lands to Indonesians, but it was clear that the colonial government would not be unbiased in its application of the law. Thus production of perennial crops on *erfpacht* lands was seriously hampered by 'the government's policy of favouring planters over peasants', and 'cases of favouritism were defended by Netherlands Indies officials with the argument that the interests of the state were best served by a strong plantation industry capable of competing on the world market'.[1] The relative scarcity of cultivable land on Java thus set the stage for a competition between native peasants and Dutch planters in the exploitation of opportunities for export production, a competition in which the legel, administrative, financial, and political odds heavily favoured the latter. In the case of the cultivation of perennial crops on the relatively less settled, unirrigated, uplands, therefore, 'the Javanese . . . were administratively barred from the bulk of their own frontier, the so-called "waste lands" . . .'.[2] In a parallel fashion, 'Dutch control of milling, legal restrictions and semi-legal pressures easily effected the . . . aim of keeping smallholders out of the cane-growing business'.[3] These restrictions on land use for commercial production by Indonesians, of course, did not bar them entirely from participation in the growth and diversification of exports, as was indicated above with regard to tea, tobacco,

[1] K. J. Pelzer, 'The Agricultural Foundation', in R. T. McVey *Indonesia*, New Haven, 1963, pp. 147, 32, 501.
[2] Geertz, *op. cit.*, p. 80.
[3] *ibid.*, p. 58.

and sugar. They did, however, by and large shape the distribution of Indonesian export production throughout the archipelago.

The process of economic development, or non-development, in the native sector on Java has been termed 'agricultural involution',[1] or again, 'static expansion'.[2] These terms refer to the phenomenon of Java's *per capita* rice production remaining more or less constant over the period 1850–1900, when population growth was rapid. This fact is combined with the intrusion of sugar cultivation on the irrigated rice lands to yield the conclusion that 'the superimposition of sugar cultivation on the already unequal distribution of *sawah* (wet-rice land) and population over Java left the Javanese peasantry with essentially a single choice in coping with their rising numbers: driving their terraces, and in fact all their agricultural resources, harder by working them more carefully'.[3] The term 'involution', here used in an economic context, is derived from anthropology where it describes 'those culture patterns which, after having reached what would seem to be a definitive form . . . continue to develop by becoming internally more complicated'.[4] A rising productivity in wet-rice cultivation, however, could not continue to match increases in population growth. Substantial imports of rice and paddy occurred in the 1880–1913 period, and local wet-rice production today still falls far short of the demand.

Why did Indonesian peasants not bridge the gap between the demand and the production of rice, displacing some of the substantial imports of Java and the Outer Islands? One part of the answer is common to Java and the Outer Islands. Simply, the evidence suggests that it was more profitable to grow cash crops for export than to grow food crops. Thus we see Indonesians planting substantial areas of potential rice land with sugar cane on Java.

At the same time, of course, a rapidly growing European-managed plantation economy found local supplies of rice more and more insufficient to feed its burgeoning labour force. On Java, the intrusion of the European sugar companies on the village *sawahs*, referred to above, was backed by the not unbiased colonial political-administrative apparatus. Thus the Javanese peasant did not have the room to expand rice production (if he had been so inclined) that was available to his Sumatran counterpart. Ironically, on

[1] See Geertz, *op. cit.* [2] Boeke, *Economics and Economic Policy*, p. 174.
[3] Geertz, *op. cit.*, p. 79. [4] *ibid.*, pp. 80–1.

Sumatra one response to the growing rice crises was the formation, in 1914, of a Dutch rice company.[1]

In contrast to the Javanese pattern, economic developments in the Outer Islands spelled a success story. In 1881 Sumatra's exports totalled some US $10 million (24 million guilders); by 1910 they had risen to about US $27 million (68 million guilders) and by 1922 to US $132 million (331 million guilders).[2] This contrast is often attributed to an inherent difference between the 'independent', 'assertive', 'economically minded' Sumatrans and the 'docile', 'servile', 'feudal', 'lazy' Javanese. Whereas there are undoubtedly some important cultural differences between the Javanese and the Sumatrans,[3] the use of such character sketches to explain economic phenomena is probably a confusion of cause with effect. More likely economic opportunities and the availability of suitable land in the Outer Islands tended to encourage Indonesian economic enterprise and innovation, while a forced kind of economic stagnation in Java's peasant sector led to a pervasive stifling of initiative and acceptance of the status quo.

The economic development of the Outer Islands derived both from European-run plantations and from Indonesian enterprise. For the plantations, amply financed by Dutch and other foreign capital, the chief problem was the shortage of labour. As late as 1915, 'the autochthonous population density in East Sumatra seems to have been less than six per square kilometers, which is low even for a swidden area'.[4] The first Western plantations, the famous tobacco estates of Deli (East Sumatra), which made their entrance on the Sumatran scene in the early 1860s, therefore had to rely on imported – mostly Chinese – labour, much of which could be recruited across the Strait of Malacca in Singapore and Penang. The abuses by planters in the recruitment and control of immigrant labour have already been referred to. Nevertheless, a substantial number of immigrant Chinese labourers did stay in Sumatra. Available data indicate that between 1888 and 1900 the total number of Chinese immigrants to the tobacoo plantations of Deli (East Sumatra) varied between about four and ten thousand yearly. During this same period, the number of labourers returned varied between some six hundred and two thousand yearly.[5] The Chinese were not the only

[1] H. Blink, *Opkomst en Ontwikkeling van Sumatra als Economisch-Geographisch Gebied*, The Hague, 1926, p. 81.   [2] *ibid.*, p. 110.

[3] Muslim influences were and are strongest on Sumatra, Indian influences on Java.

[4] Geertz, *op. cit.*, p. 109.   [5] See Cator, *op. cit.*, pp. 227–8.

immigrant labourers on Sumatra. Javanese labour was also used, and by 1914 there were some 64,400 Javanese in Sumatra,[1] while the total number of Javanese contract labourers working in the Outer Islands was about 300,000.[2]

Most of the immigrant labour was used in a relatively small area on Sumatra's East Coast, where a number of Western plantations were concentrated. The tobacco plantations in this area had obtained the use of their land in the 1860s through concessions from the local sultans (it must be remembered that Dutch political control in the Outer Islands was precarious at that time). Through these concessions the Dutch planters obtained vast control over the native population within the contracted territories. Almost inevitably, this control was used increasingly to limit the economic freedom of the native cultivator. Thus in 1884 the latter was guaranteed 'a harvest year', and by 1892, merely 'a harvest'. Originally he had been permitted to grow 'rice *and* maize', in the 1890s only 'rice *or* maize'. As with the crops, so with the land. Increasingly, the contracts limited the amounts of land open to use by the native cultivator.[3] Not surprisingly, then, native production for export did not flourish under these conditions.

Elsewhere in Sumatra and other islands land was abundant and the native cultivator was free from such restrictions. Rubber, coconuts, and coffee fitted into the traditional native swidden agriculture with fortunate ease. Rubber and coconuts especially, required very little care and could be planted simultaneously with shorter yield food and cash crops, often coffee. After about seven years' time the rubber trees would become tappable and the farmer merely had to cut away a minimum of undergrowth to get at the trees.[4] It is important to note here the relationship between the supply of arable land and the capital costs of cultivating perennials such as rubber trees and coconut palms. Neither requires a great deal of care for a product of acceptable quality, and both yield their first commercial fruits only after a number of years. On Java, where land was relatively scarce (especially to Indonesians), the opportunity cost of planting land with rubber trees was substantial, even where mixed cropping occurred. Opportunities for planting shorter-yield cash or food crops on additional land were extremely

[1] Blink, *op. cit.*, p. 78.   [2] Gonggrijp, *op. cit.*, p. 141.
[3] See Geertz, *op. cit.*, pp. 198–110.
[4] See T. A. Tengwall, 'History of Rubber Cultivation and Research in the Netherlands Indies', in P. Honig and F. Verdoorn, eds., *Science and Scientists in the Netherlands Indies*, New York, 1945, p. 350.

limited. Thus the Javanese peasant, with his meagre capital resources, had a much harder time trying to bridge the gap between the planting and fruition of rubber trees and coconut palms than his Outer Island counterpart.

On Sumatra, with an abundance of land and shifting cultivation, this opportunity cost could easily be cancelled by planting rubber trees on one piece of land (perhaps mixed with other crops), and food or cash crops on other land, until the trees began to yield. Hence the cultivation of rubber and coconut trees in Sumatra favoured the Indonesian smallholder as well as the European planter, on Java predominantly the latter. One would expect, therefore, some migration of Javanese peasants to the Outer Islands, especially to neighbouring Sumatra. No clear evidence of this, however, has been found, and it appears that cultural differences between Java and Sumatra were important deterrents to migration.

The 'take-off' of the native economy in the Outer Islands, then, derived its momentum from the smallholder cultivation of rubber trees and coconut palms, in response to attractive world prices and the ease with which both could be grown on the ample land. Commerical production in the twentieth century was facilitated by the formal end of the war with the Sultanate of Achin (in North Sumatra) in 1904, which marked the beginning of a period in which order was more effectively established and maintained, and road construction more vigorously pursued. As on Java, Chinese traders provided an outlet for commercial products which found their way to the harbours and the large Singapore market. Since the rubber produced by Indonesian smallholders was generally of low quality, the Chinese were quick to establish re-processing factories in Singapore, thereby providing the Indonesian cultivator with a link to the world market while, of course, strengthening their own economic position.[1] The Sumatran smallholder, then, had land and a market, and the only factor inhibiting the development of large Indonesian rubber estates was the shortage of labour. Importing labour, or bidding it away from the European-managed estates, required financial resources far beyond the reach of the Indonesian cultivator. Thus a growing Indonesian smallholder economy was securely linked to the world market, and stimulated by the investments in infrastructure which the Dutch agricultural and mineral interests in the Outer Islands sunk directly or elicited from the colonial government.

Why were the Outer Islands so late to link with the world market?

[1] See A. van Gelder, 'Bevolkingsrubbercultuur', in van Hall and van de Koppel, *op. cit.*, Vol. 3, p. 428.

In the first place, of course, Dutch political and military control in the Outer Islands was established much later than on Java, and remained tenuous until the beginning of the twentieth century, when the bloody war with Achin ended, and the separate treaties and arrangements of the Dutch government with the various principalities of Sumatra were replaced by the single principle of Dutch rule. The power of the principalities to create disorder and internal wars was then substantially curtailed, and as order and safety began to spread through the hinterlands, the native economy became more responsive to world market opportunities. The concentration of Dutch control on Java until the middle of the nineteenth century may well have been the most efficient allocation of political, economic, and military resources. In addition, the institution of the Culture System in the 1830s required large quantities of labour, which it would have been near impossible to recruit on Sumatra. As a result, most of the substantial government investments in infrastructure made during the period of the Culture System occurred on Java. It is hardly surprising, then, that Dutch private enterprise was slow to take advantage of opportunities outside Java. Also, the hinterlands of the Outer Islands were often rugged, inaccessible, and uninviting to the Western entrepreneur.

When order was established and roads and harbours were built, the sparse Indonesian population of the Outer Islands did not take long to take advantage of the ample available land to grow crops for export. Little change in existing land use patterns was required to grow rubber, coconuts, and coffee. In contrast to Java, there was no sugar industry to infringe on the cultivated lands (climatic conditions in Sumatra were not favourable to sugar), and the pressure on new lands by Western planters was not comparable to that exercised on Java. The low overall population density of the Outer Islands further punctuated the contrast with Java. 'Thus, as the bulk of the Javanese peasants moved toward agricultural involution, shared poverty, social elasticity, and cultural vagueness, a small minority of the Outer Island peasants moved toward agricultural specialization, frank individualism, social conflict, and cultural rationalization.'[1]

The most important foundations for future economic development in Indonesia laid during the period between 1880 and the First World War were four: a 'take-off' of the Indonesian economy in the Outer Islands, a rapid expansion of all types of infrastructure, the promotion of education, and the discovery and exploitation of

[1] Geertz, *op. cit.*, p. 123.

some of the archipelago's oil resources. We have already mentioned that the promotion of education was at the heart of the 'Ethical Policy' adopted after 1900. A final world must be said on this subject.

Education got off to a very late start, even in Java, which always got the lion's share of such funds as there were. In part, this had been due to the fiscal drain of the war with Achin. In 1882 there were only 700 native schools in all of Indonesia, with some 40,000 pupils. By 1897, largely due to the rapid growth of mission schools, the number of schools and pupils had approximately doubled. The quality of education in the native schools, however, was abominable in comparison to that in the European schools. To be sure, some natives were admitted to these schools, but in 1900 their number was not more than 2,000. In the same year, only 75,000 natives were in school on Java, or about one-quarter of one per cent of the island's native population.

Education for the Indonesians was one of the main objectives of the Ethical Policy, and the educational budget of the Dutch government in the Indies grew rapidly after 1900. Financial resources could not match the ambitious objectives, however, due in large part to the costly war being fought in Sumatra against the Sultanate of Achin. Fortunately, the awakening of a modern national consciousness after 1900 found in native education one of its most constructive outlets. By 1913, there were some 7,000 schools in the Indies, with a total of 227,000 pupils. More than half of these were village schools, only partly supported by government funds.[1] However, by comparison with other Asian countries, such as Ceylon, the Philippines or India, the record was poor. Even in 1950 only about 10 per cent of the population was literate.

In conclusion, the period between 1880 and 1913 has come into focus as one in which foreign planters and capital provided the thrust of Indonesia's response to buoyant world markets and low transportation costs. Segments of the Indonesian smallholder economy, however, also took advantage of the export opportunities, significantly increasing their share in total exports. Education belatedly began to reach growing numbers of Indonesians, and the beginnings of a modern nationalist politics became evident. Large investments were made in infrastructure.

The stimuli emanating from a dynamic world market, however, found little response among the Javanese, in contrast to the growing participation in the world economy of Indonesian smallholders in the Outer Islands. In Java, the masses of the people gained little

[1] Vlekke, *op. cit.*, p. 324, and Gonggrijp, *op. cit.*, p. 212.

from the rapid expansion of output. The sugar companies shared the rice lands with them, but sugar was always under price pressure, so that rents and wages were generally low. On the *erfpacht* lands the planters hired Javanese, but labour was plentiful and wages there were also low. Perhaps the most important gain the Javanese derived from the developments of the period was a growing exposure to modern education.

BIBLIOGRAPHY

Books

Allen, G. C., and Donnithorne, A. G., *Western Enterprise in Indonesia and Malaya*, London, 1957.
Blink, H., *Opkomst en Ontwikkeling van Sumatra als Economisch-Geographisch Gebied*, The Hague, 1926.
Boeke, J. H., *Economics and Economic Policy of Dual Societies*, New York, 1953.
——, *The Structure of Netherlands Indian Economy*, New York, 1942.
——, *The Evolution of the Netherlands Indies Economy*, New York, 1946.
Broek, J. O. M., *Economic Development of the Netherlands Indies*, New York, 1942.
Burger, D. H., *De Ontsluiting van Java's Binnenland voor het Wereldverkeer*, Wageningen, 1939.
——, *Structural Changes in Javanese Society: The Village Sphere, The Supra Village Sphere*, Ithaca, N.Y., 1956, 1957.
Callis, H. G., *Foreign Capital in Southeast Asia*, New York, 1942.
Cator, B. J., *The Economic Position of the Chinese in the Netherlands Indies*, Oxford, 1936.
Colenbrander, H. T., *Jan Pietersz. Coen: Beschieden omtrent zijn Bedrijf in Indië*, The Hague, 1948.
——, *Koloniale Geschiedenis*, The Hague, 1925–26.
Coolhaas, P. W., *A Critical Survey of Studies on Dutch Colonial History*, The Hague, 1960.
Cowan, C. D., ed., *The Economic Development of Southeast Asia*, New York, 1964.
Day, Clive, *The Policy and Administration of the Dutch in Java*, New York, 1904.
Dekker, E. D. (pseudonym, Multatuli), *Max Havelaar; or, The Coffee Auctions of the Dutch Trading Company*, New York, 1967.
Deerr, Noel, *The History of Sugar*, London, 1950.
Encyclopaedie van Nederlandsche-Indië, The Hague, 1917–21; 5 supplements, 1927–40.

281

Furnivall, J. S., *Netherlands India: A Study of Plural Economy*, Cambridge, 1939.

——, *Colonial Policy and Practice, A Comparative Study of Burma and Netherlands India*, Cambridge, 1948.

Geertz, Clifford, *The Development of the Javanese Economy: A Socio-Cultural Approach*, Cambridge, Mass., 1956.

——, *Agricultural Involution*, Berkeley, 1963.

Gonggrijp, G. F. E., *Schets ener Economische Geschiedenis van Indonesië*, Haarlem, 1957.

Gorkom, K. W. van, *Oost-Indische Cultures*, republished and edited by H. C. Prinsen Geerligs, Amsterdam, 1917–19.

Hall, C. J. J., and de Keppel, C. van, *De Landbouw in den Indischen Archipel*, The Hague, 1946–50.

Honig, Pieter, and Verdoorn, Frans, eds., *Science and Scientists in the Netherlands Indies*, New York, 1945.

Hurgronje, C. S., *Ambtelijke Adviezen van C. Snouck Hurgronje, 1889–1936*, Rijks, Geschiedkundige Publicatien, Kleine Serie, Vol. 33–35, The Hague, 1957.

de Kat Angelino, A. D. A., *Colonial Policy*, The Hague, 1931.

——, *Staatkundig Beleid en Bestuurszorg in Nederlandsch-Indië*, The Hague, 1930.

Leur, J. C. van, *Indonesian Trade and Society: Essays in Asian Social and Economic History*, The Hague, 1955.

Mansvelt, W. M. F., *Geschiedenis van de Nederlandsche Handel-Maatschappij*, Haarlem, 1924.

McVey, R. T., ed., *Indonesia*, New Haven, 1963.

Nieuwenhuijs, Robert (pseudonym, E. Breton de Nijs), *Tempo Doeloe, Fotografische Documenten uit het oude Indië, 1870–1914*, Amsterdam, 1961.

Raffles, T. S., *The History of Java*, London, 1817.

Schrieke, B. J. O., *Indonesian Sociological Studies*, The Hague, 1955–7.

——, ed., *The Effect of Western Influence on Native Civilizations in the Malay Archipelago*, Batavia, 1929.

Veth, P. J., *Java, Geographisch, Ethnologisch, Historisch*, 2nd edition, edited by J. F. Snelleman and J. F. Niermeyer, Haarlem, 1912.

Vlekke, B. H. M., *Nusantara: A History of Indonesia*, revised edition, Chicago, 1960.

Wertheim, W. F., *Indonesian Society in Transition: A Study of Social Change*, 2nd revised edition, The Hague, 1959.

Articles

Benda, H. J., 'Decolonization in Indonesia: The Problem of Continuity and Change', *American Historical Review*, July, 1965.

Higgins, Benjamin, 'Western Enterprise and the Economic Development of Southeast Asia: A Review Article', *Pacific Affairs*, March 1958.

Chapter 11

THE PHILIPPINES

by Thomas Perry Storer

I. THE PHILIPPINES IN 1880

In 1880 the Philippines stood out as an example of unexploited potential. The area was relatively large, about 114,000 square miles, and, with less than six million people (see Table 11.1) was relatively

TABLE 11.1: *Population of the Philippines**

(thousands)

	1877	1887	1903	1918
Luzon	3,346	3,548	4,013	5,279
Visayas	2,040	2,205	2,916	3,890
Mindanao	166	387	671	1,184
Total	5,552	6,140	7,600	10,353
% increase, annual rate ,total		0·7%	1·3%	2·0%
% increase, annual rate, Luzon		0·6%	0·8%	1·8%

* These official census figures are all deficient, as in the case of most undeveloped countries. Particularly in the case of Mindanao, the earlier population figures for the pagan tribes in the interior, and to some extent for the Moslems as well, were obtained only as very rough approximations by census enumerators. A more accurate idea of the growth rate can be derived from the figures for Luzon alone.

Source: Philippine Islands, Census Office.

under-populated. Given good government, it could have been a good candidate for rapid economic development in the coming years. The volcanic-ash soil was extremely fertile, and produced a variety of valuable crops. Great areas of unpopulated land existed, while at the same time certain long-settled regions already contained populations of high density, which might supply labour to clear and cultivate the frontier areas. Political conditions were reasonably stable. There were signs of growing discontentment with the Spanish régime, but three centuries of Spanish domination had at least impressed a considerable unity upon the diverse native peoples of

283

the Islands. And, in addition, there was a well-educated and economically active upper class.

Of the various agricultural products, the most important to the population as a whole was rice. Most of the peasant population carried on a purely subsistence-level cultivation of this staple, using flooded-field paddy methods. They generally managed to produce only one crop a year. Irrigation was inadequate for a second rice crop, but often vegetables were grown in the fields during the off-season. In remote regions, slash-and-burn shifting cultivation of upland dry rice was practised, but this was not a significant proportion of the total: most of the population lived in thickly settled areas where this method was not practicable. In some regions where soil, terrain and climate were not appropriate for paddy farming, maize replaced rice as the staple element in the diet, but most Filipinos regarded this food as somewhat uncivilized.

Some large landowners also produced rice on a share-tenancy basis for commercial sale, but it was generally regarded as a low profit crop. The Islands had once produced sufficient rice for export, but now, with some of the land being turned to other more profitable uses, regular importation was necessary to meet the needs of the population. In 1879, the Philippines imported 59,000 metric tons of rice,[1] and imports remained at roughly this level until the turn of the century.

The major cash crop was sugar. Export statistics for 1880–4 are shown in Table 11.2.

TABLE 11.2: *Average Annual Exports, 1880–4*

(million pesos)

Sugar	10·34
Abaca	7·15
Tobacco	1·29
Cigars	0·84
Miscellaneous	3·93
	23·55

Peasants often planted small amounts of cane to produce crude sugar for domestic use, and *basi*, an alcoholic drink. But the milling machinery necessary for production of export-grade sugar dictated that most of the production be organized on a plantation basis.

[1] Philippine Islands, Bureau of Commerce and Industry, *Statistical Bulletin of the Philippine Islands, No. 3*, 1920, p. 171.

Sugar production was already well established in 1880, some 181,000 tons being exported that year,[1] but competition from temperate-zone beet sugar, combined with the inefficiency of the archaic machinery in use in the Islands, was beginning to have its effects on the industry. The greatest cane-growing area was on the island of Negros, a district which had largely been opened up by American trading companies, who had offered loans to native planters for clearing and cultivation of the land, and installation of machinery.[2] These traders took most of the output through the port of Ilo-ilo for sale in the American market. On Negros, labour on the sugar plantations was generally on a daily wage basis, while in the older sugar districts of Luzon Island, share-tenancy prevailed, with the tenant receiving between one-third and one-half the milled output.[3]

Another agricultural product, of unique value to the Philippines, was abaca, or Manila hemp. This is a fibre obtained from the stalks of a tree of the banana family. It was extensively used in the native weaving industry, but its greatest worth was in the manufacture of rope. Manila rope made from abaca fibre was in great demand because of its strength and resistance to salt water. The Islands possessed an absolute monopoly of the product. Attempts to raise abaca outside the Philippines have met with almost complete failure.

Since capital needs in the production of abaca were slight, cultivation was undertaken on a small scale, as well as on large plantations. In earlier years, when Spanish provincial officials had obtained much of their personal revenue through franchised trading, some had forced the natives in their provinces to devote a proportion of their land to abaca.[4] The most intense cultivation occurred in the Bicol Peninsula of southern Luzon, and abaca was also grown in the Visayan Islands farther south. Trees would begin producing within two or three years after planting. There was no well-marked season for harvesting the leaves, so labour needs could be evened out over the year. It was necessary to keep the ground clear around the growing plants, but after the growing period the only significant labour involved was that of gathering the leaves and stripping the pulp from the fibre. Stripping was accomplished by pulling the stalks by hand through a crude device consisting of a blade held against a flat surface. No satisfactory mechanical stripper was ever devised. On a

1 *Ibid.*, p. 182.
2 H. M. Wright, *A Handbook of the Philippines*, Chicago, 1907, p. 233.
3 John Foreman, *The Philippine Islands*, New York, 1899, p. 313.
4 F. Jagor, *Travels in the Philippines*, London, 1875, p. 288.

small farm, the grower could perform this labour for himself. On larger plantations, strippers were employed on a share basis, receiving one-third their output.[1]

The Filipinos also cultivated tobacco extensively under the direction of the Government Tobacco Monopoly, which had controlled production on Luzon since 1781. All trade in tobacco leaf and the manufacture of cigars was also in the hands of the Monopoly, throughout the Islands. In 1880 this business provided fully one-half the revenues of the colonial administration.[2] The Monopoly was apparently efficiently run at the outset, but as time passed its manner of operation became scandalous. It expropriated peasant lands in the tobacco-growing regions, on the pretence that lands without deeds reverted to the State, regardless of the fact that deeds were almost unknown throughout the Islands. The former owners were then forced to cultivate tobacco on the expropriated lands, and no other crops were permitted. Penalties for non-fulfilment of contract were severe. In the later years of operation of the Monopoly, the cultivators received payment irregularly, if at all.[3]

Finally, in 1882, the government was prevailed upon to abandon the Monopoly, despite its importance to state revenues. The government cigar factories were sold off to private interests, and the peasant cultivators were left free to do with their lands as they wished. Most of them continued planting tobacco, and production maintained its previous levels.

Coffee was another major Philippine export, produced both by plantations and as a secondary crop by subsistence farmers in hilly regions. Although demand for Philippine coffee never reached the proportions of the South American coffee boom of this period, coffee was a large and growing industry until the late 1880s. Exports during 1880–4 averaged 6,300 metric tons per year, bringing in 5·8 per cent of Philippine export earnings.[4] At that time a devastating blight spread through Luzon, destroying the productive capacity of virtually all the coffee trees on the island. The industry never regained significant proportions. Plantation owners now eliminated their coffee trees and began production of other crops, while peasants were hesistant to expend renewed effort on an enterprise which had once come to grief.[5]

The rich soil of the Philippines produced a number of other crops,

[1] Wright, *op. cit.*, p. 198. [2] *ibid.*, p. 211.

[3] Jagor, *op. cit.*, p. 325; Foreman, *op. cit.*, p. 345.

[4] United States, Bureau of the Census, *Census of the Philippine Islands*, 1903, Washington D.C., 1904, Vol. 4, p. 77.

[5] Foreman, *op. cit.*, p. 337.

but none of these were of great significance in the export field at this time. Cocoa grew well, but its susceptibility to typhoon damage, various pests and thievery made it suitable only for secondary peasant cultivation, or else for a well capitalized plantation that could afford to absorb the risk.[1] Total production in fact was not adequate to satisfy domestic demand. Coconut trees were also common, and required little more than patience to cultivate. Coconut oil, extracted from the dried meat of the nut in crude wooden presses, was used domestically for cooking and lighting purposes, but the export market for this product was not particularly well developed at the beginning of our period.

Industry was at a low stage of development, but further advanced than in many other tropical countries at this time. The cigar industry employed several thousand women in Manila. Countless others were occupied in household weaving in the provinces, using native fibres such as abaca and pineapple fibre, as well as imported cotton and silk. Most villages had blacksmiths who could forge knives and other simple implements.

The social structure of the Philippines followed a typical Malayo-Polynesian pattern. Aside from the introduction of Christianity and central government, the centuries of Spanish occupation had had surprisingly little effect. Relatively few Spaniards came to live in the colony, compared with South American experience, and these mostly followed commercial and professional pursuits in Manila and other large cities. In general they were content to leave local affairs to the old native élite, the *datos*. These chieftains, who became known as *caciques* under the Spanish, possessed great landed wealth as well as political power and prestige. The coming of the Spaniards really strengthened this class, as Spanish land law enabled them to tighten their control over the peasantry, and intermarriage with Spanish and Chinese brought them infusions of money wealth. These *caciques* were the leading element in the agricultural economy. Foreign plantations were not numerous. Figures for the Spanish period are not available, but the Census of 1903, taken shortly after the beginning of the American occupation, reported that of all farmers owning over 100 hectares, more than 90 per cent were native.[2] Figures for smaller farms were, of course, close to 100 per cent. This probably reflects fairly well the state of affairs during the later years of Spanish rule.

Population was concentrated in tight village communities, with fields often located as far as an hour's walk away or more. This was

[1] Jagor, *op. cit.*, p. 96.   [2] *Census, 1903*, Vol. 4, p. 195.

the typical Malay practice, and it was encouraged by the Spanish since it made for more convenient administration.[1] But it also meant that the ability of the peasants to respond to agricultural opportunities was diminished, since the amount of extra land available for non-subsistence crops was rather limited by this manner of settlement.

The Philippine village was the centre of a very stable social structure. Traditional Philippine society displays no significant social ties of larger scope than the village, or the cluster of villages (*barrios*) associated with a single market town (*poblacion*). Within the village, the principal distinguishing characteristic of social life is the informal division of the population into two classes which coexist in an essentially symbiotic relationship. The *cacique* demands and receives deference in virtually all affairs, while the 'common man' receives from him a large measure of security, protection from the exploitation of others and the assurance of support in hard times.[2] Although this form of 'social contract' is primarily an indigenous institution, the introduction of Spanish Catholicism reinforced it somewhat. The incessant emphasis placed by the missionary priests on the need for acceptance of suffering in this life, as a condition for receiving the heavenly reward, gave added spiritual weight to the *cacique's* demand for deference. And in most cases the clientage relationship of *cacique* and peasant would be formalized in Catholic ritual: the *cacique* would serve as godparent at the baptism of a child, or as sponsor at a wedding. In many cases the relationship was reinforced by perpetual money debts which tied the peasant to the *cacique* in law as well as in tradition.

The boulder-like stability of this social structure lay at the root of a number of phenomena which caused contemporary observers to despair of the ability of the native Filipinos to take advantage of economic change. Their marked lack of success in commerce was often accounted to their supposed innate laziness, greed, impatience, dishonesty and simplicity.[3] In fact, both *caciques* and peasants received such benefits from their traditional agrarian, village-centred life, and would suffer such real and psychological penalties from changing it, that on the whole they saw little reason to give up the security and stability of this way of life to face the uncertain returns of commercial endeavour.

[1] Karl J. Pelzer, *Pioneer Settlement in the Asiatic Tropics*, New York, 1945, p. 110.

[2] *Area Handbook on the Philippines*, 'Social Class', reprinted in *Social Foundations of Community Development* by S. C. Espiritu and C. L. Hunt, Manila, 1964, p. 146.

[3] cf. Jagor. *op. cit.*, p. 317; Foreman, *op. cit.*, p. 182.

Most of the import-export trade in the port cities was in the hands of European companies: a few American, some Spanish, but mostly British. Occasionally these firms attempted ventures in the provinces, generally ambitious large-scale enterprises which frequently failed due to basic difficulties in dealing with labour. The American company, already mentioned, which opened up the sugar lands of Negros Island, finally was brought down by a great weight of bad debts, exacerbated by the competition of British investment houses and the steady decline in the world price of sugar.[1] In 1877, a British group invested heavily in a plan to gather cane juice from all over the Philippines, bring it to a central point near Manila by tanker and pipeline, and manufacture high-grade sugar for export, using only the most modern machinery. This venture collapsed in just three years,[2] defeated also by the falling price of sugar.[3]

The invaluable middlemen in the export trade were the Chinese, of whom there were between 65,000 and 100,000 in the Islands. Perhaps one-half of these were in Manila, and the rest spread widely through the provinces.[4] A number worked as coolie labourers, but the great majority of them were merchants and traders. Most of the coolies became merchants as soon as they accumulated sufficient capital. They managed to conduct business successfully with native producers, despite mutual mistrust. Satisfied with operating on a small margin, they easily overcame competition from any native businessmen who made the attempt. Just as commentators of this period invariably noted the commercial incompetence of the natives, so they acclaimed the skill and energy of the Chinese. Another factor in the success of the Chinese was the fact that, being outside the network of village social ties, they did not face the same range of social obligations that tended to hamper the progress of Filipino businessmen.

Friction with the native population and with the Spanish was a considerable problem for the Chinese. In earlier years they had suffered from periodic massacres and deportations. But by 1880 it was clearly recognizable that the Chinese were an indispensable part of the economic structure of the country, and the authorities generally contented themselves with heavily taxing their business activities. In 1867, Chinese shopkeepers were taxed from 12 to 100 pesos per head yearly, plus a tax of 60 pesos for permission to send their goods to the weekly market.[5]

Thus the commercial affairs of the Philippines had by 1880 settled into a well-delineated pattern. Native producers, who could

---

[1] Foreman, *op. cit.*, p. 287. [2] *ibid.*, p. 314. [3] See Chapter 2, pp. 55-6.
[4] Foreman, *op. cit.*, p. 120. [5] Jagor, *op. cit.*, p. 348.

be divided into peasants and *cacique* plantation-owners, sold to Chinese traders, who dealt with European and American export-import houses. This hierarchy was not paralleled in the political sphere, for here the Chinese stood at the bottom of the ladder. Natives and Spanish authorities were alike in the antagonism to them.

II. THE LAST YEARS OF SPANISH RULE: 1880–98

The Spanish régime may once have been interested in the development of the Philippines. Many of its early activities were of great value, and were carried on with honourable purpose. The Christianization of the natives, though attended with instances of profound cruelty, at least laid a basis for unity that the scores of tribes had not had before. The early Spaniards introduced many new crops, such as maize, tobacco and potatoes. Some efforts were made to encourage economic development: there existed, for instance, an 'Economical Society' which had once offered special prizes for the establishment of large cocoa and coffee plantations.[1]

But at the end of the nineteenth century the Spanish Empire was in the depths of decline. The Philippines, one of its few remaining colonies, was treated with little interest or concern. Rule was arbitrary and despotic. Administration was in the hands of ill-prepared governors with virtually unchecked authority. The governors, who spent only three years in any one province, were in turn dominated by priests and friars who spent their lifetimes in one village and often used their ecclesiastical offices to achieve political influence. The friar brotherhoods had accumulated vast properties, amounting to some 200,000 hectares, operated under a frequently oppressive tenancy system.

At the bottom of this lay an absence of economic interest. Philippine exports did not go to Spain, and Philippine imports from Spain were negligible. Very few Spaniards lived there. Production and trade were in the hands of Filipinos, Americans, British or Chinese. The chief Spanish stake in the Philippines was the Church, now no longer the power it had once been. In these circumstances the islands could expect at best to be neglected.

They received less than the best. Spanish rule in the Philippines had a history of restrictions on trade dating back to the sixteenth century. Until 1811 trade was strictly limited by royal edict to 250,000 tons yearly, as a result of fear among businessmen in Spain

[1] Jagor, *op. cit.*, pp. 96, 100.

that the Philippines might supersede them in selling to the Mexican market. Foreign traders worked under troublesome restrictions. Granting of loans to native producers was made highly risky due to an old law, still sporadically applied, providing that no native might be held responsible for the payment of any debt over 25 pesos. This law, originally intended to protect natives from exploitation, now made obtaining capital difficult for those Filipinos who were interested in producing cash crops. Foreign trading companies which wished to encourage domestic production for export had to adopt the rather risky expedient of buying a crop in advance at some discounted estimate of its future value.[1]

The Spanish administration made things more difficult for the British companies that handled most of the foreign trade by establishing in 1891 a high protective tariff against all but Spanish imports carried in Spanish bottoms. This policy was the culmination of a decade of increasing controls designed to improve Spain's share of the Philippine trade. In 1881 only $5 \cdot 8$ per cent of Philippine imports came from Spain; by 1893 the figure had risen to $18 \cdot 5$ per cent.[2] At the same time, the tariff and the other restrictions hindered the operations of the non-Spanish import-export firms that exported most of the native products.

More important than the things the colonial government did to hinder trade was what it did not do that would have been necessary in order to stimulate economic growth. Most significantly, progress in transportation was almost negligible. By the end of the Spanish period only one railroad had been built in the Philippines, running 196 kilometres from Manila north to Dagupan. The plans for this line were drawn up in 1875, but the franchise was not granted until 1886, and regular operation did not begin until 1892, with one major bridge still incomplete. The franchise was picked up by a British group, with a construction subsidy from the government, as well as a guarantee of 8 per cent return on the estimated investment. In fact, the actual cost went much higher than the estimate, and the company was constantly troubled by corrupt provincial officials, so that the line was slow in getting started and nearly bankrupt for many years.[3]

In spite of its difficulties, the railroad remained in operation and

[1] A. V. H. Hartendorp, *History of Industry and Trade of the Philippines*, Manila, 1958, p. 8.

[2] Schurman Commission, *Report of the Philippine Commission*, Washington, 1900, Vol. 4, p. 70.

[3] Foreman, *op. cit.*, p. 292.

was vitally effective in opening up the great Luzon Central Plain through which it ran. This region was to become an important rice and sugar producing area, but access had previously been restricted by a mountain range that cut off access to the coast. A businessman operating in the Philippines told the first American investigating commission that construction of the railroad had within a decade at least doubled the output of the region.[1]

To be sure, the Philippines' need for railways was somewhat less than in other countries. With the population spread over scores of islands, coastwise shipping could to a great extent take over the functions of rails. But the coastal regions had been populated for centuries, were characterized in general by high population densities and small-scale subsistence farming, and thus did not offer much in the way of new opportunities for export-oriented agriculture. The new opportunities, the best expanses of unutilized fertile land, existed in the interior, often cut off from the coast by mountain ranges. River travel was possible in a few regions: the Cagayan River was the principal trade route for the tobacco regions of its valley. But the mountainous terrain also limited the extent of the rivers' usefulness, and no attempt had been made under the Spanish to improve the channels.

The rapid response to the Manila-Dagupan railway indicates that a considerable encouragement to agricultural production might have been provided by additional lines on Luzon, especially a link running into the abaca-producing Bicol Peninsula, another through the rich and underdeveloped upper Cagayan Valley to the point where the river becomes navigable. Such lines existed in the general plan drawn up in 1875, but they were never brought to fruition by the Spanish administration.

The second largest island in the archipelago, Mindanao, was almost totally undeveloped. Partly this fact stemmed from the Christian Filipinos' fear of the Muslims who inhabited parts of the island and the pagan tribes that roamed the interior, but the total lack of transportation facilities only served to perpetuate this fear. Railroad penetration of the interior would have been invaluable in opening up this great frontier area. The smaller islands of the Visayas group also would have profited from short rail links; here also there were to be found fertile interior valleys and plains that awaited efficient transportation before they could be used for something more than subsistence level rice farming.

Highway development was at a minimum. The first American

---

[1] Schurman Commission, *op. cit.*, Vol. 4, p. 79.

investigating commission, sent after the Spanish-American War, reported that maps of Luzon indicated three highways totalling about 1,500 kilometres, but these were totally unusable in the rainy season, and almost impassable in places even in dry weather.[1] Port facilities were also neglected. The port of Manila was infamous for its poor facilities. In 1880 the government began levying special user taxes to pay for improvement of the docks, but work proceeded slowly, and it was suspected that most of the returns from the tax went to corrupt officials.[2]

The primitive state of transportation facilities was undoubtably the most serious hindrance to economic development, but other aspects of basic infrastructure were also in a state of decay. Education was in practice limited to the *cacique* class. The authorities were required by royal decree to provide one male and one female teacher for every 5,000 inhabitants, but even this low standard was not lived up to.[3] An excellent university had been in operation in Manila since 1610, under Jesuit administration, but fields of study were limited to law, theology, medicine and pharmacy. Little attention was paid to research or education in agricultural techniques, engineering or similar fields.

Considering the numerous obstacles, it is surprising that Philippine export trade did advance during this period, in peso value, though

TABLE 11.3: *Total Exports and Imports, 1880–1914*

Years	Average annual exports	Average annual imports	Average balance of trade	Average value of the peso, $ US	Average exports in terms of million 1903 pesos
		(million pesos)			
1880–4	23·55	22·01	+1·54	0·886	41·73
1885–9	27·35	20·59	+6·76	0·772	42·23
1890–4	30·09	23·94	+6·15	0·679	40·86
1895–9	*War period—no data*			0·491	
1900–04	55·08	60·70	−5·62	0·474	52·22
1905–09	66·69	58·87	+7·82	0·500	66·69
1910–14	94·74	104·53	−9·79	0·500	94·74

Source: Trade figures—*Statistical Bulletin*, 1920; value of the peso—*Census*, 1903, Vol. 4, p. 563.

[1] Schurman Commission, *op. cit.*, Vol. 4, p. 80.
[2] *ibid.*, Vol. 4, p. 26.
[3] *ibid.*, Vol. 1, p. 17.

TABLE 11.4: *Quantity and Value of Exports of Major Philippine Crops, and Imports of Rice, Five-Year Averages*

	ABACA			SUGAR		
	Quantity (thousand metric tons)	Value (million pesos)	Value per ton (pesos)	Quantity (thousand metric tons)	Value (million pesos)	Value per ton (pesos)
1880–4	51·17	7·15	140	171·9	10·34	60
1885–9	65·92	9·57	145	190·1	9·64	51
1890–4	78·57	11·77	150	201·6	11·08	55
1900–4	118·79	36·60	308	78·5	5·89	75
1905–9	130·22	37·78	290	128·0	10·05	79
1910–4	144·54	37·34	258	184·3	18·48	100

	LEAF TOBACCO	COPRA			CIGARS	RICE (Imports)		
	Value (million pesos)	Quantity (thousand metric tons)	Value (million pesos)	Value per ton (pesos)	Value (million pesos)	Quantity (thousand metric tons)	Value (million pesos)	Value per ton (pesos)
1880–4	1·29	—	—	—	0·84	38·28	1·26	33
1885–9	1·42	—	—	—	1·33	70·42	2·88	41
1890–4	1·86	—	—	96	1·46	60·50	1·60	26
1900–4	1·95	55·47	5·32	96	2·38	241·33	15·41	64
1905–9	2·54	76·30	10·45	137	2·31	158·17	10·08	64
1910–4	3·86	115·00	22·15	193	5·23	173·19	12·89	74

Source: Statistical Bulletin, 1920.

not in dollar value. Prices of tropical products were falling through the eighties and into the middle nineties, but in the Philippines this effect was masked by the decline in the value of the Mexican silver peso. (See Table 11.3.) The peso fell from a value close to that of a US gold dollar in the early seventies to below half that amount. This decline was stopped in 1903 by the establishment of a gold standard peso under the American administration, backed up by American reserves, at a par value of fifty US cents.

Viewed in dollar terms, the value of Philippine exports remained constant between 1880–4 and 1890–4, but in peso terms it rose, the devaluation helping the planters to pass some of the burden on to their labourers via the increased peso prices of imports. The volume of exports also rose. The greatest volume growth was in abaca, which enjoyed the strongest market. Exports of this product increased 52 per cent in ten years, at a rate of 4·2 per cent per year (see Table 11.4). This put it ahead of sugar in first place among Philippine exports. Sugar production grew only slightly, in the face of falling prices. Production of tobacco grew at a steady rate.

With the foreign exchange thus earned, the Filipinos imported chiefly cloth and clothing, and foodstuffs. Iron and steel manufactures were imported in the amount of about a million pesos per year, and imports of kerosene and other mineral oils ran about the same.[1] The Islands consistently ran a surplus in the balance of trade during this period. Evidently this surplus was balanced principally by the repatriated profits of foreign trading companies and remittances of the Chinese in the Islands. Also not to be overlooked in its effect on the foreign payments accounts is smuggling, always a great problem for the Philippines. Spain itself was not especially extractive in its relationship with its Asian colony. No tribute was collected, and in fact Spain often made up deficits in the government budget.

While Philippine production grew somewhat during the last years of Spanish rule, actual growth was slight when compared with the potential that existed. It was regrettable that the colony entered this period of great economic opportunities in the hands of a decaying régime that was incapable of providing the support necessary to stimulate development.

III. THE FIRST YEARS UNDER AMERICAN RULE: 1898–1913

In 1898, as a consequence of the Spanish-American War, the United

[1] Schurman Commission, *op. cit.*, vol. 4, p. 71.

States of America took possession of the Philippines, its first and only large tropical colony. This was a matter of considerable emotional debate at the time. Anti-imperialists at home, harking back to America's own colonial experience, condemned colonialism as an immoral adventure, and insisted that the Filipinos should immediately be given their independence. The Treaty of Paris, confirming the transfer of sovereignty, was approved in the Senate by only one vote more than the required two-thirds majority. The McKinley administration rejected the counsel of the idealists, expressing the opinion that the Filipinos were not ready for self-government, and were sure to be swallowed up by the imperial ambitions of Germany or Japan if left to their own devices; America had to accept its 'duty' to inculcate them in the ways of democracy and establish a solid, modern structure of government.

The first few years of this venture were a chilling experience for the Americans. A sizeable band of Filipinos, who had already in 1896 fought an inconclusive revolution against the Spanish, had expected that the defeat of their former masters would lead to their independence. When the Americans instead came to establish their own rule in the Islands, the revolutionaries took up arms again. Though the outcome was never in much doubt, the bitter fighting dragged on until 1901.

When civil authorities replaced the military administration in that year, the years of disorder had clearly left their mark on the land. The actual fighting had been restricted to a relatively small area, but the breakdown of civil government had much more widespread effects. A dread livestock disease, the rinderpest, spread unchecked throughout the Islands, devastating the population's work animals. It was estimated that more than 75 per cent of the water buffaloes (*carabaos*) in the country were lost during the course of the epidemic.[1] Production of rice and sugar depended particularly on these animals, and output of these vital crops declined precipitously during and after the war. Added to the consequent malnutrition, diseases also spread among the human population. Cholera was raging in Manila shortly after the new administration arrived.

The new government approached its problems with much greater vigour than the old. The American administrators set to work to establish all the appurtenances of a modern government. Education was expanded. Ports, railways and highways were developed and improved. Agricultural research and extension offices were set up and production of cash crops was actively encouraged through

[1] US Philippine Commission, *Report*, 1900–03, p. 357.

propaganda, demonstrations, fairs and so forth. Health services were built up from almost nothing. Needless to say, there were many mistakes and failures. The government was set up very much on the American model, and some institutions, adopted with naïve enthusiasm from American practice, did not perform in the Philippines as well as expected. Nonetheless, the contrast with the Spanish régime was marked.

The greatest single effort was made in education. A comprehensive system of primary, secondary and college education was set up, and hundreds of American teachers travelled to the colony to assist in its development. Accomplishment of the goal of universal primary education was incomplete, to be sure. Total primary enrolment in 1908 was 360,000 out of a total population of some 8,400,000.[1] Estimating primary-age population (grades one to six) at about 15 per cent of the total, the actual enrolment ratio was only about 30 per cent, and in addition attendance in many cases was very irregular. Also, the quality of education in a system so rapidly built up was inevitably rather low. But the difference from Spanish times, when education never reached below the upper classes, could not be ignored. The schools brought the village into contact with the outside world, and opened up avenues of social mobility. Following upon the development of the public school system, the government in 1909 established a new modern university, the University of the Philippines, with colleges of Agriculture, Veterinary Science and Engineering, as well as Law, Medicine, Fine Arts and Liberal Arts.

The government also expended a great effort on transport infrastructure. New ports were opened up and the facilities in Manila were improved. Railroad development was more effectively encouraged than under the Spanish, and total trackage increased from 196 kilometres to 1,095 kilometres by 1913.[2] A new line was constructed from Manila into southern Luzon, and several spurs were added to the original. The interiors of two of the smaller Visayan Islands, Panay and Cebu, were also opened up with rail links. These lines were built with British and American capital supported by government guarantees.

Highway construction was also intently pursued, and by 1913 the Islands had 2,200 kilometres of 'first-class' all-weather roads, in addition to 2,000 kilometres of second-class roads passable only in the dry season.[3]

The effect of government efforts in health can be seen most plainly

[1] *Statistical Bulletin*, No. 3, 1920, p. 8.
[2] *ibid.*, p. 260.
[3] *ibid.*, p. 257.

in the population figures (Table 11.1 above), which indicate a growth rate for Luzon of about 0·8 per cent per year during the Spanish period, which rose to 1·5 per cent per year during the first fifteen years of American rule.

Most of the governmental revenue for these improvements came from general taxation. A few bond issues were floated: 14 million pesos was borrowed in 1904 to purchase most of the friar estates, and from 1905 to 1913 18 million pesos was obtained for various public works ventures.[1] No direct aid was received from the United States Government.

The colonial administration decided early to concentrate heavily on various taxes levied directly on businesses for an important share of government revenue, and the growth in these collections was the greatest factor in the ability of the government to undertake increasingly large ventures. Customs revenue was always a large part of the total, but it did not grow rapidly after the duties on imports from the United States were eliminated in 1909. On the other hand, the income from the excise tax on manufactures of alcohol and tobacco products increased from 4·3 million pesos in 1906 to 8·7 million in 1913. Sales of business and professional licences went up from 2·1 million pesos to 3·5 million in the same period.[2] In 1915, the excise taxes produced 23 per cent of total revenue, licences 14 per cent, businesses run by the government 20 per cent, and customs 25 per cent.[3] The provincial and municipal governments, which shared in school operation and highway construction, relied, as in the United States, mainly on land taxes.

Attempts to deal with the land title problem began in 1902 with the institution of a system of Torrens titles, under which deeds are issued upon application after a survey and a court proof of ownership. In the following seven years only 4,000 titles were issued, mostly to foreigners and *caciques*. In order to reach the peasants, who had neither the money nor the inclination to bother with surveys and courts, a new programme was begun in 1910. Entire municipalities were surveyed at one time, and as many as a thousand cases were brought to court together at government initiative. Problems still remained in the administration of this system, but a workable solution had been begun. The administration was learning how to deal with the native Filipinos, no longer expecting them to behave exactly like Americans.

[1] Philippine Islands, Census Office, *Census of the Philippine Islands, 1918*, Manila, 1920–21, Vol. IV, p. 724.

[2] US Philippine Commission, *Report*, 1906, Vol. IV, p. 20; and 1913, p. 21.

[3] Bureau of Commerce and Industry, *Statistical Bulletin* No. 2, 1919, p. 174.

The government undertook actively to encourage the investment of foreign capital in the Islands. Exhibits were sent to international expositions, informational services were set up, research was conducted on crops of value in the American market. Members of the *cacique* class, now active in the representative legislature established by the Americans, found these efforts disturbing for a variety of reasons. In the spirit of the Revolution, they did not want to see the Philippines become merely a commercial appendage of the United States. Also, in their own class interest, they preferred not to face the competition. At any rate, actual foreign investment in agriculture proceeded at a rather slow pace during these years. Between 1900 and 1920 only sixteen American corporations, with a total capitalization of 11 million dollars, had registered in the Philippines for purposes of agricultural or mining activity. There were in addition eleven such corporations of other foreign countries, with substantially less capital.[1]

In large measure this hesitancy was due to acts of the government itself. Land holdings of corporations in the Philippines were limited by act of the US Congress to 1,024 hectares. The ostensible purpose of this law was to protect the Filipinos from the development of an exploitative plantation economy. In fact, a former American Governor-General of the Philippines contends that this law was pushed through by the domestic beet-sugar lobby which wished to cripple the development of a competitive sugar industry in the new colony. It was reasoned that 1,024 hectares was too small an area to support a modern sugar central.[2]

Prospective investors, foreign and domestic, were also discouraged by the labour situation in the Island. Native workers, it was loudly contended, were lazy, shiftless and irresponsible. The war had cut into the labour supply somewhat, and the price of rice had more than doubled in the interim, causing a proportionate increase in the going wage. The price of Philippine exports had also increased, but not so much as the price of rice. According to the statistics of Table 11.3, the percentage price increase between 1890–4 and 1900–04 was 146 per cent for rice, 105 per cent for abaca and 35 per cent for sugar. Since the large number of wage labourers on the plantations had to be paid a wage proportional to the cost of their staple food, the increase in the price of rice was a major factor in the slow recovery of the Philippine sugar industry. Smallholders, who often grew rice

[1] Bureau of Commerce and Industry, *Statistical Bulletin* No. 6, 1923, p. 255.
[2] W. Cameron Forbes, *The Philippine Islands*, revised edition, Cambridge, Mass., 1945, p. 151.

299

for subsistence, in conjunction with a commercial crop, were not so greatly affected.

Of course, there were millions of under-employed Filipinos working half-hectare rice farms in the provinces, but a substantial inducement had to be offered to entice them away from their comfortable and secure village life. Businessmen saw an easier alternative, and lobbied for the admission of Chinese coolie labour to work on plantations. Taft, the first Governor-General, opposed this idea on principle, a stance which this time met with the hearty approval of the natives. Offering the Malayan case as an example, he argued that the Chinese, if permitted to enter in quantity, would, with their greater cleverness and ambition, inevitably overshadow the native population.[1] On his recommendation, the US Congress applied the Chinese Exclusion Act to the Philippines. The businessmen's hopes for cheap, tractable labour were dashed, and there is no telling how much the commercial life of the Philippines was affected, as the flow of new entrants to its principal commercial class was thus cut off.

One further Congressional act was to have a great effect on the economic development of the Philippines, although it occurred rather late to alter the course of events in the period under study. In 1909, the Payne Tariff Act established bilateral free trade between the United States and its Asian colony. From that time the Philippine economy was intimately linked with the American. By the twenties more than 70 per cent of Philippine exports went to the United States. Filipino *caciques* again objected strenuously, foreseeing the development of a colonial economy, dependent on American markets and American import goods, but their outcries had little effect on Congressional deliberations.

The experience of the Philippines under the first years of American administration gives interesting evidence of what can and cannot be accomplished by government activity in economic development. Economic growth certainly occurred. Export value increased at an annual rate of 6·1 per cent (see Table 11.2). The greatest growth occurred in copra, the dried meat of the coconut, which finally found its market and became the Island's second largest export industry by 1913. Tobacco production doubled. Given the impetus of free trade, industries making finished products out of agricultural raw materials were beginning to grow: the rope industry, coconut oil milling, sugar refineries. The pace of industrial development was indicated by the increased quantity of imports of iron and steel products, up from two million pesos in 1903 to seventeen million pesos ten years later.[2]

[1] Philippine Commission, *Reports*, 1900–03, p. 302.   [2] Forbes, *op. cit.*, p. 121.

But there were less satisfying aspects of the picture. Abaca production grew at only 2 per cent per year, much less than the market could have taken. (Although the average unit value of abaca exports declined slightly during this period, this appears to have been due primarily to the declining net quality of Philippine exports, rather than to market weakness.) Importation of rice continued at three times the pre-war rate. This was especially damaging in the light of the fact that international rice prices had increased in the interim, considerably more than prices of Philippine export crops.

IV. THE FAILURE OF OUT-MIGRATION

With the population multiplying at an unprecedented rate, the regions of long settlement became more crowded. The government had purchased most of the friar estates, and was selling them out to the former tenants on easy terms, but in general tenancy was on the rise. In 1903, 19·2 per cent of Filipino farmers did not own the land they worked; in 1918 the figure was 22·3 per cent.[1] Later years were to see a much sharper increase. It appeared that to an increasing degree, at least in the long settled regions, much of the benefit of economic development was accruing to the *cacique* class. The *caciques* were also capitalizing on the political innovations of the American régime, establishing themselves as mayors, governors and legislators, perpetuating and strengthening their age-old political power.

Development of the frontier regions was not proceeding at the hoped-for pace. Population in the interior areas was generally quite sparse. To open them up, a large-scale migration from the coastal regions was necessary. To be sure, population was slowly seeping out of the highly populated parts of the country. Ilocanos from the crowded northwest coast of Luzon penetrated into the Cagayan Valley, Visayan Islanders crossed the straits to the north coast of Mindanao. But this was more a matter of survival than of development. Because of the backlog of needs left by the Spanish, the first great improvements in transportation facilities went into populated regions. Mindanao still had no railway and very few highways. In 1918 only 8·9 per cent of total highway mileage was found on Mindanao, and only 6·2 per cent of the first-class mileage.[2]

By way of demonstrating the considerable potential that existed for frontier settlement, we can consider the magnitude of the steady

---

[1] *Census*, 1903, Vol. IV, p. 303; 1918, Vol. III, p. 72.
[2] *Census*, 1918, Vol. IV, p. 724.

stream of migration that has taken place until the present day. Designating fifteen provinces, mostly on Mindanao, as 'frontier provinces',[1] we note that there has never occurred any sudden breakthrough in migration; instead, the frontier provinces have grown steadily in population at a rate almost double that of the country as a whole. In 1903 only 8·7 per cent of the total population of the Philippines lived in these fifteen provinces; by 1960 the figure was 21·2 per cent. During this period, 26·2 per cent of the total growth of the Philippines' population was channelled into the frontier provinces.[2] Nonetheless, it is estimated that as of 1960 only slightly more than half the cultivable land in Mindanao was being farmed (2·3 million out of 4·4 million hectares).[3]

In order to encourage the settlement of the frontier, the authorities provided for homesteading the public lands. The law was patterned after that which had so successfully opened up the American frontier. Individuals were able to claim forty-acre lots from the public domain after submitting an application with a survey to prove there was no conflict of claims. The homesteader was expected to clear and cultivate a major proportion of the land in the first five years of occupancy, or the grant would be revoked. The administrators soon found, to their consternation and dismay, that homesteading on the American model was an institution that could not easily be transplanted to the Philippines. Response to the homesteading opportunity was disappointingly small. Many peasants did not understand the law, in fact hardly knew about it. But most important was the fact that Filipino society revolved around tight village units. Very few natives were psychologically prepared to live in isolation on forty-acre tracts.[4] Some attempts were made to establish homestead colonies in Mindanao, as a way to overcome this problem, but the problems of planning and organization were overwhelming.

Nevertheless, homestead applications did begin to increase substantially after the law had been in effect for some years, about 1911. Still there were difficulties. Road-building did not keep pace, and where roads were available or planned, roadside lots were often obtained by *caciques* through political influence. They then held the land for speculation, paying labourers to improve it only enough to meet the minimum requirements.[5]

---

[1] All of Mindanao except the early settled provinces of Surigao and Sulu, plus Isabela, Nueva Viscaya, Oriental and Occidental Mindoro and Palawan.

[2] Calculated from *Census of the Philippines*, 1960, Vol. 2, Summary.

[3] Robert E. Huke, *Shadows on the Land: An Economic Geography of the Philippines*, Manila, 1963, p. 151.   [4] Pelzer, *op. cit.*, p. 110.   [5] *ibid.*, p. 112.

The failures of government action do not completely explain the slowness of the Philippine frontier movement, however. Numerous examples exist of massive peasant migration to undeveloped areas directly in response to economic incentives, without the necessity of government initiative. In Burma, for example, the period after the opening of the Suez Canal saw a rapid settlement of the previously underpopulated lowland swamp regions, in response to the expansion of the market for rice. Why did the same not happen in the Philippines? It seems that there are several additional factors at work in this case which hindered such a movement.

Government policy in the Philippines was more restrictive. The British adopted a primarily laissez-faire policy with respect to the Burma lowlands, allowing anyone to settle on unoccupied lands without going through a complicated application process. There were consequently many improprieties involved in the great land rush, but in the process the land was settled. By attempting to regulate the flow onto 'public lands', the American administration in the Philippines may have held back frontier settlement somewhat. The application process was cumbersome and cost more than many peasants could afford, and many applications were rejected because the applicant had not fulfiled various of the complex requirements. Eight thousand and ninety-five applications were received between 1904 and 1909 before the first grant was issued; in the next four years 13,873 more applications were received, and 135 grants made.[1]

However, there is no evidence of tremendous pressure on the legal machinery, in the sense that no massive government action was required to uphold the provisions of the law and prevent squatters from taking up public lands without grants. Thus this cannot be regarded as a primary factor in the failure of interior settlement. The awkwardness of the administrative machinery only meant that the government's own positive efforts to settle the undeveloped lands were ineffective; it did not act to hinder any indigenous pressure on the land. It appears that, for other reasons, such pressure did not exist in the same force as in the Burman case.

For one thing, natural obstacles were more severe. The mountainous topography of the Philippines is considerably more forbidding to trade than the Burman delta. There are great fertile stretches throughout the islands which are cut off from each other and from the sea by mountainous outcropping. In particular, the island interiors are generally poor in navigable waterways. In the Burman delta, rivers and streams were the principal means of commercial

[1] Forbes, *op. cit.*, Vol. I, p. 327.

transport,[1] but the development of the Philippine interior depended more on the establishment of land transportation infrastructure.

The archipelagic nature of the country was also a hindrance, not to trade but to human movement. The greatest settlement opportunities existed in Mindanao, which was sparsely populated even on the coast, but the worst conditions of tenancy and population pressure were found in Central Luzon. Travel within a single land mass, given strong positive or negative inducements, can be accomplished for virtually no cost, but the peasant could not go to Mindanao without cash for the boat passage. In the United States, homesteaders had had a little cash and no land; here the opposite was the case. In addition, population can spread over a land mass in stages, each generation extending the work of its forefathers; but transferral to another and distant island involves a single great leap into the unknown. Thus it was that frontier settlement of Luzon itself proceeded rapidly in certain regions close to the overcrowded Central Plain. The population of the neighbouring frontier province of Nueva Ecija increased by 69 per cent between 1903 and 1918, compared with a nation wide increase of 35·1 per cent.[2] But the settlement of Mindanao hardly got started. Its distance, coupled with the Christian Filipinos' exaggerated fear of its Muslim and pagan inhabitants, served to augment the natural conservatism of the Philippine culture.

We have already discussed above the great stability of Philippine village society, based on the symbiotic relationship of *caciques* and peasants. There was, of course, exploitation involved in this clientage relationship, but most importantly it meant that the village was socially a self-sufficient unit, with which inhabitants identified above all else except the family. Burma at this time, in contrast, was marked by a nationally integrated quasi-feudal social structure in which the village as a social unit played a relatively minor role.[3] At the same time, events had maintained the society on a rather unstable footing. As J. S. Furnivall points out, '. . . the continual disturbances never allowed custom to become a binding force. . . . Thus, when an annexation of Upper Burma brought the people into economic relations with the outer world, they had not caste system to protect them from the evil effects of unregulated competition. On the other hand, there was little to prevent them from taking advantage of their new environment so far as their knowledge and ability permitted.'[4]

[1] J. S. Furnivall, *An Introduction to the Political Economy of Burma*, 3rd edition, 1957, p. 154.
[2] *Census*, 1918, Vol. II, p. 20. [3] Furnivall, *op. cit.*, pp. 34 ff. [4] *ibid.*, p. 40.

The Philippines, in contrast, was locked into a conservative village system which had served well to maintain the stability of the society, but which now tended to minimize the response to economic opportunity insofar as it demanded severing village ties. Because the village provided a reasonably secure existence for even the most poor, there were considerable penalties for anyone who left it. He was cut off from the network of relationships which had always ensured the livelihood of himself and of his forefathers. And the farther he went, the less hope there was of being able to maintain some sort of contacts with the kinship and village groups, in case he should need assistance in an emergency. To a peasant with such a view, going to Mindanao was equivalent to making oneself an outcast and an orphan.

There were circumstances under which Filipinos could be induced to leave this social framework. Most striking was the example of thousands who went to Hawaii under contract to great sugar and pineapple plantations, starting at the time of the American takeover. Hawaiian industries took the initiative, recruited labour in the Philippines, paid the passage to Hawaii and guaranteed return passages in case of dissatisfaction. In essence, the Filipino peasant could transfer to the company the need for security which had always previously been satisfied by the village and its social structure. On his own in Mindanao, he would have no such guarantees. Perhaps there would have been much more success in opening up the interior if large corporations had been permitted to establish plantations on a grand scale. The Hawaiian experience showed that Filipinos were willing to move great distances to perform wage labour if given adequate guarantees, while they were in most cases unwilling to do do so if left to their own resources. The restrictions on land purchase, however, effectively foreclosed this alternative route to frontier development. No plantation operation could get started on a scale large enough to offer the sort of guarantees that were necessary. The government, of course, had significant non-economic reasons for wishing to discourage the large-plantation pattern of development. The American administration viewed the public lands as a national asset which should not be turned to the economic profit of the few. Viewed in this light their policy was successful, but it also slowed the process of interior settlement.

The *caciques* were certainly in a better position to carry out interior development than foreigners under these limitations, but it appears that they themselves in general had little interest in developing the frontier. With their combination of political and economic power in the settled areas, they had little desire to involve themselves in such ventures. This was, in a sense, the greatest failure of this period. If members of this leading economic and political class had utilized their returns from plantation crops to expand their business to the interior, significant results could have been achieved. As it was, the government acting alone could not accomplish much that was substantial.

V. CONCLUSION

During the period 1880–1913, the Philippine export economy did experience economic growth. Output of old crops multiplied (abaca, tobacco) and new opportunities were realized (copra). Total trade increased 125 per cent in dollar value. Yet the growth was halting and tentative, and clearly did not match up to the potential of the Islands.

Perhaps the greatest long-range factor in this experience was the uneven pattern of population distribution. Even in the absence of railroad development, economic growth was still possible in the coastal regions. Here most of the population was densely concentrated. The peasants could not take advantage of their opportunities because their small land-holdings sufficed only for subsistence cultivation. Thus the structural potential for trade, by way of the sea, existed in those areas which had least to trade. In a few places a money economy was established, with the peasants in essence paying for imported rice, and other goods, with production of export crops: for example the abaca planters of Bicol and the tobacco growers of the Cagayan Valley. In cases where extra land was available, the response could be impressive. The phenomenal growth of copra production, from insignificance to a major share of exports in a decade, was in many respects the most heartening experience of the American period, and this production was realized primarily by peasants. Coconut trees can be grown on sandy, relatively unfertile land that is otherwise unsuitable for agricultural production. Villages that did have expanses of poor, unutilized land nearby had a great opportunity to which in most cases they responded.

Tobacco, which experienced the second greatest growth during this period, had also been largely a peasant crop since the abolition of the monopoly. In this case added production was achieved by the steady expansion of cultivation up the Cagayan Valley.

But most coastal residents did not have such opportunities, and they were naturally hesitant to give up their sure subsistence by

306

diverting rice land to the production of cash crops. To provide a sure foundation for future growth, a breakthrough was necessary in opening up the interior. This did not take place. Spanish lassitude in transportation development left the interior an inaccessible and unknown place. The backlog of unmet transportation needs was still a retarding factor during the American period. But cultural factors also played a large part. Peasants responded only slowly to homestead opportunities due to innate village-oriented conservatism and fear of uncertainty. A large-scale effort was necessary to overcome such barriers, but no class in the Philippines displayed the entrepreneurship that such an enterprise required. The Chinese had never been agriculturalists. Antagonisms with the natives and legal restrictions confirmed that they could not become a productive element here. They would have only too gladly traded in the interior, given the road, had there been native producers to trade with. The *caciques*, on the other hand, were more interested in accumulating political power than in economic development. They speculated in land, but they did not expend much of their resources on substantial improvements. Finally, legal restrictions prevented the establishment of great plantations with foreign capital.

Thus the Philippines reached the year 1913 with many of the same problems it had had in 1880. There was a change of masters, the beginning of a profitable free trade relationship with a vigorous industrial economy, and great development of infrastructure. But the social hierarchy was as rigid as ever, and within the framework of that hierarchy it was doubtful that the returns from trade were being turned toward establishment of a firm base for further growth.

BIBLIOGRAPHY

Official Papers

Philippine Islands. *Guía Oficial de Filipinas*, 1892. Manila.
——. Bureau of Commerce and Industry, *Commercial Handbook of the Philippine Islands, 1924*. Manila, 1924.
——. Bureau of Commerce and Industry, *Statistical Bulletin of the Philippine Islands*, yearly beginning 1918. Manila.
——. Census Office, *Census of the Philippine Islands, 1918*. Manila, 1920–21.
Philippines (Republic). Bureau of Census and Statistics, *Census of the Philippines, 1960*. Manila, 1962–3.

307

United States. Bureau of the Census, *Census of the Philippine Islands, 1903*. Washington, DC, 1904.

——. Philippine Commission, *Report*, 1900–03, 1906, 1913. Washington, DC.

——. Philippine Commission, 1899–1900 (Schurman Commission), *Report of the Philippine Commission*. Washington, DC, 1900.

Books

Area Handbook for the Philippines, Chapter on 'Social Class' reprinted in *Social Foundations of Community Development* by S. C. Espiritu and C. L. Hunt, Manila, 1964.

Cavada, Agustin de la, *Historia Geográphica, Geológica y Estadística de Filipinas*, Manila, 1876.

Forbes, W. C., *The Philippine Islands*, revised edition, Cambridge, Mass., 1945.

Forbes-Lindsay, C. H., *The Philippines under Spanish and American Rule*, Philadelphia, 1906.

Foreman, John, *The Philippine Islands*, 2nd edition, revised, New York, 1899.

Furnivall, J. S., *An Introduction to the Political Economy of Burma*, 3rd edition, Rangoon, 1957.

Hartendorp, A. V. H., *History of Industry and Trade of the Philippines*, Manila, 1958.

Huke, R. E., *Shadows on the Land: An Economic Geography of the Philippines*, Manila, 1963.

Jagor, Fedor, *Travels in the Philippines*, London, 1875.

Montero y Vidal, José, *El Archipiélago Filipino y las Islas Marianas, Carolinas y Palaos*, Madrid, 1886.

Pelzer, K. J., *Pioneer Settlement in the Asiatic Tropics*, New York, 1945.

Taylor, G. E., *The Philippines and the United States, Problems of Partnership*, New York, 1964.

Wright, H. M., *A Handbook of the Philippines*, Chicago, 1907.

Chapter 12

INDIA

by Russell Lidman and Robert I. Domrese[1]

The purpose of this chapter is limited: one cannot write thirty years of Indian economic history in a brief essay. The purpose is confined to trying to isolate the main factors which kept down the rate of economic growth in India during this period. It will be assumed that the reader knows something about some of the major features of the Indian social landscape which changed very little at this time; about the caste system, about the peculiarities of land tenure; about the heavy indebtedness of farmers, and so on. All these are adequately described elsewhere; our primary concern is with growth factors.

As we saw in Chapter 1, nearly every tropical country with a stable and modern type of government experienced fairly rapid growth in our period, with India as a spectacular exception. We shall try in this chapter to solve this Indian enigma.

The first point to note is that the Indian record looks much better when translated from absolute to *per capita* figures. Thus between 1883 and 1913 the dollar value of Brazil's exports grew at an average rate of 4·5 per cent per annum; India's at 2·8 per cent per annum (excluding Burma). However, Brazil's population grew by 2·3 per cent per annum as against India's 0·6 per cent per annum. So the *per capita* growth rate of exports was about the same. This is not however a sufficient answer. For if we ask why India's population grew so slowly, the answer is Malthusian; population grew slowly because agriculture grew slowly, and the country was subject to recurrent famines which carried off millions of people. To be sure India also had some relatively rich areas exporting foodstuffs, but this meant nothing to the large part of the subcontinent which was still on a bare subsistence level, and unable to cope with recurrent droughts. Population grew slowly because agriculture grew slowly; so one is still left with the economic question: why did agriculture grow so slowly? As we shall see later, the rate of growth of large-scale manufacturing was not negligible; it compares favourably with manufac-

---

[1] Mr Lidman was primarily responsible for the section on Agriculture.

turing growth rates in Germany and the United States, though well below that of Japan.

The second point to note is that the period splits into two; India did badly in the 1890s, but her trade grew as rapidly as the average of all tropical countries after 1900. Very rapid expansion of the exports of manufactures contributed to the prosperity of the second half, but there was also a marked difference in agricultural prosperity before and after 1900. Valuing at constant 1913 prices, and taking the averages of exports in the three-year periods 1881–4, 1898–1901 and 1911–14, India's agricultural exports[1] grew at average annual rates of 1·3 and 1·9 per cent in the first and second periods respectively. Unusually bad weather had a depressing effect on the 1890s, but the very low prices of two leading exports, wheat and cotton, were probably even more important. These prices rose sharply after 1900, and exports rose with them.[2]

I. AGRICULTURE

The raw statistical data for agricultural output are misleading; one can use effectively only the processed versions. The latest of these is the work of Dr George Blyn,[3] starting alas only in 1891. According to Blyn, the average growth rate of Indian agriculture output between 1891/6 (five years) and 1909/14 was 1·1 per cent per annum (foodgrains 0·9, non-food grains 1·9). His figures would be even lower if he included opium, exports of which fell sharply after the agreement between China and India in 1906.

Taken together, agricultural exports grew faster than production; the average rate from 1881/4 to 1911/14 was 1·44 per cent. But there were differences between commodities; exports of foodgrains grew faster than production, whereas production of cotton and of jute grew faster than exports; this reduces comparability with other countries who were consuming very little of what they produced for export. Bearing this difference in mind, and also the difference in population growth, we note that on the average tropical agricultural exports, valued at constant prices, grew by 2·9 per cent per annum between 1883 and 1913, or at just twice the Indian rate.

Blyn's rate of growth of production of food grains can be compared with population growth; the former is 0·9 per cent, the latter

---

[1] Rice is excluded because it was exported almost exclusively from Burma.

[2] See Chapter 2.

[3] George Blyn, *Agricultural Trends in India 1891–1947*, Philadelphia, 1966. Figures used in this paragraph are derived from page 316.

0·4 per cent per annum between 1891 and 1911.[1] So the output of foodgrains kept slightly ahead of population growth, though consumption may barely have done so, since exports of foodgrains were growing rapidly (at an average rate of 2·7 per cent per annum between 1883 and 1913).

Table 12.1 shows India's principal agricultural exports in 1913, what percentages they were of agricultural exports in that year, and their average annual rates of growth between 1881/3 and 1911/13.

TABLE 12.1: *Principal Agricultural Exports, 1911–13*

	Ratio	Growth rate
Jute	21·4	2·3
Cotton	21·3	1·1
Foodgrains (excluding rice)	15·3	2·7
Hides and skins	10·6	2·3
Oilseeds, cake and oil	10·4	2·5
Tea	9·3	6·8
Opium	5·0	−3·6
Remainder*	6·7	0·4
	100·0	1·4

* In order of value: wool, lac, coffee, spices, dyes, dyestuffs, bones, rubber, tobacco and sugar.

None of these growth rates exceeds the average for world trade in agricultural commodities (3·0) except that of tea. Blyn's figure for cotton production is higher than this (3·4), but his figure for jute production (2·7) is not. Moreover, a number of crops actually lost ground. Besides opium, these included coffee (blighted by disease), indigo (driven out by synthetic dyes), and sugar (plagued by several problems, of which world competition and low prices were probably the most important). If one adds India's *export* of foodgrains to her *production* of non-foodgrains, the growth rate of this 'potential agricultural export' comes out at about 1·5 per cent per head per annum. This is definitely on the low side, in comparison with other countries, the average, excluding India, being about 2·0 per cent. Clearly the Indian farmer was not taking advantage of the great increase in world demand for tropical products.

The contrast with Japan is striking. This contrast is usually made in terms of manufacturing industry, but in manufacturing India

1 George Blyn, *op. cit.*, p. 326.

did better than most other tropical countries, though not as well as Japan. The difference in agriculture is as striking as the difference in manufacturing, and perhaps even more relevant, since agricultural exports – especially raw silk and tea – provided Japan with considerable foreign exchange for her development right up to 1929. In 1913 India's agricultural exports were about $1.70 per head. Japan's agricultural exports, starting from a much lower base some forty years earlier, were now about 60 per cent larger per head, and were growing by over 4 per cent per annum.[1] The failure of the Indian farmer to devote adequate land to cash crops is the fundamental explanation of India's relative stagnation in our period. Cotton is the only crop whose figures are impressive, and that suited only part of the country. (Tea was a plantation enclave.) If we can understand why the Indian farmer was unable to benefit as much as other tropical farmers from the swift growth of world trade in this period, we shall have found the key to India's relative stagnation.

Other exports fared better. Exports of minerals rose from almost zero in 1883 to 1·6 per cent of total exports (excluding Burma); while exports of manufactures rose in the same period from 0·7 to 19·5 per cent. As we shall see, Indian industry was making not inconsiderable strides in this period. By comparison with other tropical countries the weak spot in the Indian economy was peasant agriculture.

Sociological factors. The comparative stagnation of agriculture at this time is not a new discovery. On the contrary, most writers exaggerate it, even to the point of asserting that *per capita* food output actually fell. This would be a strange situation when the export of foodgrains was rising by over 2 per cent per year, in a free market. But this position is in any case no longer tenable in the light of Dr Blyn's revised statistics. However, we still have to ask why the growth rate of agricultural output per head, and especially the output of non-foodgrains, was low by comparison with other tropical countries.

The explanations given most frequently in the past put the blame either on the apathy of the peasant farmer, or on the rapaciousness of landlords, moneylenders and tax collectors.

The apathy explanation runs more or less as follows. The Indian peasant farmer has very low horizons. He lives in an isolated village, with few wants. His religion discourages the desire for

[1] The gap between India and Japan is not so wide if we add to agricultural exports the raw cotton and raw jute content of manufactured exports; but it is still substantial.

material success. The social system of which he is a part, with its emphasis on caste, calls for resignation. His land is small and poor, and his life is at the mercy of epidemics and famines. He is mercilessly exploited by landlords, moneylenders and tax collectors. All these circumstances induce apathy. *So even when the chance to improve his conditions exists,* he does not seize it. According to Mrs Kusum Nair[1] this state of apathy persists in some parts of India even today, when the Indian government has reduced the burden of landlords, moneylenders and tax collectors, and has made sizeable efforts, through the agricultural extension service, and the provision of credit, seeds and fertilizers, to interest the farmer in improving his condition.

Other authors deny that the farmer is insensitive to opportunity; they put all the blame on the landlords, moneylenders, and tax collectors who at this time fastened on the farmer's output, and so deprived him of incentive to increase his crops. Obviously the argument requires something more than the rapacity of these exploiters; it also requires them to be either stupid or malicious. Since it does not pay an exploiter to keep down the output which he is exploiting, one would expect that if the objective conditions existed for increasing output substantially, the exploiters would so arrange their business as to give the farmer some economic interest in increasing output. This is what happened in Egypt, where the exploitation of the peasants was also a byword. The mere fact that exploitation exists will not keep output down if additional output is shared between the producers and the exploiters. If it was exploitation that kept down Indian agricultural output, then there was something basically wrong with the intelligence of Indian exploiters.

Shortage of land. We can explain the low growth rate of Indian . agriculture without calling in either peasant apathy or exploiters' stupidity. This is neither to affirm nor to deny the reality of these phenomena. We merely affirm that the situation can be explained whether these phenomena existed or not.

The population of India was already very large at the end of the nineteenth century. The figure for 1911 was 232 million in British India, excluding Burma. At that time the net cropped area (i.e. not counting double cropping) was only 203 million acres, or roughly seven-eighths of an acre per person. Much of this area had poor yields because of inadequate rainfall; and in some other parts where yields could have been higher, farmers stuck to low-yielding grains which were more drought resistant than other high-

[1] Kusum Nair, *Blossoms in the Dust*, London, 1961.

yielding grains. Much of the land was already exhausted, through over-cropping and insufficient fallows. For all these reasons, India's yields per acre were among the lowest in the world. Famine was a terrible problem, because of the great variability of the monsoons, combined with inadequate carryover of stocks. Even in our period there were famines in 1891–2, 1896–7 and 1897–8, 1899–1900 and 1900–01, 1906–07 and 1907–08, and 1913–14. The worst famines occurred when the monsoon failed in two successive seasons; that of 1899–1901 is estimated to have cost ten million lives.

In these circumstances the Indian farmer gave the highest priority to the production of food and, since his food yields were so low, the amount of land available for non-food grain production was relatively limited. Table 12.2 shows how the land was used in the crop season of 1911–12. It shows that foodgrains, sugar, orchards and other foodcrops occupied 90 per cent of the gross cropped area. As usual this is very different from the pattern of exports, which was shown in Table 12.1. Non-foodgrains were contributing 85 per cent of agricultural exports, while occupying only 10 per cent of the cropped area.

TABLE 12.2: *Area in Crops* 1911–12*

(million acres)

Foodgrains	183·6
Oilseeds	15·3
Sugar	2·4
Orchards	4·4
Fodder	4·9
Other foodcrops	1·7
Cotton	14·5
Jute	3·1
Indigo	0·3
Coffee	0·1
Tea	0·5
Opium	0·2
Tobacco	0·9
Spices	1·4
Other non-food	2·0
	235·3
Less double cropping	32·6
	202·7

* Excluding Burma. Where not otherwise stated, the source of all figures in this chapter is the annual *Statistical Abstract of British India*.

It is not being argued that no farmer in India switched from food to more profitable crops like cotton. Some specialization did occur; only, it was more restricted than would have occurred in an economy where the farmers were not so anxious about their food supplies. Blyn's figures, implying a constant acreage per head, also involve a fall in the area cultivated in food per head, and a rise in the area per head in non-food. There was even increased area specialization. To quote Professor Gadgil:

'Thus Beras took increasingly to cotton; the irrigated tracts of the Nira and the Mutha in the Deccan took up sugar cane cultivation and the cultivation of garden crops almost entirely. Such a movement was only made possible by the facilities of transport, which opened a wider market for the industrial crops, and at the same time made the import of foodgrains from the neighbouring districts possible.'[1]

The important part played by the railway is indicated by the fact that the weight of goods carried by the railway was increasing steadily by 5 per cent per annum in the two decades before the First World War. This rate is high since the volume of commodities produced in India (plus imports) cannot have been growing by more than about 2 per cent per annum. Part of the difference would be due to the railways continuing to capture traffic from other forms of transport. But the main railway network was so well established by this time that one may safely conclude that trade really was growing faster than production, because of increased geographical specialization.

The situation is not, therefore, that there was no switching whatsoever from food to non-food crops. Some such switching did occur, but it was not enough to produce anything like the rate of growth of non-food output which occurred in the rest of the tropical world.

This situation is not unique, since in the rest of the tropical world non-food output grew rapidly more by bringing new empty lands under cultivation than by switching.[2] The main reason for India's low comparative standing was that so little new land was brought into cultivation at this time.

According to Blyn, the area cropped was increasing at an average

[1] D. R. Gadgil, *The Industrial Evolution of India in Recent Times*, Cambridge, 1950, pp. 63–4.
[2] See Chapter 1, pages 22–23.

annual rate of only 0·4 per cent, which was the same as the rate of population increase. What happened after the First World War supports this evidence. For, according to the 1951 Census, an index of the area cultivated per head in all India (i.e. including the former native states) starting at 100 in 1891, was 100 in 1911, 95 in 1913, and 77 in 1951. The fundamental obstacle to agricultural expansion in our period was the fact that nearly all the good lands were already being cultivated, in a situation where foodgrains were accorded high priority.

There were only two means by which Indian agricultural output could have been increased much faster. One was a quicker spread of irrigation. The other was by raising yields per acre through agricultural improvements. The key to Indian agriculture was, and still is water, since most of the possibilities for improvement also require more water.

India's main agricultural problem is the distribution of its rainfall, both geographically and seasonally. Geographically, a very large part of the population lives in areas which receive less than 30 inches of rain in a year; and seasonally, even where the rainfall is 80 inches or more, it is concentrated in the few monsoon months, and needs therefore to be conserved if its full benefit is to be enjoyed. In the language of Ceylon,[1] virtually the whole of India is a 'dry zone'. Tropical dry zones are difficult to develop without irrigation; they cannot carry the profitable tree crops (tea, coffee, cocoa, rubber, oil-palm, etc.), or (without irrigation) other profitable but water-demanding crops like rice, maize, yams, sugar or bananas. Very large areas of India could hope neither to feed themselves properly nor to develop lucrative cash crops, unless they could conserve their rain. The contrast between India and Egypt is instructive. In 1911 the crop area (counting double-cropped land twice) was about 0·9 acres per head of population in British India, and about 0·7 acres in Egypt. But all the Egyptian crop area was irrigated, as against less than 20 per cent in India, so Egyptian yields were enormously higher than those of India; and Egypt could both practically feed herself at a higher than Indian level, and also devote a quarter of her acreage to an export crop. Everything turned on the availability of water.

Irrigation was tackled with some vigour. The earliest irrigation works in India go back several hundred years, even into antiquity, so the idea was not novel. The British government was very concerned about the food supply of India, because it was horrified by

[1] See Chapter 9, page 235.

the immense loss of life in the recurrent famines. Even the old East India Company, which ruled until 1857, took some interest in the subject; renovated some old canals and built some new ones. But it was the famine of 1876 and 1877 which killed 5½ million people, that really spurred vigorous planning. The irrigated area rose from 29 million acres in 1880 to 47 million acres in 1913. At the latter date about 26 million acres were government works, and the remaining 21 million acres were irrigated by private works.

This was an impressive achievement; yet 46 million acres was still small in relation both to total area and to the potential. By 1965 the irrigated area of India and Pakistan together would increase by another 38 million acres, bringing the total to 84 million acres, and there would still be large plans in hand.

The question how much money to spend on irrigation became highly controversial in Indian (i.e. British) government circles around the turn of the century. Since the main emphasis was on coping with famines, the argument came to centre on whether to spend more on irrigation or to spend more on extending the railway network so that areas suffering from famine could be reached more easily. The argument is odd even in this financial setting since, according to the *Statistical Abstract*, by March 1913 the government had spent on capital account over £235 million on railways, and only £40 million on irrigation; a transfer of a few millions from railways to irrigation – if transfer were needed – would have been highly significant for irrigation, while only marginal for the railways. Bearing in mind the strong financial position of the Indian government, and the high productivity of investment in irrigation, no such transfer was involved, so one cannot be impressed by the financial argument.

Opponents of irrigation produced a catalogue of other arguments: the canals spread malaria; the ground was becoming waterlogged, or saline; it was hard to extract the water rates from the farmers. Much the most plausible explanation is that in the vast and lumbering bureaucracy of the Indian government railway building had developed a momentum over the years which carried it on and on, whereas irrigation was still something to be argued about.

England has rain throughout the year, so the average Englishman recruited and sent to India could have no idea what irrigation means to a country like India, where the rain is concentrated in such a short period, and is so variable from year to year. The benefits are severalfold. Irrigation makes possible larger crops in dry years. By doing so, it frees the farmer from reliance on drought-resistant but low-yielding grains, and therefore raises yields in good years as well. It makes fertilizing more profitable, and this brings a further increase in yield. And since the irrigation water flows throughout the year, double, and even triple cropping becomes feasible. If the Indian government had started to spend on irrigation earlier, and had spent 50 per cent more in each year, agricultural output would have risen much faster, and with this the whole tempo of Indian economic change would have been different.

Apart from irrigation, output might have been increased by a more vigorous policy of agricultural extension. At this time the government's agricultural services were rudimentary. Some provinces and states had made a beginning by establishing agricultural departments and botanic stations, but the number of scientists on hand was still minimal. Agricultural colleges made their appearance at the turn of the century and the Indian Agricultural Research Institute was founded a few years later.

It was recognised that the best hope for quick results lay in introducing and disseminating new varieties. Some progress was made with new varieties of cotton, wheat and groundnuts. According to Blyn, output per acre rose at an average annual rate of 0·5 per cent in foodgrains, and 0·9 per cent in non-food grains, but how much of this was due to better varieties, to irrigation, or to switching from less to more valuable crops, we cannot know. The technical staff available for spreading improvements in cultivation was so small that its effects must at this time have been barely noticeable, when considering Indian output as a whole.

II. INDUSTRIAL PRODUCTION

The demand for industrial products is a function of income, and this, in a mainly agricultural country, is mainly a function of agricultural output. Since agricultural output was growing only by 1 per cent per year, the demand for industrial products must also have been growing very slowly. If there was to be rapid growth of factory production this would have to be at the expense either of imports or of handicraft production, unless export markets could be opened up.

It is difficult to document what happened to handicraft production. This seems to have passed through its own purgatory in the first half of the nineteenth century, as cheap cotton yarn disrupted the spinning industry, and cheap metals disrupted the smelters. Yarn and metals are 'intermediate' products, i.e. they are the raw material of the weavers and the metal workers, who gain as cheap

318

imports reduce their raw material cost. In the textile industry the most highly productive innovations occurred in spinning. The immediate consequence in England was the disappearance of hand spinning; but hand loom weaving continued well into the second half of the nineteenth century. It is certain that Indian hand spinning was crushed by cheap imports, but the effect of imports on weaving remains doubtful. In the same way the great innovations in the metal trades occurred in smelting. Indian smelters could not withstand the competition of cheap imports, but Indian metal workers could put up a braver resistance.

By the year 1880, when our enquiry begins, most of these effects must already have worked themselves out. In the absence of censuses of population (the first Indian census was taken in 1871, and is not reliable), we cannot say by how much if at all, the proportion of handicraft workers in the population fell in the first half of the nineteenth century. Contemporary literary evidence is emphatic that the incomes of handicraft workers were greatly reduced, but contemporary literary evidence is not always reliable. In any case, a fall in the proportion of handicraft workers before 1880 would not necessarily imply a continued fall beyond that date.

By the year 1900 the contemporary literary evidence begins to change, and we begin to meet assertations that numbers have been well maintained in recent years. There was in particular much discussion about the output of cotton by handloom weavers. The Industrial Commission of 1916–18 estimated handloom output by adding together cotton yarn imported and yarn made in Indian mills, and subtracting yarn exports and the yarn equivalent of cloth made in Indian mills. This calculation gives an average rate of growth between 1897/9 and 1911/13 of 1·2 per cent per annum.[1] This seems rather on the high side when one remembers that in the same period imports of piece goods less exports and re-exports increased at a rate of 2·6 per cent per annum, and cloth production by mills at a rate of 7·7 per cent per annum. The Commission witness who produced these figures, Sir B. D. Mehta, mentioned two snags in the calculation; one was the probability that some hand spinning still lingered on at the earlier date; and the other was the increasing use of yarn for purposes other than making piece goods (e.g. making twine). The Fact Finding Committee of 1942, as quoted by S. D. Mehta,[2] allowed for both these elements. It increased the

[1] Indian Industrial Commission, 1916–18, *Report*, Appendix I, pp. 396–7.
[2] S. D. Mehta, *The Indian Textile Industry: An Economic Analysis*, Bombay, 1953, p. 89.

319

estimate of yarn available to handloom weavers at the earlier dates, and reduced the figures for the later dates. The result was an average annual growth rate of 0·8 per cent.

An alternative approach plunges us into the intricacies of the Census of Occupations. Here we meet two kinds of trouble; inconsistency in defining a man's occupation, where he has more than one occupation; and uncertainty in distinguishing between makers and sellers. To reduce potential error we work with males only, since they are classified more consistantly than females. Treading as carefully as we can, the censuses seem to say that the number of males engaged in manufacturing (excluding construction, mining, food preparation and the handling of refuse) increased from 7·88 million in 1901 to 8·52 million in 1911. At the latter date the number of males employed in factories with twenty or more workers was only about 900,000; if we suppose it to have been growing by 3 per cent per annum, it stood at the earlier date at about 670,000. By subtraction, the number of males in workshops or handicraft industries increased from about 7·21 million to 7·62 million, or at an average annual rate of 0·6 per cent. This is slightly less than the increase of the male population over fifteen years of age, which averaged 0·8 per cent.

The textile workers were the largest group of handicraft workers – some 40 or 50 per cent. Hence the Fact Finding Committee's calculation that the weavers' output was increasing at 0·8 per cent per annum, and this calculation from the Censuses that the number of handicraft workers was growing by 0·6 per cent per annum, support each other. The farmers were the main market for the craftsmen's product, and the farmers' output was growing only by one per cent per annum. Also, the craftsmen cannot have been growing at the expense either of imports or of domestic factory production, since both were growing much faster than the farmers' income. The safest conclusion about the handicraft workers is probably that their numbers were just about keeping up with population growth.

Large-scale industry. The rate of growth of large-scale industry was higher than in most other tropical countries at this time. An index of industrial production, based on six large-scale manufacturing industries,[1] more than doubled from 1896 to 1914. Between 1880 and 1896 output had tripled in cotton, jute and wool manufacturing, and had doubled in paper; so even though output was

[1] D. B. Meek, 'Some Measures of Economic Activity in India', *Journal of the Royal Statistical Society*, Part 3, 1937.

relatively constant in the other two industries, which were still small (iron and brewing), it is safe to conclude that between 1880 and 1914 large-scale industrial production increased at an average annual rate of between 4 and 5 per cent. This compared well with contemporary Germany (4·2 per cent per annum) but not with contemporary Japan (about 7 per cent). And, of course, nowadays countries with as little manufacturing industry as India then had have little difficulty in increasing large-scale manufacturing output by 10 per cent annually, through import substitution.

The broad picture is easily stated. In 1880 most of what might have been called a modern factory sector was made up of the cotton and jute textile industries, and until 1895 virtually all industrial progress was confined to these enterprises. Both industries grew dramatically after 1900.

In the twentieth century, coal mining emerged as an important industry, and other less prominent mineral industries grew as well. As modern methods and machinery began to spread to small-scale industry, engineering industries of modest size appeared and grew hesitantly. Just before the outbreak of the First World War, India began large-scale production of steel.

Thus, despite the emergence of a broad spectrum of industrial activity, rapid growth over long periods was sustained only by the jute and cotton textile industries. By 1914 the Indian economy had developed the world's fourth largest cotton textile industry[1] and the second largest jute manufacturing industry. Still, the number of persons in factories in 1911 was only about 1·1 per cent of the occupied labour force, and was still dwarfed by the number in handicrafts and small workshops (about 9 per cent of the labour force); industrial output as a whole cannot have been increasing by as much as 1·5 per cent per annum).

Just as in agriculture one can put one's finger on the decisive cause of slow growth – inadequate expenditure on irrigation – so also in manufacturing industry one major failure stands out – inadequate development of iron and steel production. In the course of establishing her railway network (the third largest in the world), India generated a very large demand for iron and steel products. Had she developed an iron and steel industry from say 1860 onwards, and the industries linked therewith (especially coal mining and engineering) she would by 1914 have been one of the largest in-

[1] The rank of the cotton industry is based on output by weight, and thus favours India's coarse grade textiles. Ranked by production capacity, India was fifth.

dustrial producers in the world. The reasons for this failure will emerge in the course of a brief survey of the major industries.

Cotton textiles The cotton textile industry sustained rapid growth after 1875, and had become India's most important factory industry by the turn of the century. In 1875 there 19 mills, most of them concentrated in Bombay. By 1880, only five years later, the number of mills had tripled to 58, and by 1914 the number had grown thirteen times, to 264. From 1880 to 1914, employment in the industry sextupled, from under 40,000 to over 260,000. The cotton textile industry would continue to dominate India's industrial development after our period. It would become the largest industry in India's private sector, and the second largest cotton-milling industry among the world's free enterprise economies by 1965.[1]

Throughout our period, the industry exhibited adaptability to changing conditions. Initially, the industry expanded its spinning capacity rapidly in response to growing world demand for yarn; Indian yarn exports, mainly to China and Japan, grew sevenfold from 1880 to 1890. As Japan, and later China, developed textile industries of their own, the Indian industry turned to domestic markets, and expanded its weaving capacity more rapidly than its spinning capacity. (These trends are all documented in Table 12.3.) By 1900 India dominated world trade in coarse grade yarn, and had captured most of the domestic market. In the final decade before World War I, India produced two-thirds of her yarn and 48 per cent of her domestic consumption of cloth.

For our decade and a few decades preceding it, the outstanding fact of the cotton industry was not that it managed to adapt to changing conditions to maintain its growth. The remarkable fact was that it was able to grow at all .The expansion took place without foreign capital. Indians not only mobilized their own capital resources, but organized and managed the enterprises with relatively little European help. Moreover, the industry was launched in competition with the world's leading cotton textile industry in Lancashire, in the face of uncongenial government policies, and without tariff protection. In 1882, import tariffs on cotton goods were eliminated and the Indian industry faced competition with British textiles in domestic markets. When a small tariff was re-imposed on British cotton goods imports for revenue purposes a countervailing excise duty was imposed on Indian output, to eliminate the appearance of protection.

[1] The ranking is based both on total production and total exports of cotton goods.

TABLE 12.3: *Expansion of Cotton Textiles*

Year	1880	1885	1890	1895	1900	1905	1907	1914
Mills	58	81	114	144	194	206	227	264
Employment (thousands)	39·5	61·6	99·2	139·6	156·4	196·4	225·4	260·8
Looms (thousands)	13·3	16·5	22·1	34·2	40·5	47·3	66·7	96·7
Spindles (thousands)	1408	2037	2935	3712	4942	5196	5763	6620
Yarn exports (millions of lbs.)	26·7	79·3	170·5	186	118	298	216	198*

* 1913–14.
Source: Based on D. R. Gadgil, *op. cit.*, and the *Statistical Abstract*.

Despite these handicaps, the incentives to invest in cotton textile production proved overwhelming. Indian entrepreneurs and the large Bombay mercantile houses were attracted by the success of the first cotton mill built in 1853, which paid a return of 20 per cent on investments in its first year.[1] Attractive profits, which offset the high risk of investing in an industry sensitive to trade cycles resulted in part from low raw-materials costs. Situated primarily in Bombay and Ahmedabad, the industry benefited from the proximity of the cotton growing tracts, and the low freight costs for raw cotton brought to the ports for export. But high profits were primarily the result of cheap labour. In Bombay and Ahmedabad, wages remained low throughout our period. Unit labour costs calculated for 1906 were less than one half the costs for weaving and one-third the costs for spinning in Lancashire.[2]

The 'boom' in raw cotton exports in the early 1860s, brought on by the American Civil War, delayed the expansion of the cotton industry by raising the price of raw cotton to prohibitive levels. (In the war years, from 1859 to 1864, the price of cotton quadrupled.) But in the longer run the 'cotton boom' of the sixties hastened the growth of the cotton textile industry, by providing a large additional lump of capital, in the form of increased profits, for later investments. From 1859 to 1865, the volume of raw cotton exported to the UK grew two and a half times, and the total value of India's cotton exports grew ten times. According to Dr Fukazawa, the boom added from 70 to 75 million pounds sterling to the wealth of

[1] H. Fukazawa, 'The Cotton Mill Industry', in *The Economic History of India, 1857–1956*, ed. V. B. Singh, Bombay, 1965, p. 228.
[2] *ibid.*, p. 236.

Bombay, over and above the normal trend growth in cotton export earnings.[1] This increase in wealth accrued mainly to the Parsee tradesmen in Bombay, and created the fortunes of several of India's most illustrious entrepreneurial families, which would later finance the expansion of the cotton textile industry.

Jute manufacturing. Like the cotton textile industry in Bombay, jute manufactures attracted investment for reasons of location, low labour costs and high profits. As world trade in agricultural commodities increased, the demand for a reliable packaging material grew on a vast scale. The industries' production and loomage trebled during the last quarter of the nineteenth century, and more than doubled again in the first decade and a half of the twentieth century. Despite competition from English jute manufacturers in Dundee, the Indian industry flourished, and in 1908 surpassed Dundee in output. Jute manufactures would continue to figure heavily in India's foreign exchange earnings in 1965. The growth of the industry is summarized in Table 12.4 below.

TABLE 12.4: *Expansion of Jute Manufactures*

Year	1880	1885	1890	1895	1902	1908	1914
Mills	22	24	27	29	36	54	64
Employment (thousands)	27·5	51·9	62·7	75·2	114·8	187·8	216
Looms (thousands)	4·9	6·9	8·2	10·0	16·2	27·2	36·1
Spindles (thousands)	70·8	131·7	164·2	201·2	331·4	562·3	744·0

Source: Based on D. R. Gadgil, *op. cit.*

One of the most concentrated industries in the world, virtually all of India's jute mills lined a sixty-mile stretch of the River Hoogly, which divides Calcutta proper from the adjacent industrial city of Howrah. The mills were thus advantageously close to the world's most productive jute fields. Equally important, the industry was managed by a collusive trade organization called the Indian Jute Mills Association.

The monopolistic character of the association probably worked to the advantage of its members and the industry as a whole. Like any monopoly the organization restricted the output of the industry below capacity levels. It also reduced competition, dampened the

[1] H. Fukazawa, *op. cit.*, p. 227.

effects of trade cycles, encouraged very high profits, afforded some security against liquidation, and possibly provided some spur to modernization in plant equipment and techniques. The Association even acted beyond the immediate activities of the industry: it subsidized the distribution of improved seed varieties to raw jute producers.

The Association restricted output by enforcing across the board under-utilization of capacity. This was accomplished either by sealing a fixed percentage of all looms in each mill, or by enforcing agreements of paid labour short-time. Barriers to entry reduced competition and guaranteed high profits. These in turn created a source of investible funds, and at the same time, by increasing the expected return on investment, made further investment in the jute industry attractive. Since barriers to entry limited the creation of new mills, most capacity expansion occurred within existing mills. The scale of operations increased, management techniques improved, and new machines were introduced. Over our period, the number of jute mills increased by a factor of less than three, while employment, the numbers of spindles and looms all rose by factors of seven to ten. To some extent, investment in large-scale operations was an investment in new, increasingly capital intensive techniques. This is suggested by the fact that, from 1895 until 1914, the number of looms and spindles increased about 70 per cent faster than the number of workers.

Coal. The main impetus behind the growth of coal mining was the growth of the railroads and of large-scale manufacturing. Despite the extensive rail network, transport and marketing costs for coal were high, and Indian coal could fill domestic needs only in the vicinity or the mining regions, in east India and Burma. Industrial and railroad demands for coal in other areas – most notably from the opposite side of the subcontinent in Bombay – had to be filled by foreign coal. In 1880, after twenty-five years of railroad construction, India was importing nearly as much coal as she produced. In that year India consumed about 800,000 tons of foreign coal and about 1 million tons of domestic coal.

The industry was already growing rapidly in the final decades of the nineteenth century. From 1893 to 1914 the pace of growth advanced considerably: output increased from 2·5 million tons to 16 million tons; employment grew from 38,000 to 150,000. The Indian coal industry became the sole supplier of the Indian railways, and began to develop an export trade, to Ceylon, Singapore, and the Malay Peninsula. Imports declined and exports grew. In the last decade of the period, exports exceeded imports by several hundred thousand tons.

The coal industry expanded rapidly once it got started, but it was a slow starter.[1] Its slow response to the demands of the railroads and of budding industries in the 1860s and 1870s is in part explained by the low quality of the coal initially mined in India, which was not suited to much industrial use. But the major explanation for the industries lagged response to growing demand lies in the location of the rail lines, which were not adequately linked to the Indian coal fields, high freight costs, and a government policy of purchasing foreign coal for its railway stores, a policy that was officially relaxed in 1883, but which in practice continued until the mid-1890s.

Iron and steel. Like the coal industry, the iron industry developed long after its time was due. The basic reason for this was very strong opposition in London against the Government of India doing anything to help the industry.

In this field, government policy was very important because the government was the largest buyer – for its programmes of railroad construction, irrigation facilities, public buildings, ordnance factories, and so on. Most of this demand was directed to English manufactures, especially as initially the government's policy was to buy 'stores' only through the India Office in London. The government did not adopt a regular policy of buying Indian manufactures until 1875, and even then such purchases were inhibited partly by the fact that the habit of buying abroad was slow to change, and partly by arguments over what percentage of value added in India to materials imported from abroad constituted 'Indian manufacture'. These controversies were to continue to the end of the century. The 'stores rules' were eroded on several occasions, but the restrictive elements, designed to protect British trade, were not finally eliminated until 1914.

For the iron industry the testing time came in 1875, when the first large-scale iron works based on coal (instead of charcoal) was established at Barakar in 1875, by an English group.[2] The company sought long-term contracts from the government, but was refused, though the government did buy from it from time to time. Following its difficulties it sought a loan, which was also refused. The company suspended operations in 1879.

[1] B. Guha, 'The Coal Mining Industry', in V. B. Singh, ed., *op. cit.*, p. 303.
[2] This section on the Barakar iron works is based on S. K. Sen, *Studies in Industrial Policy and Development of India, 1858–1914*, Calcutta, 1964, which also contains an excellent account of the 'stores rules'.

In 1880 Lord Lytton was succeeded as Governor-General of India by Lord Ripon, whose views were entirely different. Ripon was anxious to develop an iron industry, and so the Government of India bought the iron works at Barakar in 1880, and proceeded to operate them. For this Ripon was continually berated by the Home Government. He was advised by despatches from London to sell the works, but ignored this advice. But Ripon left India in 1884, and his successor was defeated in 1889, when forbidden by the Home Government to raise the capital which the works then needed. It was accordingly resold to private enterprise in that year. Thereafter the works struggled on, making some losses in the 1890s, and merely keeping alive.

The Indian iron industry was thus the victim of a conflict between the Indian Government and the India Office in London. As often happens in colonial situations, the man 'on the spot' begins to identify himself with the country he is governing, and wishes to advance its interests even at the expense of the mother country. This happened in India. Thus, in the long conflict over import duties, ranging from 1860 to the First World War, the Indian Government almost always favoured imposing duties, but it was always the Home Government which gave instructions to the contrary. In the matter of iron production the Home Goverment was equally effective right to the end of the century.

With the turn of the century *laissez-faire* ideas were no longer so all compelling in Britain, especially since a large proportion of British manufacturers, menaced by imports from Germany, were now repudiating the economic doctrines on which *laissez-faire* was supposed to rest. So, when one of India's most successful textile manufacturers, Jamshetji Tata, announced his interest in building a steel works, he was able to engage the political support not only of the Indian Government but also of officials in the India Office in London. The planning stage took several years. Attempts to interest the financial co-operation of British steelmakers failed. But eventually Tata's sons (for the old man died in the interim) got all the money they needed from other Indians, and with some German machinery, German and American experts, and a contract for 20,000 tons of steel rails per year from the Government of India, started to build their first plant. Their first pig iron was produced in 1912, and their first steel in 1913.

Conclusion. Given effective government interest, India could have completed the stage of industrialization through import substitution by 1913 – an accomplishment which was postponed for nearly half a century. The Government of India was interested, and left to itself would have imposed tariffs, would have bought more of its requirements directly in Indian markets, and would have supported nascent industries with purchase contracts. But it was restrained from doing these things by strict orders from London, which were only gradually and grudgingly relaxed.

There was a running battle on tariff policy. Even apart from industrial protection, the Indian Government needed import duties for revenue. Duties were raised significantly immediately after the Indian Mutiny, for revenue reasons. However, in 1862 revenues from other sources were buoyant; the duties on textiles were reduced in that year to 5 per cent on yarn and $3\frac{1}{2}$ per cent on fabrics.[1] Next year the duty on iron was reduced to 1 per cent. In the 1870s the Manchester Chamber of Commerce began to press that even these low duties be removed, and so in 1882 all import duties were abolished, except on salt and alcoholic beverages. This position was not tenable for long, since the government needed revenue. So in 1894 a general revenue tariff of 5 per cent was imposed. To please Lancashire, a countervailing excise tax of 5 per cent was imposed at the same time on the manufacture of cotton yarn. Since this was ineffective, a $3\frac{1}{2}$ per cent excise tax on fabrics was substituted in 1896.

Thus Indian industry was required to face the full blast of English competition without the possibility of protection, and governed by a British régime disposed to purchase only British manufactures, and unwilling to enter even into long-term contracts with local new manufacturers.

Of course, one must not exaggerate the extent of the opportunity presented by import substitution. Since the Indian farmers had only a tiny surplus, most of which they exchanged with the handicraft workers, India's import of manufactures per head was very small. It would soon have been exhausted by a large-scale industrial growth rate of say 10 per cent per annum. Continuance of this rate would have required either major agricultural change, yielding a larger surplus, or development of a large export of manufactures. Good progress was made with exports. In 1913 India's export of manufactures was as large as Japan's; but Japan had only one-sixth of India's population. For exports to have contributed substantially to India's economy, a big trade drive would have been needed, based to a considerable extent on successful iron and steel and engineering industries. Both these problems – major agricultural change and a successful trade drive – still remain unsolved, some fifty years after

[1] Sen, *op. cit.*, p. 43.

the end of our period. Still, if India had started import substitution seriously some eighty years ago, she would by 1913 have been a major industrial power.

III. INFRASTRUCTURE

The picture is brighter when we turn to infrastructure than it is when we consider either agriculture or manufacturing industry.

The brightest element was the railway system, rising to 35,000 miles of track by 1914. This led to an enormous expansion of trade. As we have already noted, during the last twenty years before the war railway freight was increasing by 5 per cent per annum; a hitherto subsistence economy was turning into a market economy, with geographical specialisation.

There is much argument as to whether the railway system was planned and operated in a manner most beneficial to the economy. Military considerations played some part in siting the lines; so also did the desire to be able to move supplies into districts menaced by famine. But it is not altogether clear that these objects were inconsistent with locations chosen on purely economic grounds; the network was, after all, very large – about one mile of track for every 46 square miles. It is also frequently argued that the rates policy of the railway system, by charging lower freights on movements to the ports than on movements from the ports, encouraged exports rather than output for domestic consumption; but since one of the principal causes of the relative stagnation of India was the failure of her farmers to adopt cash crops for export, one cannot be over-impressed by this argument.

More to the point is the failure to develop an adequate road system, linking up with the railway. Metalled roads passable all the year round expanded by only 45 per cent (1·6 per cent per annum) between 1890 and 1914, from 36,000 to 52,000 miles. These were the responsibility of the central government. Unmetalled 'second and third class' roads, financed by provincial and municipal governments, and impassable during the four months of the monsoon season, increased only 20 per cent, from 119,000 to 142,000 miles. Many roads were hastily constructed as emergency measures, and rapidly fell into disuse.

The poor quality of the roads played its part in holding down the rate of growth. To be sure, it protected the handicraftsmen in the villages, since high transport costs kept out imports. On the other hand, it reduced the farmers' incentives to grow cash crops for export, and also kept Indian factory production out of the villages as effectively as imported goods. The transformation of the economy from a subsistence to a market economy was slowed by the execrable roads.

Another bright part of the picture is the emergence of an Indian middle class, both business and professional. This is an essential factor in economic development, as well as for politics and government administration. The Indian government's record on primary education is poor. But thanks also to private and missionary effort, secondary and higher education were already by 1914 producing as many graduates as the slowly growing economy could at that time absorb, given the English domination of government jobs.

Indians had begun to receive an English university education before our period. The three Presidency universities, in Madras, Calcutta, and Bombay were founded in 1857. By 1890 some 15,000 Indians were enrolled in 135 arts and professional colleges. By 1914, the enrolment had increased to 50,000 in 196 colleges. Education, in the technical fields, needed for the growing engineering industry, also increased. Mechanical engineers were trained in one engineering college at the beginning of our period. By World War I, four engineering colleges provided training in mechanical, mining and metallurgical engineering. Another engineering institute trained skilled operatives for employment in the government-operated engineering workshops and ordnance factories. By 1914, a small number of government sponsored scholarships were offered students for technical training in foreign countries.

University education produced relatively few highly skilled Indians; it did not create an efficient labour force or turn out future captains of industry, nor was it intended to do so. The government early eschewed responsibility for the education of any more than a small Indian élite, which was intended to serve the imperial government, and itself carry the burden of educating the rest of India. Liberal arts education provided middle level administrative and clerical skills. Technical education was narrow and specialized, and was directed at providing skills needed in public works, and in the mining and milling industries. Few Indians were employed in the highest level posts, either in the government administration or in private European business.

In the long run, the education of even a small professional and intellectual élite had its effect on industrialization. The nationalist movement was first formally organized around growing numbers in the educated middle classes. The Indian National Congress – the organization that would evolve into the Congress Party – was founded

330

in 1885, with its membership comprised of these small classes. (The National Congress did not become a mass movement until Gandhi arrived from South Africa and moved into it.) From 1885 to 1900, the Nationalists' tactics of debate, discussion, and constitutional agitation reflected the values of these classes.

From the beginning of our period, the Indian nationalist movement became increasingly concerned with the economic aspects of British rule. Some of the most outstanding Nationalist spokesmen of the period were equally outstanding as economists: Naoroji, Ranade, Joshi, Gokhale, and Dutt are a few. Under the influence of these men, the nationalist movement challenged the economic policies of the imperial government more vigorously than its political and social policies. For the first time, the urban middle classes, the intellectual élites, and the nationalist politicians closed ranks behind the theme of national economic development. The abolition of poverty and the industrialization of the country became national aspirations.

In the 10 years before 1914, the *Swadeshi* movement altered the tactics but not the aspirations of the educated middle classes. To encourage Indian industrialization, the movement boycotted European manufactures, especially textiles, and channelled local capital into the founding of new enterprise. Although neither strategy produced many tangible results,[1] they did reveal widespread support of industrialization as an ideal, and the avowed determination of large numbers of the educated middle classes to speed up development in the only ways they knew.

Thus, the slow initial extension of higher education furthered industrialization in two ways. First, it provided a modicum of skills to the small number of Indians employed in the growing industrial sector. Second, together with the nationalist movement, it helped create new attitudes among the Indian populace. While neither higher education nor Indian nationalism reached much of the population – the number of college educated Indians and of active nationalists was small – they did foster the emergence of the will to modernize that would later affect both the nationalist movement and the government's policy.

Why did not the Indian government do more, especially for roads, primary education, public health and agricultural extension? Taxation was high. The tax revenue of the central government in 1913

---

[1] The boycotts probably did more to unify diverse Indian interests than to disrupt the market for British textiles, for example, and the attempts to support new industry culminated in high rates of failure. See Vera Anstey, *The Economic Development of Modern India*, London, 1929, pp. 107, 407, 435 f.

331

(excluding self-balancing items) was just under £56,000,000, which was about 6 per cent of the national income of British India. When one adds 1 or 2 per cent of national income for payments to local authorities, the Indian governments could have done well if all their money had been spent economically.

India's politicians attribute part of India's relative stagnation to what they call the 'drain' of funds from India to England. The term is misleading, since the unwary interpret it to mean that India was required to pay tribute to England. Actually it is only an all-inclusive term for Indian government expenditures in Britain, amounting in 1913 to about £20 million. The breakdown of this sum in 1913 was:

	£ million
Interest on railway and irrigation debt	9·2
Interest on general debt	2·1
Military expenditures	4·4
Pensions of retired civil servants	2·1
Purchases of commodities	1·6
Leave pay of civil servants	0·5
Miscellaneous	0·2
	£20·1

Since the railways and irrigation facilities were about the best expenditures of the Indian government (and were moreover financially profitable) the fact that interest was paid on the money hardly constitutes a 'drain' in any meaningful sense. India would certainly have been better off if it had been possible to spend more of this money in India (as indeed it was), but she was not in the position of spending money and getting nothing for it in return.

The most important 'drain' on the Indian economy was spent not outside the country, but inside the country, maintaining a large British administration, and still worse, a large British army. India had to be administered, and a great many Englishmen gave her devoted service. But a great many were also not much more than tax collectors, contemptuous of the Indian peoples, and justifying G. B. Shaw's jibe that the colonies were a form of outdoor relief for the British middle classes. If the British had been willing to employ Indians at higher administrative levels, the cost of the administration would have been significantly lower. Equally, if the British had seen their task as something greater than merely maintaining law and order and relieving famines, and had pursued vigorous agricultural and industrial policies, that would have been worth every penny.

332

But the biggest 'drain' of all was the army. Just before the Mutiny (1857), there were 39,500 British troops in India, and 311,000 Indian troops. In 1914 there were 80,000 British troops, and 157,000 Indian troops, and the military budget was consuming about 2·3 per cent of the national income. What is worse, these troops, paid for by India, were used not only for internal security, but also to fight British wars in Asia and Africa.

Thus the basic reason for the failure to spend adequately on infrastructure was not that tax levels were low, but that the proceeds were spent to an excessive and unfair extent on British civil servants and British troops, and on fighting British wars outside India.

IV. CONCLUSION

We can now attempt a rough estimate of the rate of growth of India's real national income during our period.

If agriculture grew by 1·1 per cent per annum, industry (large and small) by 1·4, and services by 2·0; and if the weights were roughly 6:1:3, then the average growth rate was about 1·4 per cent per annum. We can apply these figures with confidence only to the second half of our period. Between 1901 and 1911 the population of British India was growing by about 0·5 per annum. This makes the growth rate of *per capita* income roughly 0·9 per cent per annum. This is respectable; not as high as southern Brazil or as Japan, but not bad for a country where agricultural progress was so difficult to achieve.

This estimate can be compared with the conclusion reached by Dr M. Mukerji, after reviewing all previous estimates.[1] His results are given as real national income *per capita* in 1948–9 rupees. He gives Rs. 199 as the average of 1896–1904 and Rs. 220 for 1906–1914. This is an increase of about 1·0 per cent per annum; and is therefore a little higher than our estimate.

The startling feature of Mukerji's estimate is that he gives Rs. 216 *per capita* for 1881–9. This implies that output per head was significantly lower in the 1890s than it had been in the 1880s, and that, though rising after 1900, it did not catch up with the 1880s until about the time of the outbreak of the First World War. We have already made the point that India was relatively depressed during the 1890s, but the proposition that there was no progress from the 1880s to the outbreak of the First World War is not plausible, and is not accepted by the author himself. Between 1882/5 and 1898/1901 exports of non-foodgrains increased at an average annual rate of 1·4

[1] 'National Income' in V. B. Singh, *op. cit.*

per cent, and there is no reason why foodgrain output should not have kept up with population growth, when one averages good and bad monsoons. Our best guess is that overall output per head either stagnated or more likely rose by between 0·3 and 0·5 per cent per annum between the first half of the eighties and the second half of the nineties; then after 1900 prices rose and output grew by a little under 1 per cent per head per annum until the war.

If this is so, one must deduce that India suffered more from the 'great depression' of prices in the eighties and nineties than did other tropical countries. This is not surprising. Between 1883 and 1895 the prices of three of her leading crops, wheat, cotton and sugar fell by more than most other prices. In terms of sterling c.i.f. London, the index number of prices of all tropical agricultural exports[1] fell by 22 per cent, while cotton fell by 33 per cent, wheat by 42 per cent, and sugar by 51 per cent. The continual devaluation of the rupee during this period eased the burden for producers somewhat. Nevertheless, India's situation at this time in export markets was naturally much less bouyant than that of coffee, cocoa, rubber, or banana producers, who faced no such severe collapse of prices. Perhaps we can sum this up by saying that whereas the expansion of world trade was blowing more or less fair winds towards most tropical countries from 1870 or 1880 onwards, India did not really feel favourable breezes until the general upturn of prices after 1895. Insofar as economic expansion derived from world trade, *India was a late starter.*

Once started, she did quite well. In the first place she was doing substantially better before the First World War than she would do during and after the war when, as in Egypt, population growth caught up with acreage growth, and output per head almost certainly fell. Moreover, a growth rate per head approaching 1 per cent per annum is by no means despicable. High growth rates at this time, e.g. for the USA, and probably also for Japan if the recent revisions are correct, ran only at about 2 per cent per annum. More to the point is that the growth rate per head was respectable only because the growth rate of population was abnormally low, in comparison with other tropical countries, and was kept low by the high death rate resulting from failure to solve the agricultural problem over most of the country. (Faster growth of population and of food output would have meant lower growth of national income per head, since neither large-scale industry nor commercial agriculture was limited by population growth.) It is important to remember that India

[1] See Chapter 2.

is of continental size. Some regions probably stagnated altogether; especially those large areas in the peninsula with less than 30 inches of rain. Other areas did as well as Colombia – especially the irrigated parts of the Punjab, the jute-cultivating and manufacturing regions of Bengal, the Assam tea area, Bombay and the region supplying its mills with cotton. If India were carved into countries of Latin American size, we would find several that matched Latin American or south-east Asian performance.

One can still however ask why India as a whole did not do better, since we would still be left with enormous areas whose stagnation at miserable levels is not matched elsewhere in southern Asia or Latin America. The best answer would seem to be that over large parts of the countryside the population was already so large in relation to cultivable area by the end of the nineteenth century that the farmers felt they could spare little land for cash crops. This called for a vigorous government understanding the importance of irrigation, without which most of Indian agriculture must remain poor; and also a government which would meet overpopulation by vigorously promoting industrialization for an export market, on the basis of India's coal and iron resources. Instead India was at this time ruled by a government wedded to a *laissez-faire* philosophy, and sensitive to the vested interest of its own home industrialists.

BIBLIOGRAPHY

Official Papers

Great Britain. House of Commons, *Sessional Papers*, 1886, 1914–16. 'Statistical Abstract of British India', (C. 4730, Cd. 8157).
India. Commercial Intelligence Department, *Index Numbers of Indian Prices: 1861–1918*. Calcutta, 1919.
——. Indian Industrial Commission, 1916–18, *Report*. Calcutta, 1918.

Books

Anstey, Vera, *The Economic Development of India*, London, 1929.
Bhatia, B. M., *Famines in India*, New York, 1963.
Blyn, George, *Agricultural Trends in India, 1891–1947*, Philadelphia, 1966.
Chandra, Bipan, *The Rise and Growth of Economic Nationalism in India: Economic Policies of Indian National Leadership, 1880–1905*, New Delhi, 1966.
Darling, M. L., *The Punjab Peasant in Prosperity and Debt*, London, 1925.
Datta, K. L., *Report on the Enquiry into the Rise of Prices in India*, Calcutta, 1914.

Dutt, R. C., *The Economic History of India in the Victorian Age, 1837–1900*, reprinted from the 2nd edition of 1906, Delhi, 1960.
Gadgil, D. R., *The Industrial Evolution of India in Recent Times*. London, 1950.
Jenks, L. H., *The Migration of British Capital to 1875*, New York, 1927.
Joshi, R. M., *Indian Export Trade*, Bombay, 1922.
Mehta, S. D., *The Indian Cotton Textile Industry, An Economic Analysis*, Bombay, 1953.
Nair, Kusum, *Blossoms in the Dust*, London, 1961.
Sarkar, Jadunath, *Economics of British India*, 4th edition, Calcutta, 1917.
Sen, S. K., *Studies in Industrial Policy and Development of India, 1858–1914*, Calcutta, 1964.
Singh, V. B., ed., *The Economic History of India, 1857–1956*, Bombay, 1965.
Thorner, Daniel, *Investment in Empire: British Railway and Steam Shipping Enterprise in India, 1825–1849*, Philadelphia, 1950.

Articles

McPherson, W. J., 'Investment in Indian Railways, 1845–1975', *Economic History Review*, No. 2, 1955.
Meek, D. B., 'Some Measures of Economic Activity in India', *Journal of the Royal Statistical Society*, Pt. 3, 1937.
Morris, Morris D., 'Towards a Reinterpretation of Nineteenth Century Indian Economic History', *Journal of Economic History*, December 1963.
Patel, S. J., 'Long Term Changes in Output and Income in India, 1896–1960', *The Indian Economic Journal*, January 1958.
Thorner, Daniel, 'Long Term Trends in Output in India', in *Economic Growth: Brazil, India, Japan*, by Simon Kuznets, *et al.*, Durham, N C, 1955.

INDEX

Abeokuta (in Nigeria), export cotton industry established in (1850s) 159–60

Aburi Rubber and Kola Plantation (1902) 170

Achin, Sultanate of (in North Sumatra), wars in (1873 to 1915) 255, 278, 279, 280

Africa 13; education in 35; growth of 34; migration in 18; mines in central 15; *see also* Gold Coast, Kenya, Nigeria and Uganda

African Association 172

Agricultural Bank of Egypt (founded 1902) 216

Agriculture, tropical: dependence on water 17–18; development of, in tropical countries 33–7; necessity for expansion of 16–17; preconditions for export in 16–29; scientific revolution in 19–20

Akinola, R. A. 158

Akwapim peoples (of West Africa), introduced to cocoa farming 151, 158, 159

Alake and Council of Abeokuta, promoting cotton industry in Nigeria 160

Ali, Mohammed: death of (1849) 198; ruler of Egypt (1805–49) 198; sweeping reforms of 198

America 13; agricultural exports of 50; closing of agricultural frontier 50, 51; cotton production of 54

America, Central, expansion of coffee exports 53

American Allen type cotton, cultivated in Nigeria 161

Annuaire Statistique 57–8, 59, 60

Antioqueño culture area (Colombia) 74–5, 79, 89; coffee production in 81–3, 86, 90

Antioquia (in Colombia): industrialization in 97; textile manufacturing in 87

Arubi agricultural station, established in 1890 169

Assuantsi Agricultural Station (1907) 170

Aswan Dam, completed (1902) 205

Atjeh, Sultanate of (in North Sumatra), war of 263

Bananas 14; export of 60

Banco Nacional (Colombia), established in 1881 93

Bantam (West Java) sultan of 250

Barbosa, Rui (first finance minister of Brazil) 119

Baro-Kano railroad lines (in Nigeria) 162

Barranquilla Railway and Pier Company (Colombia) 96

Basel Mission in the Gold Coast 169

Bell, Hesketh (Commissioner in Uganda) 192, 194

Berlin Conference (1885) 147

Black, C. E. 97

Blanco, Antonio Guzman (President of Venezuela 1870–88) 143

Blyn, Dr George 310, 311, 312, 315, 318

Bolivia, tin export of 61

Bonnat, M. 149

Bosch, Governor-General van de 252

Brazil 100–25; agricultural development in 111–18; Campos Salles government in 109, 122; climate determining economic centre of 101; cocoa production in 116, 124; coffee export of 100–5; coffee valorization in 54, 104; *colonos* in 102, 104, 111; Comtian positivist doctrines in 120; cotton production in 115–16, 124; debt slavery in the rubber trade 117–18; domestic cotton industry in 116; economic policy in 118–22; education in 125; European immigrants in 102–3, 104, 105, 110, 112; expansion of the coffee industry in 113, 114, 120; failure to develop iron and coal industry in 120; first trade surplus (1861) 101; food production in 114; foreign investment in railways in 106; Indians as slaves in 112; industrialization in 119–20; land divisions in 111–13, 118; national income of 123–5; *nordestinos* immi-

*

For Product Safety Concerns and Information please contact our EU
representative GPSR@taylorandfrancis.com
Taylor & Francis Verlag GmbH, Kaufingerstraße 24, 80331 München, Germany

www.ingramcontent.com/pod-product-compliance
Lightning Source LLC
Chambersburg PA
CBHW070902080426
R18103400001B/R181034PG41932CBX00009B/17

9 781138 865167